THE
PEACE
PUZZLE

THE
PEACE
PUZZLE

AMERICA'S QUEST FOR ARAB-ISRAELI PEACE, 1989–2011

DANIEL C. KURTZER, SCOTT B. LASENSKY,

WILLIAM B. QUANDT, STEVEN L. SPIEGEL,

AND SHIBLEY Z. TELHAMI

CORNELL UNIVERSITY PRESS
ITHACA AND LONDON

UNITED STATES INSTITUTE OF PEACE
WASHINGTON, DC

First published 2013 by Cornell University Press

Printed in the United States of America

Library of Congress Cataloging-in-Publication Data

The peace puzzle : America's quest for Arab-Israeli peace, 1989–2011 /
Daniel C. Kurtzer . . . [et al.].
    p. cm.
  Includes bibliographical references and index.
  ISBN 978-0-8014-5147-8 (cloth : alk. paper)
  1. Arab-Israeli conflict—1993—Peace. 2. Arab-Israeli
conflict—1993—Diplomatic history. 3. United States—Foreign
relations—Middle East. 4. Middle East—Foreign relations—United
States. I. Kurtzer, Daniel.

DS119.76.P415 2013
956.05'4—dc23

2012009132

Cornell University Press strives to use environmentally responsible
suppliers and materials to the fullest extent possible in the publishing of
its books. Such materials include vegetable-based, low-VOC inks and
acid-free papers that are recycled, totally chlorine-free, or partly composed
of nonwood fibers. For further information, visit our website at
www.cornellpress.cornell.edu.

Cloth printing   10 9 8 7 6 5 4 3 2 1

CONTENTS

PREFACE

In 2006, the authors formed the Study Group on Arab-Israeli Peacemaking, a project supported by the United States Institute of Peace (USIP). The effort, chaired by Daniel Kurtzer and co-directed by Kurtzer and Scott Lasensky, was aimed at developing a set of "best practices" for American diplomacy. The Study Group conducted in-depth interviews with over 120 policymakers, diplomats, academics, and civil society figures and developed performance assessments of the various administrations of the post–Cold War period. An initial study, *Negotiating Arab-Israeli Peace: American Leadership in the Middle East* (USIP Press, 2008), co-authored by Kurtzer and Lasensky, served as a guidebook for American negotiators.

Given that the project had a unique set of primary sources, that official archives were likely to remain closed for many years, and that memoirs largely dominated the discourse of the period and thus created the need for an objective and scholarly account, in 2009 members of the Study Group set out to write this book. Additional interviews were conducted, and we also sought the release of select documents that offer further insight into this period; many of these documents are available in the appendix to this volume, accessible online at www .thepeacepuzzle.org.

From the beginning, the focus of our work has remained unchanged: to explain and to assess the role of the United States. Although Israeli and Arab leaders feature prominently in the book, as do political developments in the region, our assessments—by design—are limited to one and only one party. Rather than provide a definitive, comprehensive history, this book focuses on critical junctures and decision points for the United States. Although every uptick in the peace process is not covered, the book does include the most critical inflection points.

Some subjects, such as Madrid, Oslo, and Camp David II, have been studied elsewhere. For others subjects, such as critical periods in the presidencies of George W. Bush and Barack Obama, virtually no scholarly accounts exist. For this reason, in the latter cases we offer a more detailed narrative, in addition to the net assessment of U.S. policy common to all chapters. Across all of the cases, this book brings forth new source material and a common, critical analytical framework.

All five authors worked collaboratively to examine the interview material, dig through numerous secondary sources and memoirs, and then develop a common framework for this book. The introduction and the epilogue emerged from a series of workshops and exchanges between the authors in 2010 and 2011. The case studies each had lead authors: Daniel Kurtzer on the Introduction and the Madrid and Oslo breakthroughs; William Quandt on Syria-Israel negotiations; Shibley Telhami on Camp David and the collapse of the Oslo process; and Scott Lasensky and Steven Spiegel on the two chapters on the George W. Bush administration. The chapter on the Obama administration was authored by Kurtzer and Quandt.

We relied on repeated and exhaustive internal critiques as part of a review process that scrutinized and fine-tuned each case study. All the authors stand behind the underlying analysis and conclusions of the entire book.

In September 2011, the manuscript was recommended for publication as the result of a joint peer review process managed by Cornell University Press and USIP Press. We thank the publishers, particularly the lead editors, Roger Haydon (Cornell) and Valerie Norville (USIP), as well as the anonymous peer reviewers. Thanks also to Priscilla Hurdle (Cornell) and the USIP management team—Richard Solomon, Tara Sonenshine, and Abiodun Williams. Special recognition goes to Debbie Masi, the production editor at Westchester Publishing Services, and Pat Cattani, the copy editor. The book was also made possible through the able research assistance of Robert Grace, Liz Panarelli, Leslie Thompson, Surur Sanjalal, Rachel Brandenburg, Neda Afsharian, Mary Svenstrup, Jonathan Pearl, Bilal Saab, and David A. Weinberg. Britt Manzo at the United States Institute of Peace provided invaluable, boundless and thoughtful support in managing the entire project.

The authors take sole responsibility for the content of this book. Although several of the authors have served in government, this book was written in their private capacities. William Quandt worked in the White House under presidents Nixon and Carter. Daniel Kurtzer held senior positions with several administrations throughout much of the period of this book, including a role on the Obama-Biden transition team. Shibley Telhami served as a special adviser to Senator George Mitchell, President Obama's first special envoy for Middle East Peace. After this book was approved for publication, Scott Lasensky accepted a position in the Department of State.

The home for this project through its almost six years of gestation was the United States Institute of Peace. We are most grateful for the opportunities the Institute afforded us to work together on this extraordinary project.

THE
PEACE
PUZZLE

INTRODUCTION

THE DECLINE OF AMERICAN MIDEAST DIPLOMACY

The Arab-Israeli peace process has generated dozens of scholarly, autobio-graphical, and policy-oriented books, each trying to describe what happened in past negotiations, why success has eluded the parties, and what can be done to promote progress. We are adding to this small library for several interrelated reasons.

First, much of the existing literature is deeply flawed. Memoirs, incomplete personal accounts, and partisan-infused policy analyses have sometimes distorted the history of the peace process. There is even disparity among the memoirs: some firsthand accounts of the Clinton years offer honest self-criticism that is difficult to find in the first wave of memoirs from the George W. Bush presidency. Our goal, therefore, is to provide an updated, integrated, and critical review of Ameri-can policy in the Arab-Israeli peace process since the Madrid Peace Conference in 1991. Despite a voluminous amount of published material, we believe there is still the need to synthesize what is known and to seek out what actually happened and why. This book is about selected chapters in American foreign policy toward the Arab-Israeli peace process. Its inflection points cover the main lines of successive administrations' strategies and those moments when the United States tried to move things forward. It is not a comprehensive record of everything that hap-pened in the Arab-Israeli arena over the past twenty years, but rather a review of this important period in America's long-running involvement in the Middle East.

In this respect, we hope this volume will add to what we know about the policies of the Bush 41 and Clinton administrations toward the Oslo process and its relationship to the Madrid-Washington negotiations. It will define more clearly the strategic debate over policy within the Clinton administration and describe the challenges that administration faced in carrying out its policies in high-risk summitry on both the Syrian and Palestinian tracks. It will describe in some detail the degree to which Bush 43 broke ranks with the peace process policies he inherited and what that meant for his "transformative diplomacy" agenda related to democracy. And it will offer some initial observations about the Obama approach to peacemaking—well-intentioned but tactically unsound.

Second, given the strategic importance of the conflict and the peace process to U.S. national interests, it is important for policymakers to have access to and to learn the proper lessons from history. Too often, the end of a phase of peacemaking has been marked by the "blame game," assigning responsibility to one of the parties for failure to achieve an agreement. The truth usually is more textured and nuanced, with enough blame and responsibility to go around, if only the parties and the United States were to be honest with themselves. Surely, this conflict was not born of and has not been perpetuated by American diplomatic blunders or those of any single party, but neither are the United States and every other party blameless or inconsequential bystanders.

Third, given the paucity of archival and other official material, this study reflects an ambitious effort to gather firsthand accounts from a wide variety of leaders and negotiators. By their very nature, such personal accounts are imperfect and incomplete, which is why they form just one of several sources we have relied on in preparing this volume. We have also gathered an array of documentary sources, some that have never before been made public—from the United States, Israel, and Arab countries—that provide a unique window into the diplomacy of this period. We have drawn on an array of original interviews as well as on an exhaustive examination of existing sources.

Fourth, we embarked on this project because we were troubled by the increasingly partisan and zero-sum ethos that has gripped many aspects of American foreign policy, not least of which involve the Middle East peace process. This volume will remind the reader that American efforts to resolve the Arab-Israeli conflict do not begin from scratch on the inauguration day of an American president. Arabs and Israelis live the conflict daily, whereas Americans engage in fits and starts, which leads to glaring discontinuities in U.S. diplomacy. It is natural for an incoming administration to study what its predecessor did and then to choose what to continue and what to change. It is quite challenging, however, to embark on a policy predicated entirely on changing the direction of the preceding administration's policies. For far too long, American administrations have tried to dispense with what went before and to rebrand U.S. policy. Continuity in policy is not always a virtue, but it is also not always a vice.

For more than four decades, the United States has been actively engaged in trying to resolve the Arab-Israeli conflict. Every U.S. administration, even those initially inclined to maintain some distance from entanglement in Arab-Israeli diplomacy, in the end has tried its hand at peacemaking. Indeed, to varying degrees, every American administration since the 1973 Arab-Israeli War has identified Arab-Israeli peacemaking as an American interest. But no administration, with the exception of that of Ronald Reagan, has ranked it lower than that of George W. Bush, especially during his first term.

Strikingly, despite these years of effort by some of the best and brightest American leaders and diplomats, only three U.S.-assisted breakthroughs have occurred, none in the past two decades. The first occurred following the 1973 War in the region, when U.S. Secretary of State Henry Kissinger invested months in shuttle diplomacy, ultimately choreographing three disengagement agreements involving Israel, Egypt, and Syria. The achievement was significant— in the case of Israel and Egypt, the disengagement provided a foundation for the peace treaty that was agreed later in the decade. The price, however, was also high—U.S. side assurances to Israel regarding the substance and process of peacemaking as well as commitments related to U.S. engagement with the Palestine Liberation Organization (PLO) tied America's hands in dealing with the peace process during the next decade.

Kissinger's successes derived from a number of factors. The 1973 war shattered existing assumptions about power and politics. Israel was stunned by Arab audacity and the ability of Egypt and Syria to pull off a strategic surprise. A post-war Israeli commission of inquiry assailed the pre-war "concept" of regional power in its national security and defense communities, a concept that paid more attention to perceived Arab intentions than the reality of Arab military capabilities. This concept had blinded Israel's defense planners from taking seriously the threat posed by Arab military power, even while deluding Israel's political leaders from understanding the Arab determination not to allow occupation of Arab territory to become a long-term status quo.

The war also shattered assumptions made about regional leaders. After the death in 1970 of Egypt's Gamal Abdul Nasser, Israel and the United States placed little stock in the leadership qualities and the staying power of Anwar Sadat. Sadat successfully consolidated power in May 1971 through the arrest of Nasserist loyalists who had conspired against him; dismissed Soviet military advisers and sent them home in 1972; launched an economic opening designed to deconstruct Nasser's "Arab socialism"; signaled an interest in peacemaking as early as 1971, including the subsequent dispatching of his national security advisor for secret meetings with Kissinger in the United States; and when his peace overtures were ignored, displayed relatively visible signs of Egypt's military plans for war. Despite all of this, it was not until after the war that Kissinger first, and Israeli leaders later, came to appreciate Sadat as a transformational leader.

For the United States, the war challenged—it should have shattered, but did not—one of the key pillars of American strategic thinking about the Middle East. In 1970, President Richard Nixon had formulated a doctrine that effectively outsourced some of the United States' national security responsibilities in the region to two allies, Iran and Israel. Nixon and Kissinger, then the national security advisor, believed in the overwhelming power, capabilities, and deterrence of these allies in assuring American interests. Kissinger in particular believed that Israel's military superiority over all Arab foes was a stabilizing force in the region, one that would deter Arabs from upsetting de facto regional peace. It mattered little that in the 1973 War Israel ultimately reversed many of the Arabs' initial military gains: by war's end, the myth of Israel's invincibility and America's reliance on that power to stabilize the Arab-Israeli arena lay in ruins.

American diplomacy after the 1973 War was also directed at averting more wars. Indeed, the war in Sinai had ended with the Egyptian and Israeli armies dangerously intertwined, and there was no assurance that a ceasefire would last. Diplomacy needed not only to fill a vacuum, but also to prevent a continuation of war.

Against this backdrop, the creativity and perseverance of American diplomacy led by Kissinger stand out as a remarkable recovery from a failed policy. Within weeks of the start of the war, and then with growing vigor and determination, the United States—Kissinger personally—became the linchpin that would define the post-war political order. To be sure, the diplomatic breakthroughs on the road to peace required the active, creative, willing, and heroic involvement of regional leaders—Sadat in Egypt, Hafez al-Asad in Syria, and Golda Meir and Yitzhak Rabin in Israel. It was Kissinger, however, who defined the United States as the critical element in post-war diplomacy.

The 1973 War also reversed the American view of Arab-Israeli peace as an American interest. Before the war, peace was not seen as an urgent strategic interest of the United States. U.S. security was played out on an international playing field dominated by the two superpowers—the United States and the Soviet Union. However, after the 1973 War, the costs and liabilities of the absence of peace became evident to American policymakers. The heightened state of confrontation with the Soviet Union and the resulting challenge to the policy of détente; the Arab oil embargo, which was spurred by the U.S. decision to resupply the Israeli military during the war, and its economic consequences; and the American realization that the goal of assuring Israeli security had become more complex each helped transform the way American policymakers came to view the urgency of Arab-Israeli peace and its relationship to vital American interests. American policymakers suddenly needed to pay more attention to the potentially conflicting American interests of appealing to Arab leaders to assure the flow of oil at reasonable prices and of maintaining the security of Israel. From this point on, it became axiomatic in American foreign policy that the pursuit of Arab-Israeli peace was an American national interest and that persistent Arab-Israeli conflict would create uncomfortable choices for the United States.

The post-1973 diplomacy also hobbled American policy in several important respects. First, as much progress as Kissinger achieved, he did not go the distance in translating the crisis of 1973 into conflict resolution. He assessed that only limited agreements were possible, and this is what he sought and accomplished. Second, in U.S. commitments provided to Israel to seal the 1975 Israel-Egypt Sinai II agreement, the United States undertook not to recognize or to negotiate with the PLO until it recognized Israel's right to exist and accepted United Nations Security Council Resolution 242. Dealing with the thorny issue of Palestinian representation was to plague American diplomacy for more than a decade. And the United States committed to the intimate coordination of peace strategy and tactics with Israel, with no equal commitment to such coordination with the Arabs.[1] The United States provided some assurances to Egypt as well, primarily relating to assistance; however, the United States had chosen to bend quite far in Israel's direction in committing to the coordination of peace process strategies and tactics. Whatever the salutary impact for Israel of these policies, the failure to develop a comparable Arab strategy would make progress in the peace process more difficult to achieve in the years to come.

The second U.S.-assisted peace breakthrough was the Egypt-Israel Peace Treaty in 1979. The initial catalyst for progress was provided then not by the United States, but rather by the path-breaking diplomacy of Egyptian president Anwar Sadat and the responsiveness of Israeli prime minister Menachem Begin. President Jimmy Carter had entered office in 1977 interested in Middle East diplomacy and determined to try to reconvene the Geneva Peace Conference, which had met only once before in late 1973. Despite clear, early signs that neither Sadat nor the newly elected Israeli prime minister Menachem Begin was interested in Geneva, Carter plowed forward and surprised the parties in October 1977 by agreeing to a joint statement with the Soviet Union in favor of reconvening the conference. However, even as Carter engaged in his own diplomacy, the two parties had found a way to talk directly: secret meetings in Morocco in 1976 and 1977 between senior Israeli and Arab officials provided one of the backdrops for the November

1977 strategic surprise—as stunning diplomatically as the Egyptian-Syrian attack had proved to be militarily in 1973—of Sadat's visit to Jerusalem. The parties themselves had not only defined what they wanted to do diplomatically but had taken the critical, pathbreaking first step to shatter the status quo and to launch a diplomatic breakthrough.

As able as Sadat and Begin were in creating an opening for peacemaking, they proved incapable of moving bilaterally into the nitty-gritty of negotiations. The two regional leaders were too different in temperament and style, and the substantive issues that divided their countries proved too complex, at least at the outset, for strictly bilateral diplomacy to succeed. And for Sadat, a good part of the rationale for peace with Israel was to open the door to better American-Egyptian relations, and thus he surely wanted the United States to be a "full partner."

At this stage American diplomacy and determination proved to be up to the task of translating the initial breakthrough into a sustainable peace process. Carter did not wait for a "window of opportunity" to open but instead worked to create opportunities for forward movement. In so doing, he showed great agility in shifting the direction of American diplomacy—indeed, Carter had started down a track in 1977 that Begin opposed vigorously and that Sadat believed would be helpful only if the parties were able to agree on the basic principles of a settlement before the conference. After Sadat's visit to Jerusalem, Carter changed course, and he committed considerable presidential time and effort to achieve success at the 1978 Camp David Summit and the subsequent treaty negotiations. Hands-on presidential diplomacy—backstopped by a strong, diverse team of American expert advisers and extensive doses of American creativity in shaping the required mutual concessions and in crafting the language to capture progress toward a peace treaty—succeeded in translating the peace opening into a final peace settlement. It is sometimes argued that Carter brought a missionary zeal to the peace process unconnected to the importance of the issue to the United States. In fact, Carter adopted a tough approach to Israel and to Begin personally. Yet, Carter and his team also recognized a moment in which peace between Israel and Egypt could have a transformational impact in the region and beyond: not only would peace open the door to the possibility of a comprehensive settlement but it would also shift the regional balance of power decidedly in America's favor.

Although the extraordinary Egyptian-Israeli peace breakthrough changed the shape and substance of the region's political agenda and alignment for decades to come, it also carried a price for the United States. Major changes were under way in the international environment that, at least in retrospective analysis, the United States seemed to miss. For example, the run-up to the 1979 revolution in Iran occurred largely in parallel with developments on the Egyptian-Israeli peace track, and yet Carter's focus remained on peacemaking.[2] Indeed, the long-term consequences of these developments—in particular, the increasing weakness of the old Arab state order, the rise and dynamism of political Islam and the emergence of terror groups such as Hezbollah and al-Qaeda proved to be as dangerous to American interests as the peace treaty between Egypt and Israel proved valuable. American diplomacy in the Arab-Israeli conflict carried a price.

This phase of diplomacy also ushered in two concepts about peacemaking on the Israeli-Palestinian track that were to govern all efforts for the next decades. First was the idea of incremental and transitional arrangements. The theory behind the Camp David framework agreements in 1978 was that the parties would benefit from transitional arrangements and interim agreements on elements of the overall problem because final status issues such as borders, security, Jerusalem, and refugees were too difficult to tackle up front. Through the implementation of such agreements, U.S officials opined, trust would be built for the parties to tackle the final status issues. However, the real reason for the idea of a five-year transition was not so much to build trust but rather to get to a post-Begin period that might see an Israeli prime minister who was less adamant about the status of the occupied territories.

Whatever the merits of the incremental theory, it never proved itself in practice. The Palestinian autonomy negotiations stemming from Camp David were a sideshow to the more immediate challenge of implementing the Egyptian-Israeli treaty. Even so, those negotiations and subsequent efforts to construct a peace strategy based on transitional and interim arrangements, such as the initiative of Secretary of State George P. Shultz in 1988, foundered over mistrust as well as half-hearted American advocacy for the proposal in the face of rejection from the parties. Indeed, the very process designed to build mutual confidence contributed time and again to the diminishing of confidence as the parties failed to follow through on agreements reached or to implement their obligations. The success of the first Camp David process thus also begat a failed concept that was to dog peace process efforts for decades to come.

A related issue was the failure of the United States to achieve a freeze in Israeli settlement activity, even while negotiations were under way. Sadat had sought such a freeze, and Carter thought he had secured Begin's agreement at Camp David. The subsequent disagreement over what was and was not agreed soured relations between Carter and Begin and also began a long-term process of undermining Arab trust in the United States to follow through on an issue they defined as critical to peace process success.

The second concept that dominated American policy in this period was the need to advance peace prospects without the PLO, an unacceptable partner for

Israel. At Camp David in 1978 and in the autonomy negotiations that followed, Egypt tried to represent Palestinian views and positions, often adopting stances that were tougher than the Palestinians themselves ultimately were to adopt. Even so, Egypt proved to be no substitute for Palestinians representing themselves in the negotiations. Indeed, to the extent that the United States and Israel focused on this issue, they believed that it was Jordan that would be a partner for peace with Israel. The Palestinians were seen as a secondary actor, notwithstanding the United Nations decision that the PLO was the "sole, legitimate representative of the Palestinian people."

What followed from these concepts was a prolonged period of relative U.S. inactivity in peacemaking. President Ronald Reagan put forward an ambitious plan for peace in September 1982, but because Begin immediately rebuffed it and the Palestinians and Jordanians failed to agree on a common strategy for dealing with it, the United States effectively withdrew the plan. Reagan did not lobby at all for his own initiative. Six years later, in response to the outbreak of the first Palestinian Intifada, or uprising, Secretary of State George P. Shultz developed an initiative that called for an international conference "interlocked" with bilateral negotiations. This, too, failed, although elements of Shultz's plan were to reappear in subsequent American peace strategy. Reagan and Shultz also oversaw the opening of a dialogue with the PLO later in 1988, after PLO chairman Yasir Arafat accepted the three conditions stipulated by the United States: recognition of Israel's right to exist, renunciation of terrorism, and acceptance of Resolutions 242 and 338. By this time, King Hussein of Jordan had renounced his claim to recover the West Bank.

The third and last U.S.-assisted breakthrough in Middle East peacemaking occurred in 1991 with the convening of the Madrid Peace Conference. Significant changes in the international, regional, and local environment in the Middle East combined with willing leaders and creative and determined American diplomacy to create a "perfect harvest" of possibilities for diplomatic success in Arab-Israeli diplomacy. The end of the Cold War transformed an international environment previously marked by Soviet-American rivalry in regional conflicts into a U.S.-dominated international context in which the Americans and Russians found common cause to work together in resolving these conflicts. The 1991 Gulf War involved stunning and unprecedented developments, including the awesome display of American military power; America's ability to mobilize an international coalition to reverse Iraq's aggression against Kuwait; and the willingness of key Arab states, including Egypt and Syria, to join the coalition and fight alongside Western armies against an Arab country. Locally, the Palestinian Intifada that erupted in late 1987 shattered the myth that Israel's occupation of the West Bank and Gaza could continue indefinitely at little cost; and the emergence of local leaders, including the formation of a local Islamist component that would evolve into Hamas, provided the Palestinian community with a semblance of competitiveness with the PLO in determining who could speak and act for Palestinian interests.

The mortar that cemented these developments together was the determined leadership of President George H.W. Bush and the diplomatic skill of Secretary of State James A. Baker III. Emerging from the Gulf War with a variety of post-war options, Bush chose to focus his administration on Arab-Israeli peacemaking. Bush assessed that the experience of Operation Desert Storm, when Israelis and some Arabs faced the same aggressor, gave them common cause to try for peace. During the crisis following the Iraqi invasion of Kuwait, the complications from the Palestinian-Israeli conflict were visible to the Bush administration, even though the administration ultimately succeeded in organizing an international coalition. Israeli-Palestinian clashes in Jerusalem and diplomatic challenges at the United Nations over the issue opened the United States to charges of double standards, and the Bush administration put aside demands from Arab and other world leaders to deal with the Israeli-Palestinian issue with the promise to come back to the issue after the war.

As President Bush 41 told Congress after the Gulf War, "We have learned in the modern age [that] geography cannot guarantee security and [that] security does not come from military power alone."[3] Bush believed an opportunity existed for Arabs and Israelis to make progress toward peace, and he believed that peace would secure an important American national interest. He was willing to devote more attention to peacemaking than to other pressing matters, for example, regional economic or political development. His national security advisor, Brent Scowcroft, assessed later, "We thought we were remaking the map of the Middle East. . . ."[4]

Baker entered into an extended round of shuttle diplomacy in which he tried to bring together Arabs and Israelis for a conference that would launch bilateral peace negotiations between Israel and each of its adversaries as well as multilateral talks that would bring the larger Arab world directly into the peace process. To be sure, the ultimate success of this complicated diplomatic strategy rested with the leaders themselves in the region—Israeli prime minister Yitzhak Shamir, Syrian president al-Asad, Jordan's king Hussein, and others. But it would simply not have come about without the persistence of the United States during the run-up to the conference.

Baker did not approach the peace process with a predetermined plan, but rather sought to get as much as he could from the parties in order to launch negotiations. Over time, he developed trust in his team, which comprised the small circle of advisers he brought with him to the State Department and several career professionals. He knew how to use their diverse talents and encouraged dissident views. Throughout, he enjoyed presidential backing, including Bush's willingness to expend domestic U.S. political capital over the settlements-related loan guarantee issue, a crisis that developed in the midst of the most sensitive pre-Madrid negotiations. Indeed, Baker and Bush proved willing to commit the United States to high-stakes diplomacy that resulted in a diplomatic success for the United States in the Middle East.

*   *   *

As significant, far-reaching, and hard to achieve as these developments proved to be, they were also very limited in nature. The Madrid conference launched direct bilateral negotiations and multilateral negotiations, but little headway on substance was registered on any track. The fight over loan guarantees to resettle Soviet Jewish immigrants in Israel cost the Bush administration political support at home, especially among some members of Congress and some parts of the American Jewish community. The interest of the administration seemed to wane as American elections approached, and an enormous amount of diplomatic time and effort was spent on resolving procedural issues and even scheduling meetings. Bush and Baker clearly anticipated achieving breakthroughs in a second term; however, following Bush's defeat in the November 1992 election, it would take time until the new Clinton administration decided its approach, distancing the negotiations further from the 1991 breakthrough.

These three successes in U.S. peacemaking efforts demonstrated several key elements. Presidents are central to the peace process, but they do not—and cannot—operate alone. They need a strong subordinate leader and alter ego, for example, the secretary of state, who can operate with the president's confidence and thus avoid bureaucratic squabbles in Washington. The secretary, too, cannot operate alone, but needs a strong, diverse team with deep knowledge of the region and its political dynamics. And the American team, from president on down, must be fully committed to this process with persistent determination. These three successes also had their limitations. Each agreement was limited in nature and did not translate easily into a larger peace breakthrough. In the cases of Carter and Bush 41, arguments with Israel over settlements not only failed to slow down the settlement enterprise but also led to congressional concerns about whether too much pressure was being directed at Israel that would carry over into future peace process efforts.

*   *   *

We assess the transition from Bush to Clinton in chapter 1 through the prism of Israeli-Palestinian negotiations. After the Madrid Peace Conference, U.S. diplomacy encouraged direct, bilateral negotiations between Israelis and Palestinians, and U.S. diplomats focused largely on procedural issues of arranging the venues and scheduling the rounds of negotiations. The negotiations themselves lagged and became bogged down in nearly irreconcilable differences between the parties, but until June 1993, the United States offered few substantive ideas for breaking the logjam. In the meantime, Yitzhak Rabin and PLO chairman Yasir Arafat, for vastly different reasons, began reaching out to each other in what became known as the Oslo negotiations. The United States was aware of these talks but, focused as it was on the Israeli-Syrian track of negotiations, dismissed the Oslo talks as unrealistic, thereby also missing an opportunity to influence the substantive agreement that was to emerge in the 1993 PLO-Israel Declaration of Principles. The United States supported the agreement and hosted the signing ceremony, but the substantive issues and problems of Oslo were, for some time, left to the parties to resolve. This chapter assesses the U.S. role in the context of this fundamental change in Israeli-Palestinian peacemaking.

The Israeli-Syrian track of the peace process from 1993 until its collapse in the spring of 2000 is our main focus in chapter 2. Particular attention is paid to the strategic choice made by the United States to give priority to this track and to the extraordinary diplomatic "gift" given to Secretary of State Warren Christopher by Yitzhak Rabin in the form of a conditional "deposit": Rabin in fact told Christopher his bottom line, that Israel would be willing to meet Syria's territorial requirements if Syria would be willing to meet Israel's requirements on security and political relations. What happened to that "deposit" and the subsequent fits and starts of Israeli-Syrian-American diplomacy reads like a fictional mystery story, indeed like a political Rashomon tale. Each side has a different version of what happened and who did what. The only fact to emerge from this story is that an unprecedented opening for peace existed in 1993 and rose again phoenix-like in 1999–2000 finally died in the first few minutes of a American-Syrian summit: one of the main players, Israel, was not present but tried to choreograph the American role by providing the talking points delivered by President Clinton.

We look at the Camp David summit in the summer of 2000 in chapter 3 and try to sort out competing versions of why the summit failed. The American and Israeli narratives derived from the first memoirs and memories of those who participated in the summit place the responsibility for failure squarely on the shoulders of Yasir Arafat who, it is argued, would not even negotiate at Camp David. Subsequent analyses by other American diplomats and scholars are more nuanced; they fault Arafat for apparent stonewalling at Camp David but criticize Israeli prime minister Ehud Barak and Clinton as well for poor tactics, inadequate preparation, and in the views of some, too much American-Israeli collusion in developing strategy.

The Palestinian narrative counters with the arguments that what Barak offered on the critical issues of Jerusalem and refugees was woefully inadequate and that the PLO was disadvantaged in negotiating not only with Israel but also with a U.S. administration that was more interested in coordinating positions with Israel than in acting as an impartial mediator. Of particular importance at Camp David were the discussions on Jerusalem and the centrality of the refugees issue, over which the summit ultimately deadlocked, and the decision by President Clinton to blame Arafat publicly for the failure of the negotiations despite his promise before the summit not to do so. It is also curious and not entirely understandable that the Clinton administration decided to lay out substantive "parameters" for the negotiations only in late December 2000, after the U.S. election and after the outbreak of a bloody Palestinian uprising. Although President Clinton withdrew the parameters when he found the responses of the parties inadequate, the parties used the parameters to organize talks in Taba, Egypt, in early 2001. However, by that time, Barak's days as prime minister were effectively over, and the United States chose not to be present at or involved in the Taba negotiations.

We assess the peace process during the first term of President George W. Bush in chapter 4. Bush entered office with an attitude termed at the time "ABC"— anything but Clinton—and rejected the deep involvement of the American president in the nitty-gritty details of Arab-Israeli diplomacy. However, Bush did take seriously Clinton's parting words to him that laid the blame for failure squarely at the doorstep of Arafat: whereas Arafat had been the most frequent foreign visitor to the Clinton White House, he and Bush never met. Perhaps more importantly, the positive conditions for peacemaking of the 1990s gave way to a near perfect storm of diplomatic trouble. In September 2000, the Palestinians had launched the second Intifada and within a few months of Bush's accession to the presidency, Palestinian violence—including suicide bombings—and Israeli retaliation had become very deadly. Also, in early 2001, Ariel Sharon defeated Ehud Barak to become prime minister of Israel and saw as his main mission the defeat of Yasir Arafat. Especially in the midst of daily violence, Sharon had no interest in reviving a peace process that Barak had left in shambles. Equally important, the policy of the Bush administration after the terrorism of 9/11 included little interest in the peace process. Indeed, although Bush became the first U.S. president to offer official support for the creation of a Palestinian state[5] and he appointed Anthony Zinni as a security envoy, the administration during Bush's first term became ideologically fixated on the region's other problems first, including the achievement of political reform in Palestine, before considering active engagement in Arab-Israeli affairs. Sharon was given a relatively free hand to end the Intifada through military means.

Chapter 5 looks at Bush's second term, marked near its outset by the death of Arafat, the accession to power of Mahmoud Abbas, and Sharon's policy of unilateral disengagement from Gaza. The Bush administration threw its weight behind Sharon's initiative, recognizing the significance of Israel's dismantling of settlements in Gaza and the northern West Bank. At the same time, the administration did little to recognize the opening provided by the change in Palestinian leadership. By the time the dust settled from the Gaza evacuation, the administration supported—by some accounts, actively encouraged—Palestinian elections that brought Hamas to power. The result was the anomalous situation in which Bush could declare the Palestinian elections to have been "free, fair and democratic" but also vow that the United States would not deal with Hamas unless it changed its policies and its involvement in terrorism. The Lebanon War in 2006, initially supported by the administration as offering the possibility of defeating Hezbollah, gave way to Israeli despair and demands from Arab moderates for the United States to reengage in peacemaking. A clearly reluctant George W. Bush convened the Annapolis conference in November 2007 and then handed the process to Secretary of State Condoleezza Rice, who became beset by Washington infighting and backstabbing by administration officials unhappy with U.S. peace diplomacy. The administration seemed uninterested in and unprepared for potential progress being made in quiet talks between Israeli prime minister Ehud Olmert and Abbas and in the complex talks led by Israeli foreign minister Tzipi Livni and longtime Palestinian negotiator Ahmed Qurie (also known as Abu Ala'a); and George W. Bush left office in 2009 just as a bloody Israeli-Hamas war in Gaza was coming to an end, one casualty of which were potentially-promising Turkish-sponsored Israeli-Syrian talks, the first such engagement since the failed summit in the last year of Clinton's presidency.

Some preliminary observations about the peace process approach of the Obama administration are offered in chapter 6. From a heady start, at which time the president declared peace to be a U.S. national interest and appointed former Senator George Mitchell as presidential envoy, the administration stumbled for three years, careening from tactic to tactic without a sense of larger strategic purpose. As it entered the fourth year, the administration's peace process policy seemed adrift, and Israel and the Palestinians were headed in vastly different directions from those of peacemaking.

We also offer some lessons that can and should be drawn from this entire period for U.S. diplomacy in our epilogue. In general, we are astounded by America's poor performance; some advances have been made along the way (Oslo II, Hebron, Wye River, Annapolis), but these steps have not been translated into an overall success owing to alternating bouts of peace process frenzy and freeze, too much or too little presidential involvement, the persistent lack of preparations even for summit meetings, the absence of strategy at key moments, and the degree to which insider warfare in Washington undercut opportunities for making progress. Had there not been the prior moments of success for U.S. leadership in peace diplomacy, we might have concluded this book with the sad observation that the challenge is simply too great for our presidents and diplomats.

In asking these questions, we reject the argument that earlier peace process successes were simpler to achieve, grasping "low hanging fruit," whereas the current challenges are more complex. Each phase of peacemaking has been inordinately difficult in its own right and in the context of the politics and the leaders of the time. Our questions relate to American determination to articulate policy, to develop strategy and tactics, and to see through negotiations to agreements on an issue that has been of singular importance to U.S. interests for more than forty years. Having observed earlier periods of such determined, persistent, creative, and wise American diplomacy on the Arab-Israeli conflict, we are left to ponder whether that kind of American leadership and diplomatic wisdom can be recaptured. We also are left to wonder whether the supportive domestic environment in which previous administrations operated will recur, or whether congressional and public support for Israel has limited administration options and thus changed the very nature of the American role in the peace process.

Only time will tell, but meanwhile we seek in the pages that follow to provide a review of American successes and failures in the post-Cold War era in dealing with the Arab-Israeli peace process.

CHAPTER ONE

OPPORTUNITIES CREATED, OPPORTUNITIES LOST

Negotiations at Oslo and Madrid

On March 6, 1991, President George H.W. Bush addressed Congress in the aftermath of America's lightning victory over Iraq in the first Gulf War. The president, clearly basking in the glory of success in mobilizing an international coalition to reverse Iraq's invasion of Kuwait the previous August and in presiding over a quick, one-sided military victory, used the occasion of his speech to Congress to lay out his post-war policy objectives. Articulating his hope and vision for a "new world order" and resolution of the Arab-Israeli conflict, the president said,

> We must work to create new opportunities for peace and stability in the Middle East. On the night I announced Operation Desert Storm, I expressed my hope that out of the horrors of war might come new momentum for peace. We have learned in the modern age [that] geography cannot guarantee security and [that] security does not come from military power alone.
>
> All of us know the depth of bitterness that has made the dispute between Israel and its neighbors so painful and intractable. Yet, in the conflict just concluded, Israel and many of the Arab states have for the first time found themselves confronting the same aggressor. By now, it should be plain to all parties that peacemaking in the Middle East requires compromise. At the same time, peace brings real benefits to everyone. We must do all that we can to close the gap between Israel and the Arab states—and between Israelis

and Palestinians. The tactics of terror lead nowhere. There can be no substitute for diplomacy.

A comprehensive peace must be grounded in United Nations Security Council Resolutions 242 and 338 and the principle of territory for peace. This principle must be elaborated to provide for Israel's security and recognition, and at the same time for legitimate Palestinian political rights. Anything else would fail the twin tests of fairness and security. The time has come to put an end to the Arab-Israeli conflict.[1]

Thus was launched the diplomatic initiative that resulted in the convening of the Madrid Peace Conference on October 30, 1991.[2] Eight months of shuttle diplomacy by Secretary of State James A. Baker III and his team were required to bridge the differences in approach between Israeli prime minister Yitzhak Shamir and his key Arab interlocutors—Syria's president Hafez al-Asad, Jordan's king Hussein, and the Palestine Liberation Organization's Yasir Arafat—the last of whom would call the shots for a group of Palestinian notables from the West Bank and Gaza who would ultimately represent Palestinian interests in a joint Jordanian-Palestinian delegation. The conference itself launched two sets of negotiations, bilateral and multilateral, and created an atmosphere of hope that a comprehensive Middle East peace settlement could be achieved quickly.

The successes and failures of the Madrid process had several unanticipated consequences, perhaps the most important of which would be the breakthrough in relations between Israel and the PLO that occurred in 1993. After years of bitter enmity, these two parties engaged in months of secret diplomacy, under the auspices of the Norwegian government, and achieved mutual recognition and an agreed Declaration of Principles, collectively known as the Oslo Accords, signed on the White House lawn on September 13, 1993. American diplomacy opened the door in Madrid to substantive negotiations and political contacts between the parties but then played no role in the secret Israeli-PLO talks, becoming instead the host and caterer of the Oslo Accords' signing ceremony.

At the time, the Oslo Accords were seen as a critical breakthrough on the road to peace. There would be no more artificial formulas to bridge differences over who should represent the Palestinians; there would be no more excuses that the process had left out the organization viewed by the Arab states and by Palestinians themselves as the "sole, legitimate representative"[3] of the Palestinian people. Direct, face-to-face diplomacy would, from then on, take place between Israel and the PLO.

In assessing the results of the Madrid and Oslo processes, an important question revolves around the role of the United States. The United States shepherded the Israelis and Arabs into bilateral and multilateral negotiations at Madrid, but the bilateral talks that followed failed to produce agreements, and the multilateral talks faltered after a few years. The United States initiated the Madrid peace process and took one unsuccessful plunge in 1993 to bridge the gaps between the parties but then took a back seat—informed but uninterested and uninvolved in the secret Israeli-PLO contacts that led to the Oslo breakthrough. Why did the Washington talks fail, and what did the United States do—or fail to do—to try to ensure progress in the negotiations? What was it that prompted the Israeli leadership, under Prime Minister Yitzhak Rabin and foreign minister Shimon Peres, to decide to circumvent the United States, deal directly with Yasir Arafat and the PLO, and thus replace the negotiations being conducted in Washington under the Madrid terms of reference? What prompted Arafat to circumvent the Palestinian delegation to the Washington talks and agree to a Declaration of Principles that some of his own advisers argued yielded too much to Israel for the sake of gaining political recognition? Indeed, what happened to the role of the United States during this period of the peace process?

Prelude: U.S. Engagement in the Peace Process

The road to Madrid begins in 1967, if not before. The Six-Day War in 1967 changed almost all the dynamics of the Arab-Israeli conflict to that date. The Arab states, which had assumed the mantle of responsibility for the conflict after the Palestinian dispersion following the 1947–49 war, were totally defeated in 1967 in a war largely of their own making and timing. The United Nations adopted Security Council Resolution 242 in November 1967,[4] which was to become—and remains—the cornerstone of all peace efforts; and a UN negotiator, Gunnar Jarring, was appointed to try to implement that resolution. However, the Arabs had already rejected recognition of and negotiations with Israel at an Arab League summit meeting in Khartoum in August 1967,[5] and thus the UN mediation effort was stillborn. At the same time, Egypt launched the first shots in what was to become a three-year war of attrition along the Suez Canal; and Fatah, a Palestinian liberation movement launched in the early 1960s, tried to mobilize an insurgency in the occupied territories, which ultimately failed and then moved its base of operations to Jordan.

U.S. diplomacy in this nascent peace process began in 1969 with a peace plan developed by Secretary of State William Rogers.[6] Israel and Egypt rejected the plan, with the tacit encouragement of Rogers's rival, National Security Advisor Henry Kissinger, who opposed the plan because it focused on a comprehensive settlement that he believed to be unattainable.[7] Kissinger then became the chief strategist of American Middle East policy, ushering in a period between 1970 and 1973 of standstill diplomacy, predicated on persuading Israel's Arab adversaries that the United States supported Israeli strength and that the Arabs needed to adjust to this reality.

The October War in 1973 shattered any illusions in Washington that standstill diplomacy could substitute for a policy. Egypt's president Anwar Sadat had warned Kissinger that the status quo was unacceptable and unsustainable, but neither the United States nor Israel believed that the Arabs had a military option. Egypt's breach of the Suez Canal and Syria's simultaneous assault on Israeli forces on the Golan Heights proved otherwise. After a tense period of wartime diplomacy involving the Soviet Union and the conflicting parties, Kissinger turned his attention after the war to disentangling the Israeli and Egyptian armies, to structuring a Geneva Peace Conference to provide "cover" for Arab participation in peace talks, and to engaging in step-by-step diplomacy designed to achieve interim agreements between Israel, Egypt, and Syria.

What emerged from this period was the first of three peace process successes in which the United States played a significant role. Kissinger operated in a challenging global and regional environment. The United States was mired in the Vietnam War, with no end in sight. Détente with the Soviets was hanging precariously by a thread, evidenced by the Soviets' willingness to threaten to intervene militarily at the end of the October War. The United States and the West were under the pressure of an Arab oil embargo. And yet, Sadat believed that "99 percent"[8] of the cards were in the hands of the United States, discounting the role of the Soviet Union in bringing about a peace settlement that would achieve Egyptian aims. For its part, Israel, already shaken by the military setbacks suffered in the war, became nervous about what it perceived as an emerging American calculus moving the United States closer to Egypt at Israel's expense. Former Israeli defense minister Ezer Weizman later expressed his concerns this way, "My objections to excessive American involvement in the negotiations with Egypt stemmed from a simple consideration: I foresaw that US interests lay closer to Egypt's than to ours, so that it would not be long before Israeli negotiators would have to cope with the dual confrontation as they faced a Washington/Cairo axis."[9]

Despite these Israeli reservations, Kissinger was able to broker three disengagement agreements: two between Israel and Egypt, and one between Israel and Syria. He needed to devote considerable time and effort in what became almost nonstop shuttle diplomacy, and he needed to invest substantial amounts of U.S. military and economic assistance and to provide far-reaching side assurances to the parties before the deals could be finalized. Although he did not succeed in moving the conflict resolution process beyond these interim agreements, he left behind a foundation of peacemaking as well as an environment of Israeli-Egyptian competition for strategic relations with the United States. That environment became central to the dynamics of the Camp David negotiations in 1978, at which President Jimmy Carter was able to extract concessions from both sides that led to the Camp David Accords of that year and ultimately to the Egypt-Israel Peace Treaty in 1979.

As the international environment changed—the Iranian Revolution in 1979 shattered a strategic pillar of American security in the region; the Soviet invasion of Afghanistan in 1979 brought détente to an end; and nonstate, primarily Islamist actors rose to prominence in the Middle East and South Asia, especially Hezbollah and the Afghan mujahidin—American attention turned elsewhere. Initially preoccupied with Israel's 1982 invasion of Lebanon, President Ronald Reagan launched a comprehensive peace plan in September 1982, but it collapsed almost immediately when Israel rejected it out of hand and when Palestinians and Jordanians could not develop a joint approach to the plan. Over the next six years, the United States and Israel built a new relationship grounded in "strategic cooperation," and based on their agreement not to deal with the PLO until it met conditions that included recognizing Israel and renouncing terrorism. Alternative means were examined to account for Palestinian interests: Israel tried promoting rural leadership in the occupied territories under a "Village Leagues" initiative; the United States tried a "quality of life" initiative to improve Palestinian living conditions. Both efforts failed. During this period, the United States lacked a peace process strategy, and the ground-up initiatives did not work. By the end of the 1980s, the peace process was moribund, even as pressures were building up in the occupied territories over Israel's long-term occupation and its nonstop settlement policy.

The outbreak of the first Palestinian Intifada, or uprising, in December 1987 reverberated throughout Middle East politics. The Reagan administration decided that it needed a policy. Within weeks, Secretary of State George Shultz began developing a plan designed to bring about an international conference leading to direct negotiations.[10] Shultz argued for his plan until June 1988, when it collapsed under Israeli and Arab opposition. But changes in the region continued. That summer, King Hussein of Jordan renounced Jordan's claim to the West Bank, and the PLO endorsed the concept of a Palestinian state in the occupied territories and thus accepted Resolution 242. By December, under prodding from Sweden and an array of private American individuals, the PLO accepted the U.S. conditions for dialogue, and Reagan authorized the opening of a U.S. dialogue with the PLO, based in Tunis. The peace process environment inherited by President George H.W. Bush in 1989 seemed conducive to progress.

A growing library of first-person accounts offers substantial insights into the thinking of the principal diplomatic practitioners during the period under review,

1991–93.[11] There is also a significant number of academic and journalistic assessments of this seminal period in Middle East peacemaking.[12] The United States proved remarkably adept at certain aspects of peace diplomacy at the time — keeping the parties focused on the process, not allowing the process to falter as a result of bad behaviors or violations of agreements—but also proved relatively unwilling to insert itself with gusto in the Israeli-Palestinian track of negotiations.

This chapter addresses two fundamental and interrelated questions: How did the United States lose sight of the success of the Madrid process it had created and thereby drive the Israelis and Palestinians to create an alternative process of their own? And why did the United States pay so little attention to the emergence and early period of the Oslo process and thereby become an accomplice to its weaknesses and ultimate failure? In the following chapter, we examine the role of the United States in the Israeli-Syrian negotiations, which became the priority of the Clinton administration.

The 1989 Shamir Plan

The Arab-Israeli shuttle diplomacy of Secretary of State Baker between March and October 1991 followed years of effort by the United States, Israel, and the Arab world to define the process and the substantive objectives of peacemaking.[13] From the outset of his administration in 1989, Bush wrestled with Israeli prime minister Yitzhak Shamir on an array of issues, the most contentious of which involved Israeli settlement activity in the West Bank, Gaza, and East Jerusalem.

Although both leaders recognized the centrality of the other in peacemaking and bilateral relations, neither one trusted the other. Shamir was widely understood to be a status quo politician, opposed to taking initiatives and dedicated solely to the preservation of Israel's claim to the land and the security of the Israeli people.[14] He was personally attached to the settlement movement, seeing in it the dynamic vitality of Zionism and the reconnection of the Jewish people to the land of Israel. Bush, on the other hand, was a foreign policy pragmatist with long-standing personal and professional ties to the Arab world. He entered office with some interest in working on the Arab-Israeli peace process but deferred developing his own ideas until consulting with Shamir. The two leaders held talks in Washington April 5–7, 1989, but clashed immediately over the issue of Israeli settlement activity in the occupied territories.

Bush had foreshadowed his concerns in a March 13 meeting with Israeli foreign minister Moshe Arens. According to the White House record of the meeting, Bush said that "the creation of any new settlements in the occupied territories would pose a tough issue for us. . . . It was important the PM [Prime Minister] appreciate the significance of this issue here and avoid surprises."[15] But Bush and Shamir talked past each other nonetheless. During their April 6 meeting in the White House, Bush said he was "greatly upset by the fact that soon after the visit of FM [Foreign Minister] Arens here, Israel went ahead and started up new settlements. . . . This was an issue of great concern to us." Shamir, according to the White House record, said that "settlements ought not to be such a problem."[16] Shamir meant to brush Bush off, whereas Bush thought this response meant that Shamir would exercise restraint on settlements. Bush felt cheated when settlements continued, whereas Shamir was puzzled, as he never could countenance the idea of stopping settlements. Shamir tried to explain himself in a meeting with Bush later that year, where he said that the coalition agreement in Israel had stipulated that eight new settlements would be built and that Israel had thus far established five such settlements. "We have received no complaints from the Arab side," said Shamir to Bush. "It is not an important matter. Nor is it an obstacle to the peace process we are trying to advance." Bush would have none of this argument: "You and I had a frank discussion alone on this. I tried to be clear that U.S. policy is to discourage settlements. . . . Settlements are unacceptable to us. . . . What I don't understand is why just before coming here you would confront me with this embarrassment."[17] These episodes and the nonstop nature of the settlement enterprise contributed to rocky relations between Bush and Shamir that would only grow worse in the years that followed.

In response to American encouragement to initiate ideas for advancing peace, on May 14, 1989, the Israeli government approved a four-point plan whose centerpiece was elections among Palestinians in the West Bank and Gaza to determine an alternative leadership to the PLO.[18] For Shamir, circumventing the PLO's role in the peace process was a high priority. He had a deep aversion toward the PLO, which in his view was nothing more than a "foreign terroristic element."[19] With the U.S.-PLO dialogue under way at this time, the Bush administration believed it was important to start with a plan around which the Israeli political system could rally, and thus the United States endorsed Shamir's plan and sought to build support for it. Over the next seven months, Baker and Egyptian president Hosni Mubarak proposed a number of amplifying points for consideration, including a five-point implementation plan developed by Baker.[20]

It is unclear whether the administration's heart was in this effort.[21] The relationship between Shamir and Bush had gotten off to a bad start, and the administration's focus was elsewhere than on the Middle East. In May, Secretary Baker delivered a major speech to the American-Israel Public Affairs Committee (AIPAC) in which he called on Israel to "lay aside, once and for all, the unrealistic vision of a Greater Israel"; notwithstanding the fact that Baker made similar demands of the

Arabs, this speech set him on a very rocky relationship with the pro-Israel community in the United States.[22]

By early 1990, the process had moved forward a bit, but there was growing unhappiness with Shamir's policies within the Israeli coalition government. In the midst of this turbulence in Israeli domestic politics, on March 3, in comments that surprised even Baker,[23] Bush said, "the foreign policy of the United States says we do not believe there should be new settlements in the West Bank or in East Jerusalem."[24] Following this misstep, in which the administration turned the peace process issue from elections to Jerusalem, the Israeli government withdrew its support of its own peace plan. The government fell after losing a vote of confidence, but Shamir was then able to form a new, more hawkish coalition. In June, Baker told Congress sarcastically that Shamir could call the White House when he was ready to talk peace. At almost the same time, a pro-Iraqi constituent group of the PLO carried out a terrorist attack in Israel, and the PLO refused to condemn or to discipline this faction. Thus ended the U.S.-PLO dialogue that had begun in December 1988. Peace process activity stopped, particularly as a result of the deteriorating situation in the Persian Gulf and Iraq's increasing belligerency, which culminated in its August 2, 1990, invasion of Kuwait.

The United States and Israel each took away important lessons from this period of diplomatic activity. The Bush administration was vexed by the persistence of Israeli settlement activity. In response to an Israeli request for $400 million in loan guarantees, the administration secured an Israeli commitment not to direct new immigrants to settlements and to report on settlement expenditures. This Israeli commitment was to prove instrumental in the debate in 1991 over the $10 billion Israeli loan guarantee request for the absorption of Soviet Jewish immigrants. Regarding peace diplomacy, Bush and Baker had assessed that Shamir could only be attracted to a plan in which he had invested, but even this approach had failed when Shamir walked away from his own initiative. For his part, Shamir believed that U.S. objections to settlement activity were not serious, and in any event, Shamir could not countenance any restrictions on Israel's rights in the occupied territory. Both sides were to draw on these lessons in the future, often with misguided assumptions and unforeseeable consequences.

The Road to Madrid

In starting out on the road to Madrid in the spring of 1991, U.S. objectives were not well defined; they were more tactical than strategic.[25] Baker believed that a breakthrough in Arab-Israeli relations would capitalize on the changes under way globally and in the region, but his diplomacy was based around cobbling together as much as he could get the parties to agree on. Drawing heavily from some of the procedural and substantive aspects of previous U.S. peace approaches—such as the 1978 Camp David Accords, the 1982 Reagan Plan, and the 1988 Shultz initiative— Baker started building the elements of a package, including confidence building measures between Israel and the Arabs; an international conference (that would provide the visible support of the major powers and the United Nations); bilateral negotiations between Israel and each of its warring neighbors, the Palestinians, Jordan, Syria, and Lebanon; and multilateral negotiations designed to start discussing some of the region's ills but primarily intended to draw in the active participation of key Arab parties, such as Saudi Arabia and the Gulf and Maghreb states.

The United States needed to overcome formidable obstacles to achieve these outcomes. The Israeli government would not countenance the participation of the PLO. Shamir also opposed the idea of convening an international conference, even if negotiations themselves would take place in a bilateral setting. And Shamir had reservations about the U.S. role in the process. He told Baker in a July 22, 1991, meeting that he recognized the U.S. role as "honest broker" but advised against the United States taking a position on core issues once the talks began. Palestinians argued from the outset that the PLO was their representative. The Palestinians also presented Baker with several obstacles, the most significant of which was who would represent Palestinians in the peace process. Faisal Husseini, the East Jerusalem notable who led the Palestinian group that negotiated with Baker, said later that "the meetings with James Baker . . . were decided by the PLO. Both the United States and Israel know this perfectly well. James Baker met with PLO envoys."[26] Palestinians also feared that the U.S.-led process would not advance the PLO's goals of establishing a state with Jerusalem as its capital and of assuring the right of return for Palestinian refugees.[27] Syria had deep reservations about entering a process that would involve direct contact and negotiations with Israel before agreement had been reached on Israeli withdrawal from all Syrian (and Arab) territory.

In addition to the other substantive and procedural hurdles that Baker faced, perhaps none was more vexing than Israeli settlement activity. In testimony before the House Foreign Operations subcommittee, Baker said,

> Every time I have gone to Israel in connection with the peace process on each of my trips I have been met with the announcement of new settlement activity. This does violate United States policy. It is the first thing that Arabs— Arab governments—the first thing that Palestinians in the territories—whose situation is really quite desperate—the first thing they raise when we talk to them. I don't think there is any greater obstacle to peace than settlement activity that continues not only unabated but at an advanced pace.[28]

At this early stage in the pre-Madrid consultations, Israel raised the idea of a major U.S. commitment to provide loan guarantees for the resettlement of Soviet Jewish immigrants. Previously, as noted, Israel had asked for and received $400 million in such loan guarantees, but only after Baker and Israeli foreign minister David Levy had worked out an understanding by which Israel agreed not to use the loan guarantee proceeds to resettle the Soviet Jewish immigrants in the occupied territories. Because Israel kept building settlements even after receiving the $400 million in loan guarantees and because the new Israeli request was considerable—$10 billion in guarantees over five years—the issue of settlements was assured to assume prominence in the U.S.-Israel contacts on the issue.

In April 1991, Levy told Baker that Israel would not stop settlements as part of the peace negotiations, and he warned that Palestinian self-government should not become a Palestinian state in the making. In response, Baker said he needed a "credibility bank" on settlements to use with the Arabs.

Baker was not exaggerating. In a meeting in early April with the Palestinians, he heard a litany of complaints and requirements that Palestinians asserted they needed before the peace process could be launched: an end to Israeli deportations, to land confiscation, to human rights violations, and to settlement activities. During this meeting, Baker told the Palestinians to expect that "permanent status probably means to Israel something more than autonomy and less than an independent state," and he said he would consider reexamining U.S. policy on the illegality of settlements. But he also cautioned against exaggerated expectations, stressing that the "fact of life is that we cannot generate the political support to bring in the 101st Airborne to 'liberate' the occupied territories."

Baker persisted, however, and by May 1991, the elements of a package were coming together. On May 11, Baker told the press that Saudi Arabia and the other Gulf Cooperation Council member states had agreed to send observers to a peace conference, which Baker said would "break at least one major taboo" of peacemaking. On June 1, Baker felt confident enough to send letters to regional leaders proposing a peace conference, thus launching an even more intensive phase of negotiations involving Israel, the Palestinians, and Syria.

By midsummer 1991, U.S. policy challenges and choices regarding the Israeli-Palestinian track had come into sharp focus. In a pair of memoranda to Baker from Assistant Secretary John Kelly and Policy Planning Director Dennis Ross, the two officials laid out the hard choices that needed to be made:[29]

- Kelly recommended that the United States seek the "cessation of all Israeli government funded, sponsored or financed settlement activity, including roads, housing, investment and infrastructure," and the cessation of "all

activity relating to the seizure, alienation, registration or other change in
the status of lands in the territories, and the cessation of government subsidies and incentives."
- In parallel, Kelly recommended demanding that the Arabs suspend the
state of war and the Arab boycott. Ross added that Palestinians should also
be asked to "suspend" the Intifada during a settlement freeze, "suspend"
the state of belligerency, and agree to rescind the "Zionism is racism" resolution at the United Nations.
- Ross agreed that it would be hard to break the peace process stalemate
without a settlement freeze and recommended a "private assurance" be
obtained from Israel that it would stop land seizures inside the expanded
boundaries of Jerusalem.

In a critical meeting with the Palestinian delegation in Jerusalem on July 21,
Baker laid out in detail what the United States could and could not achieve in the
peace process at that time.[30] Baker reportedly said the United States was not trying
to dictate to the leadership of the Palestinians or to divide them. Rather, the United
States believed that overt Palestinian insistence on a role for the PLO, such as public
PLO selection of the delegation, would kill the process. Baker said it would not be
possible to include "outsiders," that is, diaspora Palestinians in the delegation, nor
would East Jerusalem Palestinians be able to participate in the first stage. Rather, he
noted, both diaspora and East Jerusalem Palestinians would participate in final-
status negotiations. The United States would need the "tacit acquiescence" of the
PLO in these arrangements. Faisal Husseini responded to Baker with a message
from Arafat that welcomed the American initiative. The fact that the PLO had authorized the meeting of Palestinians with Baker was a sign of good faith. But Arafat demanded that East Jerusalemites be included in the delegation. Baker, closing
the discussion, said he could not deliver this initially, "It's not a question of fairness or what is right. It's a question of reality." This last condition would have the
effect of excluding the very Palestinians with whom Baker was negotiating the
terms of Palestinian participation in the peace conference.

As this back and forth progressed, Arafat expanded his own conditions: recognition of the Palestinians' right to self-determination; the PLO must determine
Palestinian participation; Palestinians from East Jerusalem must be allowed to attend; the issue of Jerusalem must be on the conference agenda; Israeli settlement
activity must stop; and international protection must be extended to the Palestinians.[31] But the PLO lacked broad Arab support—in view of the PLO's decision
to back Iraq in 1990—and the Palestinians could not sustain these positions in
the contacts with Baker. They watched as Baker secured al-Asad's and Shamir's

agreement to attend the conference, and so in early August, the Palestinians also agreed to participate, asking for a letter of assurances from the administration that responded to some of their concerns.[32]

The Palestinian decision to participate in the Madrid conference resulted from substantial American pressure to accept limitations on their role, understood clearly by Palestinians as a sign of their weakness. Baker repeatedly told them the process would be launched with or without their participation; he argued that negotiations were the best and the only way to stop Israeli settlements; and he assessed that Shamir would use Palestinian rejection as a means to cover up his own negative stance toward peace. The Palestinians took seriously Baker's admonition not to "let the cat die at your doorstep."[33]

Baker had similar success in hammering out acceptable compromises on other core procedural issues, including the role of the conference, participation by outside parties, and the role of the multilateral negotiations. Baker provided a letter of assurances to each of the parties, but insisted in each letter that "these assurances constitute U.S. understandings and intentions concerning the conference and ensuing negotiations. These assurances are consistent with United States policy and do not undermine or contradict United Nations Security Council resolutions 242 and 338. Moreover, there will be no assurances provided to one party that are not known to all the others."[34] In so doing, Baker ensured an element of consistency in what was said to each party and maintained the status of the letters as unilateral U.S. policy statements rather than as agreements reached separately with the parties.

Meanwhile, in the midst of these complex negotiations, the issue of the loan guarantees hung over the proceedings like a Damoclean sword. Shamir perceived that the moment was ripe to gain a tangible benefit from his participation in the peace process, and thus the Israeli government pushed hard with the administration and in Congress to move the legislation forward. Bush and Baker, on the other hand, feared that loan guarantees without firm assurances against settlement growth might undercut the progress being made in advancing to a conference.

The issue put the administration in a most awkward position. The United States had been instrumental in achieving significant policy breakthroughs of direct benefit to Israel, for example, convincing the Soviet Union to grant exit visas for Jewish emigration and helping Israel establish diplomatic relations with forty-four countries, including the Soviet Union.[35] However, Israel had not fulfilled all the conditions of the earlier $400 million loan guarantee program, and thus Bush and Baker were faced with the dilemma of trying to deliver on mutually contradictory U.S. interests. For this reason, Baker pressed to postpone the $10 billion loan guarantee issue. In early September 1991, Baker told the Israeli ambassador to the United States, Zalman Shoval, that the Arabs were pressing hard for written guarantees of a settlement freeze; the United States had turned back this demand and now wanted to avoid a public debate associated with the loan guarantee issue. However, Shamir insisted on pushing forward, believing that Israel had the support it needed to prevail in Congress. It proved to be a bad miscalculation. Shamir and Bush engaged in a public clash in September, and Congress backed the administration's request for a 120-day delay before considering loan guarantees. Shamir had been very successful in obtaining agreement to the substantive and procedural demands he had made as preconditions for Israel's attending the peace conference, but he proved unsuccessful in capitalizing on this success to gain approval for the funds needed to help absorb immigrants.

The implications of this public dispute were to be of importance in the calculations of all the parties in the future. Shamir's reaction to the Senate's decision to delay consideration of the loan guarantees was sharp and far-reaching. He called the U.S. stance an attack on the "deepest foundations of Jewish and Zionist existence."[36] Bush's policies were for Shamir the antithesis of what he stood for—the ultimate incorporation of the West Bank under the sovereignty of the state of Israel. For Shamir, the clash with the United States over settlements would ultimately contribute to his defeat in the 1992 Israeli elections; the Israeli electorate made clear that it wanted its prime minister to be on good terms with Israel's major ally and benefactor, the United States.

For the Palestinians, this episode may have given rise to the belief that the United States could secure a settlement freeze if it really put its weight behind the effort. And for the United States, the issue demonstrated that a determined administration effort to try to stop settlements could get results and enjoy the support of Congress, even though the result was a hardening of congressional attitudes that was to have a longer-term impact on the administration's freedom of action regarding the settlement issue. To be sure, no one in Washington wanted a confrontation with Israel, but at the time, U.S. officials assessed Shamir's stance on this and other issues as self-defeating:

> Shamir's desire to circumvent and weaken the PLO in Tunis was defeated by his inability to hold the line against the Israeli right. Had he permitted the Palestinians in the negotiations to demonstrate that they were producing increasing Palestinian independence, had he stopped the Israeli actions that most outraged Palestinians—land confiscation, continued settlement activity, daily humiliations at checkpoints—he might have truly empowered the Palestinians from the territories and made it possible for the "internal PLO"

to become an alternative to Yasir Arafat's PLO in Tunis. But he did not. His insensitivity to Palestinian needs and concerns mirrored Arafat's insensitivity and indifference to Israeli needs a decade later.[37]

As difficult as it was to deal with Shamir, the U.S. assessment at that time was that Shamir enjoyed a strong position politically and that the Israeli Cabinet would approve Israel's participation in the Madrid conference.[38] The right-wing opposition to Shamir was seen as incapable of toppling Shamir, Ariel Sharon was seen as isolated within Likud with few options, and the left-wing Labor Party appeared "trapped in irrelevance" and would support Shamir's policies. The United States understood that Shamir had red lines, namely, to avert a role for the PLO at the conference or too much U.S. pressure on settlements, the 1967 borders, or Jerusalem. In the end, the U.S. assessment proved correct, as the Israeli Cabinet approved participation in the Madrid conference by a vote of 16–3.

The U.S. success in convening the Madrid Peace Conference extended beyond the event itself. As noted by Baker, the conference broke a number of taboos. In the mid-1970s the UN declared the PLO as the "sole, legitimate representative of the Palestinian people," whereas at Madrid the Palestinians participated in a joint delegation with Jordan, absent any PLO, diaspora, or East Jerusalem representatives. The Israelis participated despite the well-publicized declaration by the PLO that it had selected the Palestinian representatives. And virtually all Arab states—except Syria and Lebanon, which refused to participate in multilateral talks until after a comprehensive settlement had been reached—participated both in Madrid and in the multilateral negotiations that followed, despite long-standing opposition to joining peace talks before Israel withdrew from the occupied territories.

U.S. diplomacy had exploited an environment conducive to progress in the peace progress and tapped into significant interest on the part of the parties to move forward. In Israel, for example, public opinion polls indicated that 91 percent of Israelis supported Israel's decision to go to Madrid and 74 percent expressed readiness to yield territory in the West Bank and Gaza for peace.[39] In a counterintuitive twist, Bush and Baker appear to have understood the Israeli mood better than Shamir. Shamir himself, after losing the June 1992 election, said that he had intended to engage in negotiations simply as a stalling tactic. "I would have conducted negotiations on autonomy for 10 years," he told journalist Josef Harif, "and in the meantime we would have reached half a million people in Judea and Samaria."[40] Indeed, Shamir went to Madrid because of U.S. pressure, not out of a desire to make peace with the Palestinians and the Arabs. Shlomo Ben-Ami, Israel's foreign minister a decade after Madrid, puts it this way:

Shamir was practically dragged to Madrid by President Bush. The message was forcefully, by way of pressure and intimidation, brought home to him that he could have either America's friendship or the territories, not both. President Bush proved to be the architect of a formidable coalition for war. But he also showed an extraordinary diplomatic proficiency in turning that same coalition into an international alliance for peace in the Middle East.[41]

The U.S. role was instrumental in achieving success at the Madrid conference. Determined presidential leadership, a strong secretary of state who enjoyed a close relationship with and the solid backing of the president, a very positive international and regional environment, and sustained and focused American diplomacy were able to overcome the resistance of regional leaders—in particular, Shamir, al-Asad, and Arafat—and weave together a compelling peace initiative.[42] The American administration did not shy away from tackling some tough issues, such as settlements, but also judged correctly how far to push, for example, on the question of PLO representation. The United States also avoided past mistakes of monopolizing peacemaking; by bringing in Russia as a co-sponsor and inviting the Europeans and the UN to participate—a forerunner to the Quartet diplomacy a decade later—the United States built a global initiative that did not allow Arabs and Israelis to play outside parties off against each other.[43]

It is equally important to recognize the receptivity of the parties to such a U.S. role and even their dependence on the United States to exercise this role. Yitzhak Rabin, in a May 1991 speech at Tel Aviv University, emphasized the U.S. role in increasing Israel's deterrence, thereby helping Israel deal with the added risks associated with peacemaking: "The fact that the United States stood firm and was ready to become involved against an aggression in the Middle East adds somewhat to Israel's overall deterrence. It discourages initiation of war in the region."[44] Indeed, despite previously noted deep reservations about U.S. intentions and fears of U.S. pressure, Shamir would never have come to a decision to participate in a conference such as Madrid without the sponsorship of the United States. Similar conclusions can easily be drawn with respect to al-Asad and Arafat.

Although it is easy to draw particularistic lessons from the U.S. role at Madrid—that is, lessons confined to that particular time and the circumstances that existed after the Gulf War—it is also possible to draw out broader, more enduring lessons about the value of a robust, forward-leaning role for the United States in Middle East peacemaking.[45] The Bush administration started erratically on the peace process, and its first foray into peacemaking in 1989–90 failed, in some measure attributable to its own policies and statements. The administration subsequently made a decision to use the diplomatic space created by the Gulf War to forge an opening for Arab-Israeli peacemaking to get started. The administration drew heavily on the groundwork laid by previous peace efforts—in particular, Camp David, the Reagan Plan, and the Shultz initiative, rather than fall into the trap of thinking about a negotiating process to be launched "without preconditions," a Middle East code for discarding progress achieved, though not consummated, in the past. The administration proved willing to take on the settlement issue and to stand up to an Israeli government challenge with dramatic—not entirely positive—domestic political consequences. And the administration was hardheaded enough to push back Arab demands that the United States knew would be impossible to accommodate, such as engaging the PLO directly at the outset of the process. Thus the administration took what was available—a political and procedural opening, not a substantive breakthrough—and converted it into a diplomatic success. Though generations of Arabs and Israelis before and since Madrid have referred to the United States as the indispensable third party, Madrid was a moment that proved the point.

Palestinians and Israelis Negotiate

As promised at Madrid, the conference launched bilateral and multilateral negotiations, though not without serious birth pains. The Israel-Syria talks, which were scheduled to start two days after the conference, were in doubt until the last minute; Baker delayed his departure from Madrid until he was certain the two sides would meet. The Palestinians, unhappy at being in a joint delegation with Jordan for the conference, balked from the outset at having to negotiate in a joint context, and the subsequent Washington-based negotiations stalled as Palestinian and Israeli negotiators sat on a couch for weeks in a State Department hallway trying to sort out just how to enter a conference room in order to conduct formal talks. Israel initially refused to negotiate with a Palestinian delegation that included Saeb Erekat—ultimately named as chief Palestinian negotiator—after Erekat said publicly that he and the delegation represented the PLO. Israel also insisted on moving the bilateral negotiations to the Middle East and threatened not to attend talks in Washington. And Syria and Lebanon refused to participate at all in the multilateral negotiations, arguing that they had agreed to include multilateral talks in the process but would not engage Israel in this context until their bilateral issues had been resolved.

The United States played an active role in dealing with these procedural roadblocks, and ultimately the bilateral negotiations in Washington got under way. The United States also was instrumental in launching and in overseeing the multilateral negotiations, which began at a conference in Moscow in January 1992. There, agreement was reached on establishing five working groups—water, environment, refugees, economic development, and arms control and regional security—and chairmanship of the groups was divided among several international players, including the European Union, Canada, and Japan, along with Russia and the United States. The conference in Moscow also reached agreement to create a steering group in which Israel and key Arab states including Saudi Arabia—sat alongside a limited number of extra-regional parties to oversee and develop the strategy of the multilateral process.

As the Washington talks got under way, Israelis and Palestinians ultimately found their way into a conference room at the State Department in Washington, but the exchanges proved to be sterile, with both sides posturing for the press outside the room. The two sides kept State Department officials briefed on what was being discussed, but little progress was registered.

Deep differences persisted on almost every issue. Palestinians demanded jurisdiction over all the occupied territories, including full jurisdiction over matters relating to land; Israel described its approach to self-government as relating to the people, not the land, and excluded Israeli settlers and Jerusalem from consideration. Palestinians wanted an elected political authority that would exercise all powers (except security, as noted later) then held by Israel; Israel talked about delegating twelve categories of powers and responsibilities, with these subject to coordination and cooperation and with all other powers remaining as residual powers with Israel. Palestinians expected a strong executive, a legislature with legislative powers, and a judiciary; Israel defined self-government as essentially administrative and functional with no legislative power. Palestinians wanted Israel to withdraw to the 1967 line, with UN forces and special arrangements negotiated for external security; Israel talked about a local Palestinian police force, with all other security functions to remain in Israel's hands.

In March 1992, the Palestinian delegation gave the Israelis an expanded version of what they termed "Palestinian Interim Self-Government Arrangements" (PISGA), which laid out in great detail Palestinian demands related to land, powers and responsibilities, jurisdiction and other issues.[46] One month later, Israeli negotiator Elyakim Rubinstein responded in a letter that said, "there is no way whatsoever to accept on any basis your expanded outline, which would have foreclosed any option for the permanent status other than a Palestinian state."[47] Israel's counterproposal, delivered in December 1992, reflected Israel's limited definition of Palestinian governance and powers.[48]

After the intense U.S. diplomacy of 1991 leading up to Madrid, Baker and his team backed off considerably in the first half of 1992, allowing the momentum of

Madrid to languish. This decision was driven, in part, by the need to allow the parties time to engage directly and to feel out one another's positions. It was believed that too early an intervention by the United States might have fostered an atmosphere of dependency and an assumption that crises could be created in which the United States would bail out the parties. It was also a time of elections in Israel (June) and in the United States. (November). It was perceived that the Bush administration was hoping for Shamir's defeat, based on the belief that a successor government would be easier to deal with in the peace process.[49] During the summer, Baker resigned as secretary of state and moved to the White House to work on Bush's reelection campaign. The Bush administration turned its attention to other matters—the most significant of which was dealing with the aftermath of the collapse of the Soviet Union. The Bush administration assessed that an active U.S. role in the post-Madrid bilateral negotiations—coming on the heels of the loan guarantee issue—could backfire in domestic Israeli—and American—politics.

This assessment changed somewhat in the summer of 1992, following the election of Yitzhak Rabin as prime minister of Israel. The administration now believed there was an Israeli leadership intent on making progress toward peace. However, the Washington talks continued to experience two related problems that had plagued the process from the outset. First, the Palestinian delegation lacked real legitimacy. Not only was the PLO offstage, but Faisal Husseini and Hanan Ashrawi, Baker's two chief interlocutors in the run-up to Madrid, were also kept out of the talks. The Washington delegation leader, Haidar Abdel Shafi, was a well-respected figure from Gaza, but he lacked the territory-wide stature necessary to lead a fractious Palestinian delegation. Second, the PLO asserted that it controlled the delegation, but it was clear from the outset that Yasir Arafat saw the delegation as a competitor that derogated from his authority. Arafat's demand for self-legitimization took precedence over the formulation of positions in the talks to be put forward by the Washington delegation. Arafat wanted to demonstrate to both the United States and Israel that no agreement could be reached unless it were to be negotiated directly with him.[50] In this context, Palestinian decision making was "complex and opaque" and resulted in little flexibility to move forward.[51]

Madrid and Oslo Compete

The next twelve months witnessed parallel, intensive Israeli-Palestinian negotiation efforts. The Washington talks, based on the Madrid terms of reference, made little specific headway, but there were moments of high drama and potential advances. At the same time, the Oslo back channel was launched and, by August 1993, had changed the face of Middle East peacemaking.

Within a few months after launching the bilateral negotiations, the U.S. peace team understood that the talks had become deadlocked. For example, in a detailed memo to Baker from Assistant Secretary Edward Djerejian and Ross on July 31, 1992, a number of options were laid out to achieve more rapid progress. On the Israeli-Palestinian track, four possibilities were discussed; these included trying to elicit full Israeli and Palestinian models of self-government, having the United States put forward a model that would bridge differences between the parties, pursuing a unilateral Israeli decision to grant self-government to Palestinians without negotiations, or promoting elections of Palestinians in the territories who would be empowered to take decisions on self-government. The memo did not recommend one course of action over another, but the weight of the argument favored a more active U.S. approach to get the two sides to negotiate more seriously.[52]

When some Israelis were later to devise the Oslo channel, they conducted an experiment to show just how fruitless the Washington talks had become, in their view. Avi Gil, adviser to Foreign Minister Peres, assembled the Israeli delegation reports from Washington, deleted the dates and challenged Peres and others to put the reports in chronological order. The task proved impossible because, Gil argued, the negotiations were moving in circles and showed no progress or logical sequence forward.[53] Gil also noted that the public nature of the talks in Washington often gave them the character of a press conference, in which the parties appeared more interested in explaining their positions to the public and engaging in mutual recriminations than in seeing whether any ground existed to narrow differences. Critics also charged that the Washington talks were characterized by the absence of serious negotiations and mutual incentives to negotiations. Israel offered little to the Palestinians, and the Palestinians offered nothing to Israel.[54]

Israelis and Palestinians have pointed specifically to the weakness of the U.S. role in describing the failure of the Washington talks. Ahmed Qurie, later to become the chief PLO negotiator in Oslo, has said that U.S. support of Israel offered little incentive for the Israelis to negotiate seriously with the Palestinians.[55] Ron Pundak, one of the two Israeli academics who launched the Oslo process, put it this way: "[Oslo] was not an anti-American approach. Our feeling was that we could do it better alone. . . . We always compared to what was going on in Washington, which was just a disaster."[56] Notwithstanding these assessments by the Oslo architects, the negotiating situation in Washington and the U.S. role, especially between January and July 1993, actually improved somewhat.

After the Israeli elections in June 1992, Prime Minister Rabin told President Bush during a visit to Kennebunkport, Maine, that he wanted to make progress quickly with both the Palestinians and Syrians. Mindful of the prolonged violence of the first Palestinian Intifada, which started when he was the defense minister,

Rabin believed that the cost of holding on to the West Bank and Gaza had become too high for Israel. Further, he wanted the $10 billion in loan guarantees and believed he could make a credible case to Washington that settlement growth would be restrained. Bush responded positively to Rabin on loan guarantees. In the words of a senior Bush adviser, the president was willing to accept less from Rabin than from Shamir because "the difference in this case was the difference between Shamir and Rabin; Rabin demonstrated to us that he was determined to reach a [peace] settlement[;] that's why we were prepared to look the other way [regarding settlement activity on the ground]."[57]

Rabin was not particularly attached to the format of the Washington talks, but he also did not invest in changing things: surprisingly to the American and Palestinian teams, Rabin retained Elyakim Rubinstein as chief negotiator with the Palestinians, despite Rubinstein's reputation as a hard-liner on Palestinian issues.

Rabin told Bush that the Arab-Israel conflict needed to be brought to an end in order to allow Israel to focus attention on the emerging Iranian and Islamic fundamentalist threats. He shared the same message with an audience in Israel that summer, saying that Israel had a seven-year window to resolve the conflict and make peace before the Iranian threat would become real.[58]

Before entering office, Rabin had expressed to National Security Advisor Brent Scowcroft a clear preference for dealing with the Palestinian issue, where he believed progress was possible. "I believe we can make progress with the Palestinians and that the Jordanians will follow along without any problem. I am skeptical we can do as well with Syria and Lebanon. There is no basis for a compromise between us and Syria."[59] Itamar Rabinovich, later Israel's ambassador to Washington and chief negotiator with the Syrians, agrees that Rabin's initial preference as prime minister was to move first on the Palestinian track. However, Martin Indyk, who was to become the senior Middle East official on President Bill Clinton's National Security Council, disagrees, saying Rabin told Secretary of State Warren Christopher during the secretary's first trip to the region in February 1993 that Israel wanted to focus on the Syrian track. Rabin reportedly added, according to Indyk, "If the Palestinians see Syria moving it might encourage them." Indyk says that when Clinton received this report, he agreed to concentrate on Syria first.[60]

With Rabin in power, the Bush administration devoted some attention to the loan guarantee impasse and to the Washington talks. Following the president's meeting with Rabin, U.S. and Israeli officials reached agreement on several principles related to settlements: for example, that Israel would complete up to 10,000 units in the West Bank and cancel 7,000 contracts, and that government funding would not support any additional housing construction; that Israel would retain the "right" to settle and would continue to strengthen "security" settlements, giving priority to those near the Green Line; that no private land would be expropriated for settlement activity; that private individuals could continue to build in the settlements without government funding; and that Jerusalem would not be included in these provisions. Israeli ambassador Shoval added, in an earlier conversation, that Rabin would define "natural growth" in settlements in a limited manner. Indeed, within a short time, a U.S.-Israeli understanding was reached that allowed the loan guarantees to go forward. Israel agreed to deductions based on government funding it continued to direct to the settlements, and the United States agreed to trust Rabin to restrain, if not freeze, Israeli settlement growth.[61] Congress approved the $10 billion loan guarantees in October 1992 as part of the foreign aid legislation.

The Rabin government also initiated legislation to remove legal restrictions against meetings between Israelis and PLO officials, which had been banned under Israeli law since 1986. Deputy foreign minister Yossi Beilin announced the government's intention to change the law on August 9, and the Knesset in fact modified the law on January 19, 1993. Though unknown to all but a few people at the time, this change in legislation was critical in order to launch the Oslo channel.

From Bush to Clinton

The return of the Democratic Party to the White House after twelve years of Republican control marked a sea change in both foreign and domestic policy. President-elect Clinton set the new tone of his administration in a November 3 interview, published simultaneously by the French journal *Politique Internationale* and the Arabic-language journal *al-Sharq al-Awsat,* in which he was quoted as saying he would end the "pro-Arab bias" that characterized the policy of the Bush administration.[62]

Clinton was the first president to inherit an ongoing negotiations structure involving Israel and the Arabs. He appointed a relatively weak secretary of state, Christopher, indicative of the new president's focus on domestic issues. The Middle East peace team was reshaped, combining some carryovers from the Bush administration with new appointees. Martin Indyk, the founding director of the pro-Israel think tank, the Washington Institute for Near East Policy, was appointed as the senior Middle East staff member on the National Security Council, which reflected Clinton's interest in reversing the perceived tilt in U.S. policy away from Israel.[63] Samuel W. Lewis, who had served as U.S. ambassador to Israel from 1977 until 1985, was named director of the Policy Planning Staff. In other respects, the peace team reflected continuity: Dennis Ross stayed on as an adviser until being named special Middle East coordinator in May. Edward Djerejian, former ambassador to Syria, remained as assistant secretary for Near Eastern Affairs. Aaron

Miller, a member of the Policy Planning Staff, was kept in place, as was Daniel Kurtzer, deputy assistant secretary in the State Department's Near East Bureau responsible for the peace process and bilateral relations with states of the Levant.

The transition team for the Clinton administration recognized both the importance of the process it had inherited and the opportunity for translating the Madrid breakthrough into peace agreements. The paper prepared for the transition noted the favorable international, regional, and local conditions and the fact that negotiations already in progress—however roadblocked they appeared at the time—would be easier to manage than to start negotiations from scratch. The paper concluded that "the Clinton administration will inherit a Middle East that is finely balanced between two competing futures—one in which peace prevails and the other in which nuclear weapons and Islamic extremists dictate events. Working with regional allies—Israel, Egypt, Saudi Arabia, and Turkey—the Clinton administration has the ability to tip the balance decisively in favor of a more peaceful Middle East."[64]

But Clinton was also the first post–Cold War president faced with an array of challenges in trying to shape a new international order. Thus for Clinton the Middle East peace process was not an important U.S. strategic interest. He was prepared to see his administration facilitate the ongoing peace process but would not adopt this as a core concern until much later in his presidency.

During the transition, U.S. officials turned their attention to the Washington negotiations but with little success. Djerejian met with Palestinian and Israeli negotiators regularly to assess the progress of the talks and to urge practical progress, rather than to focus on principles and preconditions. From August to November 1992, when the U.S. administration was absorbed by the presidential election campaign, the core issues in dispute became clarified in the Washington talks as the situation on the ground deteriorated. Palestinians not only repeated their demand for a settlements freeze but argued for the application of UN Security Council Resolution 242 even to the interim government phase, that is, Palestinians wanted Israeli commitments to withdraw and to reverse the legal system within the territories even before final-status negotiations were to begin.

On the ground, Palestinian violence against Israeli civilians increased, leading Rabin on December 17 to order the deportation to Lebanon of about four hundred Palestinians associated with the Islamic movement Hamas. However, the deportees refused to move beyond the border area, Lebanon refused to move them, and an international media event was created overnight. The Palestinian negotiating team, already under local pressure because of toughened conditions in the West Bank and Gaza related to detainees and the economy, told the Americans that negotiations could not take place under these constraints. They demanded Israeli concessions and a more active and involved U.S. role. And yet, in mid-December, even though the negotiations appeared stuck, Israel and the Palestinians in Washington exchanged "Draft Agendas" in an effort finally to organize themselves for substantive talks after the U.S. transition.

Within weeks of the presidential transition in Washington from Bush to Clinton, Secretary of State Christopher was in the Middle East, ostensibly on a "listening tour" but also intent on resolving the issue of the deportees, most of whom were still weathering the winter on a Lebanese mountainside. During his February 23, 1993, meeting with the Palestinians in East Jerusalem, Christopher addressed the issue of the U.S. role: "There are no precise analogies to our role in the peace process. I can't promise a comparable role to the Camp David Accords, but analogous—probing, suggesting solutions, pro-active." The next day, he added that the United States will "play an active role as facilitator, honest broker, good offices, bridging gaps and asking difficult questions of the parties." Christopher reportedly assured the Palestinians that the United States considered the deportations illegal and confirmed that UN Security Council resolutions 242 and 338 remained the bases for the negotiations. Christopher reportedly told Rabin during the same visit that the United States would not supplant the parties or be a party itself to the negotiations, and it would not be an arbitrator or mediator. Rather, the United States would act as an intermediary to assist and facilitate the serious engagement that should take place between the parties. Christopher's unclear and contradictory responses to questions about the U.S. role failed to clarify a critical question that had plagued the bilateral negotiations since Madrid: Would the United States step in when necessary to break deadlocks and bridge differences? Palestinians believed they had Christopher's promise to do so; Israelis believed the opposite.

It was also during this period that the perception of Rabin's negotiating priorities—Syria or Palestinians first—became muddled. Rabin reportedly told Christopher in Jerusalem that peace with Syria would be a strategic achievement that would reduce the immediate danger to Israel as Israel prepared to confront the challenges of Iran and Islamic fundamentalism in five to ten years. Rabin said Syria had a leader who could make decisions, whereas the Palestinians lacked leadership and cohesiveness.

Within the U.S. peace team, a major debate ensued over whether priority should be assigned to the Syrian or the Palestinian track. Some U.S. officials argued that peace between Israel and Syria would be of strategic importance, removing from the conflict the second most powerful Arab state after Egypt and anchoring subsequent agreements with Jordan, Lebanon, and the Palestinians.

Other officials countered that the Palestinian issue was the core of the Arab-Israeli conflict, and that an agreement between Israel and the Palestinians would remove the biggest obstacle to a comprehensive peace settlement.

In this internal U.S. debate, Rabin's views as understood by some U.S. officials had a significant impact. In early March at the administration's first National Security Council meeting devoted to the Middle East, Clinton decided to give priority to the Syrian track, and the Palestinian track received "barely a mention."[65]

However, less than two weeks later, in an unusual meeting in Washington with the U.S. peace team, absent the secretary of state or the president, Rabin appeared to signal his interest in advancing the Palestinian track, most strikingly by indicating a willingness to bring the PLO into the peace process. In a long soliloquy, Rabin complained that the Palestinian negotiators in Washington lacked legitimacy and standing and could not move without the PLO's blessing. At the same time, Yasir Arafat showed no interest in empowering the Washington delegation because their activity undercut his own role as undisputed leader of the Palestinian people. While Rabin exhibited no fondness whatsoever for Arafat, he grudgingly noted that Arafat was the only Palestinian leader capable of making and enforcing a decision. American officials in attendance understood clearly that Rabin was expressing openness to engaging the PLO in the peace negotiations. As a first step, Rabin proposed that the United States invite Faisal Husseini to join the Washington talks, thereby reversing Israel's position on the involvement of Palestinians from Jerusalem in the talks and imbuing the talks with the legitimacy of a leader more widely recognized than Haidar Abdel Shafi.

Two explanations can be offered for what appears to be dissonance in Rabin's strategic thinking. First, this seesaw approach to negotiating priorities affirmed Rabin's intention to press forward on both tracks and to make a decision on where to focus only after seeing which track was poised for a breakthrough. There is no doubt that he was frustrated by Arafat and had a long-standing antipathy to the PLO as a terrorist movement, but Rabin also understood the challenges of dealing with a negotiating partner that was unable and unauthorized to make and to implement decisions. The second factor at play in Rabin's thinking was that the Oslo process was under way at this time. Rabin had been told that the United States was being kept informed of the Israeli-PLO contacts and thus assumed that his ruminations about the PLO would be understood in context by the U.S. officials.[66]

The following months in Washington witnessed a flurry of diplomatic activity, including a more energetic U.S. role on the Israeli-Palestinian track of negotiations. For example, in a March 17 meeting with Israeli negotiator Elyakim Rubinstein and Israeli embassy officials, Assistant Secretary Djerejian laid out U.S. views on some of the key issues being discussed. Djerejian said the United States believed the Interim Self-Governing Authority (ISGA) should have the ability to adopt legislation consistent with the agreed areas of transferred powers; that the United States supported early elections; and that the ISGA should manage land in line with its functional, not sovereign, character.

By this time, the Oslo talks were also progressing. The Oslo channel had been broached by the Norwegians in the summer of 1992. Norway's then deputy foreign minister, Jan Egeland, visited Washington and asked Kurtzer whether the United States would approve of Norway's trying to broker talks between Israel and the PLO. Kurtzer advised Egeland that it would be hard to get a formal, positive answer from the administration just months before the U.S. elections. Rather, if Norway decided to launch such an effort, it should keep the United States fully informed. Kurtzer also advised Egeland to ensure that the Israeli participants in these talks were operating with Rabin's full knowledge. The actual Oslo talks were launched in December 1992 in London on the margins of a multilateral peace process meeting. Israeli academics Yair Hirschfeld and Ron Pundak met with PLO officials Ahmed Qurie (Abu Ala'a) and Hassan Asfour. Following this and subsequent Israeli-PLO meetings, Hirschfeld and the Norwegians called the Americans— Kurtzer and, on several occasions, Secretary of State Christopher—to brief on the talks. Almost from the outset, the Israelis and the PLO started talking about a Declaration of Principles, and the Israelis prepared an early draft. The thinking was to use progress in the Oslo channel to feed into the Washington negotiations.

Thus it was that Egeland called Kurtzer March 23 from a secure phone at the American Embassy in Oslo to say there had been a "major leap forward" at the recent round of Israel-PLO talks. The two sides had agreed that the interim self-governing authority would have "jurisdiction" over the West Bank and Gaza, that final-status negotiations would begin in the third year of interim self-government, that Jerusalem would be excluded in the first stage of jurisdiction, and that elections under international supervision would be held within three months of a full agreement on principles. Several weeks later, on April 16, Egeland called again to say that Rabin had met with Peres and Beilin four times to discuss the Oslo talks, signifying Rabin's intense interest in the process. According to Egeland, Rabin had accepted the latest joint paper as a framework document, albeit with reservations about its treatment of Jerusalem. Qurie had reported Arafat's acceptance of the joint paper and interest in reaching agreement as soon as possible. During this period, Norwegian Foreign Minister Johan Jorgen Holst briefed Christopher directly on the progress of the Oslo talks.

The problem at this point became one of stage management. The Washington talks had been suspended when the Palestinian delegation refused to attend because of the unresolved issue of the Hamas deportees in Lebanon. Rabin was moving at a very deliberate pace on the deportee issue and demanded that the Washington talks resume even without a final outcome regarding the deportees. This became a test for Arafat. He became desperate to restart the Washington talks, fearing that Rabin would suspend the Oslo channel if the Washington channel did not resume; but Arafat faced resistance to restarting the talks from the Palestinian delegation in Washington, which knew nothing of Oslo and could not understand therefore why the talks should resume before the deportee issue was resolved. The challenge for Arafat was to get the Palestinian delegation back to Washington without compromising the secrecy of Oslo.

Despite Rabin's clear and growing preference for the Oslo channel, the Israelis had taken some steps to ease some of the Washington roadblocks. Rabin's government had lifted its opposition to the participation of diaspora Palestinians in the multilateral negotiations. In April 1993, the Israelis agreed that Faisal Husseini, the East Jerusalem notable with whom the United States had negotiated the Madrid terms of reference, could become the official head of the Palestinian delegation in Washington.

In late April, an unhappy Palestinian delegation—under great pressure from Arafat in Tunis and unsure why such pressure was being applied on them even though the deportees issue had not been resolved—returned to Washington to resume the talks. With Arafat having thus proved his bona fides by responding to Rabin's demand that the Washington talks resume, the ball returned to Rabin's court to deal with a PLO demand that Israel send accredited officials to the Oslo talks. By mid-May, Rabin decided to appoint Uri Savir, the director general of Israel's Foreign Ministry, to lead the talks, and Joel Singer, a trusted lawyer who had worked with Rabin for many years in the Israeli defense establishment, as the delegation's legal adviser and Rabin's "eyes and ears." Both channels, Washington and Oslo, were now in full operation, and it was a time to test the proposition that Oslo advances could be fed into the Washington talks. In fact, the opposite would occur.

Secretary of State Christopher met jointly with the Israeli and Palestinian delegations in Washington on April 27 to encourage faster progress. Christopher said that too much time had been spent on procedures and what he called "symptoms," and there was now a need to focus on substance and on creating an environment that would assist and sustain the negotiations. He said the United States was prepared to "assist and energize" the negotiations. Christopher designated Djerejian as his "quarterback" and directed U.S. officials to meet often with the delegations in order to keep an eye on developments and offer ideas. During this round of talks, the U.S. officials designated to follow the Palestinian-Israeli talks—Daniel Kurtzer and Aaron Miller—suggested a trilateral meeting and offered a draft joint statement. However, the Palestinians balked, arguing that the United

States was not even-handed and had worked out the draft in advance with the Israelis—a charge that was largely accurate. The U.S. draft statement was withdrawn from consideration.

During the next six weeks—while the Oslo talks between the PLO and Israeli officials made significant advances—the United States began working with the Washington delegations on the elements of a Declaration of Principles. This time both the Israelis and the Palestinians expressed unhappiness over the U.S. effort. The Israeli delegation said Rabin was dissatisfied with the way the American draft dealt with Jerusalem and the extent of ISGA jurisdiction; Rabin clearly preferred the emerging Oslo Declaration of Principles that treated these issues with more sympathy to Israel's positions. The Palestinians, on the other hand, said the U.S. drafts did not go far enough on Jerusalem, the full transfer of powers and responsibilities and settlements. By late June, Rubinstein was reporting that Rabin had "grave" problems with the U.S. paper, and the Palestinians were reporting that Arafat did not want the United States to surface any paper. Madrid—or, rather, Washington—had finally met Oslo, and Rabin and Arafat clearly preferred Oslo.

The Clinton administration pressed forward, trying to salvage the Washington talks. Despite the misgivings expressed by both parties, on June 30, Ross gave both delegations a U.S. draft Declaration of Principles (DOP). The U.S.-drafted DOP represented an effort to build a bridge over the growing chasm between the positions of the parties. It leaned toward the Palestinians on the key issues of jurisdiction and legislative authority, but on the issues of security and control over land, it leaned toward Israel. This was the most substantive U.S. paper to appear thus far in the Madrid process.

Rubinstein immediately responded with a long list of problems and objections; the Palestinians undertook to study the paper and responded mostly negatively over the next few weeks. The United States essentially backed away and argued no further in support of its own paper. In the meantime, Oslo was reaching a crunch point—Israel's deputy foreign minister, Yossi Beilin, told Kurtzer in late July that an agreement was within reach, and by mid-August, after a crisis in the Oslo talks had been overcome, Israel and the PLO reached agreement on the Declaration of Principles that had been negotiated in the secret talks in Oslo and which, together with an agreement on mutual recognition, became known as the Oslo Accords

What Worked—and Didn't Work—and Why

The unfolding and dynamics of the Oslo process have been described in detail by the participants and are not the subject of this analysis. Of interest here is why the

United States expressed so little interest and played almost no role in either the substance of the Oslo Declaration of Principles or in the mutual Israel-PLO recognition that accompanied the process.[67] What impact did this have on American interests, and what implications did this have for the peace process? As noted, American officials, including Secretary of State Christopher, were briefed regularly on the Oslo talks, and were privy to their launching. Kurtzer reported all Oslo-related conversations to the Secretary of State and the peace team in Washington.

The signals of Israeli interest in engagement with the PLO were also hard to miss; witness the extraordinary conversation between Rabin and the U.S. peace team in February 1993 and the proliferation of reports of meetings—in Washington, Europe, and elsewhere—of Israeli and PLO figures. Later, as the Washington talks continued to falter, the United States was receiving reports of more and more progress in Oslo. What factors got in the way of the United States understanding the shift in gravity that was taking place between Washington and Oslo?

Several factors appear to have clouded American strategic thinking. First, the PLO remained very unpopular in Washington in 1992–93, largely because of the support it had given to Iraq in the 1991 Gulf War. The U.S.-PLO dialogue, which started at the end of 1988, had been suspended in June 1990 after the PLO Executive Committee had failed to condemn and to punish a constituent organization for a terrorist attack against Israel. Second, the Clinton administration entered office with a view that the Bush administration had been too hard on Israel, as evidenced by the bilateral crisis over the loan guarantees. There was no stomach for pushing forward an initiative dealing with the PLO. Third, the Oslo process appeared to be a Peres-led initiative, and Peres's standing among U.S. policymakers had never been high. Rabin personally never briefed American officials on Oslo and never provided a clear message that he was on board the effort to test whether relations should be established with the PLO. Fourth, Rabin's earliest messages were assessed by some in the administration to assign more weight to the negotiations with Syria than with the Palestinians, and this helped to convince Washington to adopt a Syria-first approach. Only later would some American officials understand fully Rabin's strategy of promoting both tracks and seeing which track offered the best chance of success.

Another, speculative factor goes beyond the specific issues of Oslo and Madrid. Oslo can be seen as an example or case study of an American administration's lack of interest in a process that it had not initiated and in which it did not play the central role. The Clinton administration inherited the Madrid process from the Bush administration, but it was not present at the inception of Oslo. U.S. officials were busy putting together the elements of a U.S. peace strategy based on Madrid, and they appeared unable to factor in the Oslo elements that did not fit with the emerging U.S. approach. It was not a case of not knowing about Oslo, but rather an example of not paying adequate attention to a diplomatic process not conceived in Washington.

Significantly, without realizing it at the time, the United States contributed to Oslo by illustrating to Rabin in the Washington draft some of what he wanted to see as well as some of what he did *not* want to see—in a Declaration of Principles. The U.S. June 30 draft Declaration of Principles angered Rabin, for it went beyond not only Rabin's "red lines" but also exceeded what the PLO in Oslo appeared ready to accept on some key issues, such as jurisdiction. Indeed, Rabin was intent on exploiting a significant negotiating advantage relative to Arafat, namely, that Arafat was prepared to accept a weaker Declaration of Principles as long as the PLO's (and his own) role was given centrality in peacemaking efforts.

The Israelis and the PLO both assumed that the results of Oslo would feed into the Washington negotiations, that is, that the PLO in Oslo could adopt positions that the Palestinians in Washington could not, and that this would spur better Israeli-Palestinian give-and-take.[68] But in fact, Washington fed into Oslo. The Israelis found that by keeping the Americans briefed on the Oslo talks, they could gain "an accurate, updated understanding of American thinking.[69] Thus, at the outset of the Oslo channel, the Israelis and Palestinians appeared of one mind in assessing the futility of continuing the Washington talks; they did not believe the American role in Washington would change for the better in moving those talks forward and wanted Oslo to be the catalyst for advancing the talks. Although the United States was to be kept out of the talks, it was not to be kept out of the loop entirely.[70]

The United States thus played an indirect role in Oslo, in that many of the ideas that surfaced were carryovers from Camp David I, the Shultz initiative, and other U.S. plans. However, other than personal observations offered by Kurtzer to Hirschfeld,[71] the American government played no direct, substantive role in Oslo. Analysts are divided on the reasons why. Author Jane Corbin admits to not knowing why the United States did not take Oslo more seriously.[72] Washington Institute analyst David Makovsky suggests several reasons for lack of U.S. interest: the United States dismissed Oslo "as a Peres vision that stood no chance of winning Rabin's backing"; the United States trusted only Rabin and believed he would confide in Washington if Oslo were serious; Oslo was but one of several Israeli-PLO channels, so the United States had no reason to take Oslo more seriously than the others; and the United States thought its own role was "indispensable" to the negotiations and that nothing would happen without U.S. intervention.[73] Mahmoud Abbas suggests that the United States knew about the negotiations, didn't take them seriously but then was embarrassed by their success, and could not admit to having been briefed, as this would have offended the Washington negotiators who had been kept in the dark.[74] By the time Oslo should have been of greater interest to the Americans, Rabin was delivering to Christopher the "deposit" or "pocket" that held out great promise as a breakthrough between Syria and Israel.[75] When Christopher asked Rabin about the PLO talks during the same meeting as the "deposit" was being discussed, Rabin appeared to Christopher to dismiss Oslo.

Israelis and Palestinians saw no downsides in negotiating directly in Oslo and believed there were significant advantages. The Israelis believed the PLO negotiators were far more flexible than their Washington counterparts, a point echoed by the PLO officials themselves. Hirschfeld quotes a colorful example of this belief from Qurie,

> We here in Oslo are in far better shape than the Palestinians in Washington. Haidar Abdel Shafi (head of the Palestinian delegation in Washington) may think that the negotiations have progressed rather nicely in Washington and will probably consider whether he should smile in a visible way. However, before he decides, he will spend two sleepless nights wondering what his colleagues will say and how Arafat in Tunis will react to such an independent decision, and, in the end . . . he will decide not to smile. In Oslo, we can smile and laugh as much as we want, and no one will interfere.[76]

For Arafat and the PLO, the Oslo channel had distinct advantages, the most important of which was the recognition the channel conferred on Arafat's supremacy in Palestinian decision making. Arafat was clearly in a position to prevent the Washington talks from making progress; Oslo offered him the opportunity both to gain recognition and to control the pace and the scope of progress in negotiations. Oslo thus made manifest the PLO's political will to strike a deal in a manner that the Washington format could not produce. In this respect, according to the PLO's assessment, the Americans were too tied to what they had created at Madrid to understand the dynamics of Palestinian decision making.[77] Both leaderships also preferred negotiating in secret than in the semi-public atmosphere of the Washington talks.

For the Israelis, the Oslo process offered similar strategic advantages, especially if the United States was not present. First, it allowed Israel to use the prospect of progress in the Syrian track to act as a catalyst to move the Palestinians' positions. Savir admits to using this tactic when Rabin delivered the "deposit" to Christopher; essentially, Israel said to the PLO, "If you don't hurry, Syria will come first."[78] Second, it allowed Israel to use Arafat's desperate interest in gaining recognition of his status as the leader of the Palestinians as a lever to remove some critical issues from the emerging Declaration of Principles. Rabin had been particularly disturbed by the direction taken in the Washington talks and the tendency of the Palestinian delegation there to focus on issues that he did not want to deal with—settlements, prisoners, and arbitration of disputes, among others. The Oslo Declaration of Principles did not include any of the controversial issues of most concern to Rabin, including any mention of settlements.

A number of explanations have been offered to explain Arafat's reasons for not pressing to include the settlement issue (or the prisoner issue) in Oslo. Avi Gil believes that the PLO assessed its success in gaining acceptance of its foothold in the West Bank and Gaza territory as of far more importance than any reference to settlements or settlers. Because the PLO read the Declaration of Principles as promising them a state in five years, "in a way, prisoners and settlers, all these issues, will just solve themselves in time, if you do the big things."[79]

PLO foreign minister Nabil Shaath argues that the inclusion of some of these issues as agenda items in the final-status negotiations agenda was a gain for the Palestinians,[80] but others disagree strongly. In a biting criticism of the Oslo Accords, Abdel Shafi cites several critical problems with the PLO-negotiated agreement.[81] First, he says, the agreement failed to address Israel's "illegal claim" to the occupied territories. Second, the agreement enumerated some issues to be deferred until the final-status negotiations—such as Jerusalem, borders, and settlements—but there was no mention of withdrawal beyond the interim period. Complete withdrawal was never mentioned in the agreement. Third, Abdel Shafi blasts the agreement for being phrased in generalities over which there was wide room for different interpretations. Abdel Shafi argues that the Palestinian delegation in Washington stood firm on key issues, and he concludes, "I am only sorry that those who made the agreement chose to get beyond the impasse by conceding."[82] Makovsky cites Hanan Ashrawi as complaining to Mahmoud Abbas about the failure to mention settlements; Abbas reportedly replied that the PLO had made "strategic political gains" in terms of recognition of the PLO and Palestinian political rights.[83]

The other critical factor, besides Arafat's personal ambitions having an impact on his willingness to concede ground on settlements, relates to Israeli assessments and negotiating priorities. Ron Pundak, one of the two initial Israeli negotiators, has expressed the view that the Israelis were too successful in convincing the Palestinians that Rabin would stop all settlement activities, which clearly proved not to be the case.[84] Yair Hirschfeld, the other Israeli negotiator, has said that he prepared a study in 1991 on the Oslo concept and language that referred to three different negotiating models: the first model proposed to create a structure that would have enabled the Palestinian Authority (PA) to veto the creation of new settlements; this idea was rejected by the Israeli side. As Rabin's government was dependent on the support of the ultra-orthodox Sephardic party, Shas, any move regarding the settlements was perceived as being politically not sustainable, according to Hirschfeld.[85] As the Oslo Accords unfolded, Rabin also assigned the Israeli army a key role in the negotiations. For the army, the question of settlements was solely a question of security. Savir quotes Deputy Chief of Staff Amnon Lipkin-Shahak of the Israeli Defense Forces (IDF) as saying, "The IDF bears responsibility for the settlers' safety, and we must be able to say to them . . . that their security is being protected."[86] Savir goes on to say that most of the efforts of the Israeli negotiators in the second phase of Oslo were related to the security of the settlements and the movement of settlers in the West Bank.

Qurie adds an important dimension to this debate over settlements. He avers that, when the PLO delegates in Oslo asked for a settlement freeze, Hirschfeld told him that the Rabin government had halted almost all activity but could not say so publicly. Savir notes that it was he (not Hirschfeld) who brought to Qurie's attention the Israeli government decision number 360 that promised to halt expansion of existing settlements. Savir says that after showing the PLO a copy of the Cabinet's decision, the PLO dropped its insistence on requiring that the agreement stipulate the need for a settlement freeze.[87]

After the Oslo Accords were signed on the White House lawn on September 13, 1993, the Israelis and Palestinians negotiated almost nonstop for many months to translate the Declaration of Principles into a detailed agreement. The U.S. peace team played a facilitative role during this period but was largely kept away from the substantive negotiations. Norwegian negotiator Terje Roed-Larsen recalls that the Israelis and Palestinians "provided a kind of 'window dressing'" whenever meeting with Ross and the U.S. team, that is, providing enough information to keep the Americans briefed but not enough to elicit any active U.S. intervention.[88] Indeed, in one incident in Eilat, Israel, Savir and Qurie hid the papers they had been discussing when Ross entered the room, so as not to engage him in the substance of the negotiations; they provided him a general briefing, and when Ross left, the Israelis and Palestinians resumed their negotiations.[89]

For a peace process that had long been directed at producing direct, face-to-face negotiations between Israel and its neighbors, for the United States the achievement of such an outcome should have been judged a success. Several of the Israeli and Palestinian participants, in fact, assess the Oslo implementation talks in exactly those terms. Amnon Lipkin-Shahak, who became the chief Israeli negotiator in the second phase of Oslo, has said, "I don't remember a real need for a bigger U.S. involvement." For Rabin, whose views Lipkin-Shahak and the IDF negotiators represented, the Americans would have added unwanted political issues to the discussions, which the Israeli side wanted to concentrate on security matters.[90] Savir said that he favored an American role limited to "kick[ing] off the negotiations, like Madrid, but then allowing the parties to negotiate directly." In any event, Savir added, the Americans were "too much focused on Syria first . . . [and] they didn't have the same understanding that we had—that without Arafat, nothing can be done."[91] Other Israelis expressed similar views, sometimes more directly. Yossi Ben-Aharon, a former Israeli official, said, "We always had problems with American [involvement in the actual negotiations]. They were too impatient. . . . I was strong in my opposition to [such] an American role. I favored strictly bilateral talks. The American role didn't bring about any progress."[92] Needless to say, this official, like his prime minister, really did not want progress in these talks anyway.

Osama El Baz, the senior Egyptian adviser to President Mubarak who often consulted with the Palestinian negotiators, has said that U.S. involvement would only have lengthened the time it took to make a deal. "I advised against renegotiating it [the Oslo Accords] through the U.S. . . . The two sides may have been able to reach a deal with the U.S. involved, but it would have taken longer."[93] Nabil Shaath, the PLO's foreign minister at the time, has argued that the Madrid model became a "straitjacket" for the Americans, "Once the American team devised their model, they developed what could be called a 'Pygmalion complex' and couldn't let go of their Madrid formula. . . . They concentrated all their efforts on fitting everything into their cherished model rather than reexamining it and trying to build new models to deal with the actual realities."[94]

Whereas American involvement in the negotiations themselves did not apparently interest the parties, it is worth asking why neither side thought to involve the United States in monitoring the Oslo agreement. After decades of enmity and distrust, it would have seemed logical for both sides to look to a third party to monitor compliance with Oslo's requirements and to assure some accountability regarding the performance of each side's obligations. Yet, a request that the United States play this role was not made, and the United States itself does not seem to have suggested it, even when serious problems threatened the integrity of the Oslo process.

Yossi Beilin put it simply, "The whole question of who is the referee was not raised—the question of a third party to monitor and to be the referee of breaching the agreement permanently."[95] The Israelis would have opposed a U.S. monitoring role because it would have exposed practices—settlements and roadblocks or checkpoints—that would have put the spotlight on Israel. And the Palestinians would have opposed U.S. monitoring because it would cast a spotlight on Palestinian failure to take steps against terrorism.

Palestinian pollster Khalil Shikaki argues that "the U.S. has failed . . . to create a perception that its efforts are evenhanded and the overwhelming majority of the [Palestinian] elite as well as the public at large believes the U.S. is totally biased in favor of Israel."[96] Hanan Ashrawi offers stinging criticism of the U.S. role, questioning the credibility of the United States as "neutral arbiters," citing the "overwhelming Jewish representation" of the American team and arguing that the United States intervened only when Israel "needed bailing out, and becoming in effect Israel's guardian." "It was evident to me and to others that [U.S.] positions were defined on the basis of what was good for Israel from the different perspectives of the Israeli political spectrum."[97] Confirming much of Ashrawi's criticism, Aaron Miller would later write, "Far too often the small group with whom I had worked in the Clinton administration, myself included, had acted as a lawyer for only one side, Israel."[98] Ross admitted this bias in his account of the peace process:

> "Selling" became part of our modus operandi—beginning a pattern that would characterize our approach throughout the Bush and Clinton years. We would take Israeli ideas or ideas the Israelis could live with and work them over—trying to increase their attractiveness to the Arabs while trying to get the Arabs to scale back their expectations. Why did this pattern emerge? The realities dictated it.[99]

Notwithstanding the reticence of the parties—each for different reasons—to ask the United States to monitor the agreement, it is particularly curious that the United States did not insist on that role being performed. Daniel Kurtzer and Scott Lasensky conclude, "The need to 'keep the process alive,' which became the mantra throughout the Oslo years, was deemed more important than having the United States take strong positions when the parties did not comply with commitments and agreements."[100] Indeed, the parties did not comply with the commitments made to each other or to Washington. Settlement activity continued throughout this period and the population of settlements grew. Palestinians engaged in violence and acts of terrorism, and except for a brief period in 1996, the Palestinian Authority did nothing to uproot terrorist infrastructure. No one held the parties accountable for these actions, and there were no consequences for the failure of Israel and of the Palestinians to carry out their obligations.

The Consequences of American Policy

Against this backdrop, it is appropriate to ask whether a more active U.S. role could have improved the odds of Oslo's success, for example, by strengthening the

Declaration of Principles or by aligning behaviors on the ground with the substantive negotiations.[101] Palestinians dismiss this possibility: they believed the United States was biased and thus a more interventionist U.S. role would only have tipped the balance further against Palestinian interests. The Palestinians had quite specific goals in Oslo, but only some of them were fulfilled. Arafat makes this assessment in an interview during September 1993:

> The agreement we have reached constitutes, more or less, an initial step that spells out the ground rules governing the interim solution, as well as the basic components of the final solution, which must result in the dismantlement of the occupation and the complete withdrawal of occupation troops from our land, holy places and holy Jerusalem. . . . The most important component of the agreement is not the provision stating that the Israelis will withdraw from Gaza and Jericho, but rather the acknowledgement that the jurisdiction of the Palestinian authority covers all occupied Palestinian territories.[102]

Arafat's expectations and assessment went far beyond the plain text of the Oslo Accords. The Declaration of Principles did not promise a complete withdrawal of Israeli forces; it was largely silent on the question of Jerusalem, noting only that the issue would be dealt with in the final-status talks; and it did not assure Palestinians of jurisdiction over all occupied territories. The DOP did not even provide Arafat with the window dressing he sought of having a Palestinian police officer on the Allenby Bridge over the Jordan River. Savir notes that Israel was cautious about raising Palestinian expectations about the extent of territorial withdrawal in the first stage, recognizing that Palestinian expectations were exaggerated.[103] Makovsky assesses, with some nuance, that Israel and the PLO understood early on each other's bottom line: Palestinians needed to know that autonomy would lead to a state; Israel needed to be assured of security; and thus, while there was no promise of a state in the Declaration of Principles, Palestinians were led to believe that they could get a state if Israel's security needs were met.[104]

Essentially, the Oslo Declaration of Principles was a case study in ambiguities and of different expectations of the two parties. Rabin's frustration with the absence of a definitive Palestinian decision maker had led him to accept Arafat as a partner, but his personal enmity toward Arafat and skepticism about Arafat's intentions pushed Rabin to emphasize security over all else in the Declaration of Principles. For Rabin, the DOP was a significant achievement. Among other things, it also promised no definitive outcome but focused instead on five years of Palestinian performance of their obligations and five years of Palestinian efforts to build the institutions of self-governance. As Pundak has summarized, "He wanted, in my reading, to judge things to see how they develop."[105]

In Pundak's view, by focusing on security, Rabin (and Peres) also missed an opportunity to translate Oslo into a more meaningful breakthrough: "Post-Oslo, the day after the signing in Washington, Rabin and Peres should have declared unilaterally at least one time the most important element of the end game, and say that this agreement will lead to a two-state solution . . . The Palestinians can only do one Altalena, not ten. . . . This was the crucial moment when we decided who ran the show. . . . This could have united everyone around the objective of [a] two states solution."[106]

For his part, Arafat did not make things easy from the start. When he arrived in Gaza to a triumphant welcome following the Oslo agreement in May 1994, he reportedly hid a wanted terrorist under the seat of his car; the Israelis let it pass, given the symbolic importance of Arafat's return, but it left a sour impression of Arafat's commitment to the agreements he had signed.

From the perspective of Ghassan Khatib, a former Palestinian negotiator, the scorecard is far more negative:

> The flimsy agreements and their implementation, the dependent PA and the vested interests of the new elite, together with the resumption of Israeli occupation measures that exposed the real nature of the agreements encouraged opposition to the agreements and led to a gradual decline in the public position of the leadership. . . . A cycle was thus established: poor negotiations performance led to flawed agreements that negatively affected the structure and performance of the leadership which led to an increase in violence and strengthened the opposition, reducing the leadership's popularity and allowing it to be further exploited in negotiations. . . . An outcome of that cycle was that the Palestinian leadership became compromised, corrupt, dependent on Israel, incapable of facing challenges, and most important, oppressive in its response to public criticism. Its style of negotiating and leadership led it to lose its original reservoir of power—public confidence and support garnered through the years of exile and uprising—leaving it helpless before Israel's whims and dictates.[107]

In the context of Arafat's insistence on reestablishing the PLO's central role, of the PLO's distrust of the United States, of Israel's focus on security, and of Israel's realization that it could strip the DOP of much substance in return for recognizing the PLO, it is doubtful that the United States could have addressed fully the deficiencies of the Oslo Declaration of Principles, even if U.S. resolve and determination had been greater than it proved to be. For the United States, the prize was Syria, and the Palestinian-Israeli track was secondary. By the time the United States got engaged in the Washington talks, the secret Oslo channel was far progressed, and both Rabin and Arafat saw greater advantages in moving forward bilaterally than in bringing Washington into the negotiations.

Analytical Implications and Lessons Learned

A number of analytical conclusions can be drawn from this period. By all measures, the Madrid conference proved to be a very important breakthrough in process and political engagement.[108] For the first time, most of the Arab world participated actively in a peace process activity, both at Madrid and in multilateral talks with Israel. The importance of the multilaterals cannot be overstated, even though they were allowed to drift and to fade away within a few years. Until this time, Arab states had expressed the view that their own relationships with Israel were contingent on a resolution of the Arab-Israel conflict. At and after Madrid, however, the Arab states participated actively in a series of negotiations and engagements with Israel: in working groups on economic development, arms control and regional security, water, environment and refugees; and in a steering group that guided the multilateral process. In addition to the active involvement of the Arab states at this stage of the peace process, the multilateral talks also provided a platform for the engagement of outside parties, many of which eagerly sought a role in peacemaking. Canada chaired the refugees group, the European Union chaired the economic development group, and Japan chaired the environment group. Within a couple of years, the multilaterals were to stimulate a series of four public-private economic summits in Arab capitals, at which Israeli and Arab business leaders and officials rubbed elbows and planned joint business ventures.

And yet, despite the far-reaching implications of the multilaterals, senior U.S. officials paid surprisingly little attention to them and ultimately allowed them to wither away. Secretary Baker led the U.S. delegation to Moscow in January 1992 where the multilateral talks were launched, but after that other senior officials, such as Ross, were to beg off when asked to participate in the talks themselves. The Clinton administration paid almost no attention to this aspect of the peace process, in part because the multilateral talks were achieving little of substance but also perhaps because they were inherited from the Bush administration and were not an invention of Clinton's peace team.

Madrid did prove successful in dealing with potentially intractable process issues, such as Palestinian participation, that were resolved through compromise formulas that satisfied no party completely but which allowed the conference to take place. Madrid also demonstrated the best of American diplomacy: a president who was determined to translate a regional war and international military coalition into a catalyst for peacemaking and a secretary of state who was closely aligned with the president through friendship and political resolve and was willing to devote substantial time and political capital to narrow and ultimately bridge Arab-Israeli differences over the Madrid terms of reference. The Bush administration also showcased steely resolve on the politically explosive issue of loan guarantees, refusing to bend on principled opposition to settlements in favor of the expedient outcome of providing assistance to Israel.

Madrid also demonstrated the capacity of a president to exploit favorable regional and international conditions for the sake of peace. After the 1991 Gulf War, President George H.W. Bush chose to parlay his hard-won prestige into a risky peace-process gamble. Bush and Secretary of State Baker understood the salience of the peace process in regional terms as well as the degree to which larger American interests would be served by U.S. activism in the search for peace.

Nevertheless, Madrid had limited substantive reach. The terms of reference provided no real direction for the subsequent negotiations. U.S. letters of assurances to the parties provided a glimpse of what the United States would support in negotiations, but the United States gave no indication of its willingness to advance its policy positions by active engagement in the negotiations. The Washington bilateral talks between Israel and each of its neighbors went nowhere and proved to be little more than formalistic recitations of positions. On the few occasions when the United States engaged in more active intervention—for example, when the United States tabled a draft DOP in June 1993, senior American leadership was not invested in the effort, and opposition from the parties led the Americans to back away from the fray.

This case study also suggests some lessons about leadership and management of the peace process. The two presidents—Bush and Clinton—could not have been more different in style, temperament, and orientation. Bush had a strong background in and well-formed views about international affairs, and he held strong positions about some core issues in the peace process, for example, Israeli settlements. Sometimes these strong feelings worked to his disadvantage, upsetting Israel and its supporters unnecessarily and having unintended reverberations in internal Israeli politics. Clinton, on the other hand, had very little prior exposure to international issues and admitted in public speeches both during the presidential campaign and later that his views about Israel, for example, had been influenced most strongly by his pastor. Both Bush and Clinton selected lawyers with vast government experience as their secretary of state, but only Bush had a preexisting close relationship of friendship and trust with his nominee, James Baker. As

versed in foreign affairs as Warren Christopher appeared when he was appointed—
having served as deputy secretary of state in the Carter administration—he never
seemed to have the personal relationship with the president or the mandate to
move forward boldly that Baker demonstrated throughout his tenure. And the
two presidents also differed fundamentally in how they saw the basic problem in
the conflict. Bush and Baker sought to find the middle ground between Israel and
the Arabs, deferential to Israeli red lines but not bound by them; whereas, Clinton
and Christopher were to adopt an approach of precoordination of policy with
Israel so as not to expand U.S. policy beyond the lines acceptable to the Israelis.

One of the perplexing questions of this period is why the United States showed
so little interest in the emerging secret channels between Israel and the PLO, in
which Oslo proved to be the most successful. Having decided early in the Clinton
presidency on a Syria-first strategy and having no personal stake in launching the
Oslo talks, the United States largely ignored Israeli and Norwegian briefings on
the secret talks and offered no input. Rabin had alerted the Americans to his frustration over the absence of an authoritative Palestinian voice in the Washington
talks, but the Americans did nothing in response.

The Madrid-Washington negotiations produced no substantive agreements
between Israel and the Palestinians. The two sides used the talks largely to declare
formal positions and to posture before the international press. The talks almost
did not get off the ground at the outset, soon deadlocked, and made no progress.
The Bush-Baker achievement at Madrid proved to be a process success, but with
almost no substantive impact.

Another important analytical lesson from this period relates to the change in
the U.S. negotiating posture. The Bush administration initially pursued a relatively passive approach that let the peace process languish. The United States spent
much of 1989 and early 1990 developing formulas trying to advance the peace
initiative of Prime Minister Shamir to hold elections in the occupied territories in
order to empower a local Palestinian leadership. But its poorly coordinated and
halfhearted efforts contributed to the failure of this approach, as did the poor personal relations and the dispute over settlements that marked the initial encounter
between Bush and Shamir in 1989.

However, immediately after the Gulf War in 1991, Bush and Baker had set
their sights on what became the Madrid conference, and they succeeded because
of their determined pursuit of their goal, despite opposition from the parties in
the region. Sustained U.S. diplomacy, underpinned by determined presidential
leadership, marked the U.S. approach. American officials exploited a full array of
diplomatic tools, for example, extended shuttle diplomacy by the secretary of state
and side letters of assurances designed to close the deal. Following Madrid, the

Bush administration let the Washington talks falter. The administration turned to reelection politics, and the eight rounds of Palestinian-Israeli talks in Washington during 1992 were marked by a much-reduced U.S. diplomatic effort.

The Clinton administration made an early strategic decision to focus on Syria. But management of the peace process was downgraded at the same time, from the secretary of state (Christopher) initially to the assistant secretary (Djerejian) and then to the special Middle East coordinator (Ross), who was appointed in June 1993. Christopher traveled to the region quite often, but his visits lacked focus and high-level vigor. The U.S. peace team was busily engaged during this period, but its results were meager. The one exception—the U.S.-draft Declaration of Principles, which was put forward in June 1993 over the objections of the two parties—represented an effort by the Clinton administration to breathe life into the Washington talks, but the administration backed off when the parties balked at the U.S. paper.

A pattern of insularity and "dysfunctionality" also developed in the workings of the American peace team. According to Djerejian, "SMEC (the special Middle East coordinator) became a reality of its own, and it became divorced from the workings of the Department [of State], with independent channels of information and lines out that I think diminished a good foreign policy formulation toward the Middle East. . . . It was a bad paradigm."[109]

The United States played a limited role in the ongoing Washington negotiations and virtually no role in the Oslo process between Israel and the PLO; and the United States paid little attention to the deterioration of conditions on the ground. The lesson here is that an administration must not allow the situation on the ground to deteriorate if steps can be taken to prevent that from happening.

The Oslo process, built on the foundations of the 1978 Camp David Accords, was predicated on the assumption that the prospects of a comprehensive settlement would be enhanced if the parties passed through interim phases during which implementation of agreements and changes in behavior would instill confidence and build trust. This theory failed, however, when confronted with reality. Israel continued adding to settlements, and the number of settlers grew throughout this period, thus undermining confidence among Palestinians about Israel's ultimate intentions. Individual spoilers also contributed to the breakdown of trust, for example, the massacre of Palestinian worshippers in Hebron in 1994 and Rabin's assassination in 1995. Throughout this period, Palestinian terror groups attacked Israelis, both in the territories and inside Israel proper, thus engendering among many Israelis the belief that Palestinian territorial demands were not confined to the West Bank and Gaza. In response to violence, Israel built a security fence around Gaza and began to limit mobility in the West Bank through roadblocks and checkpoints, thus diminishing prospects for needed economic growth to fuel Palestinian state-building activities. And Palestinians never took institution-building seriously, giving rise to the concern that a Palestinian state would, from the outset, become a failed state. Far from building confidence and trust, the Oslo period contributed to undermining the prospects of translating interim agreements into final status.[110]

It is not certain that a more assertive U.S. role would have made a difference, for the peace process was often assessed as so brittle that there was concern U.S. pressure would drive the parties further apart. But this belief was never tested against the reality of monitoring and accountability, processes built into many agreements that, if handled properly, actually do build trust and confidence as both sides see transparently where the other side—and they themselves—stand with regard to their commitments. The Americans surely knew what was happening on the ground, and the two parties often complained to the United States about violations of the agreement by the other side. On occasion the United States would follow up in diplomatic conversations, but then nothing happened—no accountability and no consequences exacted for bad behaviors or for failing to fulfill commitments. The Clinton administration accepted Rabin's commitment to curb settlement activity and never seriously tried to stop or even slow down Israeli settlement practices that continued throughout the Rabin years and beyond. The administration always pressed Arafat on stopping terrorism but did little when terrorism continued.

The United States also failed to understand the limitations of two of the strategic concepts it had fostered in order to bring about the Madrid conference. First, the United States did not press at Madrid for any substantive reference to the territorial basis of a peace settlement. It yielded to Shamir's strong opposition to the idea of negotiations over territory, recognizing that Shamir was wedded to the Israeli definition of autonomy as relating to personal autonomy for the people, but not to Palestinian control over territory. But Shamir was defeated in 1992 and yet the U.S. concept for negotiations did not change, even when Rabin told Bush in Kennebunkport that he wanted to expedite the negotiations. Thus the Washington talks continued on the basis of Palestinian self-rule that was not rooted in an agreed transfer of territory. It was not until the Oslo Accords put forth the idea of Gaza-Jericho that a concrete territorial concept was introduced into the peace process. Not only was the end state of the negotiations left vague, but this concept left the Palestinians to try to drag out of Israel every detail of the powers and responsibilities that comprise governance. Palestinians were asked to build everything from the ground up—a state, state institutions, political and economic powers, and even the territorial scope of their future political jurisdiction—while remaining under occupation.

A related problem was that the United States remained committed to the Madrid formula for Palestinian representation long after it was clear that circumstances on the ground had changed. At Madrid, the United States needed to fashion an alternative partner to the PLO because Shamir would not accept the PLO. The United States found much support for this position within the Arab world and the international community, with everyone still smarting from the PLO's support of Iraq in the 1991 Gulf War. By 1993, however, the ability of the Palestinian negotiators in Washington to effect change in their negotiating positions had been shown to be very limited, indeed, almost totally absent. Rabin had told the Americans that although he detested and distrusted Arafat, he recognized that Arafat was the only Palestinian capable of taking and of enforcing a decision. Also, by this time, the Islamic resistance group Hamas had become a more important force on the ground, especially in Gaza, and the failure to empower the PLO was only making it easier for Hamas to make inroads among the Palestinian population. Israel, Rabin in particular, understood the implications of all these changes and thus authorized the Oslo channel. The United States, under both Bush and Clinton, took no note of these changes on the ground—it did not try to restart its own dialogue with the PLO, which had been suspended in 1990, and it paid little attention to the Israeli-PLO contacts.

One consequence of this U.S. inattentiveness both to the structural weaknesses of the negotiations and the need for a different paradigm in Palestinian representation should have been to disabuse the Palestinians of their notion that the United States would at some point "deliver" Israel. Although this notion may have contributed to the PLO decision to participate in the Oslo channel (as an additional factor to the main element, which was to gain recognition of the PLO itself), it does not seem to have affected the PLO's view on negotiations. PLO negotiators continue to believe that the United States will swoop into the talks and relieve Palestinians of the need to make consequential compromises. It did not happen throughout Madrid and Oslo, however.

Despite the pattern of U.S. behavior, there is some merit in the Palestinian assumption of what the U.S. role should have been. The U.S. Letter of Assurances to the Palestinians before the Madrid conference was quite specific about how the United States would exercise its role in the peace process.[111] The United States undertook to be an "honest broker" and committed itself to be the "driving force" in the peace process. The Americans said they would oppose unilateral actions that sought to prejudge or predetermine the outcome of negotiations, a commitment the Palestinians understood to refer to settlements and Israeli actions in Jerusalem. In other words, the United States told the Palestinians that it would play an active and energetic role in the negotiations following Madrid, and thus the Palestinians came to expect the United States to fulfill those assurances.

U.S. behavior on the Israeli-Palestinian track can be explained in part by the strategic choice made by the Clinton administration to focus on Syria first. As noted earlier in this chapter, there is contradictory evidence from the American and Israeli negotiators at the time whether this was a U.S. decision agreed to by Rabin, or whether Rabin stimulated and preferred it. Given Rabin's ambivalence toward Arafat and the PLO, it is most likely that he sent mixed signals to both the Americans and to his own associates about where his strategic preference lay. The Washington talks annoyed Rabin because the Americans kept raising issues that he wanted to avoid and he feared the United States would enter the talks more directly and favor Palestinian positions. The Oslo talks were more remote for Rabin, as they were being shepherded by Peres and his associates, and Rabin had inserted a trusted aide, the lawyer Joel Singer, to advance and preserve positions dear to Rabin. And the Syrian talks clearly intrigued Rabin, as evidenced by his surfacing the "deposit" just as the Oslo talks seemed on the verge of a breakthrough. The evidence points to Rabin's expectation of a breakthrough with Damascus, but the evidence is unclear as to what his preference was. For Israel, the military and security threat posed by Syria would always trump the threat posed by Palestinian terrorism and violence, but no Israeli would ever mistake Syria, rather than the Palestine issue, as constituting the core of the conflict in the Middle East. The Americans, however, clearly chose to focus on the Syrian track. For Rabin, the issue of who came first was instrumental; for the Americans, it became strategic.

Having made this judgment, the Americans waited too long to throw the full weight of American diplomacy behind the effort. Former secretary Baker has stated, "I think President Clinton did a great job trying to make something happen, but he waited too long. He waited until the second term when it didn't matter politically anymore, and I think that was a fundamental mistake. If he had gotten going earlier, I think he might have gotten something done."[112]

The idea of "waiting too long" could be a mask for a fundamental U.S. misunderstanding of what was happening in the peace process. Despite the intimacy of the U.S. dialogue with Rabin, the Americans never seemed to grasp either his strategy or his concept of negotiations. Indyk says revealingly,

> Had we realized at the time that Rabin had decided to go for an interim agreement with the Palestinians rather than pursue a potentially long, drawn-out peace negotiation with the Syrians, we might have acted differently. Instead of heading off for summer vacation, Christopher might have returned to Damascus to press Asad to be more immediately forthcoming, warning that if he failed to move more quickly he might be left behind. But in our excitement for the Syrian deal, we had missed what was really going on.[113]

With hindsight, many of these weaknesses in the U.S. approach to peace seem self-evident, but they were not evident to some U.S. policymakers at the time. It is instructive to note that even Israeli assessments of this period are marked by inconsistency: Avi Gil, a key Peres aide, has said that Peres warned against Israel's using its power advantage over the Palestinians to negotiate an agreement that would be seen by Palestinians as a humiliation.[114] And yet Rabin crowed over exactly those elements in an interview just days after signing the Oslo Accords:

> Two years ago, I would not have believed that these terms were attainable . . . These agreements speak of the implementation of interim arrangements, which, according to the letter of invitation to the Madrid conference, should lead to Palestinian self-government in the territories while preserving the unity of Jerusalem under our sovereignty; keeping the settlements intact; preserving our right and duty to ensure the security of settlements and safeguard the lives of all Israelis staying in the territories; and naturally, our responsibility for external security.[115]

There is a final irony in this tale, which attributes a rather large—albeit unknowing—role for the United States in the initiation of the Oslo channel. Yair Hirschfeld has noted that an economic paper by Qurie, which Hirschfeld saw a year before the Oslo talks began, persuaded him that Qurie would make a good negotiating partner. The multilateral negotiations provided useful "cover" for Oslo-related meetings to take place.

The success and limitations of the Madrid process can thus be put in perspective. As Secretary Baker put it, perhaps the most important contribution of Madrid was that it took place at all: the Arabs got the international conference they wanted; the Israelis got the direct negotiations they wanted; and a range of Arab players were brought into the process of peacemaking through the multilaterals. The Washington talks involving Israel and the Palestinians also demonstrated some of what the two sides wanted and some of what they did not want. Israel opposed devolving legislative authority and responsibility for security to the Palestinians, and the PLO opposed a process from which it had been kept out. Thus, paradoxically, the Washington talks had the effect of persuading Israel and the PLO to reach out to each other in the secret Oslo channel. Although the failure of the Washington bilateral talks and ultimately the collapse of the multilateral talks drain some of the meaning out of the Madrid breakthrough, in effect they created an environment for peace process activity that had not previously existed.

CHAPTER TWO

WITHIN REACH

Israeli-Syrian Negotiations of the 1990s

During the 1990s, the U.S. government dedicated a great deal of time and energy to Israeli-Syrian peace negotiations. As we now know, those efforts failed, and interpretations regarding the reasons for this failure differ widely. Many observers, including President George W. Bush (43), seem to have concluded that Israeli-Syrian peace was unattainable—and, in any event, of little strategic importance—based on an understanding of the events of the 1990s. The regime in Damascus was seen as weak and possibly vulnerable to ouster. The situation on the Israeli-Syrian border was quiet, so there was no sense of a crisis that needed to be addressed. For some, this meant that the Israeli-Syrian conflict could be "managed"; for others, it raised the prospect of regime change in Damascus as an appealing goal.

From that perspective, the Bush administration asked itself why the United States should encourage Israel to make peace with Syria, when there was little reason to think the effort could succeed. The administration also harbored very negative feelings toward Syria because it supported the Iraqi insurgency as well as groups the United States labeled as terrorists. As one of Bush 43's top advisers stated,

> Why would you want to give the Golan to Bashar al-Asad and make him a national hero? If you could ever get a democratic regime in Syria, how would you legitimize it? By helping it get back the Golan. But not for Bashar. Particularly when the Golan has been a remarkably quiet border. It's not in our

interest to reward Bashar, and we do try to promote our national interests, so we should try to tip the debate in Israel [against negotiating with Syria].[1]

Many of the participants in the negotiations of the 1990s, however, have come to a different conclusion. They believe that significant progress was made during the numerous rounds of peace talks between 1991 and 2000 and that a successful conclusion of those negotiations would have advanced American national interests. Although no consensus exists on why the talks ultimately failed, most participants note that the differences between Israel and Syria on matters such as the extent of Israeli withdrawal, the nature of peace, security arrangements, and the timeline for implementing an agreement had been narrowed significantly. Furthermore, the Syrians had conceded that any agreement with Israel would not be conditional on other agreements, the most important of which was a resolution of the Palestinian-Israeli conflict.

If indeed there was progress in these negotiations, why did they ultimately fail? On this point the participants have a variety of views. Not surprisingly, many are self-serving and place blame on everyone else. But in a series of interviews, some off the record, a number of the American participants in the negotiations have acknowledged that U.S. chances for success might have improved if the United States had taken a different approach on a number of matters.

Although the American role in the negotiations will be the primary focus of this chapter, this is not to say that the United States alone bears the responsibility for the failure of the negotiations. Israeli and Syrian leaders, at crucial moments, made choices that undermined the chances for success. But the American role was not incidental, and the American president had more potential clout and more freedom of maneuver than regional leaders who were suspicious, politically vulnerable, and fearful to be seen as weak.

Left to themselves, Israelis and Syrians in the 1990s would not, in all likelihood, have made peace. Over the years, they had come to an understanding on how to manage their relationship that meant that the Golan Heights was quiet and that the conflict between them was often played out indirectly in other arenas, especially Lebanon. On rare occasions, as in 1982, the underlying conflict between Israel and Syria threatened to break out in dangerous ways, but in 1990 Syria joined the anti-Iraq coalition and then, in October 1991, agreed to participate in the Madrid peace talks with Israel. Thus, throughout the 1990s there was almost always a formal structure of some sort within which Israelis and Syrians were engaged in negotiations.

It is frequently believed that parties negotiate when they are convinced that the status quo is no longer tenable and that a resort to force is not a viable option—in short, there is a "hurting stalemate."[2] If the status quo is tolerable, or if one party thinks it can use force or the threat of force to intimidate its adversary, then negotiations will not be an attractive choice. For Israel and Syria in the 1990s, it was never quite clear if the incentives to negotiate were great enough to oblige leaders to reassess their positions and to prepare for hard decisions. At times, it seemed as if they were simply going through the motions, with other goals in mind than that of reaching an agreement. For example, the Syrians were eager to improve their relationship with the United States in order to reduce their international isolation, and that was probably one of the reasons they agreed to negotiate with Israel. For the Israelis, dealing with Syria was a way of pressuring the Palestinians, with whom they were also negotiating. Despite these mixed motives, there seem to have been times when both sides thought that there was a real chance of moving toward agreement, but they both wanted the United States to play a central role in the "peace process."

With the hindsight offered by the decade of the 1990s, it seems clear that Israeli and Syrian negotiators were often rigid, too obsessed with tactics, remarkably suspicious, and very unwilling to make any unreciprocated gestures toward one another. The shadow of the Israeli-Egyptian negotiations of the 1970s was always present. The Israelis wanted a partner in Damascus like Egyptian president Anwar Sadat. They wanted public signs that Syria was ready for peace. Sadat's trip to Jerusalem in November 1977 was the model of what a peace-minded Arab leader should be willing to do. For Hafez al-Asad, however, Sadat represented an anti-model. He had given too much and gotten too little. Al-Asad seemed determined to do at least as well as Sadat in recovering his national territory but without having to pay as high a price as Egypt in "normalizing relations" with Israel.

Domestic politics played a very big part for both al-Asad—the sole voice when it came to setting the fundamental terms for the negotiations on the Syrian side— and for the series of Israeli prime ministers who engaged with him: Yitzhak Rabin (1992–95), Shimon Peres (1995–96), Benjamin Netanyahu (1996–99), and Ehud Barak (1999–2001). Domestic politics also played a part in the calculations of President Bill Clinton, the American leader who presided over the entirety of the significant moments in the search for Israeli-Syrian peace from 1993 to 2001.

This study starts from the assumption that Israeli-Syrian peace was attainable during Clinton's presidency. To get there, the American role was indispensable. On a few occasions, Israelis and Syrians have negotiated behind the back of the American government, but those efforts have also fallen short and do not suggest that the parties on their own, or with other mediators, would have succeeded. On the Syrian side, there was the hope that the United States would use its influence with Israel to press for substantive concessions, especially on the issue of full Israeli withdrawal to the June 4, 1967, line. Syria also wanted an end to U.S.-imposed sanctions; it wanted to get off the "terrorist list"; and it hoped for aid, investment, and trade as benefits that could come from better relations with the United States in the wake of Israeli-Syrian peace.

From the Israeli standpoint, the United States was important as an intermediary as long as the Syrians were reluctant to negotiate directly, and the United States would have had a role to play in security arrangements on the Golan. In addition, Israel asked Washington for (and would probably have received) a sizable compensation package if and when it made peace with Syria. For example, Barak seems to have had in mind a package of perhaps $65 billion to help defray costs of removing settlers and restructuring Israeli defenses after withdrawal from Golan.[3]

A great deal has now been written about these negotiations.[4] Many of the participants have given their own versions of what happened, most have been interviewed, and some of the primary documentation has become available. Nonetheless, there are significant gaps in the resulting narrative, and the various accounts do not come together to form a clear picture. Because there are so many different interpretations of what happened and what went wrong, it is important to get a sense of the crucial moments in these negotiations and to identify U.S. choices and the rationales behind them. This analysis leads to the conclusion—inevitably somewhat tentative because counter-factual—that had the United States played its cards more effectively, it might have made the difference between success and failure.

If this judgment is correct, then it has important implications for how the United States should act in future peace negotiations. Since our focus is U.S. policy, we will not try to explain why Israeli or Syrian leaders acted as they did; instead we will describe their positions as part of the stubborn reality that U.S. diplomats had to deal with, and we will often note how the American side tried to account for the often-puzzling behavior of the protagonists. A minor industry is devoted to casting blame on al-Asad, Rabin, or Barak and to wondering if they were sincere or whether they were capable of making the hard choices that might have ended the conflict. Many have stressed the role of Israeli domestic politics in the calculations of both Rabin and Barak, and some believe that al-Asad, that most sphinxlike of leaders, could never have afforded to break with the reassuring platitudes of pan-Arabism because of his Allawi origins. This chapter will not enter these debates because its focus is on how U.S. leaders understood the issues, perceived the parties, designed their strategies, and assessed their own performance.

During the period of ongoing negotiations from 1993 to 2000, the American side was characterized by remarkable continuity. Clinton was president throughout and had decided early in his term to make Israeli-Syrian peace a top priority of his administration. His first secretary of state, Warren Christopher, visited the Middle East more than twenty times in pursuit of this goal. Throughout almost all of this period, Dennis Ross was the special Middle East coordinator (SMEC), reporting both to the secretary of state and to the president. In addition to these three central figures, significant but lesser roles were played by Secretary of State Madeleine Albright (1997–2001), National Security Advisor Samuel Berger (1997–2001), Robert Malley and Bruce Riedel at the National Security Council (NSC), and Martin Indyk in several different roles—NSC staff, assistant secretary of state for Near Eastern Affairs, and ambassador to Israel. On the whole, the American team was a small, tightly knit group with substantial experience and continuity. This did not, however, mean that they all saw things the same way or that the team functioned well together.

Although the focus in this chapter will be on Clinton and his top advisers, one needs also to look back a bit to the George H.W. Bush (41) presidency (1989–93) and to the roles played by James Baker, secretary of state, and Edward Djerejian, American ambassador to Syria. It was they who brought Syria into the anti–Saddam Hussein coalition in 1990 and from there to the Madrid conference in 1991. And it was their assessment of Hafez al-Asad, as well as of Yitzhak Rabin, as someone "you could deal with" that encouraged the Clinton team to put such a high priority on Israeli-Syrian peacemaking.

The Substantive Issues

American leaders have been drawn to the Israeli-Syrian conflict for a number of different reasons. First, at various times in the past it seemed as if Syria could be persuaded to end some of its problematic behaviors if it could be engaged in the "peace process." For example, during the Cold War, Syria was seen as an Arab country that might follow Egypt's example of distancing itself from the Soviet Union if only it could recover the Golan, territory it lost in the 1967 War. Later, some believed that Syria might be more cooperative in "moderating" the Lebanese militant group, Hezbollah, or the Palestinian Hamas movement, if it was engaged in negotiations with Israel. Some strategists have mused about "flipping" Syria, moving it away from its alignment with Iran and toward more cooperative relations with the West. From each of these perspectives, Israeli-Syrian peace negotiations might serve broader U.S. objectives.

Among the band of "peace processors" in Washington, there has been an ongoing debate over the relative merits of pressing for Israeli-Palestinian peace—the "core issue"—or of placing emphasis on the Syrian track—the "strategic school." Those favoring the Syrian track pointed to the relatively straightforward nature of the issues that divided the two contestants, to the existence of a widely supported negotiating framework anchored in the "land for peace" formula of UN Resolution 242 (November 1967), and to a successful model in the Egyptian-Israeli Peace Treaty of 1979. Those who favored the Syrian track also stressed that Syria had a record of having negotiated with Israel, beginning in 1974, and that the resulting agreement forged by Henry Kissinger in spring 1974—the Golan Disengagement Agreement—had been meticulously respected by both sides. Finally, the strategic school argued that Israeli-Syrian peace would offer benefits such as driving a wedge between Syria and Iran. That Hafez al-Asad, and later his son Bashar, ruled with a firm hand was not necessarily viewed as an impediment to successful negotiations.[5]

The issues that needed to be resolved between Israel and Syria during the 1990s, and most likely still in any future negotiations, can be grouped into five basic categories. First, there was the issue of Israeli military withdrawal from the Golan territory that was occupied by Israel in the 1967 War and the removal of some 18,000 Israeli settlers living there. Second, there were the security arrangements that would be established between the two countries. Third, there was the issue of normal peaceful relations. Fourth, there was the issue of water. And fifth, there was the issue of the time horizon and sequencing of the implementation of the agreement.

Withdrawal, demarcation of the border, and control of water resources made up a particularly complicated package of issues. At an early date—June 19, 1967—the Israeli cabinet had decided that in return for peace with Egypt and Syria, it would be prepared to withdraw from the recently occupied territory.[6] This policy was not announced at the time, but it was an early acknowledgment by an Israeli government of the basic "land for peace" trade-off, even though Israel later stepped back from this policy and eventually declared the extension of Israeli law to the Golan Heights. In November 1967, UN Security Council Resolution 242 spoke of the "inadmissibility of the acquisition of territory by war" and of "withdrawal of Israeli armed forces from territories occupied in the recent conflict," adding weight to the notion that the Golan would eventually be returned as part of any peace deal between Israel and Syria.

If the general "land for peace" idea has been pretty well accepted as the framework for Israeli-Syrian peace, there was still the nontrivial issue of the actual line to which Israeli forces would withdraw. The so-called "international border" was established in 1923 by the British and French colonial powers, but Syria and Israel had never recognized it. The British insisted on drawing the line so that they would have full control over the Sea of Galilee (Lake Kinneret, Lake Tiberias), which meant that the border was drawn in the northeast quadrant of the lake at a distance of ten meters from the waterline. Often when Israelis talk of full withdrawal from the Golan they mean withdrawal to this line, or to one approximating it.

When Hafez al-Asad spoke of withdrawal, he invariably had in mind the so-called June 4, 1967, line. This was the line that divided Israeli and Syrian forces on the eve of the Six-Day War (which began on June 5, 1967). In 1949, after the first Arab-Israeli War, an Armistice Agreement was signed by Israel and Syria that established a ceasefire line and set up several demilitarized zones. Over time, Israeli and Syrian troops moved into parts of the demilitarized zones, establishing a new de facto line of separation—now referred to as the June 4, 1967, line. The practical significance of this line is that Syrian forces were in control of the waterline of the Sea of Galilee in the northeast quadrant, and in areas north of the lake they were on the east bank of the Jordan River. Israeli negotiators worried that a Syrian presence on the lake and on the river might lead to claims over the water supply on which Israel heavily depends.

As we will see, the June 4 line features significantly in the long-running negotiations of the 1990s. At various times, negotiators on both sides seemed to agree that the June 4 line would be the basis for demarcating the future border, but then someone, usually an Israeli or an American, would insist that no one really knew exactly where the line had run, that there was no map of it, and that a few dozen or hundred meters one way or the other was not really a big deal. But for the Syrians, and especially for Hafez al-Asad, the June 4 line did have a very concrete meaning.[7] Syrian sovereignty would extend to the shoreline of the Sea of Galilee as it had on June 4, 1967. Without that assurance, al-Asad would not make peace. (See map on next page.)

But presidents had subsequently also used the Israeli-preferred term of "defensible borders," suggesting that there might need to be changes in the pre-June 1967 lines that had been less than optimal from the standpoint of Israeli security. In addition, as part of the Sinai II negotiations in 1975, President Gerald Ford had written to Prime Minister Rabin and said, "The U.S. has not developed a final position on the borders [between Israel and Syria]. Should it do so, *it will give great weight* to Israel's position that any peace agreement with Syria must be predicated on Israel remaining on the Golan Heights. My view in this regard was stated in our conversation of September 13, 1974" (emphasis added).[8]

In short, there was no firm American position on the precise location of the future border. Anything that the parties could agree on would be acceptable to the United States. But if the Egyptian-Israeli treaty of 1979 was to serve as a guide, the withdrawal of Israeli forces from Syrian territory would have to be complete. Sadat, who had been flexible on many other issues, was absolutely rigid when it came to the question of recovering every square inch of Egyptian territory; al-Asad was unlikely to be more flexible than Sadat in this regard.

The issue of security had been dealt with on an interim basis in the Golan disengagement negotiations (1974). That agreement had incorporated demilitarized

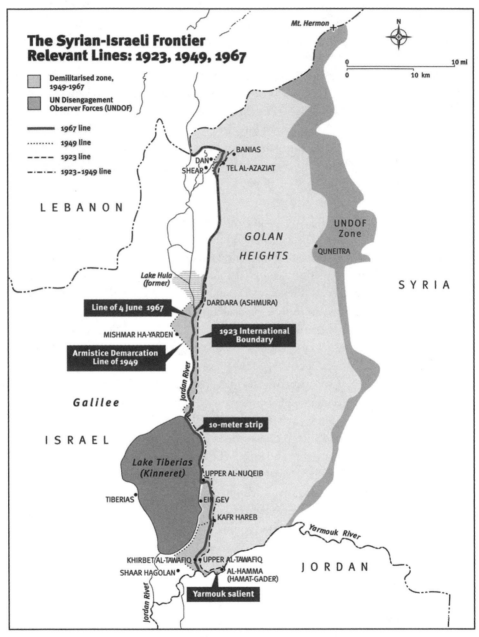

The Syrian-Israeli Frontier
Relevant Lines: 1923, 1949, 1967

Demilitarised zone,
1949-1967

UN Disengagement
Observer Forces (UNDOF)

——— 1967 line
·········· 1949 line
– – – 1923 line
–·–·– 1923-1949 line

Mt. Hermon

N

0   10 mi
0   10 km

LEBANON

BANIAS
DAN
SHEAR
TEL AL-AZAZIAT

GOLAN
HEIGHTS

UNDOF
Zone
QUNEITRA

SYRIA

Lake Hula
(former)

Line of 4 June 1967

DARDARA (ASHMURA)

1923 International
Boundary

MISHMAR HA-YARDEN

Armistice Demarcation
Line of 1949

Jordan River

Galilee

10-meter strip

ISRAEL

Lake Tiberias
(Kinneret)

UPPER AL-NUQEIB

TIBERIAS

EIN GEV

KAFR HAREB

Yarmouk River

KHIRBET AL-TAWAFIQ   UPPER AL-TAWAFIQ
SHAAR HAGOLAN

AL-HAMMA
(HAMAT-GADER)

JORDAN

Jordan River

Yarmouk salient

Map of the June 4, 1967, Line and the 1923 International Border. Prepared by Frederick Hof,
Middle East Insight (September–October 1991): 17–23. This map shows the difference between the
1923 international border, the armistice line of 1949, and the June 4, 1967, line. Also see Frederic Hof,
"Mapping Peace between Syria and Israel," Special Report No. 219, United States Institute of Peace,
Washington, DC, March 2009, www.usip.org/files/resources/mappingpeace.pdf.

zones, a UN Disengagement Observer Force (UNDOF), limited force zones, and third-party monitoring of the agreement. All of these arrangements could be adapted to a security regime. But there were bound to be difficult moments in working out the details. Israel was eager to retain its listening post on Mt. Hermon for a prolonged period, and Syria was strongly opposed. Similarly, Israel wanted the Syrians to agree to reduce the size and composition of their armed forces as part of a peace agreement, but Syria saw this as an infringement on its sovereignty. So the security issues would require some tough negotiating, but in general did not seem unmanageable. As a possible sweetener, the Clinton administration was willing to commit up to a brigade to a peacekeeping force on the Golan if the parties felt that would be helpful.[9]

Normalization of relations featured prominently in Israel's list of requirements for peace. For many Israelis, the crucial moment in the Egyptian-Israeli peace process had come when Sadat traveled to Jerusalem in November 1977 and spoke about "no more war." The Israelis were eager for words and gestures from the Syrians and also were insistent on concrete acts such as the establishment of diplomatic relations at an early date. In short, Israel wanted proof that Syria was sincere when it spoke of peace. Because the Egyptian-Israeli peace had remained a "cold peace," greater urgency was added to the Israeli demand for "normalization" and for symbolic gestures such as a face-to-face meeting with Hafez al-Asad.

From the Syrian standpoint, "normalization" was not a word that came easily. Al-Asad was ready for a contractual peace, which he seemed to see as an end of belligerency and not much else. He would frequently say (as Sadat had done initially) that he could not tell his people to embrace the Israelis. He could and would end the state of war, and time might lead to new relations, but he could not promise warm relations with the former enemy. From an Israeli standpoint, his view of peace was minimalist at best. Not for al-Asad were the grand gestures, the dramatic meetings at the summit, the cultivation of the peace camp in Israel. The more the Israelis asked for these things, the more hesitant al-Asad seemed to become.

As time went on in the 1990s, the gap on "normalization" did seem to shrink somewhat. Al-Asad was willing to speak of "the peace of the brave," and even uttered a few complimentary words about Israeli leaders. He spoke of "normal" relations with Israel, but used a word in Arabic (*'aadii*) that some Israelis interpreted as "ordinary" or "common," and understood to convey a relationship noticeably less friendly than "normal" relations. Given the deep suspicions on both sides, one could expect considerable struggle over the fine-tuning of the "normalization" issue, but there was no reason to think that the odds of agreement were insurmountable.

For Israelis, the issue of water was crucial and affected their view on the border and on security arrangements. The technicalities of the water issue were complex, but the short version of the problem was that much of Israel's water came from sources that originated in Syria and would pass through Syrian-controlled territory after Israeli withdrawal. If Syria were to return to the June 4, 1967, lines, it might be in a position to claim control over parts of the Jordan River and the Sea of Galilee. At a minimum, Israel would want assurances that Syria would not use its improved geographical position after Israeli withdrawal to disrupt the flow of water to Israel or to make claims to a share of the water in the Sea of Galilee. In the course of the negotiations, this was a serious issue that the two sides confronted. The closest they came to solving it was during a discussion that suggested that Syria would make no claim to sovereignty over the water of the Sea of Galilee if Israel recognized Syrian sovereignty over the land up to the shoreline. But this discussion was never formalized into a mutually acceptable proposition.

Finally, there was the issue of the phasing of the implementation of any agreement. In the case of Israel and Egypt, the withdrawal provision of the peace treaty was carried out over a three-year period; but already with the completion of the first phase of Israeli withdrawal, full diplomatic relations had been established. Israel would doubtless seek something similar from Syria. As these issues came into focus in 1993, Israel sought a longer time horizon for withdrawal, whereas al-Asad wanted withdrawal to be completed in a matter of months. This issue was made for haggling. Although little in the way of principle was involved, the parties started from positions that were far apart.

Other than these five bilateral issues, Israel and Syria had a number of other concerns as they engaged in negotiations. Israel hoped to get Syria to use its undeniable influence with radical movements such as Hezbollah and Hamas; Israel assumed that an agreement with Syria would be followed by an agreement with Lebanon and perhaps a normalization of relations with other Arab countries as well. Any Israel-Syria agreement, as the Israelis insisted, should stand on its own foundation and not depend on what might happen on the Palestinian front. Finally, Israel expected side payments from the United States, including the possibility of a long-sought bilateral security treaty. And both parties would expect U.S. guarantees of the terms of an eventual agreement.[10]

Syria's additional goals were largely addressed to the United States. Syria had long been listed by Washington as a country that supported terrorism, sanctions had been imposed that restricted trade and investment, and Syria often seemed more eager to engage American diplomats in discussions of bilateral ties rather than of the issues relating to peace with Israel. Finally, there was the intangible goal of showing the Arab world that al-Asad had done at least as well, if not better, than Sadat—and without having to emulate the Egyptian leaders in kowtowing to Israel, as Sadat's trip to Jerusalem in November 1977 was portrayed by the Syrian authorities. How else could Syria justify the long passage of time between its first move toward peace in 1974 and the possible endgame in the 1990s?

Setting the Stage: Baker's "Dead Cat" Diplomacy

Syria's engagement in Arab-Israeli peace diplomacy dates from the aftermath of the October 1973 War and Kissinger's shuttle diplomacy, and from that point on it had a strong U.S. dimension. Following the war and for the next five years, U.S.-Syrian diplomatic relations (which had been severed by Damascus in 1967) were resumed, President Nixon visited Damascus, and the United States had even acquiesced in Syria's intervention in the Lebanese civil war in the late 1970s. President Carter had tried to keep Syria in the peace-oriented camp and held one meeting with al-Asad in Geneva in spring 1977. But Sadat's abrupt shift of strategy in November 1977 left Syria in a lurch, and before long Syria found itself in the company of those in the Arab world who rejected Egypt's unilateral move toward peace with Israel. Inevitably, U.S.-Syrian relations cooled as Syria moved into opposition to the post–Camp David world of peace diplomacy.

During the 1980s, U.S.-Syrian relations were seriously strained and no movement toward a resumption of peace negotiations was made. The Reagan Plan of September 1982 was addressed to Jordan and the Palestinians and never mentioned Syria. As U.S. relations with the embattled regime of Iraq's Saddam Hussein improved between 1984 and 1989, U.S.-Syrian relations deteriorated. Syria found itself siding with Iran, the number one enemy of the United States in the mind of many Americans. Even some stalwart American friends of Israel were singing the praises of Saddam Hussein (secular, modern, anti-Iranian, *and* anti-Syrian), while they strongly wished for regime change in Damascus.[11]

The shock of Saddam Hussein's invasion of Kuwait in August 1990 opened the way for a new chapter in U.S.-Syrian relations and eventually for Syria's return to the "peace process" with Israel by agreeing to attend the Madrid conference in October 1991. The architect of these changes was primarily James Baker, the capable secretary of state and alter ego to President George H.W. Bush. Baker encouraged al-Asad to send a division of Syrian troops to fight alongside American troops in the aftermath of Saddam's invasion of Kuwait, a truly unprecedented development.[12]

Part of the key to Baker's success in winning broad Arab (and Soviet) support for the Desert Storm operation against Iraqi forces in Kuwait was a promise, especially to Syria and Egypt, that when the war was over the United States would turn its attention to Arab-Israeli peacemaking.[13] Baker, who played little part in Desert Storm itself, launched an intensive phase of diplomatic activity during the spring and summer of 1991. His goal was to get all of the parties to the Arab-Israeli conflict, including the Palestinians, to an international conference. To do this, he had to find a formula that would get legitimate Palestinian participants into the room without provoking the walkout of the Israelis. And Baker realized that to get Arab support for his strategy, it would be important to win over Hafez al-Asad.[14] On June 1, 1991, Bush wrote to al-Asad saying,

> I want to make clear that we will be doing so [taking on a special responsibility for making the negotiations succeed] on the only basis possible for a comprehensive peace: Territory for peace applied to all fronts, including the Golan Heights. We will not change this fundamental policy position of ours; nor will we change our non-recognition of Israel's purported "Annexation" of the Golan Heights.[15]

Fortunately, Bush and Baker had a capable ambassador in place in Damascus, Edward Djerejian, and with his help they managed to get al-Asad to agree to participate (in the person of his foreign minister, Farouq Sharaa), in what came to be known as the Madrid conference. Once Syria said yes, it was hard for Israel to say no, and soon the complex architecture of Madrid was in place. Although no one expected much from the conference per se, a major taboo had been broken— Israel was now sitting with Syrian and Palestinian negotiators, and a whole series of multilateral tracks of negotiation had been opened with broad participation from Arab countries and others in the international community.

In building support for the idea of an Arab-Israeli peace conference, Baker had several advantages. First, the Cold War was over and the Soviet Union was on the verge of collapse. Few doubted that the United States, especially in the aftermath of the Gulf War and Saddam Hussein's eviction from Kuwait, was in a commanding position of influence regionally and globally. Second, Baker was rightly perceived as having an unusually close association with the president. Third, Baker's style, sometimes folksy, sometimes cerebral, but always straightforward and blunt, served him well in dealing with Arabs and Israelis alike.

In the course of his efforts to corral the various parties to come to the Madrid conference, Baker perfected the art of what he referred to as "dead cat" diplomacy.[16] The simple version of this stratagem was to make it clear that he would not hesitate to point his finger at any party that obstructed his plans. In short, he would leave the figurative dead cat, or corpse of the peace process, on their doorstep for all to see. To emphasize the point, Baker would use the press, and especially the New York Times, to indicate his displeasure in not-for-attribution—but easily traced— comments. None of the parties wanted to be on the outs with the powerful secretary of state, so this not-so-subtle threat of finger-pointing carried some weight.[17]

Despite all of Baker's skill in setting the stage with the Madrid Peace Conference, there was little chance that negotiations would move forward as long as Yitzhak Shamir remained prime minister of Israel. Shamir's notion of bargaining with Syria was to offer "peace for peace," not "land for peace." And the idea of dealing with the PLO was simply anathema to him. Bush and Baker understood this aversion and used what influence they could—which was primarily to condition Shamir's request for $10 billion in loan guarantees on Israel's willingness to freeze settlements—to help sway the Israeli electorate to vote for the Labor Party leader in the summer 1992 elections.[18] With Rabin's victory, the peace process that had been carefully staged by Baker now had a chance to get under way.[19] But first Bush himself needed to get reelected, and that was not to be.

Syria First? Clinton's Opening Rounds

Bill Clinton did not come to the presidency with much knowledge of the Middle East. But he quickly assembled a team of advisers, some of whom had worked in previous administrations and had even participated in the strategy leading to the Madrid conference. So, despite the change from a Republican to a Democratic president, there was a likelihood that policy toward the Arab-Israeli conflict would contain strong elements of continuity. After all, Madrid provided a framework for negotiations on multiple fronts, and the election of Yitzhak Rabin the previous summer meant that an Israeli leader was in power who was known by many Americans to be a pragmatic and realistic politician.

At one of his first meetings of the National Security Council, Clinton discussed the Middle East with his advisers, and it quickly became apparent that many of them felt that progress might be made on the Israeli-Syrian front. Baker had told the new administration that al-Asad was ready to move with Rabin, and one of Clinton's key advisers, Martin Indyk, had made the case for a Syria-first strategy in a transition paper.[20] Without necessarily ignoring the Palestinian front, where negotiations were also under way, the Clinton team decided to assign priority to the Syrian front.[21] Secretary of State Warren Christopher was given the task of traveling to the Middle East to take the temperature with the leaders there and to put out a few brushfires that stood in the way of the negotiating process.

Over the next several months, Clinton and Christopher's main challenge was to see if the hints that al-Asad and Rabin were ready to do business could be developed into negotiable propositions. When Clinton met Rabin for the first time in spring 1993, the Israeli prime minister said that he knew it would not be possible to make peace with Syria without full withdrawal from Golan. Clinton then mentioned the idea of placing an American brigade on the Golan. Rabin replied that he did not "exclude the possibility" of full withdrawal in such circumstances.[22] Al-Asad was similarly hesitant to make an all-out commitment to normal relations with Israel, but he too seemed willing to consider the basic trade-off and even suggested that the United States should play the role of "repository" of the commitments by both sides.[23]

Formal negotiations stemming from the Madrid conference had been under way, with a prolonged timeout in early 1993, but little progress had been made, especially on the territorial issue, in the Israeli-Syrian track. Rabin had expressed his dislike of the Washington-based talks, and it seemed as if both Rabin and al-Asad might welcome a role by Clinton and Christopher as some kind of go-between.[24] So one more issue for the American side was to determine how to play the part that both sides seemed to favor. Would they simply be an "honest broker," passing messages back and forth, helping each side to understand the circumstances faced by the other? Or would the United States become a more forceful mediator—on the model of Kissinger or Carter at Camp David? How would Clinton and Christopher sort out their respective roles, and who would they rely on for advice?

About this time, in mid-1993, Christopher asked Ross to join his team as special Middle East coordinator. Prior to this appointment, Assistant Secretary Djerejian had played the part of lead adviser, and he was particularly well briefed on Syria, having served there as ambassador. He had made one trip for Christopher to Damascus in April, but with Ross's appointment Djerejian soon moved on,[25] briefly serving as ambassador in Israel and then leaving the Foreign Service to join Baker in establishing the Baker Institute in Houston.

Soon after his appointment as SMEC, Ross met with Rabin and al-Asad in July for a discussion of the idea of each party beginning to "meet the needs" of the other.[26] Rabin had gone so far as to say that the "depth of withdrawal will reflect the depth of peace." After his meeting with Rabin, Ross had seen al-Asad in Latakiya (Syria) and told him that "Prime Minister Rabin understands your needs. He knows that if they aren't met, if you aren't satisfied on withdrawal, there will be no deal. He wants a deal, but does not believe that you understand his needs. . . . How do you understand his needs and what would you like me to say about those needs in response to the Prime Minister?"[27] Al-Asad responded by saying that he supported "full peace for full withdrawal," so there seemed to be some potential convergence. Rabin, however, saw little new in al-Asad's formula.[28]

At this point, one might have thought that the American team would have been rethinking some of its assumptions. Contrary to the prevailing view in the Washington negotiations, they now had evidence that Rabin and Arafat were in direct communication and that progress was being made toward an interim agreement between Israel and the Palestinians. Because it was well known that Rabin did not feel he could move on more than one front at a time, and no one on the American side seemed inclined to question that judgment, this development might have indicated that the Syrian track was on the back burner for the time being, at least as far as Rabin was concerned.

Rabin's Deposit

Christopher and Ross returned to the Middle East in early August, presumably to give the impression of momentum before they went off on summer vacation. To their surprise, in a private meeting with Rabin and Rabinovich on August 3, the Israeli prime minister said that he wanted to find out if there might be an opportunity to move ahead with Syria. With this goal in mind, he told Christopher that the secretary could pose to President al-Asad "as a hypothesis" that Israel might be willing to withdraw completely from the Golan if certain conditions were met. Those conditions included normalization of relations, with an early establishment of full diplomatic relations; satisfactory security arrangements, with U.S. manning of the early-warning stations on Mount Hermon; and the safeguarding of Israel's water resources.[29] Rabin insisted that this initiative remain secret, and he and Rabinovich seemed to feel that Israel was not really committing, even conditionally, to full withdrawal, but rather simply raising a hypothetical possibility.[30] The Americans, with this in hand, were supposed to get al-Asad's response to this "hypothesis." In light of how strongly the Israeli side later expressed dissatisfaction with the way in which Christopher conveyed this message to Syria, it is surprising that there seems to have been little discussion of how it should be presented.

Christopher and Ross realized that they now had something important in hand,[31] but they also wanted to know how this fit with the rumors of progress in the Israeli-Palestinian talks. (By now, the Americans knew of the Oslo channel, but did not take it very seriously.) Rabin seemed not to attach too much importance to Oslo, so the Americans set off for Damascus determined to see what they might get in return for Rabin's conditional offer of full withdrawal.

Christopher and Ross met with al-Asad on August 4 and conveyed Rabin's conditional offer. There is no reason to think that al-Asad did not understand that the offer of "full withdrawal" would depend on Rabin's being satisfied on the other issues on his agenda, primarily security, normalization, and water. According to Ross, al-Asad said that the message from Rabin was "very important." He went on to quibble about the word "normalization." He preferred to speak of "normal peaceful relations." He then noted that security and water were issues where both sides had interests that would have to be satisfied. Significantly, he did say that the Israeli-Syrian agreement would not depend on a final deal between the

Israelis and Palestinians. He did, however, want the Israeli-Lebanese talks to move forward in parallel. Al-Asad also complained about the very long time horizon—five years—envisaged by Rabin for full withdrawal to take place.[32]

The American reaction to al-Asad was mixed. Ross saw positive elements in what al-Asad had said. Christopher, by contrast, later said al-Asad's "only verbal response was a series of nitpicking questions and contentious pronouncements that I tried to answer without displaying my irritation."[33] The following day Christopher conveyed al-Asad's response to Rabin, who was not impressed.[34] During a follow-on trip by Christopher to Damascus, al-Asad raised the question of whether Israel had any claims on Syrian territory. Christopher said they did not; Rabin was speaking of full withdrawal. Ross interjected to say, "There are no claims that we are aware of."[35] Despite the encouraging start that had been made in these high-level exchanges between Rabin and al-Asad via the American team, Christopher and Ross then returned to the United States to go on vacation, promising to return to the region the following month.

In retrospect, a number of participants in these events felt that there were missed opportunities at this moment. Some who had worked closely with Baker were sure that he would have taken the Rabin "deposit" and used it to start an intensive round of nonstop shuttle diplomacy aimed at getting agreement on the key principles of withdrawal, security, and normalization.[36] Unlike Christopher, Baker had not found al-Asad to be an unusually unpleasant negotiator—just a tough one, a view that would have been shared by Kissinger and Vance as well. It is also striking that Clinton, who subsequently was very deeply involved in the negotiations, did not make an appearance at all during these momentous few days. He did not call either of the leaders; he did not send a message directly or indirectly. If later he often seemed to get too involved, here he seemed too detached. And finally, all of the momentum in this brief flurry of activity in August 1993 was generated by Rabin, not by the Americans, who were little more than conveyers—and in Rabin's view, clumsy ones at best—of a message.

Martin Indyk has concluded that Rabin was not serious about a breakthrough with Syria in August 1993. He was simply using the offer of the deposit to convey the impression that there was movement afoot on the Syrian front, but his goal was to pressure the Palestinians, who were nearing the moment of truth in Oslo. This is one of the cases where Indyk concludes that the Americans were naïve and missed Rabin's real purpose and thereby allowed themselves to be manipulated. He imagines that if the American team had better understood what was going on, they would have pushed harder for agreement and not gone on vacation. They were aware that Rabin did not feel he could move on more than one front at a time. Rabin was now in a hurry; Arafat was desperate; and by contrast, al-Asad was patient and held out only the prospect of a long and tedious negotiating process. So, in Indyk's view, Rabin used the Americans to get the deal with Arafat that best suited his immediate needs.[37] If the Americans really had a preference for the Syrian track, they should have tried harder for a breakthrough when they had the "deposit" in hand. Few of the other Americans involved in these events agree with Indyk's interpretation of Rabin's strategy—nor does Rabin's closest confidant, Israeli ambassador to Washington during this period, Itamar Rabinovich.

Rabinovich, the only Israeli other than Rabin to be fully aware of Rabin's initiative, seems less sure than Indyk that his boss was determined to go with the Palestinian track instead of with the Syrians. He blames part of the problem, at least implicitly, on Christopher's handling of the "deposit."[38] Rabin felt, according to Rabinovich, that it had been played too quickly and unsubtly by Christopher, who got little in return. Rabin had somehow gamed this presentation in his mind so that Christopher would start with a "hypothetical" Israeli offer and see what he could get in return. If it meant anything, it would mean that Christopher could only say that Rabin was possibly considering such an offer, but had not made a final determination. It is doubtful that al-Asad would have been very impressed, and in any event, Rabin had not specifically asked that the "deposit" be presented in such a manner.[39]

In Rabin's view, it would seem that if al-Asad was forthcoming, then Christopher should have returned to Israel to get the real "commitment" that he seemed to think he already had. Rabinovich feels that a defter playing of the hand by the Americans could have made a difference and that Rabin was actually open to a Syria-first strategy, but only if it was carried out according to his rules.[40]

This moment was one of several in the peace-process narrative when the multiple versions of the same event do not quite come into focus. Ross and Christopher seem to have understood Rabin's "deposit" as a conditional offer, but they differ over al-Asad's reaction. Rabinovich, who was close to Rabin, strongly asserts that the Americans mishandled Israel's "hypothetical" offer, and Rabin, in particular, is reported to have been very annoyed with the way in which Christopher handled the deposit and with al-Asad's reply. Indyk believes the whole gambit was designed to draw the Palestinians into the Oslo agreement and was never seriously intended by Rabin to produce a breakthrough.

If there is a lesson from this phase for American policymakers, it would seem to be that moments such as August 3, 1993, when one party to a negotiation seems ready to make a significant move, must be handled with great care and there must be greater clarity with respect to the expectations of the parties. These potential breakthroughs do not come often. They should be exploited to the utmost. If there is a time for presidential involvement, it is in helping to build momentum behind such breakthroughs. Christopher should not bear the sole blame for the way he handled the "deposit" with al-Asad because Rabin gave him no guidelines on how to employ it. Even so, Christopher's decision to reveal all of what he got from Rabin is questionable, in that it gave al-Asad far too much insight into Rabin's position before the Americans and Rabin had a clear idea of how far al-Asad would go in response. For his part, Rabin was being a bit too coy with his offer. If he wanted to get any leverage out of his offer, it had to be presented as a conditional commitment, not simply one of several hypothetical possibilities.

Christopher can also be faulted for his response to al-Asad. A careful reading of what al-Asad reportedly said in response to the Rabin offer does not suggest that it was nitpicking. In fact, al-Asad made an important statement in confirming that an Israeli-Syrian deal would stand on its own. The difference between "normalization" and "normal peaceful relations" was not a deal breaker, and later the two terms were used interchangeably. And if al-Asad was asking for Israeli withdrawal on too fast a time schedule, Rabin's five years was arguably too long. This area was precisely where an effective American mediator might have begun to offer suggestions, including ways in which an American presence on Golan could be used to reduce some of the security dilemmas.

Of course, it would have helped if Rabin had been more forthright with his American allies. He could have told them more clearly that he was on the verge of making a momentous decision on whether to conclude an interim arrangement with the Palestinians. Perhaps the U.S. side would have urged him to do so and suggested that he hold the pocket offer in reserve for later when both Israel and the United States could focus full attention on the Syrian track. By not leveling with Christopher, Rabin deprived him of important information that might have affected the American strategy. Still, one cannot read over the record of this moment without feeling that more could have been done by the American side. But the Clinton administration was still new to the game, the president was in awe of Rabin, and Christopher did not have the temperament to deal with the real-world difficulties of negotiating with Middle East leaders, who regularly drive their American counterpoints to the brink of distraction.

The PLO and Jordan Go First

On learning of the Oslo breakthrough, al-Asad was doubtless annoyed that his rival, Arafat, had managed to negotiate a deal behind his back that attracted wide international support, at least initially. But for all his irritation, he does not seem to have tried to sabotage the Oslo Accords. Instead, he read them as license for Syria to move forward on its own path with little regard for the Palestinians.

The American administration hoped that the Syrian-Israeli track would be revived after a decent pause for the Oslo process to get launched, but Rabin wanted to focus on the Palestinian track. Clinton was even ready to help buy time with al-Asad by meeting him in Geneva early in 1994. That visit resulted in a few positive signals. Clinton was "elated," and agreement was reached that he would read out an approved statement that Syria was ready for normal relations with Israel. Al-Asad spoke of the "peace of the brave" and said that Syria had made a strategic choice for peace. Once again, Rabin was not impressed.[41]

By this point in early 1994, Rabin had apparently decided that his next move would be with Jordan, not with Syria. It does not seem as if the Clinton team tried to dissuade Rabin from moving ahead with Jordan, but they kept the emphasis on the front where they had the largest role to play, namely Syria. This led to a number of visits in early 1994 by Christopher and Ross to the region. Out of this came a clarification of one of the critical parts of the Syrian position—the demand that Israeli withdrawal should be to the June 4, 1967, line.

The June 4 Line Controversy

Anyone who had been listening to Hafez al-Asad over the years would have known that Israeli withdrawal from all Syrian territory was an essential ingredient of any peace agreement. The Syrians did not consider this even to be part of the negotiations—it was more like an assumed starting point. (President Sadat, as noted above, treated Israeli withdrawal from Sinai in much the same way.) But on the Syrian front there was the question of how to define the eventual border. There had never been an agreed border between Israel and Syria, only between the French and the British as mandatory powers of Syria and Palestine. Then there was the 1949 armistice line, but neither side had considered that to be the recognized border. Finally, there was the June 4, 1967, line, the position where Israelis and Syrians found themselves on the eve of the 1967 War. But even that was not incontestably demarcated.

In spring 1994, al-Asad raised the issue of the June 4, 1967, lines in one of his talks with Christopher. When this conversation was conveyed to the Israeli side on May 2, 1994, Rabin was furious because he had apparently been under the impression that withdrawal to the 1923 international border would suffice.[42] Over the ensuing weeks, Christopher and Ross pressed Israel to accept the June 4 line, and Rabin resisted. Finally, on July 19, 1994, Christopher met with Rabin and was told that he could refer to the June 4, 1967, line as a "clarification," but not as a "commitment." Christopher could tell al-Asad that it was his impression that Israel would withdraw to the June 4 line if its other requirements were met. On July 21, after having seen al-Asad in Damascus, Christopher told Rabin that his "clarification" was understood and that Syria was now ready to resume negotiations.[43]

With this significant breakthrough, the on-again, off-again talks in Washington were able to resume with a greater degree of seriousness, including participation by high-ranking military officers by year's end. Before these talks could gain much momentum, Rabin once again turned his attention to another, friendlier neighbor, Jordan, leaving the Syrians–and some Americans–with the question of whether Rabin was just playing with them to get leverage in his other negotiations. The Jordan-Israel Peace Treaty was signed on October 26, 1994, with many international dignitaries, including Clinton, in attendance.

No doubt worried by how al-Asad might react to being left on the sidelines again, Clinton agreed to visit al-Asad in Damascus just after the signing of the Jordanian-Israeli treaty. Their private session was apparently reasonably good, but in public al-Asad was unwilling to say anything positive about the Israelis.[44] This left Clinton in the awkward position of speaking on al-Asad's behalf, while al-Asad stood mute at his side.

Despite the embarrassment that Clinton may have felt during the public part of his Damascus visit, he apparently did win al-Asad's consent to setting up a channel where security issues could be discussed by high-level military officers on both sides. Meetings in Washington of the Israeli and Syrian chiefs of staff ensued in late 1994, but these talks could only go so far in the absence of an agreed political framework. Thus Ross proposed that the two sides try to identify the "aims and principles" that should guide the negotiations.[45]

Aims and Principles Document

During a March 1995 trip to the Middle East, Christopher heard from Rabin that he was now prepared to move forward on the Syrian front. After a number of additional visits by Christopher to Damascus and Jerusalem, agreement was reached in late May 1995 on the so-called "aims and principles of security arrangements" document. Because of the constant fear of leaks to the press, this document was sometimes referred to as a "nonpaper," indicating that its status was not that of a final, ratified agreement. The text of the document reads as follows:

Aims
1. The most important priority is to reduce, if not eliminate, the danger of surprise attack.
2. Prevent or minimize friction on a daily basis along the boundary.
3. Reduce the danger for large-scale attack, invasion, or major war.

Principles
1. Security is a legitimate need for both sides. No claim of security, or a guarantee for it, should be achieved at the expense of the security of the other side.
2. Security arrangements should be equal, mutual, and reciprocal on both sides.[46]
3. The two sides acknowledge that security arrangements should be arrived at through mutual agreement and, as such, should be consistent with the sovereignty and territorial integrity of each side.
4. Security arrangements should be confined to the relevant areas on both sides of the border between the two countries.[47]

The point of this somewhat awkwardly worded document was to confirm that security arrangements had to be mutual and based on a principle of equity, but that equity need not mean exactly the same arrangements on each side of the border. This issue had been long debated between the two sides, and there now seemed a basis for moving ahead toward practical discussion of the means for achieving these "aims and principles."[48] Henceforth, the Syrian side would say that there were two agreed bases for moving forward: first, the Rabin "deposit," which dealt with the border; and this "nonpaper," which addressed security. However, significant ambiguities were buried in the text of the second principle of the "aims and principles" paper, and to begin to clarify some of those, another meeting at the chiefs of staff level was arranged for late June 1995.

This second round of meetings of high-ranking military officers encountered a serious snag when the Israelis raised the issue of a long-term Israeli presence in an early-warning station on the Golan Heights. Discussion took place on whether aerial surveillance could fulfill the need, and apparently the Syrians got the impression that it could. When the Israelis returned to the topic of ground stations, they found the Syrians were adamantly opposed. On the issue of the size of demilitarized zones along the border, however, the Syrians did eventually show some flexibility in accepting a ratio of 10 to 6 in Israel's favor in a crucial sector.

In part because of the political furor caused in Israel by leaks from the talks, Rabin lost interest in the military-to-military talks. The leaks were supplying ammunition for Rabin's political adversary, Likud leader Benjamin Netanyahu.[49] So Rabin put the talks on hold until after his election campaign in 1996.[50] Once again, Rabin's irritation with al-Asad's slow pace of negotiation, and perhaps as well his unhappiness that the Americans were not quite playing according to his script, led him to call time out. The Americans apparently did not try to persuade him otherwise.

When Rabin decided to call off the talks with Syria until after his election campaign in 1996, no one could have known that his life would be cut short by an extremist Israeli Jewish assassin on November 4, 1995. Although Rabin had been slow and often mistrustful in the way he approached negotiations with the Syrians, he did have a strategic outlook that told him why it was important to try to end the conflict with his neighbor to the north. And, despite the frequent frustrations they experienced in dealing with Rabin, some Syrian officials were later to look back on him as the one Israeli leader who seemed genuinely committed to peace.[51]

For the Americans, Rabin's death was a severe loss. Clinton and the entire peace team had a very high opinion of Rabin; some, including the president, had developed close personal relations with him. They admired his personal history as a much-decorated military leader, his intellect, his tough-mindedness, and his willingness to make hard decisions. And during his brief time as prime minister (1992–95) progress had been made with the Palestinians, the Jordanians, and the Syrians. Clinton and Christopher had received the "deposit," even if Rabin periodically seemed to back away from considering that he had made a conditional commitment to full withdrawal to the June 4, 1967, line,[52] and the "aims and principles" paper provided a framework for discussing security with the Syrians. Much more would have to be done for a full peace agreement to be achieved, but Rabin had taken important first steps. Would his successor follow in his footsteps?

Flying High and Fast: The Peres Moment

When Shimon Peres suddenly became Israel's prime minister in early November 1995, many questions arose about his approach to peace talks and to the matter of the upcoming Israeli elections. Rabin's assassination had led to a strong, but short-lived, backlash within Israel against the right-wing parties, and some felt that Peres would be wise to call for early elections so that he could win a large mandate for moving forward with Rabin's fundamental policies. But Peres himself seemed to feel that early elections would make it seem as if he were exploiting the Rabin tragedy for narrow political purposes of his own.[53] He preferred at the outset to establish a record of accomplishment and then go to elections toward the end of 1996.

The American team was not sure how much Peres actually knew about the Israeli-Syrian negotiations. Rabin had kept his cards very close to his chest, but it seems as if he had informed Peres of the basic points that defined the Israeli position, including the famous "deposit." In any event, Clinton, Christopher, and Ross all met with Peres in November and made sure that he was fully aware of the record of the Israeli-Syrian talks. Based on these initial contacts, Peres decided that he wanted to move ahead quickly on the Syrian front. If he could get an agreement with Syria, he seemed to think, he could go into elections with a solid achievement in hand.

Unlike Rabin, Peres was less preoccupied with security issues and was more intrigued with a vision of a "New Middle East" in which economic relations and new technologies would be the building blocks of peace. He also saw that peace with Syria might open the way to peace with many other Arab countries. And a Syria at peace with Israel would have less incentive to support radical movements such as Hezbollah and Hamas. All of this led Peres to propose that Israel and Syria should be prepared to "fly high and fast." Peres also attached great importance to an early summit meeting with al-Asad.

Ross traveled to Damascus in early December 1995. He carried with him a letter from Peres to al-Asad. The Syrian president read it and expressed his positive sentiment toward Peres. Ross felt this was a good omen.[54] Despite his normally cautious manner, al-Asad soon agreed that talks could resume with the goal of moving quickly toward agreement.

Each new Israeli prime minister seems intent on forging a personal relationship with the American president, and Peres was no exception. In mid-December, he traveled to Washington, DC, to meet with Clinton and to reaffirm the "deposit" or "pocket" commitment of Rabin. He also spoke of his desire to move forward rapidly on the Syrian front, and Clinton encouraged him. In mid-December, Christopher and Ross flew to Damascus to propose a new round of peace talks that would take place in a much different setting. Instead of the formal talks that had previously taken place, this time delegations would meet in a secluded spot outside of Washington, the Wye River Plantation. There, all the issues could be discussed in a relaxed setting. It was encouraging that al-Asad agreed, and the first round of talks was set for the end of the month.

The Wye River Talks

Peres brought to the negotiations with Syria not only a mindset of his own but also a partly new team of negotiators. Instead of relying so heavily on Ambassador Rabinovich, he put his own aide, Uri Savir, in charge of the talks. Savir had negotiated with the Palestinians at Oslo and was viewed as fairly dovish within the spectrum of Israeli politics. It was understood that he and Ross and the Syrian ambassador, Walid al-Moualem, would meet separately at Wye to provide a kind of back channel for sensitive discussions. Meanwhile, delegations would be at work on all of the main issues—normalization of relations, security, the border and water, and the implementation of the agreement.

The first round of talks at Wye was among the most productive ever.[55] During the negotiations, the Rabin commitment on withdrawal was assumed to be in the American "pocket" but was not explicitly discussed by the Israeli side. Discussion therefore focused on the other issues. When questions of economic cooperation arose, the Syrian side suggested that President al-Asad would have to decide this issue. So, between the first and second rounds of the Wye talks, Ross went to Damascus to see if al-Asad would show flexibility in this regard. The answer was a qualified yes.

When the second round of the Wye talks resumed in late January 1996, speculation was rife in the Israeli press that Peres might call early elections, a decision that would inevitably slow down the Israeli-Syrian negotiations. Ross argued that Peres should be dissuaded from calling for an early vote. Clinton and Christopher, however, were unwilling to second-guess the Israeli prime minister. Christopher and Ross then went to the region to ask Peres what he planned to do. Peres made it clear that he would only forgo early elections if al-Asad would meet him in a summit that could produce an early agreement. Otherwise he would simply allow the Wye talks to drag on, while he proceeded with early elections.[56] When Christopher proposed the summit idea to al-Asad, he got the predictable cool response. The time was not yet ripe, in al-Asad's view, for a summit. But he would allow the Wye talks to continue.[57]

A third round of talks at Wye therefore began in late February. But a spate of terrorist bombings in Israel led Peres to suspend the talks with Syria. And when Israel carried out a powerful military strike in south Lebanon the following month, killing about one hundred civilians in Kfar Qana, the Israeli-Syrian talks came to an abrupt end. When the Israeli election was held in May, Peres lost by a narrow margin, and his successor, Benjamin Netanyahu, seemed to have little interest in talking peace with either Syrians or Palestinians.

Was Wye Another Missed Opportunity?

Although he was less involved in the Wye talks, Israeli ambassador Rabinovich identifies this period of late 1995 to early 1996 as one where a breakthrough seemed possible. One cannot read the accounts of Ross and Savir without reaching the same conclusion. Moualem, who has spoken at length about these negotiations, also seemed to feel that progress had been made. By his reckoning, about 75 to 80 percent of an agreement had been reached.

Unlike in 1993, at Wye the American side did play a more substantive role, injecting ideas of its own, trying to identify areas of agreement, and seeking to summarize the sessions in an orderly way. Ross was the primary player on the American side during these talks, and he realized the risk that Israeli domestic politics might upset the negotiations. But neither Clinton nor Christopher was prepared to weigh in with Peres on a matter as sensitive as internal Israeli politics. Nor would the Americans try to restrain Israel in the aftermath of the March 1996 terror bombings.

The primary responsibility for the collapse of the Wye negotiations lies with Palestinian radicals who were determined to sabotage the peace efforts—both on the Palestinian and Syrian tracks—and with Peres, who decided to make a show of force to bolster his scanty credentials on the security front.[58] Among the American participants in this phase of diplomacy, there is little to suggest that they saw the possibility of playing the U.S. role more effectively. Ross, who was often a polarizing figure and was frequently criticized by his colleagues for the way he managed the negotiations, is generally credited by other members of the team with handling the Wye talks quite professionally. Nor do the Syrians, who later expressed considerable dissatisfaction with his tilt toward Israel, have much negative to say about the role Ross played at Wye.

Surprisingly, the lead Israeli negotiator, Uri Savir, is the only one to put some of the blame on the American side, although he does so rather delicately. In his view, Ross and his team were generally very professional. But he notes,

> Some people in our defense establishment believed that Ross, like Secretary Christopher, was somewhat naïve about dealing with an unscrupulous Syrian regime. And it's true that the Americans—particularly in the Clinton administration—were marked by a certain innocence that is alien to our region. . . . If there was a weakness in the Americans' position, as I openly told Ross, it was their exaggerated involvement as mediator in the talks. I believe that the United States should have spent more energy defining its own broad strategic role in a peaceful Middle East.[59]

Savir's criticism seems only partially valid. Israelis and Syrians needed a mediator, and during this phase, Ross and his team played the role well. It is true, however, that for both Israel and Syria certain issues went far beyond their own bilateral relationship: Would the United States put troops on the Golan as part of the security arrangements? Would Washington offer Israel a security treaty, as Peres had requested? Could Syria look forward to a significant change in its relationship with Washington after peace? Would peace with Syria open the way for Israel to make peace with the rest of the Arab world? These were questions that could only be answered by Clinton, and he was hesitant, going into his own reelection year, to put forward ideas that might be controversial in Congress or in American public discourse.[60]

In the end, it is hard to see that the American side could have done much more to produce a positive outcome at Wye. On the whole, this period was the most productive of Israeli-Syrian peace talks to date. Bad luck, an explosion of violence between Israelis and Palestinians, and domestic politics in Israel threw the negotiations off track. Perhaps Clinton's own hesitancy as his reelection campaign got under way did have an adverse effect, but it was a secondary matter at this point. Wye came close to getting the model for successful negotiations right. With a bit more time, a bit more energy from the top levels of leadership, a breakthrough might have happened. But politics is all about timing, and the timing of this otherwise promising moment turned out to be not quite right.

Timeout: The Netanyahu Interlude

Shimon Peres did not have much luck whenever he was at the helm of the Labor Party. He led his party to its first ever electoral defeat in 1977, uneasily shared power with Likud in the mid-1980s, and then lost the election of 1996 by a tiny margin. Less than one percent of the electorate tipped the latter election to Likud leader Benjamin Netanyahu, and for the first time ever Israel was choosing its prime minister by popular vote. (Peres's Labor Party actually got more seats than Likud, but because of the new rules that had been adopted in 1992, Netanyahu had the first shot at forming a government.)

Anyone familiar with Likud's platform and Netanyahu's own views would have been skeptical about the prospects for Arab-Israeli peace diplomacy in mid-1996. And they would have been correct. There were negotiations, especially on the Palestinian track, where Clinton weighed in heavily to keep things moving forward. But on the Syrian front, there were no visible signs of progress after the suspension of the promising Wye River Plantation talks in the spring.[61]

Perhaps in response to the pressure he was feeling from the Americans on the Palestinian track, Netanyahu did eventually decide to explore the possibility of dealing with Syria. But he did so through a private American citizen, cosmetics executive Ronald Lauder, and kept the effort secret from the U.S. government. No agreement was reached, although the Syrians who were involved in the talks claim that there was some progress made. But when Netanyahu was asked for a map, like his predecessors, he was unwilling to indicate exactly the line to which Israel would withdraw on the Golan in return for peace.[62]

The Lauder initiative is important for one primary reason. Lauder later told Netanyahu's successor, Ehud Barak, that al-Asad had been prepared to accept the 1923 border rather than the June 4, 1967, line. This information reportedly had an influence on Barak's thinking. Like Rabin, Barak was willing to consider full withdrawal from Golan, but he did not want to cede the shoreline in the northeast corner of the Sea of Galilee and was therefore reluctant to reconfirm the "Rabin deposit." Lauder led him to think that the Syrians would settle for less. If al-Asad would really accept the 1923 line, that would go a long way toward solving the border problem.

The only problem was that Lauder was not reporting accurately. When the Clinton team first saw Lauder's ten points summarizing areas of agreement, Ross found them too good to be true.[63] So he checked with the Syrians, who denied that agreement had been reached on these points, especially the 1923 border issue. Eventually Lauder produced a second document of eight points, which was a more accurate account of areas of agreement, and in that document the future border was referred to, at Syrian insistence, as the June 4, 1967, line.[64] Still, for a crucial moment in 1999, when Israel's new prime minister was setting his Syria-first strategy, the inaccurate message from Lauder may have influenced his thinking and seems to have planted the seed of doubt on the American side that perhaps al-Asad would show more flexibility than previously believed on the issue of the future border. Alas, no one seems to have bothered to check with al-Asad, or when they did, they were not listening carefully. Not once in our interviews did we come across anyone who claimed to have heard al-Asad express any flexibility on the June 4 line. To him, it meant Syrian sovereignty up to the water's edge of the Sea of Galilee and nothing less.

Resetting the Stage

Ehud Barak became Israel's prime minister in May 1999 after a solid victory over Netanyahu. He was widely perceived to be a politician in the mold of his mentor, Yitzhak Rabin. Many commented on his brilliance—and his arrogance. To put it mildly, Barak was confident that whatever decisions he made were correct. One of those decisions, which had major consequences for the peace process, was that he should start with an effort to reach an agreement with Syria. His motivation seemed to be that he had promised his electorate to get out of Lebanon within one year and hoped to do so in the context of an agreement with Syria. If this meant leaving the Palestinian issue on the back burner for a bit longer, so be it.

It is rare in Arab-Israeli relations to find leaders publicly praising one another, but this is precisely what Barak and al-Asad did at the outset of this new phase.

Patrick Seale, a British journalist who was close to the Syrians, managed to get both leaders to give him interviews that included some quite generous comments.[65] Barak, however, had ideas of his own about how best to proceed. His preference was for direct and secret diplomacy.[66] Al-Asad was not enthusiastic, but he agreed to send an envoy, Riad Daoudi, to meet with Uri Saguy in Bern, Switzerland, in the presence of Dennis Ross.[67]

The Bern Talks

The Bern meeting in late August 1999 represented the first direct contact between Israeli and Syrian officials since the suspension of the Wye talks in spring 1996. The issues were much the same as they had then been. From the Syrian standpoint, the first question to be determined was whether or not the Rabin deposit—meaning the June 4, 1967, line—was still valid now that Barak was in office. Because of the confusion of the Lauder episode, there was some uncertainty on both sides about this. Prior to this meeting, Ross had been suspicious of the Lauder ten points but did not know that they represented only an Israeli draft, not an agreed position. He therefore was looking for ways to introduce some of the ideas into the discussion. Still, he cautioned Saguy at the outset that al-Asad would be expecting to hear a reaffirmation of the June 4 deposit. When Daoudi and Saguy met, the Syrian did indeed ask the anticipated question, and according to Ross, Saguy replied, "We accept the principle of withdrawal to the June 4 lines."[68] He went on to say there were some "technical questions" about the exact location of the line, and there was the question of "water and its relationship to the border" that the two sides would have to address.[69] Daoudi asked for this commitment in writing, but Saguy refused. As an alternative, Ross offered an American statement that the Rabin deposit "should guide" the final outcome and "should not" be withdrawn. Barak was willing to accept this. It was less than the Syrians wanted, but for now, it was all that the Israeli side was willing to offer.[70] The next step would be a visit by Madeleine Albright, who had replaced Christopher as secretary of state in 1997, to Syria and Israel.

Albright managed to get agreement from the parties to resume secret talks in the Washington area in mid-September. On September 13, Ross met with Barak in Israel to prepare for these talks. Barak showed no interest in a summary of points prepared by Ross. Instead, he wanted to know if al-Asad would accept a border that did not touch the northeast corner of the Sea of Galilee and the Jordan River to its north. If so, he thought that an agreement could be quickly reached. He sketched on a map what he had in mind.[71] Based on everything the Americans had heard in the past, Ross should have bluntly said that al-Asad would most likely not accept. But Ross's concern was of a different order. He thought Barak was rushing things and urged him to let the talks in Washington go forward and to focus on Ross's draft document.

Talks in Bethesda, New York, and Washington

The June 4 issue would not go away. When the parties next met for secret talks in the Washington suburbs, Daoudi and Saguy, joined by a Syrian general, went in detail over a map of the border region. When Daoudi asked again if Israel accepted the principle of withdrawal to the June 4 line, Saguy responded positively but added that Israelis needed areas to the east of the Jordan River and to the east of the northeast part of the lake.[72] The Syrian general bristled, saying, "You want Syrian land." Shortly thereafter, the meeting broke up.[73]

Perhaps in the hope of easing the strain, Daoudi in private reportedly said to Ross that in regard to the northeast corner of the lake, there was no real difference between the June 4 line and the international border.[74] (The border had deliberately been drawn by the British ten meters off the shoreline.) Ross then showed Daoudi the map where Barak had sketched his preferred line and asked him if Syria could accept a small strip of land east of the lake under Israeli control. Ross claims, but Syrian sources deny, that at this point Daoudi said it might be possible to accept something like 50 meters off the lake.[75] Ross then conveyed this information to Saguy. Indyk, who was present, cautioned that "al-Asad will need nominal sovereignty over the area around the lake that you want."[76] The net effect of these exchanges was to make the American side optimistic that a deal might soon be reached, including on the vexing border-water issues. Ideas were being discussed about distinguishing between "sovereignty" and "control," but no one claims that agreement along these lines was ever reached.

That impression was not to last for long. Foreign minister Sharaa was in the United States and was planning to meet with President Clinton. Barak wanted the American side to press Sharaa to accept the idea that the future borderline should not touch the water of the Sea of Galilee. Ross, using one of his favorite concepts, decided to try to "condition" Sharaa "to the idea that Israel needed to retain a small piece of land area off the lake to show its public that its control of the water was not in jeopardy."[77] Meeting initially with Albright and Ross, Sharaa said that Syria required sovereignty up to the June 4 lines, but that Israel's concerns for water could be met by other means.

During his meeting with Clinton, Sharaa agreed that an American-manned early-warning station could be established on the Golan Heights, preferably under a UN flag—a concession of considerable importance. Clinton also pressed him hard to accept Barak's need for the small strip of land around the lake. Clinton then introduced an idea first heard from Saguy that perhaps a "peace park" could be established, with free access to both Syrians and Israelis, in the sensitive area along the edge of the lake. Sharaa agreed to consider the idea as long as there was no question of Syrian sovereignty over the land. Barak showed no interest in the "peace park" idea, although it had originated with one of his own negotiators. In his view, Israel needed sovereignty over the strip of land but would graciously allow Syrian farmers to have access to the lake for their fishing and irrigation needs.[78] In short, the gap between the two sides on the border—by now clearly the crucial issue for both—was still substantial conceptually, if not in terms of the amount of territory. Just as clear was that the American side was leaning strongly in Barak's direction.

What is puzzling at this point is that Ross seemed to engage in both wishful thinking and advocacy in ways that were particularly questionable. First, ignoring al-Asad's repeated statements about the June 4 line, he appeared to believe that the Syrians were beginning to move away from that long-held position toward something the Israelis might be able to accept. And then he threw his weight behind the position that Israel was right to insist on a land corridor under its control in the northeast quadrant of the Sea of Galilee. Not surprisingly, al-Asad came to the conclusion that Ross was no longer an honest broker.

The Endgame

Barak, who had initially favored the idea of secret talks where everything would be discussed, suddenly lost patience with this approach and decided that Clinton should be used to administer a "shock" to al-Asad. In his view, Clinton should simply go to Damascus and tell al-Asad that negotiations must be resumed at a political level; if al-Asad said yes, then Clinton could reaffirm the Rabin deposit. Ross and all of Clinton's advisers thought this was a terrible idea. By now Barak was calling Clinton whenever he felt like it, and Clinton would take the calls.[79]

It was fairly obvious to the Americans that al-Asad was not in good health. In addition, Sharaa had fallen ill and was out of commission for several weeks. So, although Clinton did write to al-Asad explaining that political level talks were now warranted to deal with the small difference over borders, the relationship of the border to control of water, and early-warning stations, al-Asad was slow to respond.[80] And when the reply finally came, it was stiff and unhelpful.[81] This led Barak to propose his "shock therapy."[82] It was finally agreed that Albright and Ross would see al-Asad and try to persuade him to resume negotiations. If necessary, Albright would tell al-Asad that the Rabin deposit was still in the American pocket.

As it turned out, al-Asad agreed to resume negotiations at the political level without any such assurance.[83] Sharaa, now recovered, was to travel to Washington for preliminary talks. On the Israeli side, Barak would lead the negotiating team.

Talks in Washington

Barak's shock therapy approach to negotiating took an unusual turn as the highest level political talks between Israelis and Syrians began. In this case, the shock was administered not to the Syrians, but to the Americans. Barak, who had pressed so hard for a summit and was always talking of swift movement toward agreement, now told the Americans when he arrived in Washington in mid-December 1999, "I can't do it because my political circumstances have changed."[84] The "it" was the Rabin deposit—full withdrawal to the June 4 line. And, to Ross's astonishment, he even said that he would not agree to any one-on-one meetings with Sharaa.[85] His rationale for this about-face was evidence of growing opposition to a deal with Syria within Israel and his obsessive fear of leaks.

With Barak in such a frame of mind, one might have wondered what the preliminary talks in Washington could accomplish. The idea was to agree on a plan for an intensive round of negotiations, beginning January 3, 2000. But before such procedural matters could be discussed, Sharaa insisted on reviewing the entire history of the Rabin deposit and the importance of the June 4 line. Barak sat and listened and responded by saying, "While my government has made no commitment on territory, we don't erase history."[86] This was as close as Sharaa could get for the moment to a reaffirmation from Barak of the Rabin deposit. The parties then agreed that when they reconvened in January, talks would take place in four working groups: on security, on the border, on water, and on peace. In the course of discussing these groups, Sharaa reportedly made a comment to the effect that you "cannot find the June 4 line in any map in any book." Ross was encouraged by this comment to believe that the Syrians might indeed be a bit flexible on exactly where the border might run along the lake, the key issue to which the two sides kept returning.[87]

On to Shepherdstown

On January 3, 2000, the Israelis, Syrians, and Americans convened in Shepherdstown, West Virginia, for an intensive round of diplomacy aimed at bridging the gaps that remained between the two adversaries. Barak and Sharaa represented their respective countries. On the U.S. side, Clinton participated frequently, and Albright, Ross, Berger, and others joined in the effort to forge a peace agreement.

If ever there was a promising moment for diplomacy to resolve the Israeli-Syrian conflict, this would seem to have been it.

American accounts of Shepherdstown converge on two points. First, Sharaa is portrayed as having made a number of forward-leaning proposals. Second, Barak is viewed as the reticent party, holding back for domestic political reasons. Barak, with a general's mindset, seems to have viewed these negotiations as a process to isolate and then to overpower the adversary. From Barak's standpoint, Clinton's role was to be one of the prime minister's shock troops. The American president would pressure the Syrians to make the concessions—especially on the strip of land along the lakeshore—that would clinch the deal.[88]

From the outset of the talks, the issue of the June 4 lines had to be confronted. Berger, among others, understood that nothing much would happen until Barak openly confirmed the Rabin deposit directly to the Syrians. There had been so much dancing around on this issue—it finally had to be resolved. And if Barak would not do it directly, Ross felt that Clinton should nonetheless state that his own position was that June 4 should be the basis of the final border negotiations.[89] Barak rejected both alternatives, and added a new condition of his own. Now he insisted, without much apparent logic, that the Syrians must allow the Israeli-Lebanese talks to begin immediately.[90] No one on the American side thought this was a serious issue, but Barak was stubborn in pushing forward one more hurdle for the Syrians to get over to prove their good intentions and to ease his domestic problems. It was a strange way to negotiate if one genuinely wanted to resolve the conflict.

Contrary to previous rounds of negotiations, this time the United States was ready to put forward a draft of its own on how the key issues should be resolved. The American team would use the technique of bracketed language where the two sides disagreed. Because the United States felt it had a commitment not to "surprise" Barak, the draft would be shown first to him. Apparently, there was no reciprocal Israeli commitment not to surprise the United States, which Barak repeatedly did with his new demands and his backing away from previous promises.

According to Ross, the Israelis were doubtful that Sharaa really had authority to clinch a deal. Barak seemed to have in mind that only a summit with al-Asad would allow for a final agreement, and until then he would hold firm on not putting the Rabin deposit on the table. Ross asked what it would take to show that Sharaa had authority, and one of the Israelis said that a clear statement that Israel would have sovereignty over the water of the Sea of Galilee would be an important sign.[91]

When Albright and Ross met with Sharaa, Ross outlined the positions of both sides. According to Ross, Sharaa listened carefully. "On the question of whose sovereignty applied where, he was straightforward and unequivocal: *The Israelis would have sovereignty over the lake; the Syrians would have sovereignty over the land, at least all the land to the east of the 10 meters off the shoreline.*"[92] By this time, Ross seemed to be assuming that the Syrian position made no distinction between the June 4 line (on the waterline) and the 1923 border (ten meters off the lake) in the northeast corner.[93] Perhaps some of the Syrian negotiators had implied that there was no important difference here, but no one claimed to have heard this directly from Hafez al-Asad, who without a doubt was the ultimate authority on the Syrian side.[94]

Sharaa, in Ross's view, was showing considerable flexibility, even on the issue of an American presence on Mt. Hermon to manage an early-warning station. But Barak, while acknowledging Sharaa's constructive approach, was unmoved. He would offer nothing new.

To salvage the situation, the American side decided to offer to send a letter to al-Asad saying that the Rabin deposit was still in Clinton's pocket and that Barak did not intend to withdraw it—in other words, he might play it at the very end, but not quite yet. This was not exactly music to al-Asad's ears, it would seem, because he had been told the same thing on numerous occasions and seemed to have the idea clearly in mind that the June 4 issue had to be resolved up front, before everything else could fall into place. Ross concluded from this episode that the president was being "overused" at Shepherdstown. Barak was relying on Clinton to keep the Syrians on board while he held out.[95]

On January 7, Clinton finally presented the American draft peace treaty. On the crucial issue of the "commonly agreed border," the purported Syrian position was that it should be "based on the June 4, 1967 line," whereas the presumed Israeli position simply said the border should take into account "security and other vital interests of the parties as well as legal considerations of both sides," which really committed the Israelis to nothing at all. By contrast, on peace and normalization, there was no bracketed language, implying that the two sides were in agreement.[96] Sharaa's reaction was predictable. He complained to the Americans that Israel had failed to deliver on the June 4 issue, "June 4 was the ignition; without it the car won't start."[97]

With this document on the table, the parties then convened in subgroups to try to narrow their differences. In the border meeting, the Syrian general reportedly suggested that in some areas the border could be adjusted as much as fifty meters to meet mutual needs and concerns, provided that June 4 remained the basis for demarcating the border. Ross characterizes these talks as showing considerable flexibility on the Syrian side, for which they were getting nothing in return.[98] Because little more progress seemed possible at this point and Barak was eager to get back to Israel, the parties agreed to suspend Shepherdstown, with the intention of resuming after a break. During their last meeting, Sharaa asked Barak directly if he would confirm the Rabin commitment. Barak just smiled.[99]

As it turned out, the fear over leaks from the conference was warranted. On January 9, a well-informed article describing the two sides' positions had appeared in London-based Arabic newspaper *Al Hayat*.[100] Much more devastating, however, was the appearance of the complete text of the American proposal in the Israeli newspaper *Ha'aretz* on January 13. Particularly embarrassing was the revelation that the Israelis, according to the document, had made no commitment whatsoever on withdrawal (except to a "commonly agreed border"), while the language suggested that the Syrians had already agreed to normal peaceful relations with Israel. When Clinton spoke to al-Asad just after the leak appeared, he found the Syrian leader in a foul mood about the Shepherdstown negotiations. Whatever respect al-Asad had once held for Barak seemed to be fading as the Israeli position on the Rabin deposit remained ambiguous.

Evaluating the U.S. Role at Shepherdstown

While the January 2000 talks were not quite the end of the road for Israeli-Syrian peace talks on Clinton's watch, they did represent a particularly propitious moment. Never before had the Syrians shown such flexibility and willingness to reach an agreement. Could the United States have done anything differently that might have improved the chances of success?

The key issue that kept the parties from reaching agreement was the question of the extent of Israeli withdrawal. On the one hand, there were ample reasons to believe that the gap between the two sides was not too large. Rabin had said, Peres had confirmed, and Netanyahu had reportedly hinted that the June 4, 1967, line would be the basis for the future border, provided that Israeli needs on security, water, and peace were all met. Barak came tantalizingly close to reaffirming this commitment, but he would not do so explicitly and he would not do it directly to the Syrians unless he could have his much-hoped-for summit with al-Asad.

Before calling for the Shepherdstown talks, Clinton would have been well advised to get Barak to confirm the Rabin deposit. Some ambiguity about the exact demarcation of the border still would have existed, and the Syrians might have been willing to show some flexibility, once the principle of the June 4 line was affirmed. After all, for the Syrians, and especially for al-Asad, it was the principle of recovering all of the land they lost in 1967 that seemed to matter.

Barak had made it clear that his objection to the June 4 line was that it would put the Syrians on the shoreline of the Sea of Galilee and that might lead them to claim rights over the water as well. No real security issue was involved regarding whether Israel would maintain a 10- or 50- or 200-meter strip along the northeast corner of the lake.[101] Israeli troops would not be deployed there under any conceivable scenario. Nor would Syrian troops. This strip of land would be part of a demilitarized area that both sides had already agreed on. So the issue was water, and the Syrians had hinted, and then at Shepherdstown confirmed, that sovereignty over the lake would go to Israel.

Although it would have taken real American leadership and negotiating skill to pin down these two points—water to Israel, land to Syria—this was the only reasonable outcome to the stalemate that arose every time the parties met. Rather than put American prestige on the line by hosting a meeting where the chances of success would be slim unless this trade-off were achieved, Clinton could have refused to host the Shepherdstown talks until each side had moved toward basic acceptance of the proposed June 4 land-water compromise. Al-Asad seemed eager to get an agreement, so he might have been willing to confirm the point about the water; Barak, if he thought he could get most of the remainder of what he wanted on water and security including bilateral commitments from the United States, might have also been willing to accept the June 4 line without quibbling endlessly over exactly where it was.

True, Barak's pollsters (some of whom also happened to be Clinton's!) were telling him that the Israeli public would not back him if he made such compromises, but one could never be sure what the impact of an actual peace treaty would be. Clinton was willing to help sell it, and Barak would most likely be able to point to significant gains in the U.S.-Israeli relationship as part of the peace package. His political standing could hardly have gone down much further than it already had; it might, in fact, have risen substantially.

One of Clinton's top advisers who joined him at Shepherdstown said,

> The fundamental reason why Shepherdstown failed, and ultimately the Syrian track failed, was that Barak did not share with us his strategy that Shepherdstown would be kabuki. Barak felt once he had the Syrian commitment to engage that he needed not to look overeager, and so he never had an intention of making much progress in Shepherdstown. . . . We sort of got snookered by the same pattern in Geneva where Barak really didn't share with us until the very last minute the proposal that he wanted us to put to al-Asad and he wound up giving us a proposal which was not something al-Asad accepted and probably one that we should have pushed Barak to sweeten. Now, we should never have let ourselves get in that position. . . . We should have been more prepared to push back on Barak. Now, Clinton saw his role very much as a facilitator and in these negotiations . . . his

approach was that of an honest broker . . . and in Geneva we had the Israeli proposal, and the President felt that it needed to be presented to al-Asad without any gloss, but I think we should have pushed back on Barak and said this is just inadequate, I'm not going to al-Asad with it.[102]

Indyk looks back at this period and argues that it would have made sense to have had a Barak-al-Asad summit in January.[103] Whether al-Asad would have come is doubtful, but the rest of Indyk's criticism is pertinent. He notes,

But we were led astray by our all too well-developed habit of seizing on a procedural fix to overcome a substantive roadblock. Because of al-Asad's dilatory tactics, this had become so ingrained in Dennis's [Ross] approach to Israeli-Syrian negotiations over the twelve years that he had devoted to them that it had become a natural instinct. But it was particularly ill suited to this moment when al-Asad's health was so frail and he seemed so eager to make peace, when the clock on Clinton's term in office was already ticking, when Barak was rapidly losing political altitude, and when the Palestinians were growing impatient because their negotiations were being ignored. . . . In hindsight, we shouldn't have allowed Sharaa to go home empty-handed; Clinton should have pressed Barak to be more forthcoming at that moment, not later. But Clinton had always been particularly sensitive to the political situation in Israel. . . . There was also a predisposition in Clinton's peace team to avoid second-guessing Israeli leaders who were committed to taking risks for peace.[104]

It also appears that the Americans were too quick to assume that Syria was willing to cede to Barak's desire to keep a strip of territory along the lakeshore. On this issue al-Asad had made his views known on many occasions, and if there were to be a change of position, then it would have to come from al-Asad himself. True, the June 4, 1967, line may not have been on any official map, but everyone knew that before the Six-Day War Syria had control up to the waterline in the northeast quadrant of the lake. That was the meaning of the June 4 line, after all, and that was why Barak was so reluctant to repeat the June 4 formula.[105]

When hints of flexibility were reportedly given by the Syrian side about the precise demarcation of the border, Ross was led to conclude that Barak's "need" for the strip of territory could be met, and that all that remained was to determine how wide the strip would be. With this thought in mind, he was not insistent on pressing for clarity about the June 4 point.[106] This stance undervalued the symbolism of June 4 for al-Asad. Unless al-Asad could hear clearly that Syria's sovereignty would be restored up to the June 4 line, meaning the shoreline, he was unlikely to move forward.

One may decry al-Asad's lack of flexibility and imagination on this point, but this was al-Asad's long-standing and well-known position. Clinton should have been aware of this, and so should Ross. And they should have said to Barak that they would not waste their time or energy on trying to clinch the deal between Israel and Syria unless Barak was prepared to accept the June 4 line. The worst that could have happened was that Barak stood firm, and there would have been no agreement. But at least then there would not have been the major investment of American time and energy, while the Palestinian-Israeli track was put on hold. And the outcome would have been the same—no agreement.

But it is also possible that Barak would have decided to play the "Rabin deposit" card and would have settled for iron-clad guarantees on water and large side payments from the United States. Clinton then could have pushed the Syrians hard on security issues and accelerated normalization, and the pieces might have fallen into place, including the much-talked-of Barak-al-Asad summit to finalize the deal. But Barak kept introducing distractions, such as the Lebanese track, and he pulled back from positions that had been taken by his predecessors, all of which were simply maneuvers designed to help him on the home front. Clinton was too patient and too understanding of Barak's politics—and of Barak's infuriating style of negotiating.

If the Americans were too sensitive to Barak's problems, they seemed almost aloof from any deep effort to understand what it would take to bring al-Asad to the point of decision regarding peace. They knew he was ill and sometimes thought that might be an incentive for him to move quickly. Clinton engaged in telephone diplomacy with al-Asad, but even his own team thought he was inclined to mislead al-Asad about how forthcoming Barak was prepared to be when they spoke on the phone.[107] In Ross's memoir, he recounts endless hours in consultation with Barak, and with a number of Barak's aides as well. But there is no comparable record of such close consultations with the Syrians. In Israel Clinton had an ambassador who could deal with Barak effectively and who was really part of the U.S. team. The same was not true in Damascus. One rarely hears of any important role being played by the ambassador there, and yet it was al-Asad who had to make the final decisions on his side and Clinton needed to understand his thinking as well as possible. And based on Sharaa's bitter final summation at Shepherdstown, where he accused Barak of reneging on his professed willingness to reaffirm the Rabin deposit and to discuss the border, there was no reason for the wishful thinking that seemed to persist about Syrian flexibility on the June 4 line.[108]

Only one Arabist was on the American team, Gamal Helal, and his role was that of translator (plus occasional adviser on Arab affairs). Present at most of the meetings with al-Asad, Helal claims that he did not believe that an Israeli-Syrian deal was possible unless al-Asad got back every centimeter of land.[109] But he was a junior member of the team and was not regularly consulted. So this insight into al-Asad's insistence on the principle of full withdrawal was not given sufficient prominence. Wishful thinking was allowed to win out over inconvenient truths.

The Geneva Summit: One Last Gasp

Having invested heavily in Israeli-Syrian peace, Clinton and his team were still not ready to give up after the Shepherdstown disappointment. When Clinton spoke to al-Asad, however, he got little encouragement. The Syrian leader said that Barak was always adding new demands. The Syrian president could not figure out what Israel really wanted. He did not close the door on future talks, but the Syrian leader made it clear that the border would first have to be agreed on before any formal negotiations could be resumed.

At this point, the Saudi ambassador to Washington, Bandar ibn Sultan, who was on good terms with Clinton, offered to help. He would go see al-Asad if Clinton wanted him to. Clinton agreed (without informing Albright or Ross in advance), asking the Saudi to tell al-Asad that a deal was still possible. According to Ross (who was not present at the meeting), Clinton said that Bandar could tell al-Asad that he, Clinton, would want to see al-Asad "when we had what we needed from Barak."[110] Bandar apparently then told al-Asad that if Clinton were to ask to meet with him it would mean that he had gotten from Barak the necessary concession on the June 4 line.

Ross met secretly with Bandar in Geneva on January 28, 2000, to hear what al-Asad had said. Bandar had met with al-Asad for more than three hours. He had a piece of paper with the Syrian position spelled out, which Ross summarizes as follows:

> Al-Asad was determined to do a deal, and had thought he had a partner in Barak for that purpose. Now he was not sure. Barak, he felt, had played a game at Shepherdstown. Al-Asad was not Arafat; he could not be treated this way. The two sides should take their bitter pill together and not stretch things out. He could not afford to have his people coming and going in multiple rounds. They should get together in one round and stay until they finished. The border could be demarcated in secret and not revealed until the deal was done. But it must be demarcated. The Israelis did not want him to negotiate over their security requirements; they could not expect him to bargain over June 4.[111]

Ross asked Bandar if he thought al-Asad would show any flexibility on the June 4 issue, at least on the actual line if not on the principle. Bandar was not sure, but thought that he might. He claimed that al-Asad had agreed that there was no complete consensus on the exact location of the line. Ross maintains that he was uneasy about what Bandar had said about al-Asad's flexibility on the June 4 line. "I had a feeling that Bandar told me what I wanted to hear on the issue of flexibility on the line versus flexibility on the principle."[112] Still, Ross concluded that another effort had to be made to determine if a deal was possible.

The key to success in the American view was to get Barak to reveal to them his bottom line position on withdrawal. If it was close enough to meeting al-Asad's presumed needs, then Clinton would seek a meeting with al-Asad for a "make-or-break" session. At this point, Barak was talking about a line some hundreds of meters off the Sea of Galilee. Ross began to think that the gap between the two sides might be bridged with a gimmick. The level of the Sea of Galilee had receded over the past thirty years, so the current shoreline was some distance to the west of where it was on June 4, 1967. Maybe al-Asad and Barak would agree on the old shoreline of June 4 as the border, which would still leave a strip of land under Israeli control, just as Barak wanted. Barak insisted, therefore, that Ross show the Syrians a map based on the 1967 shoreline rather than a current map.[113] No one apparently thought to try this idea out with al-Asad before the summit meeting, and in any case Barak was asking for a much wider strip of land, one that would actually place the border well to the *east* of the 1923 international border. How Clinton and Ross expected that al-Asad would actually agree to this proposed new border was difficult to imagine. They apparently paid little heed to the message that Bandar brought from al-Asad.

Barak was now impatient for Clinton to see al-Asad for the "make-or-break" session. He was willing to go a bit further in revealing his bottom line but still seemed to think that Clinton would simply set the stage for a Barak-al-Asad summit, and only there would he finally reveal his real bottom line. It was all a bit too complex and hypothetical, and it did not take seriously the point that al-Asad had made that negotiations would only resume once the border issue was resolved.

Clinton tried to arrange a meeting with al-Asad in early March, but found the Syrian president to be standoffish. The idea of sending Albright to Damascus to help prepare the summit was suggested, but Barak was adamantly opposed to the idea, and Clinton inexplicably backed down. Finally, Clinton and al-Asad agreed to meet in Geneva on March 26.[114] Clinton would be returning from a trip to South Asia. Meanwhile, Ross continued to try to get to Barak's bottom line. Ross and Indyk were not persuaded that Barak was offering enough to win al-Asad's agreement,[115] but Barak promised to come up with an improved formulation that he would communicate directly to Clinton just hours before he was to meet with al-Asad in Geneva. Amazingly, Clinton was willing to proceed this way.

The phone call between Barak and Clinton on the morning of March 26, about one hour before Clinton met with al-Asad, broke no new ground. Barak was insistent that the President follow his script. Clinton, who was not feeling well after his trip to South Asia, may not have taken enough time to think through how best to explain Barak's position. Nor was he inclined to argue with Barak. Some of Clinton's team later complained about the poor preparation for this important round of negotiations. One senior adviser strongly felt that Clinton should have pushed back harder when Barak laid out his position. Even Albright says in her memoir that Barak's last-minute demands on Clinton were "patronizing."[116] On the face of it, what Barak had to offer was still quite far from what al-Asad—or any other Syrian official—had said they could accept. And al-Asad had been led to believe by Bandar that Clinton would only be coming to see him if he had the June 4 deposit in his pocket and ready to be played.

The meeting did not go well. According to Ross, Clinton said that Barak, based on "a commonly agreed border," was prepared to withdraw to the June 4 line as part of a peace agreement. But al-Asad reacted badly to the phrase "commonly agreed," asking what that meant. If, as Ross claims, Clinton did also mention the June 4 line, al-Asad's reaction would seem to be surprising. But Albright, who was also present at the meeting, has Clinton making a slightly different statement at the outset. In her version, Clinton only says that "the Israelis are prepared to withdraw fully to a commonly agreed border."[117] Clinton, in an interview with Ahron Bregman, also recalled that "I opened the meeting and said that Barak was prepared to withdraw to a commonly agreed border."[118] If this is indeed what Clinton said, it was a repeat of the language used to describe the Israeli position in the draft treaty submitted at Shepherdstown—in short, it indicated no movement at all toward the Syrian position. Al-Asad would have had reason to be both surprised and disappointed if the Clinton and Albright version is accurate. Given how important this exchange proved to be, it is remarkable that the Americans who were present do not have a common version of what was actually said.

All of the American accounts of what happened next have Ross showing al-Asad a map with Barak's proposed border on it. For Clinton, always willing to split the difference, this was not Barak's final offer, but just one more move in the endless game of negotiation.[119] If al-Asad were to respond positively, then Clinton would get a new position from Barak. But al-Asad looked at the map, with its four hundred-meter strip of land under Israeli control along the northeastern shore of the lake and its proposal for a land swap further south along the lake, and said,

"Then he doesn't want peace. It is finished." He apparently also made a remark to the effect that "there were no Jews between the June 4 line and the water" before 1967—which was true in the northeast quadrant of the lake—and any line that gave the Israelis a presence there would not be acceptable.[120]

Clinton apparently felt that Barak had made a reasonable offer and that his demand for a strip of land along the shore of the lake was justified.[121] In Clinton's view, al-Asad was now the one who was not being reasonable. According to Indyk, "Clinton had emphasized that there would be no deal without the strip of land around the lake in Israel's hands. 'Then things will stay as they are' was al-Asad's nonchalant response. Clinton agreed: 'The land is in Israel's possession and they can keep it for a very long time.'" After two hours of haggling, Clinton gave up.[122] Israeli-Syrian peace was not going to happen on his watch.

Evaluating Geneva

When previous Israeli-Syrian negotiations ended without success, it had always been possible to pick up the pieces eventually and to try again. But not after Geneva. This was a high-profile failure. It affected Clinton's reputation as a negotiator; it cast a shadow over the chance for success in later Israeli-Palestinian negotiations; it affected the way in which Barak proceeded to withdraw from Lebanon, which gave a big boost to Hezbollah's reputation; and it no doubt gave ammunition for Barak's critics. Not surprisingly, there is a very wide range of assessments concerning who was to blame for the failure and what role the Clinton team played in the debacle.

The dominant theme on the American side is that al-Asad got cold feet at Geneva, refused to negotiate, and could not have been persuaded by anything Clinton did or said to be forthcoming. If there was a time for a deal, it was at Shepherdstown. But that was when Barak hesitated because of the bad poll numbers he had just received, according to Ross.[123] Others, including some members of the Syrian delegation, also believe that Shepherdstown, not Geneva, was the moment for an agreement.[124]

Interviews with most of the American participants, and some of the Israelis and Syrians as well, reveal a more complex picture of what happened at Geneva. A significant number of participants in the talks believe that al-Asad was indeed ready for a deal, but only if the June 4 issue was resolved up front. Without that, he would not continue to play the game. There is really no way of knowing which school of thought is right about al-Asad's state of mind. We should note, however, that he did agree to go to Geneva. As one Israeli negotiator noted, if he had wanted to say no, he could have stayed home. And he went to Geneva with a very large coterie of advisers, as if he would be prepared, as he had told Bandar, for one last push to conclude an agreement.

Clinton was crucial to the outcome of the Geneva summit. Several of his traits seem to have worked against success. He tended toward optimism, as well as a belief that he could charm people into agreeing with him.[125] He hated to second-guess Barak, for whom he had a great deal of empathy, even when he disagreed with him. He seemed oblivious to the way in which time was running out for Barak, for al-Asad—and for himself.[126] One of Clinton's top advisers felt in retrospect that Clinton should have presented an American proposal at Geneva rather than simply parrot what Barak had dictated to him an hour before the summit began.

What if Clinton had tried a different approach after the collapse of Shepherdstown? Let us imagine the following scenario:

- Clinton concluded after Shepherdstown that a Syrian-Israeli peace was still obtainable, that it was still in the American national interest, and that he was prepared to use some of his remaining time and political capital to achieve it.
- Clinton and his team determined that the final trade-off would have to involve Israeli withdrawal to the June 4, 1967, line without any gimmicks or ambiguity.[127] If Barak was willing to make this commitment, then Clinton would work to get a clear Syrian commitment to Israeli control over the lake itself; an agreement on water resources more generally; firm security arrangements on the Golan, including an early-warning station manned by American personnel; and the key elements of normal peaceful relations that the two parties had been discussing. In addition, Clinton would offer to provide American troops for a peacekeeping force on the Golan if both sides requested it, he would consider a bilateral U.S.-Israeli security treaty, and he would offer a generous military support package to help Israel redeploy its forces from Golan.
- If Barak were to turn this proposal down, or insist on keeping territory along the shore of the lake, Clinton should simply tell him that in those circumstances the United States did not believe that a summit meeting between Clinton and al-Asad was warranted. Other means—perhaps an Albright trip to Damascus with Barak's "best offer" in hand—could be used to see if the Syrians could be persuaded to accept less than the June 4 line, but Clinton would not use his prestige for such an unlikely venture.

- If Barak were to agree to this approach, then Clinton should have moved quickly to clinch the deal. Then instead of speaking from Barak's script, Clinton should have made something like the following presentation to al-Asad:

Mr. President, I believe that the key elements of an Israeli-Syrian peace are now at hand. You have long insisted on a reaffirmation of the "Rabin Deposit." Today I am authorized by the Israeli prime minister to say that Israel is prepared to withdraw to the June 4, 1967 line, provided all elements of a peace agreement are agreed upon. This will mean that Syrian sovereignty will be restored up to the shoreline of the Sea of Galilee, as you have requested. As you mentioned to Prince Bandar, there will now be a need for an Israeli-Syrian group to work in secrecy to delineate and demarcate the exact location of the border. But on the principle of the June 4 line, you can be assured that Syria's position has finally been accepted.

In return, Israel has several requirements that I would like to spell out. The water of the Sea of Galilee must be under Israeli control, even if the shoreline is under yours. I would hope that both parties could work out arrangements for your access to the water and theirs to the land in conditions of peace. We discussed some constructive ideas along these lines at Shepherdstown and a team of experts might usefully focus on these issues as well. But for Prime Minister Barak, control of the water of the lake is fundamental. In addition, a group from both sides should work out a water–sharing formula that will be fair to both Israel and Syria.

On security, your military men and their Israeli counterparts have discussed the need for demilitarized zones, limited force zones, and early-warning stations. These are all building blocks of the arrangements that will provide both sides with security and assurance against surprise attack. My country is willing to make whatever contribution you deem helpful, including troops for a peacekeeping force and manning of an early-warning station that will provide assurances to both sides that the terms of the agreement are being observed and that neither side is posing a threat to the other.

Finally, on the issue of normal, peaceful relations and the time period for implementation of the agreement, we believe that the differences between you and the Israelis have been significantly narrowed. It is my understanding that Prime Minister Barak is prepared to come to Geneva immediately to finalize all of these arrangements. He is ready to meet directly with you or your representatives, or to communicate with you through us. The point is to reach an understanding quickly on all of these points. If you are ready to proceed, I am prepared to stay in Geneva for another day or so. Ideally, we could then have a three-way meeting in public—Barak, you and I—to announce that agreement on the principles of Israeli-Syrian peace has been reached.

If you are prepared to go forward with this scenario, I will also commit to discussing immediately ways in which the U.S.-Syrian relationship can be improved. In conditions of regional peace, there are many ways in which our two countries can cooperate.

It is, of course, possible that al-Asad would have still found some reason to say no to such a presentation by Clinton. But based on what he had told Bandar, he was inclined to say yes if his condition on the border was met. Barak might have refused to go as far as Clinton would have gone in this scenario, in which case the summit would never have taken place, and most likely there would have been no breakthrough. Barak would still have had to figure out what to do in Lebanon and to decide whether to go ahead with negotiations with the Palestinians, but at least Clinton would not have damaged his own prestige in a futile attempt at summit diplomacy.

One of Clinton's advisers, and the one most committed to the Syria-first track, seems to believe this approach might have worked. While sharing the Ross-Albright-Clinton view that al-Asad was primarily to blame for the failure of the summit,[128] Indyk in the end draws a striking set of conclusions:

Herein lies another lesson for future American peacemaking efforts; when the rare moment arises that an Arab leader indicates a willingness to make peace, and reveals a sense of urgency, it is essential to capitalize on it immediately and pursue the opportunity relentlessly until the breakthrough is achieved and the deal is closed. . . . Notwithstanding all of al-Asad's shortcomings, there remains the nagging sense that Clinton could have done more to move him at that critical moment in Geneva. Clinton might have focused on what we knew from long experience was al-Asad's stubborn approach to the line around the lake. It was predictable that Barak's requirements would become a stumbling block for al-Asad. . . . Clinton could have refused to take no for an answer. . . . He could have told him that if the line around the lake was the problem he would summon Barak to Geneva to work up a different arrangement (Barak was waiting for the call). It should not have been beyond the capabilities of American diplomacy to bridge the gap. When we see the extraordinary lengths to which Clinton went a few months later at Camp David and after to persuade Arafat to accept his proposals, it remains puzzling why he didn't try harder.[129]

Perhaps one reason that Clinton did not "try harder" was his own sense of frustration in dealing with the interminable haggling of both Israelis and Syrians, neither of whom showed a Sadat-like willingness to rise above the squabbling to make peace. But there was probably more to it. Many of Clinton's advisers did not really believe that the Syrian track was where Clinton should be devoting his remaining time. They were eager to move on to the Palestinian-Israeli negotiations.[130] The irony, of course, is that the dramatic failure at Geneva made it even more difficult to imagine that the much more complex set of issues that existed between Israelis and Palestinians could be resolved in short order. In brief, the combined failures at Shepherdstown and Geneva took a very high toll on U.S. interests and credibility in the Middle East.

Conclusion

Israeli-Syrian peace could have been achieved in the 1990s, not easily, not on the cheap, but with a sophisticated and sustained dose of U.S.-led diplomacy. And it would have made a great difference for the entire region—for the parties themselves, for Lebanon, for radical Islamic movements, for Iraq and Iran, and for the chance of Israeli-Palestinian peace as well. Instead, failure on the Israeli-Syrian front set the stage for numerous other failures and contributed to the belief in the Bush 43 administration that Arab-Israeli peace was no longer possible or of much importance. Historians of the future will look back and wonder why a difference of a few hundred meters along the shore of the Sea of Galilee was allowed to block the way to a peace agreement. They will be right to wonder if more could have been done to bridge the gaps that existed.

A number of lessons can be derived from this case. *First*, it is very costly for a mediator to allow himself to become an advocate, and sometimes an apologist, for one side of the conflict. Although Clinton's empathy for the Israelis was not a problem per se, it should not have led to his willingness to accept Barak's backtracking at Shepherdstown or his micromanaging of the Clinton-al-Asad summit. *Second*, when major substantive breakthroughs are in hand, don't go on vacation. When Rabin first gave Christopher his "deposit," the American team should have recognized that it was a time for intense shuttle diplomacy. Kissinger and Baker would have understood that. Clinton and Christopher did not. *Third*, Clinton's team of advisers did not serve him particularly well. There was the normal competition among them, exacerbated by the high stakes of the approaching endgame. But the advisers also never should have let Clinton go into a summit meeting with al-Asad as poorly prepared as he seemed to be, especially with a proposal from Barak that they had already judged to be inadequate. Someone should have had the guts to tell the president that he should either go back to Barak and get an improved proposal or drop the idea of the summit altogether. Allowing Barak to dictate his position to the president one hour before the meeting with al-Asad was to begin was a disservice to Clinton and to the chances for peace.

Most of the people we interviewed, as well as our own reading of these events, lead us to the conclusion that Israeli-Syrian peace was within reach in 1999–2000, if not before. If the lessons highlighted here had guided U.S. policy, Clinton might have been able to use his obvious political and personal skills to broker an agreement of historic significance. Instead, his failure at Geneva set the stage for his subsequent failure at Camp David, a topic covered in the next chapter. Of course, these failures were also the responsibility of the Syrian, Israeli, and Palestinian leaders, but they, more than Americans, were captives of their insecurities and ideologies. We had the chance to help them transcend their parochial concerns, but we failed. And the cost has been incalculable.

CHAPTER THREE

THE COLLAPSE OF THE ISRAELI-PALESTINIAN NEGOTIATIONS

The collapse of the Camp David negotiations in July 2000, the subsequent rise of the al-Aqsa Intifada, and Israel's measures in the West Bank and Gaza in the following months were hugely consequential to the prospects for Middle East peace, to the regional order, and to American foreign policy. These events put an end to a paradigm that began with the end of the Cold War, the successful reversal of Iraq's invasion of Kuwait, and a significant American military presence that seemingly ushered in a new era of American influence in the Middle East.

When, a year later, a horrific attack was perpetrated on American soil, the changed environment had already limited the regional and global support for American foreign policy choices. Much of the debate focused on whether the attacks by al-Qaeda terrorists had anything to do with the Arab-Israeli conflict, but that debate missed the point entirely. Had the attacks taken place in an environment of Arab-Israeli peace and cooperation or even during the limited hope that prevailed from 1993 to 1995 following the Madrid Peace Conference and the Oslo agreements, regional reaction and American choices likely would have been different. There is little doubt that the ensuing decade would have looked markedly different, not only for the Middle East but arguably for American foreign policy and the post–Cold War global order. At a minimum, Arab public opinion would have been far more receptive to America's war on al-Qaeda, and the Arab-Israeli conflict would not have been a distraction to American foreign policy.

How did the players allow what seemed to be a historic opportunity for peace to turn into a failure of major proportions? The roots of the answer can be found at the Camp David Summit.

Much has been written in the past decade on these events by scholars as well as participants from all three sides,[1] but during this time, much more has also been revealed by the key players—information that challenges conventional wisdom and requires a reassessment of previous failures. It is our aim in this chapter not to retell the entire story of these negotiations, but to provide some broader perspective, to shed light on the key issues of contention by making use of additional interviews we have conducted with many of the participants, and to draw some conclusions that might help in future mediating efforts.

The Strategic Environment of the Negotiations

Although the process, structure, and the personalities involved in the negotiations are important and deserve examination, they cannot be fully understood, and their relevance to the outcome of the negotiations cannot be properly evaluated, without fully understanding the strategic environment and the distribution of regional and global power in the context of which the negotiations took place. To gain that perspective, it is useful to contrast the strategic context of the 1990s American role in the Palestinian-Israeli negotiations with that of the 1970s American role in mediating the Egyptian-Israeli negotiations.

Even aside from the strategic weight that Egypt, the most populous and powerful Arab state that had just fought a credible war, could bring to bear in its negotiations with Israel, the global picture was dramatically different for the United States, the primary mediator between the parties. The Cold War was very much in place in the late 1970s, with the Soviet-American competition for influence in the Middle East a critical part of the calculus. The United States had suffered the consequences of the Arab oil embargo a few years earlier. While Egyptian president Anwar Sadat used to say that 99 percent of the cards were in the hands of the United States, he believed that the United States also needed Egypt in the larger picture of Soviet-American competition in the Middle East.

In this respect, Israel worried about the broader American calculus moving the United States closer to Egypt at Israel's expense. Former Israeli defense minister Ezer Weizman expressed his concerns this way, "My objections to excessive American involvement in the negotiations with Egypt stemmed from a simple consideration: I foresaw that U.S. interests lay closer to Egypt's than to ours, so that it would not be long before Israeli negotiators would have to cope with the dual confrontation as they faced a Washington/Cairo axis."[2]

Indeed, the Israeli-Egyptian competition for strategic relations was not only credible but one of the central dynamics of the Camp David negotiations in 1978, with each party prepared to leave without a peace agreement as long as it consolidated stronger strategic ties with the United States at the expense of the other. This dynamic provided President Jimmy Carter with leverage that he employed to extract concessions from both sides, which ultimately led to an agreement.

The importance of that agreement in anchoring a political order in the region that was advantageous to the United States is often taken for granted; had the Iranian Revolution just months after Camp David taken place in the shadow of failed Egyptian-Israeli negotiations and revival of conflict, the picture for the United States (and the Soviet Union) would have been dramatically different.

In contrast, President Bill Clinton ascended to the American presidency in a changed global environment that moved American priorities to the home front. As noted earlier in this volume, the United States had won the Cold War with the Soviet Union and emerged as the world's sole superpower. In the Middle East, the United States had just exhibited its influence and power through the post–Cold War era's first major crisis, the Iraqi invasion of Kuwait. By assembling the largest global coalition to date, the United States successfully forced Iraq out of Kuwait and instituted a tough international sanctions regime that vastly undermined Iraq's influence. In the process, the United States managed to win the support of the largest Arab coalition in history, including Syria. The net result was also the dramatic expansion of America's military presence in the Middle East in a manner that limited the power of Iran, which was already weakened by nearly a decade of war with Iraq.

When Clinton assumed office, a somewhat halting Middle East peace process started in Madrid by the Bush Administration was already in place, which at a minimum managed to restructure regional priorities and to establish a new set of relations between the United States and a good number of Arab states. Clinton ran on a domestic agenda—primarily the economy—at a time when most analysts expected that Washington would have fewer incentives to focus on international issues and instead would turn inward. And while the Clinton administration continued the Madrid process started by the previous administration, there was little sign of urgency or of making Middle East peace a White House priority.

When Israel and the Palestine Liberation Organization (PLO) secretly negotiated a breakthrough agreement in Oslo, the Clinton administration saw an opportunity with little downside. To his credit, President Clinton jumped on this opportunity that Oslo provided, adopted the agreement, and had it signed in a memorable ceremony on the lawn of the White House on September 13, 1993. Without his backing, it is unlikely that the Palestinian-Israeli peace process would have progressed, as it did in the early years after the signing. But there can be no mistake about how Yasir Arafat, the leader of the PLO, made it to the White House: through the consent of an Israeli prime minister. When Arafat was ultimately kept out of the White House after his last visit to Washington in January 2001, it was also largely because of the collapse of his relations with Israel—even though Arafat's own behavior had contributed to the loss of trust of the United States and particularly of President George W. Bush.[3]

Thus the American relationship with the Palestinians from the outset of the Clinton administration was in large part a function of American-Israeli relations—though not entirely. In the two years, 1997–99, following the election of a rightwing Israeli government headed by Prime Minister Benjamin Netanyahu, Arafat was more welcome in the White House than the prime minister of Israel. Backers of the assassinated Yitzhak Rabin in Israel and the United States were suspicious of the new prime minister; some (including Rabin's widow, Leah Rabin) even accused Netanyahu of fanning the flames that tragically consumed Rabin. More to the point, most in Israel and in the United States continued to believe that Arab-Israeli peace was a viable, maybe even inevitable, option and that there were genuine Arab partners, and therefore they saw Netanyahu as a temporary obstacle. But aside from the symbolism and public posture, the structure of relations between the United States on the one hand and the Palestinians on the other, did not change much even in that period.

The bottom line is that the increasing role of Clinton in the Arab-Israeli peace process was not a function of an elevation of the Palestinian-Israeli conflict as a compelling national interest of the United States. In part it was a function of the relationship with Israel. In part it also became an issue of what Clinton hoped would be his legacy as president. Certainly there was awareness that it had some ramifications for U.S. relations with the rest of the Arab world, but there was no evidence that the latter was a central point at a time when the United States seemingly commanded unprecedented power and influence in the region. And throughout much of the Clinton years, the strategic outlook in the Middle East focused on the policy of "dual containment," which envisioned maintaining balance in the Gulf region in the aftermath of the 1991 Gulf War by containing both Iraq and Iran.[4] An Arab-Israeli peace was seen in part as a mechanism of gaining both Arab and Israeli support for this policy.

Adding to this picture was the sense, perhaps spread by the very picture of Yasir Arafat and Yitzhak Rabin shaking hands under the watchful eye of the American president, that the Palestinian-Israeli conflict was on its way to resolution. As noted in the introduction to this volume, however, the Clinton administration policy went through three phases, at least in terms of presidential involvement.

Up until the assassination of Yitzhak Rabin, the general White House assumption was that the Israelis and Palestinians were already on their way to resolving the conflict and that the need for presidential involvement was minimal. By the time Rabin was assassinated, Clinton had also developed close personal ties with Middle Eastern leaders, particularly Rabin himself and also King Hussein of Jordan. More importantly, Rabin's assassination and the subsequent election of Benjamin Netanyahu, who had opposed the Oslo Accords, as Israel's prime minister, meant that the process was unlikely to proceed without more presidential involvement, which was particularly critical in the Wye River negotiations. Finally, when Ehud Barak was elected prime minister in 1999, an opportunity was opened for Clinton to try to mediate a deal in his remaining two years in office, but this phase required even more presidential involvement.

* * *

Between 1993 and the Camp David negotiations in July 2000, there were ups and downs, outbreaks of violence and expansion of settlements, shifts in domestic politics, and varying degrees of American presidential involvement, but the trajectory seemed in one direction and the betting was on an agreement that would end the conflict. It is probably for this reason that throughout the 1990s the conflict itself did not seem to be central in global priorities even outside the United States. Later, Secretary of State Hillary Clinton, in remarks at the dedication of the S. Daniel Abraham Center for Middle East Peace in April, 2010, contrasted global attitudes in the 1990s with the trends in the previous year in this way,

> One of the striking experiences that I had becoming secretary of state and now having traveled something on the order of 300,000 miles in the last 15 months and going to dozens and dozens of countries, is that when I compare that to my experience as first lady, where I was also privileged to travel around the world, back in the '90s when I went to Asia or Africa or Europe or Latin America, it was rare that the Israeli-Palestinian conflict was raised. Now it is the first, second, or third item on nearly every agenda of every country I visit.[5]

Reflecting on the Clinton administration's efforts to mediate Arab-Israeli peace, a former American official articulated the approach of the administration this way, "We hadn't defined this so much as our interest. It was an Israeli and Palestinian interest in which one of the two sides was prepared to take risks and the other one wasn't, and we were facilitating their effort. We were not sort of driving and telling 'you better do it for us,' we're helping you do it, and one side is prepared to go much further than the other, at least in our perception, because of where we had started."[6]

In that regard, there was a decided difference between the reasons that propelled the Bush 41 administration to initiate the Arab-Israeli negotiations in Madrid and Clinton's adoption of the Oslo agreements. The Bush administration moved a reluctant Israeli prime minister, Yitzhak Shamir, at a time of unprecedented presidential popularity and international prestige after the 1991 Iraq War, as it had concluded that the issue was important to American interests. In mobilizing Arab and international support to compel Iraq to leave Kuwait, the United States faced constant demands to address the Palestinian-Israeli issue; the first Intifada was raging and the violence in Jerusalem nearly derailed the American efforts at the United Nations and played into the hands of the opponents of the American-led war. The efforts that went into persuading Israel not to respond to the missile attacks from Iraq during the war also highlighted the complications that the conflict brought to American policy in the Middle East.

By the time Clinton came to office, the United States was seen as having won the Cold War and the Iraq War, and the urgency of the Arab-Israeli conflict had receded. This perspective on Arab-Israeli peacemaking is indispensable to understanding how the Clinton administration ultimately evaluated the prospects, the options, and—up to a point—even the way the negotiating teams were structured. More than anything else, it determined the failure of the American mediation efforts.

American Mediation and the Distribution of Power

When the Clinton Administration took it on itself to help implement the Oslo agreements, important factors were beyond its control. Certainly, there is much to criticize about the American strategy and tactics, but two big factors hampered the American efforts. First, the actual terms of the Oslo agreements, on which the United States had no say, made implementation challenging. Second, an extraordinary inequality of power existed between Israel and the PLO. The mediation task was particularly challenging for the United States given its dual role in the negotiations as mediator and as Israel's most important ally.

Mediators almost always face somewhat unequal parties to conflict. And every party has leverage in negotiations, though rarely equally. But the kind of inequality of power that the Clinton administration faced as the PLO and Israel started negotiations is also rare. There is again some utility in comparing the environment the Carter administration faced when it mediated between Israel and Egypt in the

1970s with the environment for Clinton's mediation in the Palestinian-Israeli conflict.

Egypt had more capacity to fight Israel effectively than any other Arab country, and demonstrated that capacity just a few years before entering negotiations with Israel, in the 1973 War. Israel's leverage primarily came from holding Egypt's Sinai Peninsula, which it occupied in the 1967 War. But Israel had no historic claims to Egyptian territories and always saw these territories as a lever to take Egypt out of any war coalition against Israel. Although there was much more to it than that (the settlements that Israel had built in the Sinai in the meantime, the linkage to the Palestinian issue, and the ramifications for Egypt's relations with the rest of the Arab world), each side had significant leverage even aside from the American role. Each side could afford failure, but both would also pay a heavy price if they failed.

The picture was very different for Israel and the PLO in 1993—and this difference was consequential for the American mediation effort. Certainly both sides had something to gain from an agreement and much to lose if they failed. And each side had at least theoretical leverage: neither side had been able to resolve the conflict unilaterally despite multiple wars and much suffering. But Israel controlled all the Palestinian territories on which the PLO hoped to establish a state; the PLO had no territorial control anywhere, especially after moving its forces out of Lebanon and its headquarters to Tunis. The PLO's regional influence and financial support had declined following the Iraq War, when Yasir Arafat angered many Arab states, including Saudi Arabia and Kuwait, by maintaining his relations with Saddam Hussein, who clearly attempted to exploit the Palestinian issue in Arab public opinion. The PLO's influence with the Palestinian people was also diminishing. The influence of Hamas in Gaza was expanding and, even among the PLO supporters, those who were leading the Intifada on the ground were ascending in importance—although it was still clear that the PLO leadership in Tunis remained in charge. For the American mediation role, this entailed that the PLO had minimal leverage in its relationship with the United States, even aside from the reduced Palestinian leverage with Israel. At most stages in the negotiations, it was easier for the United States to seek concessions from the Palestinians than from Israel.

For Israel, the defeat of Iraq, the engagement of Syria in negotiations, and the primacy of its American ally in the Middle East had all significantly shifted the regional environment to its favor with little prospect of a regional war that threatened its security. The biggest threats were clear: the Intifada that had started in 1987; the costs of occupation, especially in Gaza; the rise of Hamas; and simply not being able to bring about a solution to its occupation in the West Bank and Gaza alone. And in the post–Cold War environment of American foreign policy, the elevation of domestic politics in the formation of American foreign policy favored Israel and increased the domestic costs for an American president seeking concessions from Israel.

This structural inequality between Israel and the PLO was not only consequential for the negotiations but also for the psychological mood of both Israelis and Palestinians. And it made American mediation efforts far more difficult.

From Oslo to Camp David

Despite their flaws, the Oslo agreements should not be underestimated.[7] Above all, they signified Israeli and Palestinian mutual acceptance and opened the door for a two-state solution to the Israeli-Palestinian conflict. They changed the regional global perspective on the Arab-Israeli conflict from betting on failure and conflict to betting on the inevitability of resolution. They changed the regional environment, particularly toward Israel, with a number of Arab states from the Gulf to North Africa starting cooperative, mostly commercial, relations with Israel.

Despite the near-euphoric optimism that followed the signing of the Declaration of Principles in September 1993, American mediation efforts faced extraordinary obstacles from the outset. In the first place, there was the violence of the opponents of the agreement on both sides. On February 25, 1994, Jewish settler Baruch Goldstein shot and killed up to thirty Palestinians at a mosque in Hebron during Friday prayers. Following the attack, a mood of pessimism prevailed among Israelis and Palestinians as several security incidents took place. In an attempt to break the cycle of violence, on May 4, 1994, Israel and the PLO, with some last minute help from the United States, reached an agreement in Cairo on the initial implementation of the 1993 Declaration of Principles. The document specified Israel's military withdrawal from most of the Gaza Strip, excluding Jewish settlements and land around them, and from the Palestinian town of Jericho in the West Bank. The agreement also contained potential serious challenges. It envisaged further withdrawals during a five-year interim period during which solutions to the difficult issues were to be negotiated—issues such as the establishment of a Palestinian state, the status of Jerusalem, Jewish settlements in the occupied territories, and the fate of Palestinian refugees—and followed by the establishment of a Palestinian state. Following the agreement in Cairo, Arafat left Tunis in July 1994 to take up residence in Gaza and assume his new position as head of the Palestinian Authority (PA), the representative body formed under the Oslo agreements. Stimulated by the progress being made on the Palestinian-Israeli track of negotiations, Jordan and Israel signed a comprehensive peace treaty on October 26, 1994.[8]

The first year of Palestinian self-rule in Gaza and Jericho in 1995 was hampered by difficulties. Bomb attacks by Palestinian militants killed dozens of Israelis, while Israel blockaded the autonomous areas and assassinated militants. Israeli settlement activity continued. The PA quelled unrest by instituting mass detentions. Opposition to the peace process grew among right-wingers and religious nationalists in Israel. Against this background, peace talks were laborious and fell behind schedule. U.S. mediation efforts picked up during this period in an effort to prevent Oslo from collapsing. On September 24, 1995, the so-called Oslo II agreement was signed in Taba in Egypt, and four days later it was counter-signed in Washington. The agreement divided the West Bank into three zones: Zone A comprised 7 percent of the territory (the main Palestinian towns excluding Hebron and East Jerusalem) going to full Palestinian control, along with 55 percent of the West Bank Palestinian population; Zone B, where 41 percent of the West Bank Palestinian population resides, comprised 21 percent of the territory under joint Israeli-Palestinian control; and Zone C, with 61 percent of the West Bank encompassing settlements, army facilities, public land and roads, and many Palestinians, under Israeli security and planning control. Israel was also to release Palestinian prisoners. Further handovers followed. Oslo II was greeted with little enthusiasm by Palestinians, while Israel's religious right was furious at the "surrender of Jewish land." Amid an incitement campaign against Rabin, Yigal Amir, a Jewish religious extremist, assassinated him on November 4, 1995, sending shock waves throughout the world. Shimon Peres succeeded Rabin as Israel's prime minister.

The assassination of Yitzhak Rabin may have had more impact on the failure of the peace process to move rapidly than almost anything else. Many of those who were involved in the process continue to believe that this event was the single most significant setback for reaching a final-status settlement between Israel and the Palestinians. Rabin had unquestionable security credentials, was there from the inception of Oslo, was close to Bill Clinton, and by the time of his assassination had developed a credible working relationship with Arafat. Clinton himself later reflected on the implications of Rabin's death this way, "Nor has a single week gone by in which I have not reaffirmed my conviction that had he not lost his life on that terrible November night, within three years we would have had a comprehensive agreement for peace in the Middle East."[9]

Conflict returned early in 1996 when a series of devastating suicide bombings in Israel was carried out by the Islamic militant group Hamas (on March 3, 1996, a Hamas member conducted a suicide operation killing nineteen Israelis on a Jerusalem bus; two days later, another Palestinian suicide bombing took place in Tel Aviv killing twelve people), and Israel conducted a bloody three-week bombardment of Lebanon. Peres narrowly lost elections on May 29, 1996, to the right-wing Benjamin Netanyahu, who campaigned against the Oslo peace deals under the motto "Peace with Security." Netanyahu soon inflamed Arab opinion by lifting a freeze on building new settlements in the occupied territories and by opening an archaeological tunnel adjacent to the compound of al-Aqsa mosque.

From the American point of view, the most opportune time for a serious initiative would have come early in Clinton's second administration—just the time Netanyahu came to office. As White House official Bruce Riedel put it, when Clinton was in the best position to get something done in the Middle East, "he had a partner in Bibi [Netanyahu] who was not interested, basically, in a deal . . . , who had profound doubts about the whole hostile process and whose domestic constituency was not enthusiastic about proceeding."[10] Netanyahu had opposed the Oslo agreements altogether and had a testy relationship with Bill Clinton throughout his tenure as prime minister.

In this challenging environment, the Clinton administration rose to the task with increased presidential involvement to save the peace process. Despite his antagonism toward the Oslo Accords, Netanyahu, on January 15, 1997, under increasing U.S. pressure, agreed to transfer control of the West Bank City of Hebron to the Palestinian Authority (Protocol Concerning the Redeployment in Hebron).[11] Unlike earlier withdrawals from the West Bank, 20 percent of the city—the central area where more than 400 Jewish settlers lived among 130,000 Palestinians—would remain under Israeli control. Palestinians cheered the withdrawal, but Jewish settlers felt betrayed by Netanyahu. A year later, Netanyahu signed the Wye River Memorandum on October 23, 1998, outlining further modest withdrawals from the West Bank. The Wye River Memorandum allowed for the building of an international airport in the Gaza Strip, and Israel agreed to pull back from an additional 13 percent of the West Bank and to release 750 Palestinian security prisoners. The PA agreed to combat terrorist organizations, arrest those involved in terrorism, and collect all illegal weapons and explosives.

Although prospects of a final-status settlement between Israel and the Palestinians were viewed as diminishing, the Clinton administration spent much energy on the Palestinian-Israeli conflict during this period. (President Clinton never got as involved in the negotiations as much as he finally did during the Wye River talks). Its primary aim at the time, however, was preserving the Oslo Accords and maintaining momentum—not a full resolution.

Netanyahu's right-wing coalition eventually collapsed in January 1999 in disarray over the implementation of the Wye deal. He lost elections on May 18 to Labor's Ehud Barak, who pledged to "end the 100-year conflict" between Israel and the Arabs within one year. The five-year interim period defined by Oslo for a final resolution passed on May 4, 1999, but Arafat was persuaded to defer unilateral declaration of Palestinian statehood for a chance at negotiations with the new administration. On September 4, 1999, Barak and Arafat signed the Sharm el-Sheikh Memorandum.[12] This memorandum provided that accelerated permanent-status negotiations would commence no later than September 13, 1999, and that the goal of these negotiations would be to reach a framework agreement on permanent status within five months and a comprehensive permanent-status agreement within one year. It also set out a timetable for additional redeployments of Israeli forces in the West Bank and the transfer of areas to Palestinian control in several phases, to be completed by January 20, 2000. The first phase was carried out on September 10, 1999.

However, initial optimism about the peacemaking prospects of a government led by Barak turned into skepticism, further withdrawals from occupied land were hindered by disagreements, and final-status talks (on Jerusalem, refugees, settlements, and borders) got nowhere. Frustration was building among Palestinians who had little to show for five years of the peace process. And many Israelis felt that the agreements allowed Palestinian militants to intensify attacks against Israel. Barak concentrated on peace with Syria—also unsuccessfully, as seen in chapter 2. But he did succeed in fulfilling a campaign pledge to end Israel's twenty-two-year entanglement in Lebanon. After withdrawal from Lebanon in May 2000, Barak's attention turned back to the Israeli-Palestinian track, and he persuaded Clinton to pursue a high-stakes Israeli-Palestinian summit that was resisted by Arafat.[13]

By the time the Camp David negotiations commenced, President Clinton was dependent on two men, Yasir Arafat and Ehud Barak, for potential success, and the timeline for an agreement was urgent as the United States was in the middle of a contentious presidential election campaign and Bill Clinton was on his way out. Despite being handed the Oslo agreement early in the first year of Clinton's first term, the American team had failed in mediation efforts over the succeeding seven years to conclude a final-status agreement that the Oslo Accords had anticipated could be accomplished in three years and implemented in five.

By 2000, the mutual trust between Israelis and Palestinians that was supposed to have been bolstered by the process of implementation of the Oslo Accords had all but disappeared. No issues eroded trust more than the continued construction of Israeli settlements for the Palestinians, and the continued Palestinian violence, especially suicide bombings, for the Israelis. The process launched by the Oslo Accords, which was intended by design to gradually build mutual trust, generated the opposite propensity as it left too many opportunities for extremists on both sides to erode trust instead.

One central reason for the failings of the process was that the incremental approach of trying to negotiate and to implement interim agreements without a pre-agreed final target was bound to face daunting obstacles. As Arie M. Kacowicz put it, "The Israeli and Palestinian narratives of Oslo reveal . . . profound disillusionment with the behavior of the [United States] in failing to meet the expectations arising from the peace process. The very gradual and piecemeal characteristics of the process were intended to build trust and confidence, deferring the most difficult issues (Jerusalem, refugees) to the end of the negotiations. In practice, the result was the opposite: confidence undermining, instead of confidence building."[14] For one thing, a lengthy and precarious process was inevitably going to be particularly vulnerable to extremists on both sides. But even for leaders who aimed for a peace agreement to end the conflict, there was a built-in Catch 22: The more concessions they made in the interim, the weaker their position would be in negotiating the more important final-status issues. And each leader would have to pay an internal political price for the interim concessions, depleting the domestic capital they would need for selling their publics a final deal. This was an almost insurmountable flaw, particularly when leaders had minimal trust in each other. The PLO, and later the PA, gave up the use of force by agreement, but its leadership also recognized that the limited existence of some militant groups kept the pressure on the Israelis and that shutting them all down would be costly at home and could reduce the leverage as the big issues were negotiated. The Palestinians were always fearful that Israel retained enormous leverage with them by virtue of its occupation, while their instruments of leverage in the interim were miniscule in comparison. On the Israeli side, there was always a sense that every Israeli interim withdrawal, action to limit the construction of settlements, and release of Palestinian prisoners would be costly in domestic politics and would reduce what the Israelis could offer to get maximal Palestinian concessions on such final-status issues as the right of return and Jerusalem. And on most occasions, Palestinians and Israelis did about the minimum to keep the process moving, at the cost of eroding trust and public confidence.

Ehud Barak's tenure was an extreme version of this logic. As he aimed for a final-status agreement quickly, he reneged on commitments to withdraw from Palestinian territories and to release Palestinian prisoners in a manner that significantly underlined already strong Palestinian mistrust in him personally and in Israeli intentions broadly. But his logic was clear: to complete the withdrawal and release prisoners, he would have to pay a high political price at home and in the process he would give up something he could offer to the Palestinians as an inducement for final-status concessions. It was also a mechanism of hedging his bets in case of failure. Therefore, the central flaw was an Oslo process implemented incrementally over a long period of time and having an indeterminate ending dependent on what the parties did in the interim. And this flaw was severely compounded by an insurmountable gap in the leverage that each side wielded toward the other.[15]

It is also often suggested that the Oslo process was flawed in part because there was no effective monitoring mechanism to hold the parties responsible when they failed to implement their part of the agreements.[16] There is much to be said for that view and future negotiations will have to consider it. But what was said about the Israeli and Palestinian calculations could also be said about the calculations of the United States or any third party: Does one want to jeopardize the whole process by making an incremental step a central issue of contention and undermine what leverage may be needed in mediating the more important final-status issues? The mindset during the Oslo years is summarized by a former American official,

> You're interpreting how these people are gonna act like we all went to Harvard Law School. I understand accountability, but you know, the way the party, everybody understood that there was fudging and cheating and moving and it was, but the thing was moving in the right direction and so maybe there should have been more accountability. I can't, I don't know how to think about it except that when you sit with all these guys, just the security negotiations, we had violations all over the place, but the general trend was very good, very good. So I think both we, the Israelis and the Palestinians just kept saying let's keep moving. Now maybe that's the wrong way to do it, but let's keep moving because we understand that perfect is the enemy of good."[17]

The dilemma is that if one assumes that one must tolerate violations in the short term with the eye on the bigger prize ahead, the trust required for parties to take the kind of risk they need to take in the end will erode, and the mediator can lose credibility and control of the process.

A second significant problem for the American mediation effort in the Palestinian-Israeli negotiations during the Oslo process was the discourse about "concessions" and obligations and how these were packaged. The Palestinian starting point was anchored on core positions. The first is that by virtue of accepting Israel in its pre–1967 War borders, they were forfeiting 78 percent of the whole of Palestine, all of which they had claimed for the first four decades of conflict with Israel. The second position was that the Palestinian-Israeli negotiations, like other Arab-Israeli negotiations, were from the outset over territories occupied by

Israel in the 1967 War and from which Israel is fully obligated to withdraw. Any part of that territory kept by Israel would be a major concession given by the Palestinians.

Although the Israelis officially accepted UN Resolution 242 as a basis of negotiations with the Arab states (and provided their own interpretations of what that resolution entailed), in effect, the Israelis treated the West Bank and Gaza as if they were at best disputed territories and, in the case of east Jerusalem and the annexed suburbs that were incorporated into the Jerusalem municipality, as Israeli territories. The fact remained that Israel was in control of these territories and had the power to keep them. Thus when Israel agreed to offer the Palestinians withdrawal from 90 percent or more of the West Bank, it was seen by Israelis as a generous offer, whereas the Palestinians saw it as a demand by Israel to keep 10 percent of what was rightfully theirs.[18]

This differing approach also corresponds to the public discourse in both polities. Separate from the reference to UN resolutions that Palestinians almost always make, the right of return issue, so profoundly central in the Palestinian experience and narrative, is always a reminder of the claims that went beyond the West Bank and Gaza and reinforces the view that to limit a Palestinian state to Gaza and the West Bank is a major historic compromise on the part of the Palestinians. In Israel, the discourse, at least since the 1970s, with changing reference to the West Bank and Gaza as "Judea and Samaria," highlighting the biblical link, added another dimension to Israeli perceptions. Perhaps more importantly, the Israeli justification for a deal with the Palestinians that would result in relinquishing control in the West Bank and Gaza was primarily based, not on international law or UN resolution, but on preserving Israel as a Jewish state. So the starting point in the Israeli public view was the following question: What is the minimum that needs to be done to end a costly occupation and preserve Israel as a Jewish state? These public postures reinforced negotiating attitudes and a propensity to dismiss "concessions" of the other side.

For American mediation efforts, these differences between Israelis and Palestinians on what constituted concessions and the starting frame of reference provided additional challenges because it was easy for each side to dismiss the gestures of the other as "concessions" given their differing interpretations of the status quo.

Issues of Contention

In the multiple accounts of what transpired at Camp David and who is to blame for the failure, there are a few central issues of contention: the setbacks in implementing the Oslo Accords in the intervening years, the timing of addressing the final-status issues between Israel and the Palestinians, preparations for Camp David, the American style of mediation, Arafat's and Barak's aims, what transpired on the crucial issues of Jerusalem and refugees, Clinton's move to blame Arafat after the summit, and the prospects of success between the end of the conference in July and the end of the Clinton administration in January. We will offer some perspective on these issues of contention.

The Elevated Role of Leaders and their Relationships at Camp David

By the time Ehud Barak was elected Israeli prime minister and formed a government, only a year and half was left in the Clinton presidency. Two things resulted. First, time became of the essence, and how the negotiations were sequenced was bound to affect the ending. Second, it ushered in a new relationship between Clinton and the new Israeli prime minister that significantly affected the course of negotiations.

In contrast to Netanyahu, Barak was in a hurry to try to clinch peace deals with both the Syrians and the Palestinians. The excitement in Washington was hard to miss. Barak's victory resulted in a mood of celebration that was displayed in all its splendor in the semi-state White House dinner on July 18, 1999, that was held for Mr. and Mrs. Barak with hundreds of guests. And in hearing Barak's ideas and intentions Clinton was "like a kid in a candy store."[19] The resulting relationship between the two was essential in understanding much of what transpired in the American mediation efforts for the duration of the Clinton administration.

For one thing, Clinton saw in Barak the best hope to accomplish a major achievement in his last months in office. For another, Barak's talk of compromise on both the Syrian and Palestinian tracks, of taking political risks at home, was music to the ears of a president who had labored hard just to keep the Oslo Accords alive in the previous two years. The result was a most unusual relationship between an American president and a leader of another country: a direct line with practically no limits, which often sidestepped the normal protocol of first going through the national security advisor or the secretary of state.[20] In the process, unprecedented deference was made to the wishes, tactics, and strategies of an Israeli prime minister who was seen to be ready to take enormous risks, in a manner that shaped a series of decisions ranging from pursuing the Syrian track first, to the Geneva meeting between Clinton and President al-Asad, to the timing and structure of the Camp David negotiations, to the decision to declare failure and assess blame at the end of the Camp David negotiations.[21]

Clinton and Barak hardly knew each other before Barak became prime minister. And unlike the relationship between Clinton and Rabin, which became warm and much like a "father-son relationship," Barak and Clinton needed each other. There was something of "anything but Netanyahu" built into Clinton's attitude, and Clinton felt sympathetic to Barak's democratic domestic politics, ultimately spending much of the time in his conversations with Barak discussing this issue.[22]

This relationship was important for another reason. Despite the diversity of the American, Israeli, and Palestinian political systems, the top leaders were the central players at Camp David. On the Palestinian side, Arafat was always the central player when it came to decisions on key issues, and he alone made these decisions, even though he often listened to key advisers, and was sometimes even swayed by them. By the assessment of the American team at Camp David there were primarily two people who could have had more sway with Arafat and with whom American officials could have dealt directly, Mahmoud Abbas (Abu Mazen) and Ahmed Qurie (Abu Ala'a). Mahmoud Abbas had to leave Camp David to attend his son's wedding. As for Qurie, a high level White House official put it this way, "Abu Ala'a gets very angry when Clinton dresses him down, when the Israelis put down maps and the Palestinians wouldn't put down a map, they said 'they've got to establish 67 first, and then we'll talk about maps,' and he blew up as you know at that point.[23] And Abu Ala'a was very embarrassed by that, and he retreated. And I think that's unfortunate because the two principal subordinates to Arafat who had his trust and confidence—to the extent that anyone had Arafat's trust and confidence—were somewhat out of the picture."[24] There were certainly other senior and influential members of the Palestinian realm, including Saeb Erakat, Yasir Abd Rabbo, Nabil Shaath, and Muhammad Dahlan who were trusted by Arafat and who played important roles on the negotiating committees, but none commanded the kind of clout that could sway Arafat on the big issues and were not authorized to go beyond what Arafat instructed. Another high-level American official provided this assessment,

> There's that, but then there's also then the courting of Dahlan and the younger members as being bolder in decision . . . But it was partly just cultural. They were more your own peers. They were kind of younger, they were more, I don't know if they were more Americanized, but they were more a peer level group, more the same age of the American team and the Israeli team, if you think about it . . . And I think it was thought to be useful in giving a support structure to Arafat. But it was definitely a strong dynamic in the meetings. The question there is, was that right? Is that where Arafat would draw his support from? Or was it really from his peers?[25]

And except for some reports pertaining to Dahlan and other mid-level Palestinian officials as being more willing to compromise, there is little indication that this was generally true among senior members of the delegation.[26]

As for Barak, his domestic political picture, as is always the case in Israeli politics, was very complicated, as he constantly needed to work hard to keep his coalition together.[27] Even while at Camp David, he spent much of his day calling home to maintain political support. But Barak's leadership style was very much to keep his cards close to his chest and, on many issues, even away from his close advisers. And his theory about Israeli politics was always that it would be much easier to get public support once you had an agreement that ended the conflict once and for all.[28] At Camp David, what the Israeli team was going to accept, especially on the crucial issue of Jerusalem, was up to Barak personally. And Barak had already cultivated a close working relationship with President Clinton, whose personal role was essential.

Arafat and Barak, on the other hand, had practically no relationship. Arafat deeply mistrusted Barak. Some of this mistrust goes back to a personal issue. Barak was reportedly the man in charge of a 1988 Israeli military operation that killed Arafat's deputy Khalil Al-Wazir (Abu Jihad) in the PLO's headquarters in Tunis. But much of the suspicion had to do with what transpired in the months following Barak's election. Arafat was frustrated that Barak did not meet with him prior to the formation of his government. He felt betrayed by Barak's pursuit of a Syrian-Israeli agreement before a Palestinian-Israeli agreement, and he particularly resented Barak's refusal to implement what was already agreed in handing over three Palestinian villages outside Jerusalem and refusing to free a large number of prisoners.[29] According to a senior Palestinian negotiator, Arafat despised Barak because he felt that Barak was always trying to outsmart him. He thought even Netanyahu could be trusted more than Barak. Toward the end of the Clinton term, Arafat was even of the opinion that he would rather deal with Sharon than Barak. All the while, Arafat didn't believe the polls that predicted Sharon would be elected.[30] Even on the second day of the Camp David conference, after a tough day of negotiations, Arafat went to Clinton to express his fear of being set up to be blamed for failure and to express his distrust of Barak, "Let me remind you that he voted against Oslo. He wants to form a government of national unity in Israel with Likud."[31]

Barak, on the other hand, viewed Arafat as someone who would never make a concession or a decision until he absolutely had no way out and therefore must be cornered and squeezed; furthermore, it must be made clear to him that the alternative to making the "right decision" was far worse. In that regard, Barak preferred that the conversation with Arafat be conducted through Clinton. Barak's attitude toward Arafat determined not only his approach to the negotiations but what turned out to be the basic setup at Camp David. Enderlin describes it this way,

> Nothing must be concluded as long as there remains even one point of difference. To avoid having the Palestinians transform Israeli positions into firm commitments, his [Barak's] proposals will be submitted through American mediation. He himself will not have any face-to-face meeting with Arafat who might seize on some minor verbal discrepancy and have it influence the talks. On several occasions, at critical moments of the summit, his advisers will suggest that he speak directly with Arafat. Barak will refuse. At meals he will regularly and openly ignore him, an attitude that the Palestinians will take as an insult and an unwillingness to negotiate.[32]

This condition set up a relationship that highlighted Clinton's personal role, not only as a mediator but also as a conveyor of the positions of one side to the other, and in particular the Israeli position to the Palestinians. Clinton's strong assets and liabilities were on display throughout the negotiations. One of Clinton's strengths was his demonstrated ability to empathize, even with his opponents. On most occasions, this ability served him well. On other occasions, it may have been a detriment because he was unable to bring himself to weigh in forcefully with both Barak and Arafat when necessary, as Jimmy Carter had done with Menachem Begin and Anwar Sadat during the Israeli-Egyptians negotiations. Despite being let down by Barak at Shepherdstown and Geneva, he failed to prod Barak to share with him more about his bottom line prior to the start of the Camp David Summit. One of his White House advisers put it this way,

> I think the President was—he obviously pushed back and he influenced him, etc. But he was pretty tolerant of what Barak's clock was, what he thought he could do, what he thought his politics were. I think that's to some extent characteristic of the President, and I admire him for it. One of his great strengths is even with his enemies he could put himself in their circumstances. And I think one of the reasons, it didn't work here, but one of the reasons he is effective is he could project . . . empathy in the best sense. He could really imagine what were the constraints on even his opponents. When we were negotiating with the Republicans it drove me crazy, but he could see what was influencing them, what was constraining them, what was possible, what was not. So I think he built in a lot and trusted Barak in that sense to understand the kind of political pace at which he could operate.[33]

On another occasion, he was less insistent with Arafat when he needed to be. On this point, Dennis Ross was direct in his criticism. According to Ross, in a meeting with Arafat during the Millennium Summit in New York in September 2000, "the President did not do his [job]." Despite having been briefed to firmly reject the idea of sovereignty over Jerusalem by the Organization of the Islamic Conference by both George Tenet and Dennis Ross, Clinton "did not convey that message in the meeting with Arafat . . . The President shied away from confronting Arafat . . . Moreover, the President as much as told him that the blunt talk he'd heard from George and me [Ross] separately did not matter."[34]

As former Israeli foreign minister Shlomo Ben-Ami has pointed out, it was not entirely unusual to have a mediating effort between enemies who do not have a working relationship. In the Israeli-Egyptian negotiations at Camp David in 1978, Israeli prime minister Begin and Egyptian prime minister Sadat had to be separated for much of the negotiations after a stormy start. But even aside from the significantly different strategic environment in which they were negotiating, their attitudes toward each other and toward the United States were vastly different. The problem was not at its core one of deep mistrust. Indeed, even when many around the world, and certainly in the Arab world, lost hope in the prospects of a peace deal between Arabs and Israelis following the election of Begin as prime minister of Israel—the first right wing government in the history of the state— Sadat saw in Begin a strong leader that he could deal with, and Begin thought that Sadat could compromise easily because he was an authoritarian leader who could bring his public along. Moreover, unlike at Camp David, the Israeli team had politically strong members in Moshe Dayan and Ezer Weizman, who were trusted enough by the Israeli prime minister to carry out negotiations with the American president and the Egyptian president; furthermore, they had the capacity to persuade the prime minister—although it was still clearly the case that Begin was the ultimate Israeli decision maker.

Even before Camp David, Barak himself led the negotiating efforts on both the Syrian and the Palestinian fronts, which was not unusual for an Israeli prime minister. Most prime ministers saw negotiations with Arab interlocutors as top-level issues that required their personal attention. And so they also viewed Israeli relations with Washington, which are considered by Israelis as perhaps the most crucial foreign policy issue for any Israeli government. As a consequence, the Israeli ambassador in Washington is typically the prime minister's man, and not the foreign minister's agent.

In Barak's case, he had appointed David Levy as foreign minister, in whom he had no apparent trust, and who was not seen by the United States to have Barak's confidence. As a consequence, the role of the American secretary of state, Madeleine

Albright, was diminished as she did not have an empowered counterpart on the Israeli side. One White House official put it this way,

> I wouldn't underestimate the consequences of there not being a functioning Israeli foreign minister. Because a lot of things would have happened at the Albright-Levy level that was dysfunctional, not because of Albright, because of the Israelis. So there wasn't [a functioning foreign minister yet], Madeleine played an important role at Camp David, but she was handicapped by the fact that she didn't have an interlocutor, David [Levy] didn't even come to Camp David. So that enhanced Dennis's role. Had there been a, what I call a 600-pound gorilla functioning, then I think his role would have been different.[35]

However, the State Department interpreted the diminished role of the secretary of state differently. One former American official put it this way,

> The problem is we don't have a good system for dealing with systems where there's a prime minister and a president. If the PM can call the U.S. president whenever, it's hard to get the secretary of state involved. The next president shouldn't spend so much time on the phone with the prime minister. It puts the secretary out of the loop and puts the national security advisor in the lead. This arrangement makes regular diplomacy harder to achieve. Everyone in other countries is trying to divide State and NSC.[36]

President Clinton also had a long-standing relationship with Yasir Arafat, who frequently visited the White House in the years following the signing of the 1993 Oslo agreement. By most accounts, Arafat personally liked Clinton and even trusted him. Furthermore, Arafat trusted Clinton more than any other member of the American team, and he also had a favorable view of former Central Intelligence Agency Director George Tenet. But there is much evidence that he never trusted Dennis Ross and Martin Indyk.[37] And he never saw Secretary of State Albright and National Security Advisor Samuel Berger as the central drivers on this issue, seeing them as primarily deferring either to Ross or to the president. One former American official put it this way:

> Usually how Arafat saw Madeleine or Sandy [Samuel Berger] or Dennis or anybody else, this would change, depending on which week you're asking, and what is the political issue at any given time. But when it comes to Clinton, I really believe that Arafat saw in Clinton the American President who

can actually deliver the Palestinian state. He thought that Clinton has the charisma, the power, the understanding, the devotion to make this happen. But what Arafat failed to do, and a lot of Arab leaders unfortunately do the same thing, is they think that "this is enough, now I sit back and relax, do nothing, and the other guy will deliver it for me."[38]

Clinton clearly believed that Arafat was genuine in his pursuit of a final-status agreement and capable of delivering it—although there were always frustrations with his behavior and style. On this point, a top-level American official observed, "So I think Clinton was torn between looking at Arafat as a figure who can deliver, or at least he hoped that he can deliver, and the conduct or the misconduct of Arafat that sort of took away from the personal relationship."[39] Despite the interpretations that emerged after the end of the Clinton administration, it was the consensus among the American team that Arafat and the Palestinians were interested in and capable of reaching an agreement to end the conflict with Israel. Two views were also part of the American consensus. As one American official put it, "Arafat wanted this to be seen as a negotiating continuum, so that Camp David was not the final stop on the train, it was one stop on the train, and we were going to negotiate. I think Arafat would have preferred to negotiate, negotiate. So I think we made the decision . . . that this was an action-forcing event for both sides."[40]

The second view was that Clinton (and the American team) apparently shared Barak's assessment that Arafat would never be ready to make a decision unless he was forced into a decision-making mode and that, even then, there was no way to know which way he would go. Whether this assessment was based on Clinton's own interactions with Arafat or was principally influenced by Barak's interpretation and the interpretation of the American team is not entirely clear. One former American official suggested that Clinton "was so goddamn ill-advised by the people around him, it is sickening."[41] The American team had no full appreciation for Palestinian domestic politics and, somewhat more surprisingly, no full understanding of Israeli politics.[42] In addition, Arafat's conversations with Clinton were profoundly different from those between Barak and Clinton. With Barak, Clinton was on the receiving end of a barrage of ideas and proposals and strategizing and coordinating how to push those ideas forward both with the Palestinians and in Israeli politics that Clinton understood and followed closely. When Arafat met with Clinton, he usually came to hear ideas, not to propose them. And when he did initiate a conversation, an American official who typically sat in on those meetings put it this way, "There was frustration always with Arafat because he was a master at victimhood, at grievance, and you'd listen to him for hours at a time talking about how poorly the Palestinians had been treated."[43] Thus much of Arafat's lengthy complaints and description of grievances were often seen by members of the administration as being part of a ritual.[44] One official described Clinton's outlook toward the two leaders this way: "I think that Arafat was a foreign leader. Barak was sort of a political kindred spirit. He was a politician, not a long-term politician but he was at that moment a politician, a kind of social democrat. He was more of a kindred spirit; I think they probably had an easier relationship."[45]

Arafat was seen to be passive in his negotiations throughout the Oslo process, not just at Camp David. According to a former American adviser, "The idea of coming up with an initiative was always surrounded by fear and suspicion. If anybody else comes with the idea, they feel—the Palestinians, that is, and Arafat in particular—that there is a trap in it somewhere, they just have to figure it out."[46] It is not that the Palestinian team didn't make some compromises on issues ranging from borders to refugees. Some of the concessions made by the Palestinians to the Israelis during the Camp David Summit included accepting settlement blocs in the West Bank under Israeli sovereignty; an acceptance that the Jewish neighborhoods of East Jerusalem and the Jewish Quarter of the Old City would be Israeli; an agreement to Israeli early-warning sites in the West Bank; an acceptance of the principle of swapping Israeli territory for the Palestinian territory Israel wanted to annex, which was markedly different from Egyptian and Jordanian precedents; and agreeing to a cap on the number of Palestinian refugees permitted to return to Israel.[47]

But Arafat's style on the big issues was to expect American and Israeli proposals and then to respond to them. Even aside from the substantive negotiations, Arafat specifically and the Palestinian team more generally were rarely initiators of proposals, of ideas for the process, and of conversations with the Americans and the Israelis. According to a former American adviser, "The traditional Palestinian position and the traditional Arafat position was to stick to your position on permanent status, for example, and you can't and should not deviate from that. And that becomes your maximum and your minimum at the same time. And it does not work in negotiations, and I think it was an important setback for the Palestinians during Camp David itself."[48] This passive style was particularly true of the Palestinians when Barak became prime minister and was in sharp contrast to Rabin's style. Despite having a longer relationship with Bill Clinton and one that survived not only the assassination of Rabin but also the difficult Netanyahu years, Arafat rarely initiated a call to the President, and when the two of them did talk on the phone, usually on Clinton's initiative, it was typically brief, intended to sell Arafat some idea or proposal. Barak, in contrast, felt he could call Clinton on issues big and small—and was thus able, far more than Arafat, to influence the agenda.

Even when the Palestinians made important concessions, they failed to propose them in a manner that highlighted their willingness to compromise. One Clinton administration official put it this way,

> But in terms of even what I consider as Palestinian compromises, [these] were not really presented in a way where they can capitalize on [them] and maximize [the benefits from] these ideas. For example, the whole concept of swap. The whole concept of swap, when I look at it as somebody who has worked in this process for years and dealt with various countries that had some territorial issues with Israel, that's a huge Palestinian compromise. Because what the idea tells you is that "I am willing to accept 100% of the territories, but not the same exact 100% that I lost in 1967." Certainly that did not happen with Egypt, did not happen with Jordan, and probably most likely will not happen with Syria. Yet even though I see this as a huge Palestinian compromise, it was never ever packaged, presented, articulated as a Palestinian compromise. Therefore now, 10 years later, the Palestinians are begging the Israelis to accept it, and say 'please accept the swap and accept the one-for one-swap.' This is just an example of how they poorly managed initiating anything and making that thing a part of a bigger picture, and where would it fit."[49]

When Arafat and the Palestinians had an idea, it was usually conveyed to Clinton indirectly, most typically through Dennis Ross and his team. Thus the Office of the Special Middle East Coordinator (SMEC) played a critical role in interpreting the Palestinian mood and Arafat's mindset. And yet, it is equally clear that the Palestinian team and Arafat in particular had little trust in Ross and saw him more as delivering the Israeli point of view.[50] One former American diplomat who had been in close contact with Arafat (and, after his retirement, represented the PLO in Washington) observed,

> I would say that increasingly Arafat resented Dennis and the American approach and that he felt that Dennis was too much of an advocate, from his point of view, for Israeli perspectives, and did not sufficiently understand the kind of pressures that Arafat was under in terms of his own public opinion.[51]

There is little evidence that the White House understood the full extent of the long-standing Palestinian distrust of Ross or the Palestinian perception that he was primarily conveying the Israeli positions. Asked if he or Clinton were aware of the Palestinian perception, a former American official replied," [We had] a little bit [of sense of the Palestinian mistrust of Ross], but some of that I think is post-hoc rationalization from the Palestinians. At no point did any of the Palestinians come to me and say 'we don't want to deal with Dennis.' "[52]

Barak's relationship with Clinton drove much of the agenda, from the decision to pursue the Syrian track first to the meeting between Clinton and President al-Asad of Syria in Geneva, to the Camp David conference. And in every episode with Barak leading up to Camp David, Clinton experienced frustration and sensed that he was being manipulated. A White House official put it this way,

> A greater skepticism I think crept into the relationship after Geneva . . . where Barak really didn't level with us. It left Clinton in a very awkward position in Geneva, when we sat in Geneva in the hotel room waiting for Barak to call us with his bottom line, which he finally did, and his bottom line was not something that was acceptable to our side. So I think Clinton felt that he got manipulated a little bit by Barak . . . [At Shepherdstown] Barak didn't come prepared to do anything, and Clinton was really upset about that. And at some point at Camp David, he says to Barak,
> "I went to Shepherdstown, nothing happened. You left me hanging in Geneva, nothing happened. I'm not going to let that happen again."[53]

To understand this presidential predicament, we need to examine the role of the SMEC, not simply at Camp David but in the process leading to the summit, as it may have been critical in shaping the White House perceptions about the Israeli and Palestinian positions long before the negotiators arrived at Camp David.

The Role of SMEC and of Dennis Ross

Retrospective accounts offer both praise and criticism of Ross and the SMEC staff. Ross's team was small but deeply experienced, and had personal relationships with many of the key players on both the Israeli and the Palestinian sides. Situated as it was outside of the normal State Department hierarchy, the SMEC had direct channels to the secretary of state and the president, which bolstered its clout during negotiations. The SMEC's negotiating strength was further augmented by key policymakers' collective confidence in Ross and his team, up to and including President Clinton.

But the expertise that Ross and his staff held on Israel was not matched by a corresponding expertise or experience with Palestinian, Arab, or Islamic needs.

The SMEC was so lacking in this department that during Camp David II, State Department translator Gamal Helal was made a key interlocutor with the Palestinian delegation. Further, many years of frustrating negotiations took their toll on personal relationships. By Camp David, the U.S. team (and Ross in particular) was viewed by the Palestinians as strongly biased toward Israel. Finally, SMEC's special bureaucratic situation at the State Department and Ross's tendency toward secrecy were thought by many to have had the practical effect of cutting out key assistant secretaries, ambassadors, and interagency support structures from the process, and of creating a culture where little was committed to paper, resulting in a dearth of written analyses, records, and methodical preparation.[54]

Dennis Ross had helped to shape and to implement American diplomacy toward the Arab-Israeli conflict throughout the decade, and his ideas and role were also important at Camp David where the White House staff played a more central role. He had impressive experience in the Department of State, the National Security Council, and the Defense Department that dates back to the 1970s; he worked for both Republican and Democratic administrations and was widely respected in Congress.

Ross was one of the few senior political appointees from the Bush administration retained by President Clinton in 1993. Although the Office of the SMEC, created in May 1993, was housed in the Department of State, Ross was reporting to both State and the White House. One former assistant Secretary of State described the relationship this way,

> Albright was doing a very aggressive and quite effective job managing the process and SMEC earlier on, but over time Berger gradually took over. Toward the latter part of the Clinton administration, Berger was doing her job and Ross was reporting more to Berger than to Albright. The breaking point here was probably Albright's London trip—this trip occurred during the Netanyahu administration and the basic story is that Albright was particularly hard on the Israelis and it had political reverberations. It was at this point that Berger started to take a more active role.[55]

Despite the direct involvement of the president and his staff at Camp David, which reduced the roles of the State Department and in some ways of SMEC, Ross's role was still critical. In particular, both Clinton and Berger had come to rely on Ross's judgment. While Berger's relationship with Ross "was complex, it was rare for Berger to take a position that was hostile to Ross's position."[56] And even aside from the direct input that Ross had at Camp David, his own interpretations of the environment on the ground, of the outlooks of Israeli and Palestinian leaders,

and of what the process could or could not bear had already influenced the outlook of the president, the national security advisor, and the secretary of state.
Above all, Ross had more information than anyone else and that made him indispensable. One senior White House official described his centrality at Camp David
this way,

> Dennis had the most hands-on face-to-face experience, up to and including
> Madeleine. . . . Sandy had a lot of faith in Dennis. Dennis had the most in-
> formation . . . people did have different perspectives on substance, tactics,
> personalities, but Dennis had the advantage of controlling what was per-
> ceived as the most granular information about the players. Which is good
> and dangerous . . . So it's good and it's dangerous, because the danger is,
> particularly with someone like Dennis who has a certain kind of certainty
> about where people are going to land, is that if they miss in their calculation,
> you can go down a blind alley, if not a bad path.[57]

Ross's near monopoly of information was partly by design. According to one
high-level State Department official who worked closely with Ross, there were
many occasions where participating staff were told that they couldn't let certain
people know about developments in negotiations. Though they had their own
bosses, had they not complied, they would have lost their roles and influence, because Ross was calling the shots.[58] Remarking on Ross's tendency to keep the records in his own head, a former assistant secretary of state remarked that "I don't
think there's any paper trail. You can ask the historian, but I believe that the paper
trail is Dennis's book."[59]

According to a senior White House official, even though a lot of people personally did not like Ross, they dealt through him anyway because he was the president's
point man. Ross was very much in charge, did not write much down for the record,
and played everything close to the chest. But Ross kept the White House informed
of everything he did, down to the minutiae—but almost always he did this by
phone. Ross did not, however, do this with the rest of the State Department.[60]
There was a sense among others in the State Department that Ross seemed to have
little use for the information and the reports they were producing about the situation on the ground. According to a former U.S. diplomat, "Dennis basically didn't
listen to people. Dennis kind of had an attitude of what should be done and how
to do it and he essentially had a closed mind, I think."[61] It was no secret that Arafat
and many Arab and Palestinian officials did not trust Ross. A former Jordanian
foreign minister reported that King Hussein did not trust Ross at all and that he
thought that Ross's starting point was always the Israeli bottom line. He suggested

that this is largely why Hussein did not want to tell the United States about his moves with Israel (toward the 1994 Jordanian-Israeli Peace Treaty).[62] According to an Israeli participant at Camp David, "Arafat said once or twice to Clinton that Ross and others on the US team were 'working for the Israelis, not for you.' "[63] But this official disputed that these perceptions were well founded or that they had the impact Arabs assumed they did on American behavior: "At the end of the day, the image of the biased US negotiator has done more to hurt the Israelis than the Palestinians because it forced the US to overcompensate."[64] Another Israeli participant argued that although the Palestinians did not like Ross and Indyk, the charge that the pair had a pro-Israel bias was just an excuse. On some issues, Ross and Indyk expressed opinions that were totally different from those of the Israelis.[65] A former American official involved in the negotiations argued that it is natural that many people came to distrust Dennis Ross because this is the natural course of human events when somebody is put in the middle of two warring parties. Over time, both sides come to resent that person.[66]

Still, criticism of SMEC and the entire American team has been sometimes sharp, and in one case coming from Ross's own deputy, Aaron David Miller, who argued that the American team, including Miller himself, behaved as if it were "Israel's lawyer."[67] Regardless of the basis of Ross's own assessments and positions, in reading his own account, it is hard to miss that he trusted Barak far more than Arafat and that he was skeptical of Arafat's gestures and tended to interpret Barak's behavior more benignly.[68] This is not to say that other American officials differed substantially in their interpretations, but Ross was the most knowledgeable and served as a trendsetter.

Although Ross's role was unmistakable throughout the Israeli Palestinian negotiation process, an argument could be made that the very reliance on SMEC and on a special envoy to deal with the negotiations was itself a symptom of the issue not being a national security priority for the president, even though the president's personal interest and involvement evolved over time. One former American official, argued that contrary to what has become conventional wisdom that the appointment of a SMEC shows U.S. dedication to be deeply involved in the Middle East peace process—the creation of a SMEC was only to assert a minimal U.S. role and keep tabs on the process. Rather than showing U.S. determination to make a big push, SMEC reflected a realization that the United States was not in the driver's seat during Oslo and, in fact, Ross's appointment was a downgrade of sorts of U.S. involvement (from the presidential–secretary of state level) to the working level.[69]

The Camp David Summit

The path to Camp David started in earnest after the failure of the Syrian-Israeli negotiations that followed the troubled meeting between Clinton and al-Asad in Geneva on March 26, 2000. Ehud Barak envisioned a summit that would deal with all the issues at once and had Clinton's support.[70] There were some differences within the American team, particularly after the failed experiences at Shepherdstown and Geneva.[71] Arafat visited Clinton in the White House on April 20, 2000, and was concerned about the idea of an "end all" summit. An administration official who attended the meeting observed, "Arafat came here to Washington, I think near the end of April, the last 10 days of April. And we started talking to him about having some kind of a meeting that hopefully can produce an agreement. Arafat's concern at that time was that if the meeting fails, he would be blamed. And he was assured by President Clinton at that time that he would not be blamed."[72] By June, the pressure mounted for a July peace conference and Secretary of State Madeleine Albright and other members of the American team visited the region to garner support for the conference.

> What encouraged the administration very much at that time, and what encouraged President Clinton, was Prime Minister Barak, who actually was driving this very hard, pushing for it with a simple logic that everybody bought at that time, which was "we will go to Camp David, we'll lock ourselves in, we'll just meet day and night until we find the solutions. The leaders will be there, Clinton will be there, and there will be no excuse." . . . So based on that, we went to Arafat in June to tell him "listen, you have to come." And Arafat was still driven by the misgivings and the fear and the concern that he would be blamed. Some cynically would say because he was determined to come to Camp David and not to agree to anything, so he knew that he would be the bad guy, and therefore he wants to secure the fact that he should not be blamed. But I don't necessarily subscribe to this. . . . We all knew that what Arafat was saying was right. But what is the alternative? The alternative is you don't do it now, you don't do it for the next six months, you don't do it for the next eight months, there is no time limit.[73]

The Camp David Summit was a cause for concern among members of the American team. Berger worried about the bad precedents of Shepherdstown and Geneva.[74] Others worried about the lack of preparation. Still others worried about the political risks of a failed conference and one, Aaron Miller, suggested a parallel path in case the summit failed, but he was shut down by Berger.[75] In part, the risks were seen by the White House to be primarily political risks, not strategic ones, and there was a sense that the president was prepared to take that risk. Scheduling also became an issue in the waning months of the Clinton presidency, and so July was selected as the best opportunity to meet. Whatever the reasons, by multiple accounts, the American team was ill prepared for the summit, with many participants on the American side, as well as others, describing the American team as "dysfunctional."[76]

As the Camp David negotiations commenced on July 11, 2000, several features of the negotiating environment that were bound to affect the outcome were already salient. Arafat profoundly mistrusted Barak, and Barak disrespected Arafat. On the one hand, Barak was determined that this round—where nothing is agreed until everything is agreed—would end all negotiations. The Palestinians, on the other hand, feared that there was not enough preparation for an end-of-conflict agreement; Arafat had argued for the secret talks under way in Stockholm to be given more time to generate possible openings for agreement and wanted Camp David to be only another round of negotiations. Barak avoided making any direct offer to Arafat and wanted all to be presented to him by Clinton. Arafat feared that the aim of Camp David was to trap him into making concessions on Jerusalem that he was incapable of making—and was in the end probably the only one in the world to believe Barak's narrative after the Camp David failure that the whole exercise of Camp David was just to prove to the world that Arafat was incapable of making peace.[77] The crucial Jerusalem issue had never been discussed in detail during the negotiations up to that point, not even between the Israelis and the American mediators.

The problems became apparent to some members of the American team early on. One senior official put it this way,

> Well, I think that the first couple days created some confusion. Because we started to feel, at least I started to feel that the rationale that drove us to Camp David has not been manifested yet. Before going to Camp David, I thought that we would be spending like six, eight, to ten hours of constant, non-stop negotiations between the Palestinians and the Israelis with an American presence. Then we would take a break to draft, to do something, then come back again and continue. That was my assumption based on everything that I heard before that. When that did not happen, the first day, the second day, I felt that there was something seriously wrong here. Because the logic that encouraged Clinton to make the decision and allowed us to sort of like push Arafat to come to Camp David did not manifest itself. There were no meetings, nothing happened. Arafat did not meet with Barak

at all, except once, over an event sometime midway during Camp David, and it was not even a meeting, it was some kind of a tea or something that was useless. So I think Barak decided he's not going to do this. And as a result we all got stuck . . . by "this," I mean what he told us, that the leaders would sit down, day in, day out, every hour, round the hour, to negotiate permanent-status negotiations and reach solutions. That did not happen.[78]

The Nonpaper

Instead, Clinton was the go-between for Barak and Arafat. Yet, unlike the 1978 Camp David Summit, to which the Americans brought a draft agreement hammered out after extensive contacts with the parties, in 2000 the American team arrived at Camp David with no formal proposal to put on the table and no extensive preconsultations to draw from. On the second day at Camp David, Dennis Ross asked legal adviser Jonathan Schwartz to prepare two documents: a principles paper and a draft agreement that would be presented to the president so he could decide which the American team should present to the parties.[79] Aaron Miller, Gamal Helal, Martin Indyk, John Herbst, Bruce Riedel, Robert Malley, and Dennis Ross went over the drafts together. Ross described this process, "We heard that the Israelis had their draft ready. We got it and John [Schwartz] went to see Gidi Grinstein at midnight to hear his explanation of what it contained. But the paper had many points that had never been raised with either the Palestinians or us. For us to incorporate them would signal to the Palestinians that this was not our paper, but an Israeli paper. John was able to take a few of the Israeli comments, and I decided to have him produce only one draft, not two."[80]

After reviewing the drafts, Ross decided to go with the draft agreement and received positive reactions on this idea from Albright and Berger. On the following day, Ross briefed members of the Israeli team on the content of the document and read to them the parts he considered most sensitive.[81] The Israelis rejected the part of the paper that the border would be based on the 1967 lines with modifications taking into account the demographics and strategic needs of the Israelis. "This was surprising because it. . . . was literally taken from the language Shlomo [Ben-Ami] and Gilad [Sher] had put in their non-paper in Sweden with Abu Ala and Hassan Asfour."[82] They also did not like the refugee section, objecting to language that suggested that Israel, along with others, had a responsibility to help resolve this question once and for all.[83] The Israelis preferred putting the American language in brackets effectively turning the document into an "I" and "P" paper representing Israeli and Palestinian suggestions.

Later in the day Ross met with members of the Palestinian team, and "without going over the details of the draft, I went over the categories and structure of what we were planning to present."[84] Abu Ala'a wanted to make sure there was enough specificity in the document, especially about Jerusalem.

According to Ross, when Clinton read the draft, he felt it was more prudent to go instead with an I and P paper, with suggested solutions as well, because he felt it was "premature to force something down Barak's throat."[85] The American team proceeded to prepare such a draft.

In the rush to get going, the team presented a draft of the document that had not been proofread to the president. "The President went over it with Barak but did not allow him to read it, saying we had changed our whole approach to accommodate Barak's concerns, and he needed to present it to Arafat. Barak did not resist."[86] Dennis later handwrote in the word "expanded" to modify "municipality" after the Israeli team objected that that the last point in the paper on Jerusalem was not in brackets and it implied that there could be two capitals in the existing municipality of Jerusalem.

Arafat was visibly upset when reading the paper. Gamal Helal, the American adviser and translator who had developed a close relationship with Arafat, reported on his meeting with the shaken Palestinian leader. Arafat believed that this was an Israeli paper and pointed to the inserted word on Jerusalem as an indication.[87] Shortly after, Abu Ala'a and Saeb Erekat came to see Albright and complained about the I and P paper, saying that it was not what they expected and that it was unfair.

The irony is that the Israelis were also having second thoughts about an I and P paper, and two of them, Shlomo Ben-Ami and Gilad Sher, remarked to Ross the morning of the fourth day that the Americans should have stuck with the original draft agreement, despite the initial Israeli objections.[88] In response to the Israeli concerns, the United States withdrew the paper, and it never resurfaced during the summit. Nor did the Americans present any other paper during the summit. Indyk notes that the Israelis "informed us later that Barak's strong reaction to the preview of the first paper was a bargaining tactic. They never imagined that we would respond to their negative comments by dropping the paper altogether."[89] By then, it was too late to go back.

Final-Status Issues

For the remainder of the negotiations, the issues were taken up by three negotiating committees: the territory and security committee, the refugee committee, and the Jerusalem committee.[90] While the Jerusalem issue was in the end the central obstacle to an agreement at Camp David and is therefore the central final-status issue analyzed in this chapter, it is important to note that there was some limited progress made on other issues, including refugees[91] (which is further discussed later in this chapter with the regard to the Taba negotiations), territory,[92] and security.[93]

The Jerusalem Issue

There is near consensus among scholars as well as participants from all three sides that the primary reason for the collapse of the negotiations at Camp David was the issue of Jerusalem,[94] even if other important issues such as refugees, borders, and Israeli settlements remained unresolved. This was particularly ironic as Jerusalem was the single issue over which there was no previous discussion or any serious preparation—not that the centrality of the issue was unpredictable.[95]

It is also striking how the American team had limited information about the Palestinian or the Israeli bottom line positions, particularly with regard to Jerusalem. This omission was particularly notable given Clinton's experience with Barak at Shepherdstown and Geneva—and given that Barak saw in Clinton a partner who delivered his positions to Arafat and structured the summit in a manner to leave the Palestinian leader nothing but the narrowest of choices. This partnership contrasted with that in the negotiations between Israel and Egypt in 1978, when President Sadat perceived Carter as a "partner" and shared with him a prepared document that he did not share with most of his own Egyptian delegation, outlining how far he was prepared to go—which was a central factor in Carter's belief that a deal could be had.

Part of the reason for the absence of American probing was the perceived consensus in Israeli politics about Jerusalem (and even in the U.S. Congress). National Security Advisor Samuel Berger described the sentiment at a dinner he attended in Israel in May 2000 this way: "I don't know about Yossi Beilin, but everybody at that dinner said 'Jerusalem is a red line which no Israeli prime minister can cross, and if he does, he'll be out of office.' "[96]

It is clear that the Palestinians worried that the Israelis were structuring the negotiations in a manner that would force unacceptable choices on Jerusalem. Arafat's confidant, Akram Haniyeh, described Arafat's strategy at the outset of Camp David,

> Arafat was carrying out a three-pronged tactical offensive on Jerusalem. First, he strove to get across the idea that there could be no deal that deferred Jerusalem (Clinton soon seemed convinced of this logic). Second, he aimed at getting the "Abu Dis as substitute capital" idea dropped by making clear that Jerusalem for the Palestinians means the Old City and the neighborhoods

outside its walls such as Musrara, Shaykh Jarrah, Salah al-Din, Suwana, Wadi al-Juz, al-Tur, Silwan, and Ras al-Amud. Thanks to his insistence, the rumors peddled for months by the Israeli press and officials that the Palestinians had agreed to give up East Jerusalem for Abu Dis ended. From then on, the focus of the discussions shifted to the Old City. Finally, Arafat rejected any fragmentation of the negotiations on the Jerusalem issue and stuck to the Palestinian insistence on Palestinian sovereignty over all of East Jerusalem.[97]

Although it was of course hard to know how far either side would go in the negotiations, particularly since the parties had not discussed Jerusalem in detail previously and neither had shared its bottom line positions with the Americans, there was an unmistakable lack of understanding of the importance of the Jerusalem issue to the Palestinians and to Arabs and Muslims more broadly. Arafat reportedly said shortly before falling ill in 2004, "Had they given me Al-Quds and the Al-Aqsa Mosque, I would have given them everything."[98] The shortage of American experts on the Palestinians, Arabs, and Muslims at the negotiations was most apparent on the issue of Jerusalem. According to one White House official,

[There was a] lack of reflection I think on the American side about how to deal with Jerusalem. It was dealt with, there were position papers that were written . . . but they were not advanced enough if you compare them with where we are today. So that was a learning experience, we had not matured in terms of our reflection on Jerusalem. That I think—were people missing on the team? What I've said is I think the people missing on the team were people who could have, and I'm not in favor of quotas, but people who could understand the Palestinians' experience. . . . Do you need a Muslim on the team? I don't know. But you could have someone on the team who was particularly sensitive to Palestinians of all stripes, Christian, Muslim views of Jerusalem. You certainly had that in terms of sensitivities to the Jewish, Israeli views; you didn't have that on the other side. I don't know who in the State Department or elsewhere could've done that.[99]

But another high-level White House official saw the picture somewhat differently and stressed the presence of members of the team who, in his view, had a good sense of the Palestinians and what was transpiring within their delegation,

I think Gamal [Helal] is a good channel for us in terms of what's going on among Arafat's people. There were a lot of different channels here, it was not just Clinton and Barak and Arafat, it was Dahlan and Shlomo Ben Ami, and there were a lot of conversations going on, but Gamal was our best source of information and some analysis of what was going on the Palestinian side. But you know Rob [Malley] has a good sense of that, Aaron [Miller] has a good sense of that, Dennis [Ross] had a good sense of it, so it's not like we were without people who were knowledgeable.[100]

Although the U.S. government has always had a good number of experts who understood Arab politics and culture and the Palestinian side of the story—regardless of their ethnic and religious backgrounds—few had full command of the culture and language. In a report by the Public Diplomacy Committee that the State Department later commissioned,[101] it was noted that in the diplomatic services only a handful of diplomats were found to be fluent enough in the Arabic language to appear on the Arab media. But the State Department's Near East Bureau has always had well-trained experts with widespread knowledge of and extensive experience in the Middle East (including staff at Intelligence and Research, the consul general in Jerusalem, and ambassadors in the region). Most were absent from the peace process and were not at Camp David, beyond the core group that had worked directly on this issue.[102]

The absence of preparation on Jerusalem became clear early on with the frantic attempt to draft a nonpaper. It also became clear that the leadership needed to be brought up to speed quickly on conceptualizing different approaches to the Jerusalem issue and for that, the team turned to Jonathan Schwartz.

At the request of Dennis Ross, Schwartz, a State Department legal adviser, played an important role in drafting the nonpaper circulated by the American team. He was asked to "educate" the leadership about the issue of sovereignty and to draft a paper about the different gradations of sovereignty to see if any could serve as a basis for the status of different parts of Jerusalem. He identified ten such possibilities.[103] These ideas became central as the American team grappled with ways to address both Israeli and Palestinian concerns on Jerusalem.

Negotiating Jerusalem

From the outset, both Barak and Arafat, each for his own reasons, wanted Jerusalem discussed. Whether or not, as Schwartz later assessed, it would have been wise to delay negotiating Jerusalem, it was probably unlikely that both Arafat and Barak would have gone along with postponing the Jerusalem issue.[104]

According to Ross, at the outset of the Camp David, the American team took a "conceptual" tack on Jerusalem.[105] On the evening of the first day of the Camp

David talks, Clinton and his team met with Arafat and Erekat. Clinton raised the issue of Jerusalem with Arafat.[106] Arafat's suggestion was "East Jerusalem for us, West Jerusalem for the Israelis. It will be the capital of the two states, and there will be a joint commission for water, roads, electricity . . . " but Clinton took the view that Israel would never give up sovereignty over East Jerusalem.[107] Arafat stressed the centrality of Haram al-Sharif to Muslims worldwide (it is widely considered to be the third holiest site in Islam).[108]

Clinton stressed the difficulties Barak faced on the issue of Jerusalem and that Barak wanted "an open city, an enlarged Jerusalem under Israeli sovereignty. The solution would be extended city limits including the two capitals. You would have the rights over the Islamic holy places and also certain districts."[109] Arafat demanded sovereignty over both Muslim and Christian places in the city.

On the fifth day of the negotiations, Barak wanted to put Jerusalem on the table. According to Ross,

> What, he asked, did I think the Palestinians needed? I said, in addition to clear control of the Haram, they needed some sovereignty in a part of existing East Jerusalem. Al-Quds could not simply be Abu Dis and the villages outside of the existing municipal boundaries of East Jerusalem. Here again, he [*Barak*] took a tough position. What he [*Barak*] had signaled to the President on Jerusalem he now seemed to walk back on, saying he [*Barak*] could not give more than autonomy for the outer villages like Bayt Hanina and Shua'fat. When I pressed on this point given our earlier conversation, he [*Barak*] said it simply was not possible to do more in the outer villages.[110]

Later that day, Ross met with Sher and shared with him a draft of the paper which the president had not finalized. He asked him not to share it with anyone as it was not finalized. Ross described the paper's key elements as follows "On Jerusalem, we will propose Palestinian sovereignty in the outer neighborhoods of Bayt Hanina and Shua'fat; for the inner neighborhoods, there will have to be real autonomy, meaning that they get planning and zoning; on the Old City, there will need to be shared responsibilities; and the Palestinians will get jurisdiction, not sovereignty, on the Temple Mount/Haram."[111] Sher raised questions about zoning in the inner neighborhood in Jerusalem and objected to unlimited Palestinian building in the area. Ross assured him, "Remember, these neighborhoods are staying under your [*Israeli*] sovereignty—that's the big thing and there has to be some selling point for such an agreement."[112]

The Palestinians were focused on Jerusalem from the outset. On day six of the negotiations, Sher reported to Ross on his meeting with Palestinian negotiators and noted that they were unresponsive on any issue except Jerusalem. "Saeb proposed that East Jerusalem be divided, with all the Arab neighborhoods becoming Palestinian and all the Jewish neighborhoods becoming Israeli."[113] Later the same day, when Israelis and Palestinians met prior to their meeting with Clinton, there was little discussion of the refugee issue as the Palestinians continued to draw attention to what they had proposed on Jerusalem, "emphasizing that this was a big move and a logical one."[114] In contrast, the Israeli team members, Sher and Ben-Ami put forth additional and more detailed ideas,[115] but as the president met with Arafat later in the day, the Palestinian leader again returned the centrality of the Jerusalem issue. While belittling the proposed ideas on borders and Jerusalem, Arafat gave Clinton a letter in Arabic, which was translated by Gamal Helal. In the letter, Arafat left no uncertainty on how highly he ranked the Jerusalem issue, "I agree that the ratio of exchange will be in accordance with the agreed-upon size of the settlements. I will leave it up to you if we can guarantee a solution to East Jerusalem for you to determine the ratio."[116]

Whereas Arafat's position could have been interpreted as his idea of a grand bargain—if the Israeli side could meet Palestinian requirements on Jerusalem, then the Palestinians would allow the Americans to determine the territories and border issue—Ross interpreted Arafat's letter as simply a clever move by Arafat. "Even with the most favorable interpretation, we were being told, give us sovereignty over East Jerusalem—effectively all of East Jerusalem including the Jewish neighborhoods and then you can decide the annexation and the swap. We might be able to produce on borders and territory for Barak, but it would come at an unacceptable price to him."[117]

On the seventh day, Ross and Helal came up with another idea inspired by Schwartz's discovery that after the 1967 War the Israelis had offered to give the UN personnel diplomatic status in the holy sites in Jerusalem. The Americans proposed to offer the Palestinians "permanent custodianship" over the Haram, which would be conferred by a committee composed of the five members of the UN Security Council, the Vatican, and Morocco as the chair of the Jerusalem Committee of the Organization of the Islamic Conference. Ross notes that the Israeli team had come up with a similar idea on its own.[118]

When the Clinton saw Barak later that day, Barak had a prepared paper that he wanted presented to the Palestinians as an American idea. The paper constituted a retreat from the positions that Barak and his aides had already presented.[119] Instead, Ross drafted a query to Arafat, "If he could get sovereignty over the outer neighborhoods, sovereignty over the Muslim Quarter in the Old City, and the custodial role over the holy sites, would he be prepared to proceed on that basis? I did not mention the inner neighborhoods, but I was now signaling that he could get sovereignty over one neighborhood in the Old City and I was introducing the custodial idea."[120] But when the president made the proposal to him, Arafat's verdict was clear: he would accept nothing short of sovereignty over East Jerusalem.

One reason why the American team was frustrated with Arafat was the sense he was not moving far enough toward the Israeli positions. Certainly the reference point was not the extent to which he was making more concessions on 1967 boundaries than did Egypt and Jordan or than Syria ultimately insisted on at Geneva. And on Jerusalem, there was a sense that it really was up to Arafat—and not so much a broader Palestinian, Arab, and Muslim opinion—to accept or to reject what was offered; at least the assumptions about public opinion in the Arab and Muslim world were that they allowed Arafat to make far more concessions on Jerusalem than he was prepared to do.

In contrast, the Israelis appeared flexible and eager to present multiple ideas on Jerusalem, provided that Israel retained sovereignty according to its definition. More importantly, Barak moved far more than many members of the American team believed he could, and he also broke taboos in Israeli politics that were hard to ignore, especially by an American team and an American president who were especially mindful of Barak's domestic politics and his upcoming elections.

Barak's flexibility was particularly clear on the eighth day when one hour after Clinton met with Arafat, he met with Barak who was now prepared to share more of his bottom line on Jerusalem. Barak accepted for the first time the idea of Palestinian sovereignty within the walled Old City of Jerusalem over the Christian and Muslim Quarters; sovereignty over seven outer neighborhoods; and planning, zoning, security, and law enforcement powers (but no sovereignty) over the inner neighborhoods; and "custodianship" over the Haram. Barak's bottom line on Jerusalem was presented by Clinton to Arafat, who went on to say in a private meeting with Clinton that "he would consider everything the President said and come back with an answer." Arafat's team came back to Gamal Helal with a number of questions, including the meaning of custodianship for the Haram and the issue of sovereignty.[121]

On the ninth day, as the president was preparing to leave for Asia, the Palestinians requested a two-week break before responding to the president's ideas so that Arafat could consult with Arab leaders, then return to the negotiations. According to Ross, "The Sandy [Berger]-led group response was that there would be no break; we needed an answer on the U.S. ideas: were they a basis for concluding an agreement, yes or no. The answer was 'no.'"[122] The Jerusalem issue was not further discussed substantively until the thirteenth day of the negotiations.

On the thirteenth day, Arafat met with George Tenet, one of the American mediators he trusted, to react to the ideas the president had put on the table. After the meeting, Tenet reported that Arafat had given a qualified yes to the president. Arafat was saying yes provided he got several additions: the Armenian Quarter in the Old City and contiguity with sovereignty in all the inner neighborhoods. Barak would certainly interpret this as a no.[123] By that time, Barak had retracted his offer of Palestinian sovereignty within the walled Old City.

With the conference on the verge of collapse, Shlomo Ben-Ami suggested that Clinton meet the two leaders and give them bridging proposals on Jerusalem. He suggested "limited sovereignty" for the Palestinians over the inner neighborhoods and a "sovereign compound" in the Muslim Quarter with the Palestinians having "sovereign jurisdiction" over the Haram, or Temple Mount.

By the end of the day, it became clear that all the creative ideas short of clear sovereignty over the Haram were not going to work with Arafat. He also rejected deferring the Jerusalem issue. Despite last-ditch efforts that went on until early morning with "Hail Mary" type proposals by Clinton, the gap on Jerusalem was too wide to bridge. Arafat sent a letter to Clinton, saying, "I appreciate your efforts . . . , but these proposals could not constitute the basis for a historic reconciliation."[124]

Blaming Arafat

In the assessment of the Camp David negotiations, two issues are often conflated: the failure to reach a final-status agreement, which was the aim of the conference, and the American decision to interpret the conference as a failure and to place the blame squarely on Yasir Arafat. The two issues are somewhat related, but they are not identical and must be separated conceptually. Each had implications, but the latter may have had more immediate ramifications than the former and thus must be examined carefully.

On the thirteenth day, the Camp David negotiations finally broke down, primarily over the crucial issue of Jerusalem. As mediators, the Americans had a consequential decision to make: to take stock of what had been accomplished through the summit, claim progress, and call for another round of negotiations; or to declare failure and place blame. Barak's position was obvious from the outset. He felt that any proposals that were made at Camp David were made in the context of an end-all agreement, and he did not want the Palestinians to "pocket" his concessions and then face another round in which he would have to make further concessions. In contrast, the Palestinian position from the outset was not to view Camp David as an end-all episode and to hope for a positive interpretation of the outcome; this view was expressed in their initial public presentation and in later statements made by Palestinian negotiator Saeb Erekat on the American television show Nightline on the day the negotiations ended.[125]

As it was already becoming apparent that Camp David could end in failure, one member of the American team was tasked to prepare a statement reflecting what had been accomplished. The prepared draft statement highlighted the progress and the concessions made by each side and did not declare failure, and as such did not place blame for failure. Another member of the American team who had been present when Clinton promised Arafat that he would not be blamed, advised Clinton personally against blaming Arafat for failure.[126] The American team also attempted to persuade Barak that this summary statement might be the wise way to go: "We did try to persuade Barak, when it became apparent on the last day, and this really did go up to the end as you know, that this was not coming together, we went to Barak and said 'let's structure something so that there is a second act here,' and Barak refused. Whether that was well considered on his part or just a matter of his temperament at that point, which was dark and angry, I don't know. But we did try at the end."[127]

Upon review by the president and the national security advisor, a determination was made to go in a different direction. The extent to which extensive discussion took place among multiple members of the American team is not entirely clear, but one former American official recounted this moment,

> I think it was Clinton's decision. There was not a lot of discussion during this period. We had this session on the twelfth night that went way into the morning when the President cajoled, pleaded, induced, did everything he could with Arafat, and Arafat said "if I sign this deal I will get killed" . . . I think the President had felt that (a) Arafat had not been forthcoming and (b) I think he was concerned about Barak's politics and did not want Barak politically to collapse, and so some combination of the two. But, I don't recall this was the result of a lot of discussion.[128]

These two issues—concern for Barak's politics, and anger over Arafat's apparent passivity—were clearly the key to understanding Clinton's response. Regardless of the merits of Clinton's conclusions, there is little doubt that the act of blaming Arafat was hugely consequential, for the Palestinians, the Israeli public, and the American role in the coming months and years. Regarding Clinton's personal commitment to Arafat that he would not be blamed regardless of the outcome of Camp David, Berger has opined, "I think it was Clinton's intent going in that we would not blame Arafat if it failed. I think that was necessary to get Arafat there. I don't think it was cynical on Clinton's part. It ultimately was not the way things played out. But I don't think that he was disingenuous with Arafat at the time, I think as things unfolded he went in a different direction on that."[129]

It is not clear how blaming Arafat could have helped Barak politically. The emerging narrative, according to another American official,[130] was that Barak was a "sucker":[131] he had offered Arafat more than any other Israeli leader ever had, maybe even more than the Israeli public was prepared to accept, and Arafat simply pocketed the concessions and gave little in return. And although Palestinian-Israeli negotiations continued throughout the summer and even after the onset of the al-Aqsa Intifada in September 2000, the resulting Israeli and Palestinian moods—and Barak's own coalition politics—made a deal increasingly unlikely. As the Israeli elections came nearer, Barak himself increasingly sensed that the Camp David failure narrative was bound to hurt him in the elections, so much so that he put together a public relations initiative to persuade the Israeli public that he knew from the outset that Arafat was incapable of making an agreement and that his own compromising posture was only to prove to the Americans and to the world that Arafat was not really a peace partner. However, there is no evidence that he ever expressed such a view to American officials prior to Camp David. Eran Halperin and Daniel Bar-Tal note that "Barak even openly explained later on that the negotiations that continued until the elections of 2001, including the Taba talks, were not genuine but kept going only because of 'general political considerations' so that Israelis should not be held responsible for the cessation of the political process before the end of Clinton's tenure in office."[132]

Thus, the American analysis that blaming Arafat would help Barak deserved far more discussion, not only given what ultimately transpired in the Israeli elections, but because it also altered the relationship between Arafat and the member of the American team he trusted most, Bill Clinton. It also betrayed a failure to understand Arafat and his propensity when he felt cornered.[133]

At Camp David, Arafat increasingly believed that Barak and Clinton were ganging up on him and sensed that he had no further options. When Clinton then laid the blame for failure at his doorstep, contrary to what he had promised, Arafat probably concluded that he needed to change direction. Negotiations during the previous seven years had not produced much for the Palestinian cause; at the same time, Israel's unilateral withdrawal from Lebanon in spring 2000 had been hailed as a victory for the armed resistance of Hezbollah. In Arafat's mind, these factors added up to produce what may have been his biggest strategic blunder, one that ultimately made a deal between him and the Israelis impossible: namely, Arafat embraced the al-Aqsa Intifada that started in September 2000, probably believing that a measure of violence could be employed as a complement to negotiations in order to persuade the Israelis that there were consequences for not reaching an agreement.

The narrative of failure that is ultimately blamed on Palestinian leadership also had a consequence for the mood of the American political mainstream and the

Israeli political mainstream with the election of an Israeli government headed by Ariel Sharon that was less willing to compromise and with the election of an American President, George W. Bush, who saw little possibility for a Palestinian-Israeli breakthrough.

It is important to reflect on the American conclusion that Arafat was passive and unresponsive to the multiple proposals that Israel had put forward to him through Clinton. It is not that the Palestinians did not put ideas into the mix, as previously noted in this chapter. The real source of American anger was Arafat's posture on the issue of Jerusalem: from the outset the Palestinians feared that the Israelis and the Americans did not fully understand the importance of Jerusalem to them, and that the whole summit, its timing and its structure, was aimed at pressuring them to make concessions on this issue. In and of itself, Arafat's passive style was nothing new, having been the pattern prior to Camp David. What was new was the active involvement of President Clinton in pressuring Arafat to accept Israeli ideas that the Americans described as breaking Israeli taboos but which fell short of Arafat's requirements. Thus it was really targeted anger related to Arafat's unyielding position on the issue of Jerusalem in the face of changing Israeli attitudes on the issue and fueled by odd remarks by Arafat claiming that the Temple Mount, the holiest site in Judaism, was not under the Haram al-Sharif mosque, but instead in the city of Nablus. On the latter, one member of the American team later observed that he believed that Arafat was simply trying to mislead, "He knew better. But if he were to admit any Jewish claim to the area under the Haram al-Sharif, it would undermine his insistence that the Palestinians alone had the right to sovereignty there. That would breach the defense he had created for himself."[134] But this position was not new for Arafat as he had stated it on multiple occasions long before Camp David.[135]

Yet, that very puzzlement betrayed a lack of understanding of the Palestinian position in the negotiations. The American team already had a mindset that accepted Israel's redlines on Jerusalem, while underestimating how important the issue was to the Palestinians. Palestinians, like all Arabs, treated every inch of the territory occupied by Israel in 1967 territory from which Israel was legally obligated to withdraw, including East Jerusalem.[136] Israel, which had extended Israeli law, administration, and jurisdiction to Jerusalem after its occupation in 1967, claimed Jerusalem as Israeli territory. Although the American position never accepted the Israeli de facto annexation of the city and was always mindful of the consequences of the American position on Jerusalem for the broader Arab and Muslim worlds, the American posture in the mediation effort was closer to the view that East Jerusalem is a contested city, not an occupied one. For the Palestinians, what Israel kept out of any part of the territories occupied in 1967 was a

Palestinian concession, and that view applied equally to East Jerusalem. On the Israeli side, starting with the assumption that all of Jerusalem was Israeli territory, any part that Israel agreed to have come under Palestinian sovereignty would be an Israeli concession. This viewpoint colored the American interpretation of who was doing more or less or offering more or less. Seen from that perspective, Arafat was prepared to offer a number of concessions in accepting the principle of Israeli sovereignty over Jewish neighborhoods of the city that were occupied in 1967 and in the Jewish quarter of the Old City as well as the Wailing Wall.[137] These attempts at compromise, however, were hardly seen as major concessions by the Israelis or the American team. It was part of a mindset that took years to develop and certainly preceded the start of Camp David. To contrast the Palestinian position with that of Egypt at Camp David in 1978, it serves to recall that Egyptian president Anwar Sadat too was absolutely intransigent in the face of a barrage of Israeli proposals to hold some of Egyptian territory and maintain settlements in the Sinai. His position, however, was not seen as a sign of passivity or lack of responsiveness but was understood for what it was: Sadat was prepared to compromise a great deal on many issues, but not when it came to matters of sovereignty on territory occupied in the 1967 War. The same could be said of King Hussein of Jordan, who concluded a peace treaty with Israel that was anchored on full sovereignty over Jordanian land; and of Syrian president Hafez al-Asad, who ultimately refused to sign a peace deal over a few hundred meters of Syrian lands occupied by Israel in 1967.

Regardless of the American team's anger with Arafat and the worries about Barak's political fortunes, it is remarkable how little thought in the end went into assessing the consequences of failure and of blaming Arafat for it, on American interests in the region, which in retrospect, as noted earlier, were far-reaching. The only way to understand this outcome is to return to the strategic context in which the entire negotiating process was taking place: this process was not perceived to be driven by an elevated importance of the Arab-Israeli conflict in America's strategic priorities or by worries about the consequences for America's broader regional policy if the process failed. It was first and foremost a process born out of an opportunity (the Oslo Accords), out of a close U.S.-Israeli relationship, and in the end, a possible historical accomplishment for the Clinton presidency. This strategic context may also explain why, even throughout the process preceding the negotiations at Camp David, there was so little interagency coordination to compare notes, to read diverse perspectives, or to assess possible consequences for American interests. Of course, failures of process and of style matter, and they did at Camp David. But these were more likely to happen once one assumes that strategic stakes were not too great. This mindset underlay the process in the decade following the end of the Cold War and the aftermath of the 1991 Gulf war.

There is a sense that part of the failure at Camp David was a function of Clinton's personality and style. As White House official Bruce Riedel put it, Clinton had incredible strengths as a negotiator but not the ability to twist arms thoroughly, and you could not get a final deal without really hammering people.[138] Clinton's approach may have undermined his ability to influence both Arafat and Barak. But at Camp David, he hammered Arafat particularly hard on more than one occasion, including on the day before the conference ended, when he reportedly told Arafat, "You won't have a state and relations between America and the Palestinians will be over. Congress will vote to stop the aid you've been allocated, and you'll be treated as a terrorist organization."[139]

Although Clinton lectured Barak too, particularly on not sharing more with him on how far he was prepared to go, there was no evidence that he ever threatened the Israeli prime minister. "I think we had more leverage over Barak than we used," noted a former American official.[140] Part of this unequal treatment had to do with the fact that the American mainstream, especially Congress, was far more supportive of Israel, and as one former secretary of state put it, the Israeli prime minister can always go directly to the American people and Congress.[141] But most of it had to do with the fact that Clinton was far more in agreement with the Israeli narrative than the Palestinian one—which was in good part a function of the way the American negotiating team was structured and the filtered interpretations the president had received.

The Intifada, the Clinton Parameters, and Taba

Despite the sense of failure at Camp David, the blame placed squarely on Arafat, and the further loss of trust, the negotiating efforts continued throughout the remaining months of the Clinton administration and even beyond, partly through American mediation, partly through the bilateral Israeli-Palestinian negotiations taking place at Taba, Egypt, on the eve of the Israeli elections, January 21–27, 2001, without the presence of American mediators. But just over a week later, the picture had dramatically changed in both Israel and the United States. Ariel Sharon was elected in Israel to replace Ehud Barak as prime minister, just two weeks after George W. Bush replaced Bill Clinton as president of the United States. The players, the strategic picture, and the political environments had changed dramatically.

After Camp David, notwithstanding the collapse of the summit, Israelis and Palestinians negotiated almost continuously throughout the summer. Enough progress was being made that the Americans started crafting "parameters," or guidelines, within which the U.S. team would argue the negotiations should proceed. However, the Americans did not surface the parameters over the summer or in intensive talks during the annual UN General Assembly meetings in New York in September. By late September 2000, with the absence of a breakthrough in the talks and pressure building on the ground, the stage was set for a dramatic punctuation point to this phase of the peace process—the outbreak of the al-Aqsa Intifada.

The Intifada was triggered by the visit of Ariel Sharon, then a Likud Party candidate for prime minister, to the very place that derailed the negotiations, the Haram al-Sharif/Temple Mount, on September 28, 2000. Although the Intifada was primarily spontaneous, Arafat embraced it as he came to believe that it could serve as an instrument of pressure on the Israelis. For more than four years, both Israelis and Palestinians suffered under the impact of terrorism and reprisals.

The Intifada also carried serious consequences for the peace process. First, mutual trust collapsed, and the Israeli "peace camp" virtually disappeared. Second, the paradigm of the inevitability of the two-state solution collapsed. Third, the Jerusalem issue, as well as the rising power of Hamas as an Islamist organization putting forth a militant alternative to the failed negotiations, helped change the discourse from a nationalist discourse to a religious one. Fourth, the expansion of suicide bombings propelled the Israelis into the mode of confronting what was perceived to be an "existential" threat. Fifth, the events essentially assured the election of a right-wing Israeli government led by Ariel Sharon in February 2001.

Bill Clinton continued the American mediation efforts even after the outbreak of the Intifada. He persuaded Egyptian president Hosni Mubarak to convene a summit in October in order to try to bring the Intifada to a stop; the meeting failed. Clinton then put forth the "Clinton Parameters," constituting the most detailed American vision for the outline of a two-state solution that any administration had developed before or since.[142] He presented these ideas on December 23, 2000, that is, during the transition following the American presidential elections. The parameters went far beyond anything that had been agreed before between Israel and the Palestinians in laying out principles for resolving the final-status issues.

Clinton summoned Israeli and Palestinian negotiators into the Cabinet room on December 23 to present his parameters. Although he made it clear that he was prepared to discuss his ideas, he warned that he would only accept refinements, that he would give the leaders four days to respond, and that "if these ideas are not accepted by either side, they will be off the table, and have no standing in the future."[143] As soon as the president departed, Ross went over the presentation with both sides, apparently at dictation speed. "Nearly as soon as I began going over the words, Saeb and Sher—as if to show that they each had real problems, began to complain about specific formulations."[144]

On December 28, 2000, the Israeli government decided that "we consider these ideas to be a basis for discussion" but appended a list of reservations that were conveyed in a letter dated January 5, 2001, by Gilad Sher, chief of bureau of the Israeli prime minister, to Samuel Berger.[145] On the same day of the Israeli government's decision, Arafat sent a letter to Clinton thanking him for his ideas but asking questions. After consulting with President Mubarak of Egypt and with other Palestinian leaders, the Palestinian team formulated an official response that was presented to Clinton in a meeting with Arafat on January 2, 2001, in the White House.[146]

Arafat told the president that the Palestinians accepted his ideas but with a long list of reservations. After Arafat reviewed his reservations, "he reiterated to the president that he still wanted to get the deal done on Clinton's watch, but suggested that the two sides should continue the negotiations based not just on the president's parameters but also on Arafat's 'views.'"[147] Despite the delay in the Palestinian response and the long list of Palestinian reservations, Clinton's initial reaction was to see the Palestinian response as positive, and "Clinton believed that it was still possible, within a few days, to reach an agreement on a document in the spirit of his plan."[148] But upon further discussions within the American team, the view was that the reservations went beyond the parameters. According to Ross, the Palestinian reservations were different from the Israeli reservations in that the latter "were within the parameters, not outside them."[149]

As one Clinton White House official put it, "The administration saw [the Israeli and Palestinian reactions] too much as black and white, but there was a difference and I think all members of the team who were present at both occasions saw it extended beyond the parameters. For example, the official Israeli position was that Clinton's ideas were a 'basis of discussion'." The Israeli letter specified that "The President's ideas regarding both the Old City and Har Habayit are different from Israel's." But the American team chose to disregard the letter, seeing it as an effort to protect Barak in case the talks failed. The administration felt that Arafat's initial acceptance, in contrast to Barak's, was always qualified.

Much has been written about the timing of the Clinton ideas, coming so late in the day.[150] Certainly, one can argue that the parameters were almost bound to fail because they were put forward just before Clinton left office. If these parameters had been presented as a working American proposal at the outset of Camp David, or even in August 2000, there might have been enough time to fully explore the parties' reactions and reconvene another meeting to bridge the gap.[151] But by December, everyone was focused on the contested outcome of the American elections with the possible win by the Republican candidate, George W. Bush. Each side had to decide whether the new president would back whatever was agreed and as a consequence hand the outgoing president a crowning achievement. In Arafat's case, he believed that Bush would be more "even-handed" toward the Middle East, a view that was common in the Middle East not only among Arabs, but also among Israelis who were passionately hoping for the victory of the Gore-Lieberman ticket. But it is important to note that Arafat was also given advice to the contrary, according to the former Egyptian ambassador to the United States, Nabil Fahmy, who accompanied the Saudi ambassador to the United States, Prince Bandar. The two met with Arafat at the Ritz-Carlton Hotel in Washington during Arafat's last visit in early January 2001.[152] Bandar had just visited the president-elect in Texas to assess his stance on the Middle East as they had known each other for many years. Arafat was anxious to hear Bandar's report. Bandar reported two things to Arafat. The first was that he could not expect the new president to be more forthcoming on the Palestinian-Israeli issues; the second was that Bush would not stand in the way of an agreement if Clinton managed to clinch it before his departure. But Arafat may have had his own analysis of American politics.

Nonetheless, the Clinton Parameters remain important in historical perspective and may yet be central in future negotiations, even if they were unlikely to lead to a breakthrough in the days before Clinton left office. The ideas put forth by Clinton were the most specific and bold American positions on the two-state solution to that date. They called for a solution that allocated between 94 and 96 percent of the West Bank to an independent Palestinian state, along with all of Gaza, and a land swap of 1 to 3 percent. The capital of the Palestinian state would be in East Jerusalem with sovereignty over all Arab suburbs and the Arab quarters of the Old City, including Haram al-Sharif. Israeli security concerns would be addressed through the presence of an international force that could be withdrawn by the agreement of both Israelis and Palestinians. An agreement would clearly have marked the end of the conflict and its implementation would put an end to all claims. Clinton's ideas were particularly detailed on the issue of the Palestinian "right of return" and settlement of Palestinian refugees. Noting the importance of the "the right of return" to the Palestinians at the same time as recognizing the dilemma it posed to Israel's Jewish character, Clinton proposed that both sides would recognize the right of Palestinians to return to "historic Palestine" or to "their homeland." He identified five possible final homes for refugees: the West Bank and Gaza, areas acquired by Palestinian state through land swaps, host countries, third countries, and absorption into Israel. While settlement in the new Palestinian state would be a right for all refugees, settlement in Israel, host countries, and third countries would depend on the policies of these countries.

The impact of these ideas was already visible in the Taba negotiations that took place in February 2001. The United States played no direct role in them. Indeed, Ross argued that the real aim of the Taba talks for the Israelis may not have been an agreement.[153] Nonetheless, progress was reported beyond what was achieved at Camp David on a number of issues, but notably not on the critical issue of the Haram al-Sharif/Temple Mount. Although there is no official record of the negotiations, and certainly no American account as the United States was not represented, there is a credible unofficial account by the European Union representative of what was agreed.[154] But whatever progress was made was rendered mute by the increased violence between the Palestinians and Israelis on the ground, the huge political shifts in Israel and the United States, and the ascent of Hamas in the Palestinian territories. Above all, the belief that dominated local, regional, and global attitudes that the path started at Oslo was bound to end the conflict between Israel and the Palestinians was gone, replaced by a bet on continued conflict.

Conclusion

The failure to conclude an agreement at Camp David proved to be immensely consequential not only for the prospects of Arab-Israeli peace in the following decade but also for American foreign policy in the Middle East. The failure of the negotiations had its roots in a process dating back to the early days of diplomacy to implement the Oslo agreements—and maybe even to the terms of those agreements themselves, as noted earlier in this volume. Many of these problems were outside of American control, including the internal politics of Israel[155] and of the Palestinians, to the particular flaws of Arafat and Barak and their mutual antagonism. The assassination of Yitzhak Rabin in 1995 and the outbreak of the al-Aqsa Intifada in the fall of 2000 may have had the most consequential impact on the prospect of negotiations. The behavior of both sides, particularly the Israelis continued construction of Jewish settlements in the occupied territories and the Palestinian failure to stop suicide bombings, had an enormous impact on mutual trust and on the prospects for peace. But there were also failings of American diplomacy.

Some of these failings, particularly in the early years of Oslo have been discussed by many, including the authors in an earlier work.[156] But at Camp David, there were a number of avoidable mistakes.

First, one of the striking things about the Clinton administration's attitudes toward the negotiations, given what turned out to be the consequences of failure, was that there was little consideration of the strategic impact of the different options including the two critical decisions at the end—to blame Arafat for failure and to reject the notion that Camp David was a relatively successful episode of negotiations that could be continued in another, possibly final, round, perhaps in August or September. The mindset was that the risks at hand were simply a matter of political consequences for the president himself, and Clinton was prepared to accept that. A former senior American official put it this way, "It's more fair to say the consequence of failure was a political failure on his own part, which he [Clinton] was willing to risk, rather than a strategic failure on the country's part, which I think wasn't well mapped out."[157]

For that reason, there was no full discussion, let alone an interagency analysis, of the strategic implications of failure at Camp David for the United States, or of preferred paths for the president to take should the summit fail. Clinton White House official Bruce Riedel put it this way, "The Clinton administration saw the Arab-Israeli issue as a humanitarian and political issue but not as a national security issue and thus the national security bureaucracy was by and large not involved in decision-making. The national security principals did not meet to consider the options and the ramifications."[158]

Second, the Clinton team was unable to get more information about the bottom-line positions of both the Israelis and Palestinians before going to Camp David. Although it is not realistic to expect that either side would reveal its full hand prior to the talks, or even that they themselves knew in advance how far they were prepared to go, the lack of information on critical issues such as Jerusalem not only made it difficult to address the issue comprehensively during the summit but also made it difficult to solidify Arab support during the critical days of negotiations—which had already been made a difficult task by the limited Arab involvement in the negotiations leading up to Camp David. Had there been more preparation and had the Clinton Parameters been the type of working proposal that the United States put on the table at the outset of the Camp David negotiations, the outcome may have been different. In this respect, it is also important to note how little use was made of allied diplomacy during this period. The United States failed to keep key Arab partners, such as Egypt, Jordan, and Saudi Arabia, briefed during the Camp David Summit and thus denied itself the assistance these countries could have provided in dealing with Arafat.

Third, the American team allowed Ehud Barak to drive the agenda and the timing—sometimes against the better judgments of members of the American team. This is hard to understand, given the experience with Barak at Shepherdstown and Geneva just several months prior to Camp David.

Fourth, given the Palestinian team's inability throughout the negotiating process to formulate initiatives and proposals, Clinton would have done well to couple his promise to Arafat not to blame him in case of failure with an Arafat promise to come to the table with his own ideas and proposals. At some level, Clinton was unable to put his foot down with either Barak or Arafat in the same way that Jimmy Carter did in mediating Egyptian-Israeli peace in 1978.

Fifth, the failure to stick with a detailed American proposal, even in the face of pushback by both Israelis and Palestinians, was the most critical reason the American team lost control of the negotiating process. The Americans had not discussed with the parties or produced a draft before the summit, and then backed away from the draft tables at the summit at the first sign of resistance by the parties.

Sixth, the decision to blame Arafat at the end was flawed and consequential and reflected a lack of understanding of both Israeli and Palestinian internal politics. On the Israeli side, it may have doomed Barak's prospects in the Israeli elections. On the Palestinian side, it reinforced Arafat's biggest fears about being cornered by the United States and Israel and contributed to his most critical decision in the weeks after Camp David to embrace the al-Aqsa Intifada in the belief that violence could be used as a lever in the negotiations. In retrospect, had there been a two-week break in the negotiations as the Palestinians had requested, and a return to the table sometime in August, progress may still have been possible.[159] Even on this point, one can imagine the Clinton Parameters prepared immediately after the Camp David Summit and put on the table at the outset of a second round. Had Camp David been seen in historical perspective simply as one important round of negotiations, rather than as an end-all summit, it would have been assessed as a remarkably successful episode, where historic compromises were put on the table, and issues that were considered taboo in the past, such as Jerusalem and refugees, were discussed. In the end, however, the Clinton administration went along with Barak in rejecting the idea of another round of negotiations. The irony in this narrative is that Israelis and Palestinians took another shot at these negotiations on their own at Taba, Egypt, in January 2001, by which time it was clearly too late.

CHAPTER FOUR

GEORGE W. BUSH RESHAPES AMERICA'S ROLE

George W. Bush was a president with a new approach to foreign policy, a leader conscious of his predecessor's failed peace bids, and a commander-in-chief who was seized after 9/11 with a missionary zeal to fight terrorism and to transform the broader Middle East. Taken together with the difficult negotiating environment during his first term, these factors aligned to set the stage for a dramatic departure from the post-1973 American approach. For three decades, the United States conventionally placed priority on Arab-Israeli diplomacy and emphasized active mediation. Bush returned to Ronald Reagan's more hands-off policy. Intense internal divides also characterized foreign policy debates within his administration. Infighting left its stamp on U.S. policy, at times leading to inaction and weak follow-through, and at other times imposing limitations as policy settled on the lowest common denominator. Dissension also provided additional openings for outside actors to lobby and to shop around for the most sympathetic ear within the administration.

This chapter and the next offer both a critical analysis of and new insider information about the Arab-Israeli policies of the Bush 43 years.

Bush's Background

Bush had campaigned against much of the Clinton foreign policy legacy and as his advisers (the "Vulcans") scorned multilateralism, arms control, "nation-building," and the Oslo process. Therefore, it was no surprise that he would turn decisively away from Bill Clinton's policies—not to mention his father's own legacy of internationalism.[1] "You had a desire to differentiate . . . from both presidents," according to one former American official.[2] In the campaign, Bush was critical of Clinton's "nation-building" endeavors and his diplomatic dealings with authoritarian leaders and unsavory regimes. He implied that he would pursue a more restrained foreign policy. For example, in a debate with Al Gore, the Democratic Party candidate, Bush stated, "I think what we need to do is convince people who live in the lands they live in to build the nations. Maybe I'm missing something here . . . I mean, are we going to have some kind of nation-building corps from America? Absolutely not."[3] Bush entered office with a strong unilateralist streak, having promised to withdraw from the Anti-Ballistic Missile (ABM) Treaty and having pledged to undo Clinton's commitment to multilateralism and international institutions. These signals to the Republican neoconservative wing contrasted with a more traditional Republican emphasis on managing "Great Power" relations.[4]

It is stunning how different Bush 43 was from Bush 41 in his attitude toward the Middle East. George H.W. Bush was a traditional "realist" in orientation; his son was a throwback to the more elementary view, a Ronald Reagan school of American politics that defines the world in terms of good and evil, right and wrong. Of course, compared to his father, George W. Bush was more conservative, more Texan, and more driven by religion. He was heavily influenced by neoconservative ideas and the 9/11 trauma. Moreover, he took office as head of a party that in the eight years since it lost the White House had itself become far more aligned toward Israel's policies, perhaps even the Likud's version of those policies. Others who had served in the first Bush administration, most prominently Vice President Dick Cheney, would reemerge in far more strident incarnations. Some, such as National Security Council (NSC) staffer Elliott Abrams, worked tirelessly to reorient U.S. involvement in Arab-Israeli affairs and to make a clean break from the approach that Nixon and Kissinger pioneered in the early 1970s, an approach that had been followed by every administration since then.

Bill Clinton and the Oslo process were held in particular disdain by Abrams and a cadre of neoconservative advisers.[5] This cadre was highly motivated and its views reinforced the president's own predisposition not to engage. This orientation closely aligned with Israel's own conservative camp, which would dominate Israeli foreign policy during the initial Bush years. At its core was a deep-seated skepticism that Arabs would ever accept the legitimacy of Israel.[6] It was Clinton's parting advice, together with the public blame heaped on Arafat, that even further emboldened the neoconservative view—both about the shortcomings of the traditional American approach and their own distrust of Arab intentions.

Bush's policies led to few measurable election gains; his support among Jewish-Americans increased by 6 percent from 2000 to 2004, according to the Pew Research Center.[7] In the same period, however, he gained 10 percent of the Evangelical vote, partly owing to his support for Israel.[8] This raises a puzzle for some of his closest advisers. No doubt his policies on Israel reinforced support among a small cadre of major Jewish donors, such as Mel Sembler and Sheldon Adelson. But more important, his approach aligned with a major shift in Republican politics. By the mid-1990s, there was a growing indifference, even hostility, within the Republican Party—especially Evangelical Christian activists and neoconservatives—toward the notion of pressuring Israel or establishing a Palestinian state (which was gaining traction internationally and within the Democratic Party).

The Bush 43 presidency thus marks a turning point in the politics of U.S.–Middle East policy, with strong currents pulling Republicans away from the more realpolitik, activist approaches of Nixon, Ford, and Bush 41, which placed a high priority on Arab-Israeli peacemaking. The September 11 attacks accelerated this growing partisan shift, with Bush and many of his supporters seeing the "root causes" of terrorism and anti-Americanism as emanating from the region's democratic deficit, a position also championed by Israeli prime minister Benjamin Netanyahu in his address to a joint congressional session in 1996.

Until late in the administration, the president rejected any notion that the Arab-Israeli conflict was linked to a solution for other problems elsewhere in the region.[9] As had progressively become the pattern, the Republicans in Congress and in several pro-Israel groups—Jewish and Christian alike—would oppose policies and even at times agreements designed to promote the peace process through congressional resolutions and strong statements. Bush pursued his own path, and his views usually coincided with those of his supporters. But it would be an overstatement to suggest that his policies were defined by core constituencies, especially Evangelical Christians, who advocated on a wide variety of issues, mostly domestic. Since the administration never succeeded in pushing the peace process forward in a measurable way, however, he never had to worry about strong and organized opposition to his policies. Instead, the preconceptions of Bush and his top advisers determined the direction in which policy toward the Arab-Israeli dispute moved.

"Anyone But Arafat"

U.S. policy on the peace process—already severely challenged by worsening Palestinian Intifada violence and Israeli responses—was effectively in limbo as George W. Bush entered office. "Condi [Condoleezza Rice] and Steve [Hadley] had previewed in the week [before the inauguration] that there was going to be a change from peacemaking to conflict management," said senior NSC official Bruce Riedel; "they would also put it in terms of 'this President's going to need time to decide what his policy is.'"[10]

Many in the Arab world assumed—wrongly—that George W. Bush would pursue an activist and less pro-Israel approach to the Middle East as his father had done—and thus they were pleased at the outcome of the contested U.S. election. But Arab leaders would be in for an unwelcome surprise. True, early statements by the White House and the State Department sought to contain the fighting and promote the idea of a cease-fire. The strongest defender of engagement early on was Secretary of State Colin Powell, who came to office with a more traditional, activist orientation and was given broader latitude in the early months of the administration.

However, Bush's own predispositions against active mediation efforts were reinforced by the chaos unfolding on the ground, as well as his predecessor's parting advice. Vice President Cheney reports that on Inauguration Day, Clinton spoke at length to him and Bush about the Middle East and repeatedly blamed Arafat for the failure of the negotiations.[11]

On January 30, 2001, ten days into the new administration, the president met for the first time with the principal officials of his NSC. He made it clear he had no intention of continuing intensive Arab-Israeli diplomacy. "We are going to correct the imbalances of the previous administration on the Mideast conflict. We're going to tilt it back toward Israel," reports Bush treasury secretary Paul O'Neill, who was present. "And we're going to be consistent. Clinton overreached, and it all fell apart. That's why we're in trouble."[12] Recalling his helicopter tour with Ariel Sharon, "Looked real bad down there," Bush said. "I don't see much we can do over there at this point. I think it's time to pull out of that situation," O'Neill reports the president saying.[13] Powell protested that disengagement by the United States would equate with allowing an unhindered Sharon to derail any hope of peace negotiations and use extreme Israeli military force against the Palestinians. Bush mused, "Maybe that's the best way to get things back into balance. Sometimes a show of strength by one side can really clarify things."[14]

In early February, following Sharon's election, the administration publicly affirmed that the Clinton Parameters were no longer U.S. policy.[15] Of course, Clinton had made that decision easier by declaring that the parameters would not be operational after he left office. For some, Sharon's election placed a damper on any hope for renewed peacemaking. "Ariel Sharon was not elected to bring peace with the Palestinians," Rice said in retrospect.[16] In addition to disavowing the Clinton plan, the Bush administration was careful not to appoint a special envoy in order to ensure no parallels could be drawn with Clinton, who relied heavily on Dennis Ross in that role.

Bush reports that he spoke to Arafat three times in his first year as president; the first time in February 2001. "He was courteous, and I was polite in return. But I made clear we expected him to crack down on extremism."[17] At Sharon's first meeting with Bush in mid-March, he was warned by the new president not to expand settlements. It was not surprising for an American president to oppose settlements. But Bush also sounded a different note, signaling a turning away from the Clinton approach and the notion that the United States would put forward a peace plan. In a brief joint appearance, Bush stated, "I assured the prime minister my administration . . . will not try to force peace."[18] Bush reportedly also assured Sharon in private that the United States would protect Israel by force if needed—much to Sharon's astonishment and pleasant surprise.[19]

Ambassador Martin Indyk reports that during a private lunch, Sharon spoke to the president at length about terrorism, Osama Bin Laden, Hezbollah, and Iran in particular. He argued that terror "is a strategic threat to regional stability in the Middle East."[20] As Indyk reports, Sharon urged the president to "lead a coalition of Western states" in the fight against terrorism. The prime minister warned that it would be highly dangerous not to do so. Sharon's arguments may have presaged Bush's later policy after 9/11, but at the time, "Sharon's appeal fell on deaf ears. The president simply smiled and said nothing."[21]

In a larger meeting with aides, Sharon reinforced his reputation as iron-fisted. Speaking of Palestinian terrorists, he promised to "remove them from our society." Later, Bush remarked to Indyk, "I think we've got the picture, . . . there's no Nobel Peace Prize to be had here."[22] When Sharon was elected in early 2001, he did not appear to be a leader with whom the United States could easily work. But a combination of Arafat's misdeeds, the post-9/11 context, and Sharon's somewhat surprising willingness to make concessions at critical periods that helped turn Bush decidedly toward Israel. It did not hurt Sharon that as foreign minister he had hosted Bush on his first trip to Israel in 1998. Bush was predisposed to give Sharon the benefit of doubt because of this meeting, where Sharon took Bush on the helicopter tour of the immediate area and made clear his policies. "He said that when he took that tour and he looked down, he thought, 'We have driveways in Texas longer than that,'" said Ari Fleischer, a former White House press secretary. "And after the United States was attacked, he understood how it was for Israel to be attacked."[23] Thus, during Sharon's first prime ministerial visit, Bush told Sharon that he would use force to protect Israel. One person present later commented that it "was kind of a shock to everybody . . . It was like, 'Whoa, where did that come from?'"[24]

Despite Bush's intention to radically alter the U.S. approach, Powell prevailed in convincing the president that it was important to try to end the violence—both the Palestinians' escalating terrorist attacks and Israel's harsh retaliatory responses. As the situation worsened over the spring and into the summer, U.S. efforts to achieve a cease-fire gradually increased. For Arab leaders, months and months of nonstop media coverage and a mounting Palestinian death toll led to demands that Washington take stronger actions. In April, King Abdullah of Jordan appealed to Bush during a White House meeting to end the violence. Although Bush declined to get personally involved, Powell was charged with trying to contain the fighting. The Israeli Defense Forces (IDF) made their first extended incursion into Gaza in mid-April, entering areas of exclusive Palestinian control (dubbed "Area A" per the 1995 Interim Agreement) but withdrew almost immediately following a stern warning from Powell.[25]

But Sharon was also careful to cultivate Bush and administration hard-liners, even portraying himself as a moderate. Indeed, in a meeting with an American official shortly after he became prime minister, Sharon explained that the United States would be able to work with him. He argued that he was not of the left (like Ehud Barak) or the right (like Benjamin Netanyahu), but a centrist, as the United States would discover.[26]

Four months after Bush became president, one of Clinton's final acts returned to the spotlight. The previous October, at an emergency summit in Sharm el-Sheikh with Mubarak, Barak, and Arafat, Clinton had committed the United States to organize an international fact-finding committee charged with examining events surrounding the outbreak of violence in late September. The effort, which came to be known as the Mitchell Commission, as it was led by former senate majority leader George Mitchell, concluded with a final report released in early May 2001 in New York.[27] The commission did not lay sole blame for the violence on Sharon's visit to the Temple Mount, as Arabs had claimed; nor did it point a finger solely at Arafat, as Israelis and many pro-Israel supporters in the United States had done. The report's recommendations included a complete Israeli settlement freeze and a Palestinian clampdown on violence as preconditions for resuming negotiations.[28]

In perhaps its first real test, the administration embraced the report, but without making clear where the United States stood on some of the more controversial issues, such as a settlement freeze.[29] In May, Powell named Assistant Secretary William Burns as a special emissary and again appealed to Israelis and Palestinians for an unconditional cease-fire. But Powell also went out of his way to emphasize that Washington would not be "putting forward a peace plan."[30] In the following months, Mitchell's recommendations for ending the violence would be reinforced by at least two additional envoys—George Tenet, director of Central Intelligence, and Anthony Zinni, retired Marine Corps general. Tenet's ideas to restore security cooperation were quite pragmatic, based in part on his experience following the 1998 Wye River Memorandum, when Clinton asked the Central Intelligence Agency (CIA) to play a central role in maintaining security ties between the two sides.

But the cycle of violence between Israelis and Palestinians steadily intensified, and the administration's narrowly defined efforts to achieve a cease-fire were often lost in the carnage. A June 1 suicide bombing at a Tel Aviv disco killed twenty-one young Israelis, mostly teenagers. Under U.S. pressure, Sharon showed restraint, but the mood in Israel was turning grim. In June, a divide was emerging between the Bush administration and Sharon on how to get to the "cooling-off" period called for in the Mitchell report. Sharon was not enthusiastic about the report, especially the recommendation for a complete settlement freeze. Sharon's call for "absolute quiet" before diplomacy could begin was viewed by some in Washington as a major impediment and an unrealistic expectation.[31]

By late June, Sharon continued to dig in his heels. Following a meeting with Bush in Washington, the Israeli leader began to speak of "ten days of quiet," in contrast with the administration's emphasis on bringing down the violence to a "realistic" level.[32] Even before Sharon left Washington, Powell traveled to the region to see Arafat and to meet with other Israeli leaders, including foreign minister Shimon Peres. On the trip, Powell emphasized the importance of the Mitchell report, "describing it as embraced fully by the international community."[33] Still, U.S. efforts seemed to go nowhere.

Israel was uneasy with Powell's diplomacy, as well as with the Mitchell and Tenet plans, largely over the question of sequencing. Sharon would not budge from his insistence that Palestinian violence must end before a political process could be resumed.

Despite Bush's disinclination to get involved, outside pressures kept building. For months, Saudi crown prince Abdullah was the administration's harshest critic among Washington's Arab partners. In an extraordinary July phone call initiated by former president Bush, with the sitting president in the room, Bush 41 reassured Abdullah that his son's "heart was in the right place" when it came to the Middle East.[34]

But it was Sharon, not Arab leaders, who was making the strongest inroads with the new president. Despite Powell's efforts to press for a cease-fire and pursue an even-handed approach, Bush spoke out in August in what was interpreted as the administration fully accepting Israel's preconditions for renewed negotiations—and placing full blame for the ongoing crisis on the Palestinians. "The Israelis will not negotiate under terrorist threat," said Bush.[35] As suggested by the president's statement, it was difficult for Arafat to gain much sympathy in the United States because of the Palestinian turn toward violence, considered by most Americans—even before 9/11—as meaning that it was the Palestinians who had caused the crisis in Israeli-Palestinian relations.

Almost immediately, this perceived alignment with Sharon generated a furious response from Saudi Arabia. In a lengthy letter hand-delivered by longtime Saudi ambassador Prince Bandar, Abdullah challenged the White House to do more. If not, Abdullah threatened, Riyadh would reconsider the very nature of its ties with Washington.[36] As a sign of their seriousness, the Saudis even cancelled planned defense exchanges with Washington.

The Bush White House was alarmed. In a hastily drafted two-page response, the president assured Abdullah that the United States remained committed to a peace settlement. He further stated, "I firmly believe the Palestinian people have a right to self-determination and to live peacefully and safely in their own state."[37] The crown prince reacted favorably to Bush's reply, and the two governments reportedly began discussing how to turn Bush's assurances into public pronouncements.[38]

Although some observers, typically Bush defenders, point to this letter as a major breakthrough in U.S. policy—a step that would foreshadow the president's post-9/11 public endorsement of Palestinian statehood—it was still a half-measure, designed to buy time and calm the Saudis rather than break new ground in advancing those Palestinian aspirations for statehood. According to an American official, "The motive was basically to get the Saudis to climb down out of the tree and it wasn't to break a huge amount of new ground conceptually."[39] Confrontation with Riyadh would come again on this issue the following spring, but for the time being a crisis of confidence was averted.

The Post-9/11 World

The restored relative calm in U.S.-Saudi relations was shattered just days later by a new but far more serious crisis: the September 11th terrorist attacks on New York and Washington, in which most of the attackers were Saudi citizens. In the aftermath of the attacks, world leaders rushed to offer their support to Washington. Messages from Israel were extremely sympathetic, as could be expected. Arafat sought to join the chorus of condemnation of the attackers, even offering to personally donate blood to assist the rescue efforts. Syria's new president, Bashar al-Asad, promised support to Bush and cooperated in sharing intelligence on al-Qaeda and Islamist militants.[40]

Amid the disarray of dealing with the horror of 9/11 and before a full-fledged strategy could be developed, there was an immediate sense in the administration that ongoing Israeli-Palestinian fighting had to be addressed more visibly in order to garner as much regional support as possible for its counter-terrorism efforts. This was not a carefully tested theory, but rather a snap judgment. Meanwhile, there had been long-standing demands from the Europeans and Arabs for greater American involvement in the peace process.

Israel suddenly announced an end to offensive military operations and began to pull back from Palestinian areas that were recently reoccupied, reportedly following "severe" U.S. pressure. For his part, Arafat declared a Palestinian cease-fire. Although months of on-again, off-again U.S. efforts had failed to produce a cease-fire and restart peace talks, the 9/11 attacks clearly caught the attention of Arabs and Israelis.[41] But the lull would not last. Palestinian violence quickly resumed. Sharon would also revive his demands for absolute "quiet."

Just two weeks after the attacks, the U.S.-Jordan Free Trade Agreement was ratified and signed into law, after languishing for some time. The immediate post-9/11 diplomatic environment therefore understandably worried Sharon. He was nervous, fearing Israel would be asked to pay the price of improved American ties with the Arab world. In a speech in early October, Sharon compared Bush to Neville Chamberlain appeasing Hitler, causing a bitter, if brief, row with the White House. "I call on the Western democracies," Sharon said, "and primarily the leader of the Free World, the United States, do not repeat the dreadful mistake of 1938 when Europe sacrificed Czechoslovakia. Do not try to appease the Arabs at our expense. Israel will not be Czechoslovakia. Israel will fight terrorism."[42] Sharon's speech elicited an enraged rebuke from the White House, and he was forced to apologize for his outburst.[43]

Some analysts predicted a new crisis in American-Israeli relations, given the presumed pressure on the United States to enhance relations with the Arabs, following 9/11. In their first phone call after the attacks, Bush asked Sharon to allow foreign minister Peres to meet with Arafat, an idea that was floated previously but vetoed by Sharon. A meeting, Washington believed, might calm the situation and project the right signal as the United States planned its response to the catastrophic terror attacks. But Sharon refused again.[44] The U.S. ambassador to Israel, Daniel Kurtzer, met afterward with Sharon and pressed him again to agree to Bush's request. Sharon demurred, saying he feared the United States would then ask Israel to do more.[45] But he soon relented, and Peres met Arafat on September 26. Three days before, in a speech in Latrun, Sharon for the first time expressed support for a Palestinian "state."[46]

It turns out Sharon need not have worried about his relationship with Washington. "9/11 strengthened Sharon's hand," said a former American official, "and it strengthened the hand of the others in the administration who didn't want to do [the peace process] at all."[47] By mid-October, following the assassination of Israel's minister of tourism, Rehavam Ze'evi, by the Popular Front for the Liberation of Palestine (PFLP), Israel was again ready for major military actions against Palestinians. Israel identified the perpetrators and informed Arafat through intermediaries, but Arafat refused to act. As a consequence, Sharon's tough response, including targeted assassinations, elicited barely a criticism from Washington. Indeed, 9/11 had quietly ushered in a new American approach to counter-terrorism: whereas the United States had traditionally opposed targeted assassinations, after 9/11 the United States dropped its opposition and tacitly approved Israeli actions.

But then on November 10, 2001, Bush announced that his administration was prepared to support a two-state solution. "We are working toward the day when two states—Israel and Palestine—live peacefully together within secure and recognized borders as called for by the Security Council resolutions," Bush said before the United Nations General Assembly.[48] Other than Bill Clinton's brief endorsement in his late December 2000 parameters and a stray comment by Bush to a group of congressmen, this was the first time Washington went formally on record in support of a sovereign Palestinian state.[49]

In retrospect, the statement at the UN was more an early indication of the administration's trust in speeches and stated policy rather than a sign of renewed commitment to negotiate Arab-Israeli peace. Given how little progress was subsequently achieved and given what is now known about the depth of resistance inside the administration to Arab-Israeli peacemaking, the endorsement of statehood in a speech largely devoted to 9/11 and the war in Afghanistan suggests that Bush was ready to use the term when Sharon had already done so.[50] But in reality, he acted as if he did not much care about the Palestinian state. By contrast, Clinton may not have talked a lot about a Palestinian state, but he treated Arafat as if he were the head of one.

On November 19, Secretary Powell made a major speech in Louisville, where he elaborated on Bush's recent endorsement of a two-state solution. After an extensive discussion of the issues in dispute, he said clearly, "Israel must be willing to end its occupation, consistent with the principles embodied in Security Council Resolutions 242 and 338, and accept a viable Palestinian state in which Palestinians can determine their own future on their own land and live in dignity and security. They, too, will have to make hard compromises."[51]

But Powell had to struggle to give the speech; National Security Advisor Rice was trying to postpone the address up to the last moment.[52] "The White House vetting ensured [the speech] would break no new ground," said Powell adviser Aaron Miller.[53] Powell was able to announce the appointment of former U.S. Central

Command (CENTCOM) commander, retired marine general Anthony Zinni, as a special security emissary. As a military figure, it was felt that Zinni would carry considerable weight, especially with the Israelis. As a former CENTCOM commander, he also had close relationships with many Arab leaders.

From the outset of his mission, there were signs that Zinni's political support would be limited. There was an impression, said Zinni, that the effort to achieve a cease-fire and renew negotiations did not have a "White House seal of approval."[54] "[It] became clear to everybody in the region, both the Palestinians and particularly the Israelis . . . that this was Secretary Powell's [project] and when they weren't happy with something, they made end-runs around the Secretary."[55]

November and December 2001 were particularly deadly months, with scores of Israelis killed in suicide bombings and intensifying Israeli retaliatory strikes, including against Arafat's headquarters. Zinni, accompanied by Ross's former deputy, Aaron Miller, shuttled repeatedly between Israelis and Palestinians, and also visited several Arab capitals. Some modest steps were taken, including Arafat's closure of Hamas and Islamic Jihad offices, and partial Israeli military withdrawals in some West Bank cities. But the situation remained extraordinarily tense, as the Palestinian attacks continued and as Israel moved in December to isolate Arafat in his West Bank offices. An uneasy cease-fire went into effect in mid-December. On December 30, four Israeli soldiers killed six Palestinians whom the army accused of preparing to attack Israeli settlements in the Gaza strip.

Bush's Break with Arafat

The administration's efforts to stop the violence and resume a political process were interrupted by Israel's capture of a ship containing arms destined for the Palestinians, the Karine A, in early January 2002. After the Israeli navy captured the ship, they waited to announce the seizure and the evidence of Arafat's complicity. Zinni returned to Israel on January 3 and was briefed on the arms ship by Sharon and his defense advisers. He asked Sharon to let him break the news to Arafat in person, when he traveled the next day to Ramallah. Sharon agreed. Zinni confronted Arafat, but the Palestinian leader waved off the incident as an Israeli setup, even going so far as denying any Palestinian involvement in a letter he later wrote to President Bush.[56] Yet Israel had amassed more than enough evidence to implicate top Palestinian officials, which it used to press its case against Arafat with the Bush administration. This act was a major issue because under the terms of the Oslo Accords, Arafat was not allowed to bring in arms.

The Karine A episode "put Sharon in a great bargaining position in his [Bush's] mind," said Zinni, who reported that his Palestinian counterparts—clearly embarrassed at being caught red-handed—were much more cooperative afterward. "They had egg on their face," said the U.S. envoy.[57] Sharon sought to use the Karine A to his advantage in bargaining with the United States and the Palestinians. He was successful. For Bush and his team, the Karine A affair was a turning point—one that culminated in Bush's June 24, 2002, speech calling for "new" Palestinian leadership. If there was suspicion toward Arafat before the Karine A, then afterward it became outright distrust and hostility. "The Karine A fed into the anti-terrorist vision, or policy," said NSC adviser Elliott Abram; "the President had no relationship with Arafat anyway."[58] Rice further stated, "Then an incident in the Red Sea cemented our already dim view of Arafat's 'leadership.' I never met him, and neither did the President, but it was absolutely clear that he was not going to lead his people to peace . . . In January 2002 we added 'committed terrorist' to the list of offenses."[59] One could argue that this is an odd conclusion from the Karine A incident. It demonstrated that Arafat was devious, not a man of his word, a liar, and so on, but it did not actually show anything new about whether he was a committed terrorist. For that conclusion, the evidence was much older.

Vice President Cheney was taken "aback," according to a former American official, who said there was also evidence of connections to Hezbollah terrorist Imad Mugniyah and Iran's Islamic Revolutionary Guard Corps. "Our office pushed very hard for as robust a response as possible," he added.[60] "There was no doubt in my mind," Cheney writes in his memoir, that Arafat was responsible.[61]

"Arafat sent a letter pleading his innocence," says Bush, "But we and the Israelis had evidence that disproved the Palestinian leader's claim. Arafat had lied to me. I never trusted him again. In fact, I never spoke to him again. By the spring of 2002, I had concluded that peace would not be possible with Arafat in power."[62]

In early 2002, the administration's divide on how to deal with Arafat was worsening. Powell still felt it was necessary to engage Arafat. Others, including Cheney and secretary of defense Donald Rumsfeld, did not, and increasingly the president himself disagreed with Powell as well. Sharon and his government encouraged the administration to cultivate other Palestinian interlocutors, but it would still be some months before the White House formally gave up on Arafat once and for all.

Sharon did not make it easy for the administration, but it was still Arafat's repeated failures and misdeeds that led Bush to an increasingly uncritical relationship with Israel. Arafat, as seen within the administration, could not be trusted.[63] "Sharon was chomping at the bit throughout these months to do something against Arafat," Ambassador Kurtzer said. "The administration made it clear Arafat could not be harmed or exiled, but Karine A gave Sharon the opportunity to make Arafat persona non grata in the peace process."[64]

There were other developments at the time that might have been interpreted differently by another administration—one less traumatized by 9/11 and less riven with internal fault lines. On January 14, 2002, Israel broke the month-long cease-fire by assassinating Raed Karmi, who had been involved in numerous attacks against Israelis as an operative of Tanzim, a militant faction of the Fatah movement. By then, the Karine A crisis had erupted and the first Israeli deaths of the year occurred on January 9, when two Palestinian gunmen raided an Israeli outpost in the Gaza Strip and killed four Israeli soldiers before they were subsequently killed. Though the Palestinian Authority (PA) condemned the assault, Sharon held Arafat personally responsible.

The Karmi targeted killing was widely viewed as a sign of Israeli escalation. And there is no doubt that Sharon exploited the Karine A incident to rally American support. "I had proof," Sharon said later in an interview, "Arafat is the father of terror. He's the initiator of terror . . . It proved without doubt Arafat was directly linked to terrorism. He was arming himself against us. We found so many weapons . . . The tables have turned. They used to put pressure on me. Now it will be him."[65]

Throughout winter 2002, as Colin Powell and his emissary General Zinni pressed for a cease-fire, the violence and counter-violence dynamic on the ground intensified. In February, Saudi crown prince Abdullah revealed details of a new peace initiative, which would become known as the Arab Peace Initiative (API) at the late March Arab League summit in Beirut. Abdullah's plan was notable in that he tied a two-state solution along the 1967 lines to full Arab normalization with Israel. On the surface, it appeared to be a breakthrough—having Saudi Arabia's de facto leader extend an olive branch to Israel amidst what by then was a year and a half of unremitting violence. But it was brushed aside by Sharon, who was coping with the worst month of suicide bombing thus far, and barely noticed by the Bush administration.[66]

March was a particularly deadly month for Israelis—139 were killed in Palestinian attacks—leading to demonstrations and a government decision to build a "separation barrier."[67] In the middle of the month, Vice President Cheney went on a major Middle East tour to build support for the administration's anti-terrorism campaign and to discuss military action against Iraq. Toward the end of Cheney's trip, he visited Israel but did not meet with Arafat. Cheney held out the possibility of seeing the Palestinian leader but attached a series of conditions about ending violence and adopting the Tenet security plan.[68] Cheney's offer was designed to balance out Sharon's tough position, which effectively had Arafat cornered.

Throughout Cheney's tour, Arab leaders complained about the lack of American engagement and appealed to Cheney to convince Israel to allow Arafat to travel to the forthcoming Beirut summit meeting where the Arab Peace Initiative (API) would be approved. In the end, Cheney did not see Arafat, and Sharon did not allow the Palestinian leader to travel. Despite the tough line on Arafat, Cheney's visit did seem to exert a degree of restraint on Sharon, who ordered limited Israeli military withdrawals in the West Bank at the end of the vice president's trip.

By late March the pressure was building on all sides. General Zinni was pressing the Israelis and Palestinians to accept a cease-fire in light of the increasing violence, but to no avail. Despite pressure from the international community and many Arab states, Sharon approved a cease-fire proposal that Zinni negotiated with the two parties for weeks, but Arafat could not bring himself to accept it and time ran out.[69]

The Arab League's adoption of Abdullah's peace plan in Beirut became inseparable from a horrific Palestinian suicide bombing the next day in the Israeli town of Netanya, killing scores of Israelis celebrating the Passover Seder at a local hotel. Violence against Israeli civilians had been escalating for months, but the scale and setting of the Netanya suicide attack shocked the world. Under intense U.S. and international pressure, Arafat immediately called for a cease-fire and pledged to adopt the Tenet plan. But it was too late. The bombing sparked Sharon to launch a massive military assault to reoccupy major Palestinian cities in the West Bank. The Israelis had had enough. The Bush administration was not interested in restraining Israel because key officials, including the president, were outraged by the attack, even if they sensed the political and diplomatic problems the Israeli retaliation would create.

In the wake of the Netanya bombing, Zinni returned to the United States for his daughter's wedding and did not return to the region. The administration's conclusion that it was not possible to do business with Arafat was intensifying.[70]

"I was appalled by the violence and loss of life on both sides," Bush writes of this period in his memoir, "but I refused to accept the moral equivalence between Palestinian suicide attacks on innocent civilians and Israeli military actions intended to protect their people. My views came into sharper focus after 9/11. If the United States had the right to defend itself and prevent future attacks, other democracies had those rights, too."[71]

The Quartet Is Born

If there was ever a moment of truth in Bush's early encounters with the Arab-Israeli realm, it would be in the wake of the Netanya bombing and Israel's reoccupation of the West Bank. The level of violence spiked, the death toll was rising, Israeli forces surrounded Arafat's headquarters in Ramallah, and Palestinian militants holed up in Bethlehem's Church of the Nativity—causing deep concern among Christian communities worldwide. There was also widespread apprehension that Arafat would be killed by the Israelis and a growing fear that violence could spill over into neighboring countries. The administration went into high gear and over a five-week period used a variety of means to pull Israelis and Palestinians back from the brink. This period showed what the administration could accomplish when focused, but it also revealed many fundamental weaknesses—a disengaged president, an administration at war with itself, and an inability to follow through and to execute its own policies.

Bush made a dramatic statement from the Rose Garden on April 4, which demonstrated disillusionment with Arafat but not the Palestinian cause. The president denounced terrorism and placed blame squarely on Arafat ("the situation in which he finds himself today is largely of his own making"). Yet he reaffirmed support for a two-state solution and called for a "viable" Palestinian state. Bush had words of praise for the Saudi peace plan but also chastised Arab states for not recognizing Israel or confronting terrorism ("It is not enough for Arab nations to defend the Palestinian cause. They must truly help the Palestinian people by seeking peace and fighting terror.")[72] Although Bush's statement applauded the Saudi initiative, the American government did nothing to build the initiative up, instead simply chastising the Arabs for not doing more. By taking the approach to the Saudi plan that it did, Washington allowed an intriguing opportunity to slip through its grasp.

The themes that came through the strongest in his statement were Bush's condemnation of terrorism, evocative of 9/11 ("suicide bombing missions could well blow up the best and only hope for a Palestinian state"), and Israel's legitimate right to respond ("America recognizes Israel's right to defend itself from terror"). Yet the president called on Israel to halt its campaign. He demanded an "immediate cease-fire."[73] Asked later in the week about his call on Israel to stop its military assault, Bush added "without delay." Asked later by reporters to elaborate on Bush's demand, Rice said "it means now."[74]

In the April 4 speech, the president also announced that Secretary Powell would be dispatched to the region in an effort to halt the escalation and achieve a cease-fire. Some in the administration—such as Secretary Rumsfeld—opposed sending Powell. On his way to the region, Powell first sought to build a broader international consensus about how to reach a cease-fire and resume negotiations. This effort led to one lasting achievement from this period, the formation of the diplomatic "Quartet"—the United States, the European Union, Russia, and the United Nations—in mid-April. Sensing a need for greater multilateral coordination, and increasingly boxed in at home, Powell launched the Quartet in Spain and the ad hoc grouping quickly became the prime vehicle for coordinating international policy on the Arab-Israeli issue.[75]

Powell met with Sharon on April 12, and then with Arafat in his besieged compound in Ramallah on April 14. In the meeting with Arafat, Powell told him that the administration's patience was at an end; he would be the last administration official Arafat would ever see if Palestinian violence did not cease.[76] Arafat promised to act, but he never satisfied the administration and never again saw a high-ranking American official in the two-and-a-half years he had to live. Powell had hinted to Arafat that he himself did not even have full support within the administration to see the Palestinian leader, and indeed administration infighting hampered Powell's mission from the outset.

According to a senior American official, "Everyday [Powell was] getting these course corrections out of the NSC, which reflected the bulk of the thinking within the Administration" and that thinking did not agree with Powell.[77] Before departing, Powell had hoped to announce that a peace conference would be convened. However, Stephen Hadley, the deputy national security advisor, "called to tell the Secretary he was not going to be authorized to give a statement that included explicit reference to a political process . . . [Rumsfeld and Cheney] were not willing to support this idea, they were also taking a lot of heat over this domestically from the pro-Israel community and from the President's conservative base." There followed a call from Rice emphasizing that Powell did not have the authorization; Powell was "very agitated," but all he could do was gloss over the failure of his mission in his press conference.[78]

At a Quartet meeting in Washington in early May, Powell again tried to move forward with the notion of an international conference—getting international buy-in where he lacked support from his own colleagues. "We discussed how best to begin to prepare for an international conference meeting this [past] summer," Powell told a news conference after meeting with his Quartet counterparts. But according to Vice President Cheney, Powell had overstepped his guidance from the White House. "The president had not agreed to this and it was a bad idea," Cheney writes in his memoir, adding that he told Rice to inform Powell that he was "once more out of line with the president's policy."[79]

After Powell's abortive April mission and the May flap, Rice effectively took over the Israeli-Palestinian account for the rest of the term, establishing a secret channel with Sharon's top aide, Dov Weissglas. Still, the administration's efforts continued to seem disjointed. Bush's repeated calls on the Israelis to pull back fell on deaf ears, though private warnings to Israel against killing or deporting Arafat were more effective.[80] More typically, in the middle of Powell's trip, the president surprised many by calling Sharon a "man of peace" on April 18.[81] As the administration's own messaging seemed pulled in two directions, Jewish-American advocacy groups were gearing up for a renewed campaign of "solidarity" with Israel. Days before Bush's statement about Sharon, a massive rally was held in Washington featuring strident speeches by former New York mayor Rudy Giuliani, former Israeli prime minister Benjamin Netanyahu, and others. The Bush administration was represented by Deputy Secretary of Defense Paul Wolfowitz, who was booed and drowned out with chants of "No More Arafat" when his remarks touched on Palestinian suffering.[82]

As the administration was facing political pressure at home from Israel advocates to give the Jewish state a free hand, it was also confronting mounting diplomatic pressure to end the fighting. This pressure peaked in late April 2002, when Saudi Crown Prince Abdullah visited Bush at his ranch in Texas and sought immediate action. Referring to Sharon, the crown prince asked Bush, "When will the pig leave Ramallah?"[83] Abdullah gave Bush an eight-point plan for an Israeli pullback, and when Bush gave no sign he would do more to pressure Sharon, the crown prince asked to consult his foreign minister and ambassador privately. A few minutes later Bush heard from his translator and adviser, Gamal Helal, that the Saudi team was preparing to leave in frustration.

"Does it matter if they leave," Bush asked Rice, who responded that "it would be a disaster."[84] Bush offered the crown prince a tour of his ranch because his briefing notes suggested that the Saudi leader "loved his farm." Abdullah accepted and the tour began immediately. When they reached a remote part of the property, a wild turkey was blocking the road. Bush reports that the crown prince grabbed his arm suddenly and said, "My brother, it is a sign from Allah. This is a good omen."[85] Meanwhile, Powell pressed Bandar to stay. "This will take some time," he told Bandar, "The President is engaged and we'll get this resolved and [the crown prince] can't simply leave and get in [his] plane and fly away."[86] Asked by Bush to help resolve the standoff, Rice retreated to other quarters to negotiate by phone with British and Israeli colleagues about the siege on Arafat's compound.[87] Whether Powell's intervention or the president's ride with the crown prince was responsible, the meeting resumed successfully. As Bush reports, "For the rest of my presidency, my relationship with the crown prince—soon to be king—was extremely close."[88]

In the wake of the president's meeting with the crown prince in Crawford, American and British officials on the ground helped move the parties toward an end of the standoff in Ramallah and at the Church of the Nativity. In early May, the Israeli military partially pulled back from its forward positions and withdrew from Arafat's compound after several wanted Palestinians were transferred to an improvised, British-run prison facility in Jericho. American diplomats on the ground, working closely with British counterparts, found a formula that allowed Israel to end the siege at the Church of the Nativity in Bethlehem on May 10, after the Palestinian militants inside were given safe passage to Europe.[89]

During a visit to Washington, Sharon promised Bush he would not "kill" Arafat. Sharon later weighed options for forcibly deporting Arafat, but quickly ruled out the idea when military advisers told him they could not guarantee that the Palestinian leader would not be killed in the cross fire.[90] At the same meeting with Bush, Sharon said he accepted that "a Palestinian state may involve some significant territorial concessions" and that Israel would be willing to dismantle settlements. "Bush loved it," said a former Israeli official.[91] With the situation on the ground still tense, at least the parties appeared to be stepping back from the brink.[92]

But international pressure was building on Bush to take further steps. In typical fashion, pressure would peak and the administration would offer a speech, statement, or other action but avoid the hard-bargaining required of Arab-Israeli diplomacy. The president would make a major address on the Middle East in June, but even that would turn into a pitched battle within the administration. Yet what emerged was a dramatic statement that reshaped U.S. policy. From January 3, 2002, when Israel seized the Karine A, to the disastrous Powell meeting with Arafat on April 14, the President's disillusionment with Arafat became complete. For Bush, the logical next step was to call for regime change in Palestine.

The Rose Garden Speech

As the president stepped into the Rose Garden on June 24, flanked by his foreign policy team, he did more than just recast U.S. policy. Bush's speech also revealed each of the themes that would define his administration's approach to the Middle East: an aversion to becoming deeply enmeshed in the give-and take of negotiations; ideational goals that trumped the Arab-Israeli question; an administration divided; and an inability of the administration to follow through on its policies.

Bush wanted to strengthen U.S. support for a Palestinian state but also sideline Arafat. "The idea sparked controversy, starting in my administration. While Condi and Steve Hadley supported it, Dick Cheney, Don Rumsfeld, and Colin Powell all told me I shouldn't give the speech," Bush writes in his memoir. "Dick and Don were concerned that supporting a Palestinian state in the midst of an intifada would look like rewarding terrorism. Colin worried that calling for new Palestinian leadership would embarrass Arafat and reduce the chance for a negotiated settlement."[93]

In the lead-up to the speech, Israel transferred new intelligence to the White House, claiming to prove Arafat's complicity in terrorism. According to NSC staffer Flynt Leverett, Vice President Cheney said the material was a "'smoking gun'— proof that Arafat was supporting and funding terrorist attacks against Israelis . . . The U.S. had no choice but to 'write off Arafat.'"[94] Weissglas confirmed to the authors that he passed "a piece of intelligence" before the speech that "clearly proved Arafat's personal involvement in financing terrorism."[95] Cheney says he "urged that we move beyond Yasser Arafat."[96]

Dozens of drafts were passed around in the final days and hours, up until the morning of the speech—with the final version reportedly drawing considerable input from the president himself. Sharon had inputs as well.[97]

"[The] June 24th speech . . . is really two speeches in one," said former NSC official, Robert Danin, "papering over the fundamental cleavage within the administration between those who wanted to park the issue and those who believed that there should be an activist approach to the issue."[98]

At the front end of the speech, Bush shocked many by declaring in no uncertain terms that "peace requires a new and different Palestinian leadership . . . I call on the Palestinian people to elect new leaders, leaders not compromised by terror," the president said, adding, "I call on them to build a practicing democracy, based on tolerance and liberty." An administration that embraced the idea of active "regime change" in places such as Iraq was calling on Palestinians to effect their own form of regime change—even as they remained under Israeli occupation.

Bush not only signaled that the United States had given up on Arafat once and for all—effectively echoing Prime Minister Sharon's position—but he created a new sequence in which Palestinians were expected to "have new leaders, new institutions and new security arrangements with their neighbors" before Washington would support the creation of a Palestinian state—whose borders and sovereignty, Bush added, would be "provisional."[99] Only then, according to the president's vision, would final-status talks begin. Then, in stark terms, the president tied the post-9/11 war on terror to the Arab-Israeli conflict. "Nations," Bush stated in an oft-repeated view, "are either with us or against us in the war on terror . . . Every nation actually committed to peace will stop the flow of money, equipment and recruits to terrorist groups seeking the destruction of Israel—including Hamas, Islamic Jihad, and Hezbollah."

This speech was the most important statement on the Arab-Israeli conflict by George W. Bush in his eight years as president. He linked here his opposition to terror with his broader proposals for the region and showed his willingness to defy international opinion and conventional wisdom. "A Palestinian state will never be created by terror —it will be built through reform," he said. "There is simply no way to achieve that peace until all parties fight terror."[100]

But the implication of the speech was that the Arab-Israeli conflict was somehow tied to the "root causes" of terror, a linkage long rejected by "neoconservative" thinkers who opposed a Palestinian state because they believed Arabs are not prepared to truly reconcile with Israel. Bush went so far as to tie the Palestinian fate to the world as a whole. "If liberty can blossom in the rocky soil of the West Bank and Gaza, it will inspire millions of men and women around the globe who are equally weary of poverty and oppression, equally entitled to the benefits of democratic government." Bush went even further, connecting his approach to Palestine specifically with the future of the region. "This moment is both an opportunity and a test for all parties in the Middle East: an opportunity to lay the foundations for future peace; a test to show who is serious about peace and who is not."

And one new factor was introduced that few have noted. Earlier administrations' policies of peacemaking inherently involved two parties: the Arab actors and Israel. You could not try to negotiate peace effectively without Israel being part of the discussions. A policy championing reform, however, seemed to relieve Israel of responsibility in the process. Indeed Bush's later embrace of Natan Sharansky's views on democracy promotion threatened to create just such an impression in the region.[101] By making reform the principal diplomatic goal, a peace strategy was reduced to an internal Arab agenda. This view left reconciliation with Israel outside the process, to its own and to America's detriment, but at the time, to the relief of the Israelis because it meant avoiding frontal conflicts with Washington. It is no wonder that Israeli-American relations improved following the speech: there was less for the two sides to argue about. The focus was on Arab, and especially Palestinian, responsibilities to reform, and the U.S. bar was lowered for Israeli behavior. Israel got a free pass on the peace process until the Palestinians achieved reform, and Israel was not even really expected to do much to enable that reform, despite increasing Israeli control of the West Bank.

The latter part of the speech placed responsibilities on Israel as well, including a statement that "consistent with the recommendations of the Mitchell Commission, Israeli settlement activity in the occupied territories must stop." Israel was asked to restore freedom of Palestinian movement, to release frozen Palestinian revenues, and to take steps to allow for the emergence of a "viable" Palestinian state. The Mitchell Commission language on settlements was even stronger, calling for a total freeze, including "natural growth." But though there were calls on Israel to take major steps, the focus was on a change of Palestinian leadership. Israel embraced the speech, while Arabs were downbeat.

Rice said she immediately reached out to Bill Burns, head of the Near East Affairs Bureau at State and a trusted adviser from her days in the first Bush presidency, to check on the Arab reaction. "Pretty rough," is how Burns put it. Later that evening, a scheduled call with Jewish leaders turned into a "love fest," says Rice.[102]

In recalling the speech, Bush seems surprised that "my support for a Palestinian state was overwhelmed by my call for new leadership," seemingly forgetting that he had already supported the idea of a two-state solution, only now adding

conditions. That was the news. It was therefore a bit odd that he said of his preparations for the speech, "I would be the first president to publicly call for a Palestinian state as a matter of policy."[103] He had already done so. Bush also rejected what
had been the longtime conventional wisdom that Arafat, despite his blemishes,
was the only Palestinian leader capable of making a deal. "While I considered Arafat a failed leader, many in the foreign policy world accepted the view that Arafat
represented the best hope for peace."[104]

These skeptics included his parents. "Shortly after the speech, Mother called.
'How's the first Jewish president doing?' she asked. I had a funny feeling she disagreed with my policy. That meant Dad probably did as well. I wasn't surprised."
The next day Bush headed for the annual G8 summit in Canada and received
more criticism. He told his detractors that he was "convinced Arafat would never
prove a reliable partner for peace."[105]

The Road to the Road Map

Bush's speech did little to change the worsening situation on the ground, which soon
began to spiral out of control. Violence peaked again and Israel renewed its siege of
Arafat, this time largely destroying the Ramallah compound where he was housed
with a small cadre of aides. As it did the previous April, the administration viewed
Arafat's death or expulsion as a red line. Despite Bush's antipathy toward the Palestinian leader, it was decided that an Israeli move against Arafat would be too risky
and that the potential for a wider conflict too great. Israeli actions against Arafat
would also harm U.S. efforts to gain Arab backing for the planned invasion of Iraq.

In September 2002, following a terrorist attack by Hamas in Tel Aviv, Sharon
ordered the IDF to return to the Muqata in Ramallah and to start demolishing buildings, creeping ever closer to Arafat's headquarters. On instructions from the White
House to see the Israeli prime minister immediately, Ambassador Kurtzer met with
Sharon on Saturday, September 22, and demanded assurances that Israel would
pull out from Arafat's headquarters and not threaten his person, which Sharon
initially resisted.[106] Weissglas was dispatched to Washington, but heard the same
message from Rice in no uncertain terms on September 27.[107] On this issue, the
administration was united in its messages to Sharon, who then acceded to the U.S.
government's appeal. Within hours of Rice's reproach, Israeli forces were ordered
to pull back from Arafat's compound. In return, a senior administration official
told Weissglas that Israel's swift action in keeping its promise had "upgraded our
relations."[108] For the Bush team, more than others, keeping commitments was a
critical factor in maintaining relations, and Sharon—in the eyes of the White
House—kept his word, albeit after giving the White House a six-day scare.[109]

Over the summer and fall, Arab entreaties—particularly from Jordan—convinced the administration it needed a concrete plan as a follow-up to Bush's June speech. According to Marwan Muasher, the Jordanian foreign minister at the time, at one point he "asked the president for a 'road map' that would include benchmarks, timelines, obligations, and a monitoring group to measure performance." "He listened," writes Muasher, "but did not react." King Abdullah made the same appeal. "More than outlining steps," Muasher reports Bush saying, "we need progress on the ground first."[110] But in the months to follow, Bush would relent on this point, and he gave the green light for his administration to develop a more detailed peace initiative—the debut of which would come after the invasion of Iraq.[111]

By late 2002, the administration was consumed by its preparations for war against Saddam Hussein. In the face of mounting European and international opposition, Bush would not budge and the White House went ahead with its war plans. For some in the Arab world, a U.S. invasion was a fait accompli, and therefore they turned their attention to advocating for greater American engagement on the peace process. President Bush faced some of his sharpest international criticism from Paris. Just as a major transatlantic rift was emerging over Iraq, the Arab-Israeli conflict was being dragged in. In December, French president Jacques Chirac—one of Bush's toughest critics and opponents on Iraq—sought to gain American commitment to a plan to establish a Palestinian state within three years. Bush rejected the idea, and the administration managed to kill it.

But when a similar appeal for action came from Bush's Iraq War ally, British prime minister Tony Blair, the White House was more receptive. Blair was facing intense anti-war sentiment at home, and sought U.S. action on the peace process as a way of assuaging his critics. Blair's appeal added momentum to the Road Map process. It is indicative of Bush's approach that having issued his "vision" of a future Palestinian state, he was content to settle back and wait until someone listened, and was even reluctant to provide a plan for implementing what he himself had set out to do. In the speech, he had offered to help, along with others in the international community, "the Palestinians organize and monitor fair, multiparty local elections by the end of the year, with national elections to follow."[112] The deadline was repeatedly postponed; the priority was simply not there.

Although Iraq remained the priority, the administration was willing to display greater engagement on the peace process if it would help Blair and potentially ease the rupture with other international actors opposed to the U.S. invasion. The bulk of the drafting of the Road Map was done by David Satterfield and Terje Roed-Larsen and the timing of its release was influenced heavily by Tony Blair. By the time it was finished, the Palestinians, Israelis, and other parties in the Middle East were consulted but did not directly participate in the plan's creation. The Quartet was also involved.[113] But throughout the fall, the administration stalled on releasing the plan, which Sharon did not favor and which he hoped would be delayed.[114] Sharon's unease could not be easily dismissed by the administration. Israel also figured in the Iraq War plan. Just as Bush 41 had pressured Israel to stay out of the conflict in 1990–91, Bush 43 wanted Israel to remain outside the fray.[115] For this, Israel needed reassurance and guarantees, some of which would culminate months later in April 2003, when the administration asked Congress to approve a $9 billion package of loan guarantees.

Some Road Map advocates, such as Jordan, became impatient as the initiative kept getting delayed, apparently because of Israeli concerns. Muasher recounts being "livid" over one specific delay, telling a White House official that he "failed to understand how Rice could tell me at the end of October that there would be no delay in announcing the plan, how Satterfield could subsequently reiterate this in mid November, and how this all could be reversed because of one meeting the administration had with Dov Weissglas."[116]

The drafters of the Road Map were faced with a fundamental conflict between Israeli demands for Palestinian "performance" measures up front (principally on security), and Palestinian and Arab insistence on a timeline, Israeli pullback, and a settlement freeze. Each side wanted the other to act first. In an attempt to satisfy everyone, all elements were included. There were sequences, mutual responsibilities, and parallelism. In Phase I, there would be PA reform, an end to Palestinian violence, an Israeli settlement freeze, an end to incitement by official institutions, and Israel's withdrawal from Palestinian cities. Phase II called for the establishment of an independent Palestinian state with provisional borders, the renewal of multilateral talks, and the restoration of Arab states' pre-Intifada links to Israel. Phase III would involve a comprehensive peace deal, including a final agreement on all outstanding issues. All phases were to take place within two years.

As the diplomacy was focused on the Road Map, it became clear that the emphasis on reform in the June 24 speech struck a chord with many Palestinians who were long tired of Arafat's autocratic ways and the endemic PA corruption. Over summer 2002, the PA had adopted a provisional constitution, which had support from many reformers. Also, the Quartet established a task force on Palestinian reform. Despite much unease among America's partners, Bush's June 24 speech did have a major impact on the international community's approach to the conflict. PA reform would now be indelibly marked on the agenda. Arafat found it particularly difficult to resist Western pressures to reform, given the Palestinian Authority's increasing dependence on foreign aid—a situation that had worsened over the previous eighteen months because of the dramatic fall in tax revenue and

Israel's frequent impounding of Palestinian funds in retaliation for continuing Palestinian suicide bombings and attacks.

Under intense outside pressure, Arafat acceded to the creation of the post of prime minister, to which he appointed Mahmoud Abbas (Abu Mazen). There were no illusions about where ultimate power still lay, but with Abbas's appointment there was hope that over time Arafat's monopoly on power could be broken. More immediately, Abbas's selection was important in that it provided a way for Sharon to enter into negotiations. The administration began to ask Sharon to take more steps to bolster the new PA prime minister—including prisoner releases and troop redeployments.

On April 30, 2003, on the heels of the creation of the new position of Palestinian prime minister, the Quartet released the Road Map publicly.[117] Abbas's government accepted without reservations. Sharon's government accepted the document as well, but with fourteen "reservations" that focused largely on such issues as demands for the complete cessation of violence, Arab states' taking action against terrorist activity, and American management of any monitoring mechanisms. Not wanting to lose Palestinian and Arab support, the administration acknowledged Israel's reservations, but formally made no changes to the plan.[118] Washington and Jerusalem simply agreed to disagree on whether these points should be in the peace plan.[119]

The day after the Road Map was released, the president delivered his famous "Mission Accomplished" speech. Saddam Hussein had been quickly overthrown, and the Iraqi military had melted away. These were heady times for the administration, and it began to look for "something big" on the diplomatic front. Rice gathered senior members of the foreign policy team in her office for brainstorming sessions about what might be done on the Israeli-Palestinian track.[120] It was decided that the president would travel to the region to meet with Arab and Israeli leaders as part of twin summit meetings designed to boost support for the Road Map and renew high-level Israeli-Palestinian contacts.

The trip was a curious affair. In early June, 2003, Bush made his first visit as president to the Middle East. On June 3, he met with a host of Arab leaders in Sharm el-Sheikh. They discussed Iraq, but also gave a strong signal of regional support for the Road Map. Bush then went to Aqaba, where he met with Sharon and Abbas. As part of a highly choreographed summit, U.S. officials were deeply involved in drafting the statements each team would present. The scene was a stark contrast with the violence and acrimony of previous years. Abbas pledged in no uncertain terms to use peaceful means to attain Palestinian goals, while Sharon agreed to remove settlement "outposts" and to support a Palestinian state with "territorial contiguity"—a phrase the Americans coaxed out of him with some difficulty. Behind the scenes, Bush seemed to favor Abbas over Sharon, alarming the Israeli prime minister that Abbas might chip away at Israel's special ties with Bush.[121]

In what many interpreted as a new sign of Bush's commitment, he said he would "ride herd" on the parties until they had reached agreements.[122] But he then spent a good part of the summer at his Crawford, Texas, ranch, having appointed a little-known career-diplomat with no prior Middle East experience—John Wolf—to serve as the Road Map monitor. Wolf's lack of familiarity with the region led many to wonder why Bush would send someone so inexperienced. Moreover, as with Zinni before him, Wolf seemed to be stepping into a job without clear White House backing. "They're not backed up by anything," a former senior American official would later say about envoys under Bush, "It's almost as much public relations as it is substance."[123]

The afterglow of the twin summits did not last long. A wave of Palestinian terrorism and Israeli targeted killings, and the absence of effective monitoring, which held no side accountable and exacted no consequences for lack of "performance," effectively brought Road Map implementation to an end. "I would learn valuable lessons about how frustrating it can be to get the Israelis to actually carry through on promises relating to the Palestinians," says Rice about Israel's failure to carry out its commitments to Bush at Aqaba.[124] In early September, Abbas suddenly resigned as prime minister, citing lack of support from the United States and Israel and "internal incitement" against his government.[125] "We missed an opportunity with Abu Mazen [Abbas]," says Zinni, "there should have been more done to empower him."[126] Arafat had scored a coup. The United States was left as a bystander.

In practice, nothing worked. When neither side fulfilled its obligations, the administration seemed helpless or uninterested in holding the parties accountable. "The Roadmap, like the June 24 speech," says Aaron Miller, who worked on early drafts of the plan as an adviser to Powell, "became a convenient administration talking point and guidepost, pointing toward what the parties needed to do."[127]

Perhaps the entire venture was doomed from the outset. "The whole idea of putting the Roadmap together and having the Quartet involved, it was all designed as a holding place, because the administration was not prepared to do anything," according to one former American official.[128]

Gaza Disengagement and the Death of Arafat

After the false starts of the preceding years, fate seemed to offer the Bush administration unexpected opportunities for success in the 2004 to 2005 period: Sharon's

Gaza disengagement proposal, Arafat's death, and Abbas's accession to power. But these opportunities would also be squandered.[129]

In the fall of 2003, with Abbas's resignation and the Road Map stalled, there was a vacuum. The administration was suddenly informed by Sharon that he was contemplating leaving the Gaza Strip. The prime minister told Elliott Abrams about his plans in November 2003.[130] Sharon's move was unexpected in Washington, even if the prime minister had evacuated the settlers in the Sinai, as part of the Egyptian-Israeli Peace Treaty. After all, he was an early and consistently vociferous patron of the Israeli settlement movement.

Yet Israel had long wanted to rid itself of Gaza, which was difficult to control. Gaza's large Palestinian population also gave meaning to the growing argument that Israel's future would be in doubt due to demographics if it held on to the occupied territories. Although Sharon denied repeatedly that he placed any stock in the demographic argument—that Arabs would soon outnumber Israelis between the Jordan River and the Mediterranean—the issue began to weigh heavily on Israeli politics during this period.

At the same time, a group of Israelis and Palestinians launched the Geneva Initiative, an unofficial peace plan that was gaining widespread attention. Geneva showed signs of popularity with the Israeli public.

With Abbas now gone and with little Israeli interest in fulfilling the Road Map, Sharon needed an alternative approach to Geneva that would allow Israel to redefine the diplomatic landscape; unilateral withdrawal from Gaza seemed to answer the problems Israel faced as the Intifada wound down. Sharon went public with his Gaza withdrawal idea in December 2003 at the Herzliya Conference, an annual policy event which includes appearances by major Israeli cabinet ministers. However, his statement was unclear, and many in the audience had a hard time understanding precisely what the prime minister had in mind.[131] There was no question that the plan itself was not fully developed and indeed it would not be for several months. Thus, in early 2004, Weissglas came to Washington to discuss Sharon's thinking on Gaza and to propose three variations: a withdrawal from all of Gaza, a withdrawal from Gaza plus four settlements in the West Bank, or a withdrawal from Gaza plus more extensive withdrawals in the West Bank.[132]

The Bush administration reacted with some hesitation. First, the move was so unusual for Israeli behavior.[133] There was also a concern that Palestinians might think the withdrawal from Gaza was a trick intended to allow Israel to annex the West Bank—treating Gaza the way Begin had treated Sinai. Some in the administration thought a unilateral withdrawal would signal to the Palestinians that the Intifada worked and would therefore result in greater violence. Others mentioned the danger that Hamas or Arafat would get the credit. A different view was that renewed negotiations would now be all the more important so that the withdrawal would avoid these negative scenarios.

The administration was quick to embrace Sharon's idea, yet also careful to push for a limited West Bank component. Israel had considered going further than just four small settlements on the West Bank. Sharon had even showed Hadley and others more detailed maps, reflecting more extensive withdrawals.[134] But the Bush team settled for the symbolic West Bank withdrawal of four isolated settlements in the north, even discouraging Sharon from going further.[135]

Sharon had unleashed a firestorm at home and caused a political upheaval in his own party. It soon became clear that he wanted something in return from the Americans for his withdrawal. He sought unequivocal U.S. backing, as well as assurances on the core issues in the peace process for several reasons: (1) in order to present the Israeli public with an attractive package of benefits to compensate for the lack of an agreed withdrawal with the Palestinians, (2) because of the traditional Israeli disinclination to relinquish bargaining chips up front, and (3) to counter what he expected would be a backlash from settlers and the right wing of his own party. Sharon's desperate need for U.S. support suddenly gave Bush additional leverage—yet it would prove to be potential influence that largely went untapped.

If there was any disbelief left in the administration that Sharon was not the "centrist" that he had portrayed himself to be in his first meeting with Bush in 2001, the Gaza plan put it to rest. Key figures in the administration—most notably the president himself—viewed Sharon's plan as courageous. His willingness to take on so many constituencies in his political base bought him kudos in Washington. "The President had his closest relations with foreign leaders who in his view took risks, were strong leaders, used their power to do something: Koizumi, Blair, John Howard, Sharon," said Elliott Abrams. "The huge opposition in Likud, losing votes in Likud organs, having to split the party he was a founder of, all of this really impressed the President, so he wanted to help. That's what led to the April 14, 2004 letter."[136]

In Washington, the question then turned to what sort of political compensation could be provided to Sharon to enhance his ability to implement the disengagement plan at home. The allure of the Sharon plan to Bush's team was simply too great. The Road Map was stuck, and Sharon was promising to remove settlements, something that was never achieved even at the height of the Oslo process.[137] The United States and Israel, in their discussions in the early spring, finally produced an agreement in an exchange of letters between the two leaders. On April 14, at the White House and with all the ceremonial trappings of a major event, Bush offered public support for Sharon's disengagement plan.

In his letter to Sharon, Bush declared that Israel should be able to keep existing "population centers" in the West Bank, which for Israelis was code for the large settlement "blocs."[138] As the president put it, "In light of new realities on the ground, including already existing major Israeli populations centers, it is unrealistic to expect that the outcome of final status negotiations will be a full and complete return to the armistice lines of 1949, and all previous efforts to negotiate a two-state solution have reached the same conclusion. It is realistic to expect that any final status agreement will only be achieved on the basis of mutually agreed changes that reflect these realities." Basically, the president of the United States had endorsed Israel's position that the major settlement blocs alongside the 1967 border would remain inside Israel. There were almost no Israelis, however dovish, who would disagree with this position.[139]

But the president went even further. On the sensitive issue of refugees, he took the Israeli position when he announced that Palestinian refugees should be resettled in Palestine, not Israel.[140] His precise words were as follows: "It seems clear that an agreed, just, fair and realistic framework for a solution to the Palestinian refugee issue as part of any final status agreement will need to be found through the establishment of a Palestinian state, and the settling of Palestinian refugees there, rather than in Israel."[141]

On the surface, these appeared to be major shifts in American policy, both in substance and in style—the issue having only been discussed with Israel. The Arab reaction was predictably negative and hostile.[142] No administration had gone as far in a bilateral discussion with Israel (though Bush's commitments were generally consistent with points in the Clinton Parameters, which were offered to both Israelis and Palestinians).[143]

In a press backgrounder later that day at the White House, administration officials tried to downplay the statement—which, with a lawyer's lens, could be interpreted as less of a departure from previous American policy than first appeared to be the case. But as with so much else in Arab-Israeli diplomacy, perception is key—and the perception in virtually every quarter was that Bush made major concessions and offered Israel unprecedented assurances on final-status issues in an effort to help Sharon's political fortunes at home.

Of course, the Israelis had wanted more. Nonetheless, some in the administration felt that Bush gave too much. "We gave away a lot more than we needed to," says an American official, "I don't think that we needed to pay as big a price as we did."[144] Some questioned what the United States received in return from Israel, besides strengthening Sharon's support at home for disengagement.

As might be expected, the Arab world interpreted the Bush-Sharon letters much in the same way the senior official did. The Arab view was that Washington had interfered in what should be issues for the negotiations and had made concessions to Israel without the consent of the Arab parties. A former senior American official recalls how he kept working to tone the letter down, "so my problem wouldn't be too severe."[145] The two parties effectively reduced the process to a negotiation between themselves, a much easier, but less productive task than involving the Arab side.

Sharon also provided a note to Bush on April 14, but the more important letter came on April 18, when Weissglas offered a written commitment to Rice. Weissglas promised that "within the agreed principles of settlement activities, an effort will be made in the next few days to have a better definition of the construction line of settlements in Judea and Samaria" and to jointly define the construction line outside of which Israel would no longer build.[146] He also promised the removal of "illegal" settlement outposts and a range of other positive commitments on such issues as mobility restrictions on the Palestinians in the West Bank, Palestinian revenues, and the "security barrier" the Israeli government was building between the West Bank and Israel.

Beginning as early as 2003 in private discussions between the United States and Israel over the latter's reservations to the Road Map, the two countries had begun to discuss the settlement issue. The primary Israeli figures involved were the prime minister himself as well as his trusted adviser, Weissglas. In 2003, there were deliberations on a four-part draft in which a contingent understanding emerged that settlement building would be allowed, if confined to already built-up areas. Stephen Hadley, the deputy national security advisor, led the behind-the-scenes effort to reach a deal with Sharon. He says there was a tentative understanding based on four principles: no new settlements, no more confiscation of Palestinian lands, no further subsidies to settlers, and no construction "outside the construction lines."[147]

Hadley said the understandings were designed to end further taking of Palestinian land, which was important for Palestinians. The idea, he says, was that the Israelis could "build up, not out."[148] With these earlier "understandings" now codified in the Weissglas-Rice exchange, the task turned to defining the built-up areas of the settlements. According to the letter, Ambassador Kurtzer would be responsible on the American side for defining the construction lines. After Sharon returned from Washington, Kurtzer and his Israeli counterparts set about trying to negotiate the details of the tentative understanding and to develop a mechanism for delineating the built-up areas. But this effort failed to progress, as the Israelis became increasingly uncomfortable with implementing what was agreed, and the administration lost interest.[149]

In the end, despite their commitments to Bush about "outposts" and building restrictions, Israel was never held accountable. Although part of a long pattern of

U.S. ineffectiveness on settlements, the Bush failures were more notable given the concrete commitments they had from Israel.

The problem was that Israel began to act in accordance with its own interpretation, as if the deal had been consummated. In reality, the so-called "understandings" were never codified. Certainly the split inside the administration was very deep. Some worried that for the United States to monitor settlement activity was to draw Washington into the settlement operation and to engage in a painstaking enterprise that only seemed to legitimate settlements, which the United States had long opposed. For these critics, a settlement freeze including natural growth, as delineated in the Mitchell Commission Report and the Road Map, was preferable.[150]

In this administration, as we have seen previously, disagreements often resulted in deadlock, as no one, including the president, was prepared to resolve disputes between competing officials. Those opposed to an idea could win simply in their opposition, balancing against those who wanted to proceed in a more positive direction, thereby stalemating policy. This predicament prevented what might have become a major settlement achievement. It also undermined the possibility of new openings toward Iran and Syria. As these examples suggest, splits within the administration often served the goals of the neoconservatives in the administration.

But even if it had been united, this administration, generally weak on follow-up, simply did not pursue the plan on settlements with the Israelis that had been agreed on. On top of it all, many Israelis were cool to the idea of delimiting a settlement construction line, once they realized it wouldn't be just a symbolic action. The outcome of the Rice-Weissglas exchange solidified to the Israelis the message that they could make promises to the Bush administration but would not have to worry about implementing them. Like the June 24 speech and the Road Map, statements for this administration acquired a special standing, regardless of what happened next.

Despite the Bush letter to Sharon, which was in part intended to allay the fears and opposition of right-wing critics in Israel, to Bush's dismay a Likud Party referendum turned down the Gaza disengagement proposal on May 2. Although Sharon was subsequently able to circumvent this hurdle by gaining Israeli government approval of a slightly amended plan, thereby bypassing Likud, it indicated the difficult domestic problems facing Sharon. Indeed, the parties (both in Israel and the region) were to spend the next fifteen months wrangling over disengagement.

Given Arab outrage at Bush's commitments to Sharon and the deterioration in the U.S.-Palestinian relationship, it was therefore not surprising that the next Arab leader to visit Washington a few weeks later, King Abdullah of Jordan, was showered with effusive praise to compensate for Arab fury. On May 6, the king was greeted with a letter of his own from the president. Referring to the Gaza withdrawal, Bush told Abdullah, "This bold plan can make a real contribution toward peace." In seeming contradiction to the letter to Sharon, Bush stated that "The United States will not prejudice the outcome of final status negotiations, and all final status issues must still emerge from negotiations between the parties in accordance with UN Security Council Resolutions 242 and 338." Suddenly the promises to Sharon on refugees and settlements were not as solid as they had seemed. In a clear attempt to allay Arab fears that the Gaza withdrawal would trump the Road Map, Bush reaffirmed his commitment to a Palestinian state alongside Israel living in "peace and security." "The Roadmap," wrote Bush, "represents the best pathway toward realizing that vision, and I am committed to making it a reality."[151]

"The exchanges of letters between the monarch and Bush expressed a clear preference for negotiations over unilateralism," wrote Muasher. "The text reaffirmed that the United States would not prejudice final status talks on any issue, implicitly including those of refugees and borders."[152] The administration hoped that these actions would reassure its Arab partners. But the perception remained that the commitments to Sharon were far stronger. Palestinians and Arabs continued to fear that Gaza disengagement would replace the Road Map, an anxiety fueled by comments from Sharon's own advisers.

In October 2004, an interview with Dov Weissglas confirmed what many critics of the disengagement plan had feared, that it was an Israeli scheme to divest itself of the troublesome Gaza Strip and to cement its grip on the West Bank. "The significance of the disengagement plan is the freezing of the peace process," Weissglas said, in comments that caused a stir in the United States and across the Middle East. "The disengagement is actually formaldehyde . . . It is the bottle of formaldehyde within which you place the president's formula so that it will be preserved for a very lengthy period."[153] It was an argument that was focused on Sharon's domestic opponents, but it had a devastating impact in the region itself, confirming many Arabs' worst fears about Gaza disengagement. It even caused some consternation in the United States. At a Senate hearing on the Middle East, for example, a senator quoted Weissglas and pressed U.S. officials to explain the obvious inconsistency with the administration's position on the Road Map.[154]

But as domestic opposition in Israel grew, the Bush administration became more and more preoccupied with Sharon's political problems and what could be done to strengthen his hand. The "illegal outposts," which Israel had previously committed to remove, but did not, virtually disappeared from the agenda once Sharon pledged to dismantle full-fledged settlements in Gaza and once the administration became obsessed with bolstering Sharon's political fortunes.

Even as this discussion of the proposed withdrawal from Gaza was occurring, Israel also began building a barrier separating the West Bank from Israel. The barrier did not follow the Green Line, the 1949 armistice line between Israel and the West Bank that lasted until the June 1967 war, but was constructed to meet Israeli security needs, including the incorporation of as many settlements as possible. The Palestinians complained bitterly that the result was the seemingly arbitrary divisions within Palestinian locations (such as within farms or towns). The Israelis responded that they had done what they needed to do to stop the violence. They had not started the bloodshed, but they would certainly take whatever measures necessary to protect their people.

The Bush administration had conflicting reactions to the barrier. At times, key officials, including the president, noted the basic hardships the barrier and other Israeli steps caused Palestinian residents of the West Bank, but at other times they stressed that stopping the violence was part of the war on terrorism, and if the barrier proved effective, so be it. President Bush called the wall a "problem" in July 2003, but then endorsed it on April 14, 2004, only to criticize it obliquely again during a visit by Abbas to Washington in late May 2005.[155] In his memoirs, Bush says, "The fence was widely condemned. I hoped it would provide the security Israelis needed to make hard choices for peace."[156]

On July 9, 2004, the International Court of Justice (ICJ) ruled that Israel's West Bank barrier was illegal.[157] The United States reacted with considerable opposition. White House spokesman Scott McClellan stated that the administration believed that the court was not the appropriate forum to resolve a "political issue."[158] It was not surprising that the administration had little faith in the ICJ, but the administration achieved a limited degree of success in terms of shaping Israeli policy. The administration's policy developed around four key principles:[159]

- The United States supported—in principle—measures Israel felt it needed to take to ensure its security. The barrier was such a measure that fit the category of enhancing Israeli security.
- The United States would not support the barrier as unilaterally defining Israel's boundary, that is, would not support any political significance that Israel might attach to the barrier.
- The United States expected Israel to minimize the amount of the West Bank included between the barrier and the 1967 line.
- The United States would oppose any routing of the barrier that impacted negatively on daily Palestinian life, including access to fields, movement, and the like.[160]

To be sure, the key factor in Israeli decisions to revise the routing of the barrier was the Israeli Supreme Court, which ruled often in favor of Arabs whose property and lives were affected by the barrier. However, Bush administration intervention, on occasion, helped to persuade Israel to reroute the barrier.

Following Bush's reelection in November 2004, the opportunities for progress grew immeasurably. Just a week after the election, Yasir Arafat fell ill and died. Both Bush and Sharon had claimed since they had assumed office in 2001 that Arafat was a main impediment to progress. Suddenly, Washington and Jerusalem had the more moderate Mahmoud Abbas to deal with, as he was quickly elected PA president in January 2005 with a resounding majority. He would also assume Arafat's role as chairman of the PLO Executive Committee. Yet, because of the continuing turmoil in Gaza, Palestinian instability, caution about the strength of Abbas, and a general aversion to negotiations in the administration, there was virtually no attempt to capitalize on the Palestinian leadership transition.[161]

Despite a range of ideas proposed by American diplomats, the White House was not interested in using the new circumstances brought about by Arafat's death on November 11, 2004, to chart a new course with Palestinians.[162] The administration was focused on the Israeli disengagement plan and more interested in assuring a smooth transition for Abbas. The Bush team was also concentrating on Iraq and the hope of a successful election there, and ultimately on broader democracy-promotion goals.

But most important, perhaps, as Arafat's death occurred a week after the American presidential election, the administration was preoccupied with reorganization. On November 10, 2004, Secretary Powell was informed that he would not be kept on in a phone call from the president's chief of staff Andrew Card, though Powell later agreed to claim the resignation as his own.[163] Condoleezza Rice was nominated to replace him on November 17.

Conclusion

Given Bush's inexperience in foreign affairs, it was difficult to predict what he would actually do in office. For all of his later visions of the end of terror and a reformed Middle East, his policies often led to inaction or merely a change in rhetoric, except in waging wars. But even in war fighting, his early successes in both Afghanistan and Iraq dissipated as a consequence of failed diplomacy, inadequate planning, and poor implementation. Similarly, infighting within his administration made it all the more difficult to produce policies that sustained effective diplomacy between Israel and its Arab counterparts.

This was a president who viewed traditional statecraft and the give-and-take of negotiations as diminishing, rather than enhancing, American power. Jacob Weisberg has described Bush as "a bit of cowboy, with little use for international law or the United Nations, when using them did not suit American interests."[164] Promoting a peace process meant compromising Bush's ideals by dealing with and legitimating problematic regimes such as Bashar al-Asad's Syria or Yasir Arafat's Palestine. This Bush would not do. Instead, the reorientation of American foreign policy toward ideals and principles refashioned U.S. involvement and allowed for Bush's particular unilateralist approach to wielding power and influence abroad.

Another factor inhibited this president and the peace process: the president's leadership style. Bush was reluctant "to get involved in that kind of detailed, mind-boggling nuanced negotiation and diplomatic activity," said a former senior American official, "whether it was arms control or the Israeli-Palestinian conflict."[165] But the details of the peace process, as every president since Nixon, except Reagan, would testify, are hard to avoid. "President Bush was not a hands-on leader," said a former official from his administration. "He did not know much about details, and unfortunately when it comes to the Middle East, it's all about details."[166]

Moreover, for a president obsessed with political capital at home, there were few political incentives to pursue a different approach, given the circumstances of his inauguration, "The president himself from early on had the sense that he had very limited political capital and he had to be careful how he spent it," said Ambassador William Burns, one of Bush's top Middle East officials.[167] At the end of the day, though, it was Bush's worldview that was decisive, not domestic or international capital.[168]

Bush's arms-length approach was cemented by President Clinton's last-ditch and failed peace efforts, coupled with Clinton's own warnings to the new administration about Palestinian leader Yasir Arafat. Bush "saw how much time Clinton had spent on it and it all blew up in his face," said a former American official, "and so he had no inclination, from the very beginning, to start down that road in any way, shape, fashion, or form."[169] Of course, he could as easily have concluded that he could succeed where Clinton failed, as he did on other issues, but instead his predecessor's frustration fit perfectly with his own passive predilections on the peace process.

Bush reversed the logic of peacemaking. As he says in his memoirs, by mid-2002 he had developed a "game changer." In previous administrations, the fundamental concept was that Arab-Israeli peacemaking was the ticket not only to stability, but to American standing and gains in the region, whether the goal was containing the Soviets, stopping terrorism, or protecting critical energy supplies.

However, Bush and his advisers pursued a different logic, particularly after 9/11. They believed political reform and democratization, including by the Palestinians, should precede peacemaking. As the Bush team saw it, why would the United States go out of its way to help dictatorial, duplicitous regimes cement their power through American mediation? Further, they felt that the stability of peace would depend on the domestic accountability and transparency of the parties. After his first year, a year framed by 9/11, Bush's thinking evolved—with his own, distinctive emphasis on democratic reform.

Because the administration was adamant not to repeat the Clinton experience of overinvolvement, the U.S. role was downsized to the point of impotence, undermining the very prospects for success. "I didn't blame President Clinton for the failure at Camp David or the violence that followed. I blamed Arafat," Bush wrote in his memoirs.[170] Nonetheless, Bush and his team were adamant not to repeat what they viewed as Clinton's transgressions—particularly the overinvolvement of the president and the tight embrace of Arafat. For example, under Bush, Washington generally sat out negotiations, deferring to the parties to negotiate the core issues. This posture also satisfied the strong currents in the administration that opposed any hint of pressure on Israel.

It should be said that Bush was not immune to outside pressures, as with Saudi Crown Prince Abdullah's passionate entreaty for U.S. engagement before 9/11, or more notably British prime minister Tony Blair's linkage of support for the Iraq War with U.S. action on the peace process. But even in these cases, when external pressures did move Washington, the response was minimalist and, more important, without determined follow-up.

It was not that Bush was insensitive to Middle East peace (though it is clear several key advisers, especially Cheney and Abrams, viewed the process with disdain), but rather he believed the prospects for peace depended on the pursuit of his broader agenda. If Richard Nixon and Jimmy Carter sought to gain advantage in the Cold War through Arab-Israeli peacemaking and if George H.W. Bush and Bill Clinton believed Arab-Israeli peacemaking could be a driving force that could transform and stabilize the Middle East, George W. Bush saw democracy promotion, institution building, and the defeat of terrorists as necessary precursors to settling the region's hostilities, including the Arab-Israeli conflict.

American policy was also shaped significantly by administration infighting. "A culture of distrust and dysfunction," is how Secretary Rice describes a deeply divided national security team.[171] The rifts would show up on Arab-Israeli questions, but they ran much deeper than the Middle East, reflecting the two competing poles within the Republican establishment, the personalities of the Bush team, and the president's own inability to build a team that worked well together. Powell and his allies in the State Department who argued for a more traditional American approach found themselves consistently outmaneuvered by a dominant neoconservative camp that emphasized other priorities, such as regime change in Iraq, and viewed Israel's challenges as America's own. Powell was undercut by others in the administration, particularly Cheney and Rumsfeld, who felt Arab-Israeli peace was a lost cause.

Rumsfeld, who had been Middle East envoy for a time (1983–84) during the Reagan administration, took the diametrically opposite position from Powell on Arab-Israeli diplomacy. Powell also clashed with Rice when he strove to get the president more involved.[172] Moreover, senior advisers—such as Douglas Feith at the Department of Defense, Elliott Abrams at the NSC, and Lewis Libby and John Hannah in the vice president's office—harbored deep-seated suspicions toward a negotiating process and had been long-standing opponents of Clinton's support for the Oslo process and any notion of Israeli territorial compromise.

There were key developments on Arab-Israeli policy when the president overruled Cheney, including the June 24, 2002, Rose Garden speech (which Cheney opposed) and Rice's 2007 Annapolis initiative. Cheney was more directly focused on other issues, including overall national security policy, Iraq, Iran, the "global war on terrorism (GWOT)," detainee policy, and the creation of the Department of Homeland Security (DHS). Still, when it came to Arafat, Cheney's views were particularly tough. "As far as I am concerned, you can go ahead and hang him," he reportedly told one Israeli leader.[173]

Both 9/11 and the Iraq War dominated the first Bush term. During the Clinton administration, the Arab-Israeli peace process had been the primary issue in the region for American policy. Now it was a relatively backwater problem—influenced deeply by the other two priorities—but also causing problems of its own for the Bush team's dominant interpretation because of the Intifada initiated by the Palestinians. The intensifying Intifada also heavily reinforced the message from outgoing President Clinton during the transition that Arafat was not to be trusted.

The global war on terrorism progressively led the president and many of his team to identify with Israel's struggles to thwart Palestinian suicide bombings and Israel's tough counter-terrorism measures against them, especially after suicide bombings spread in Iraq as well. Israel's discovery of the Iranian ship, the Karine A, headed toward Palestine with arms, reinforced these attitudes at a critical point in the formation of the administration's views just four months after 9/11. Similarly, Syria was seen as an adversary when it began to assist Iraqi opponents of American intervention. The reliance on military force to solve fundamental political problems manifested itself in both the administration's reaction to the Palestinian and Iraqi issues.

But the utilization of sweeping measures in both the GWOT and Iraq also reflected a preference for big ideas grandly offered with too little consideration of the consequences for implementation or the politics of the area. Typical of grand plans with no specific strategy for follow-up were the repeated calls for an independent Palestinian state that would live alongside Israel: the June 24, 2002, speech—with its insistence that political reform in Palestine should precede a serious peace process—and the Road Map. When the Israeli prime minister produced a specific plan that showed promise of implementation—the disengagement from Gaza—months of negotiations followed that were still under way when Bush's first term concluded.

Grand plans without specifics made it difficult for the administration to react to unexpected developments such as the Arab Peace Initiative and Arafat's death. Those in the administration who tried to pursue specific positive efforts on the Arab-Israeli peace process, led by Colin Powell, were usually unsuccessful. Indeed, Powell himself was often handled harshly and even humiliated on his trips to the region, especially in his effort to organize an international conference to address the problems created by the Intifada, in his attempts at engagement with Syria, and in his pursuit of diplomacy and the hiring of envoys on the Arab-Israeli front. Powell succeeded only in being allowed to establish the Quartet as a focal point for diplomatic efforts.

The president did not share the meanness of spirit of those on his team who handled the secretary of state with contempt, but Bush was also not ready to back most of Powell's efforts for diplomatic advances, frequently making it clear that "he was on his own"—if there were any problems, Powell would be held responsible. The kinds of practical measures the secretary was pursuing would necessitate compromises in cherished preferences, and that was not this administration's "cup of tea."

Thus, the preferred method of the first term was innovative ideas and big visions, but the Road Map was not followed, the April 2004 letters with Israel did not result in a major breakthrough, and the term ended with Israeli disengagement from Gaza still not achieved and not at all coordinated with Abbas so that the new Palestinian leader might gain some credit and influence there. Additionally, no strategy adjustment took place when Arafat died, and Syrian-American relations and the Arab Peace Initiative remained in limbo in early 2005. Indeed, for all the presentations, prophecies, and pronouncements, the only takeaways from the first term on the Israeli-Palestinian front were the idea of political reform in Palestine and the establishment of the Quartet. The second four years would determine whether the president's visions could be made into practical policy in more substantive ways.

CHAPTER FIVE

THE ANNAPOLIS DENOUEMENT

The second term of the Bush administration was still dominated by the aftermath of 9/11 and the Iraq War; by political reform in the Middle East; and by the creation of new institutions for Palestinians, including a new security force trained and largely funded by the United States. But the major change was the new secretary of state. Colin Powell was never close to the president or to many of the top officials such as Vice President Richard Cheney and Secretary of Defense Donald Rumsfeld. The new secretary of state, former national security advisor Condoleezza Rice, was one of the closest officials to the president himself—perhaps the closest. She was a confidante with a shared global view and common interests—especially in sports. She was also close to her former deputy, Stephen Hadley, the new national security advisor, which gave her more room to maneuver.

Powell had to contend with Rumsfeld, but Rice was more fortunate to have Robert Gates as the secretary of defense from late 2006 onward. He and his aides were more sympathetic to engagement in Arab-Israeli matters. But major disputes still arose within the administration around the Annapolis process. Elliott Abrams, Rice's former deputy at the National Security Council (NSC), frequently sought to counter her on many initiatives during the second term.

Rice was just as committed to the Arab-Israeli peace process as her predecessor. It would now be far more difficult for other centers of power within the administration to counter her efforts to move the peace process forward.

And, yet, despite these advantages, the administration still had difficulties with turning its declarations into actions and taking advantage of diplomatic openings. Events in the region, internal divisions, and the power of the president's enduring belief that the best way to achieve peace was to create democracy throughout the region were in the end too powerful—even in the wake of the partnership between the president and the new secretary of state.

Expanding Reform and Finishing Disengagement

The first step by Bush in the second term was to identify a broader democracy program, which largely focused on the Middle East. The rhetoric on democracy promotion in Bush's second inaugural was soaring. The White House also publicized his meeting with Natan Sharansky, the Soviet dissident turned Israeli right-wing politician. Sharansky had just published a book, *The Case for Democracy*, which Bush read, praised, and highly recommended.[1] He personally even bought a copy for Tony Blair. The argument in support of freedom everywhere left Israel as the major beacon for the United States in the region, though others, especially Turkey, could make a claim. Moreover, Sharansky argued that without internal political reform in Arab states, there could never be peace. Referring to the book, Bush describes in his memoirs how Sharansky and his fellow prisoners "were inspired by hearing leaders like Ronald Reagan speak with moral clarity and call for their freedom." He goes on to say, "I considered it America's responsibility to put pressure on . . . the world's tyrants. Making that goal a central part of our foreign policy was one of my most consequential decisions as President."[2]

In practical terms, the democracy campaign was pursued, but an effort to engage Arafat's successor, Mahmoud Abbas, in a political process that could capitalize on the Palestinian leadership transition was not. The timing of Bush's campaign may have had considerable immediate merit for Iraq, but it was unfortunate in adapting to opportunities presented by post-Arafat Palestinian politics. Yet the administration did not perceive the link in this way. Instead, it was still concentrated on Israel's Gaza disengagement. That left plenty of time for Abbas to enter center stage later, or so the administration seemed to think. The preoccupation with Gaza and Israeli prime minister Sharon's political fortunes resulted in the administration failing to leverage the Gaza withdrawal as a way of renewing diplomacy and strengthening Abbas ahead of Palestinian legislative elections, which were planned for early 2006. In short, the administration had no peace process strategy.

When Rice sat down at Camp David with the president before the inauguration to discuss her appointment, she told him that she wanted to make movement on the Israeli-Palestinian issue a high priority. Bush agreed, says Rice.[3] Thus, 2005 was her debut, when she confronted the post-Arafat political moment, even while the Gaza withdrawal hung in the balance.

For most of 2005, the administration was intensely focused on Sharon's Gaza disengagement plan, helping the Israeli leader overcome his formidable domestic opponents. By mid-year, with Abbas firmly in control, Washington had resumed high-level contacts with the Palestinian Authority (PA), as well as direct financial assistance. The rise of Abbas, and the looming Gaza withdrawal, led to a brief warming of U.S.-Palestinian relations, particularly in comparison to the intense friction of the 2001–4 period under Arafat.

Thus, Arabs, Israelis, and the United States took several important steps toward improved relations. General William (Kip) Ward was appointed in early February as a new Middle East security coordinator to facilitate the training of Palestinian security forces, a step that would accelerate under his successor, Lieutenant General Keith Dayton, appointed in December 2005.

On February 8, Abbas and Sharon met in Sharm el-Sheikh for their first summit after the Palestinian presidential election, together with Egyptian president Hosni Mubarak and Jordan's king Abdullah. The Israeli and Palestinian leaders declared an end to violence, marking the close of the Second Intifada. In the weeks that followed, Jordan and Egypt returned their ambassadors to Israel. Sharon promised prisoner releases and a transfer of security responsibility in the major West Bank cities. He said the Gaza disengagement would lead to implementation of the Road Map. Perhaps most important, at Sharm el-Sheikh, Sharon said the changes in Palestinian politics could "become the new starting point for a coordinated" process.[4] Indeed, Israeli and Palestinian "technical" committees began to meet, but progress was difficult and the big-ticket issues related to the withdrawal— security, border control, and movement—remained unresolved.

The Bush administration backed the appointment soon thereafter of James Wolfensohn as Quartet envoy for economic matters. The former World Bank president was charged with following through on Sharon's suggestion about coordination and ensuring that economic arrangements were in place so that Gaza and its population would benefit from the Israeli withdrawal. The backdrop to Wolfensohn's mission was also to ensure that Abbas benefited as well. His party, Fatah, would soon be up for election to the Palestinian Legislative Council.

On May 26, Abbas traveled to Washington, where Bush rolled out the red carpet. The Palestinians had not seen this kind of positive attitude in Washington since before Camp David, and Bush rewarded Abbas by asserting that "changes to the 1949 armistice lines must be mutually agreed to."[5] Although this type of phrase was also tucked into the bowels of the April 2004 Bush-Sharon exchange, and the subsequent letter to King Abdullah of Jordan, it was greeted by the Palestinians and others in the Arab world as a positive development.

By June, Rice was announcing that there was an Israeli-Palestinian agreement to destroy settler homes in Gaza after the Israeli withdrawal so that the areas could be used for more appropriate Palestinian housing.[6] But Palestinians were frustrated at the glacial pace of negotiations. Sharon and Abbas met at the Israeli prime minister's residence in Jerusalem in late June. It was an acrimonious meeting. An internal Palestinian account said "the summit consisted of a recycling of the Sharm el-Sheikh arrangements."[7]

As the date of withdrawal drew closer, Sharon seemed to become progressively less interested in negotiating withdrawal with the Palestinians. The Israeli prime minister was afraid that in talks with Abbas, the Palestinian leader might well ask for more, and he did not want the withdrawal to be seen as a result of concessions made to the Palestinians.

Israel even hinted it might retain a strip of territory (code-named "Philadelphi") along the Gaza-Egypt frontier. Washington opposed anything short of full withdrawal, and Sharon dropped the idea. But Washington failed to convince Sharon to step up his coordination with Abbas and renew negotiations.

At the G8 summit in Gleneagles, Scotland, in July, wealthy nations pledged $3 billion to Palestinian economic projects—a testament to Wolfensohn's ability to fund-raise, Blair's need to look influential on an issue that resonated with the British public, and the Bush administration's willingness to step up foreign aid. Skeptics would call it a substitute for meaningful political action.[8]

In mid-August, Israel began the unilateral withdrawal from all Gaza settlements and four small northern West Bank settlements. Despite some settler protests, the withdrawals went far more smoothly than had been anticipated. During the immediate post-withdrawal Palestinian euphoria, the Gaza-Egypt border was breached and Palestinians enjoyed a brief period of free movement. Egypt quickly reinforced the border, partly relying on steps authorized via amendments to the 1979 Israel-Egypt Peace Treaty—a process encouraged by Washington.[9] In response to a request from Rice, Sharon announced on August 29 that there would be no further unilateral Israeli moves. All future steps would fall under the rubric of the Road Map.

But there were already ominous signs that pointed to problems. Envoy Wolfensohn had negotiated the preservation of the valuable Israeli greenhouses in Gaza that were to be evacuated by the Israelis. These were costly assets that could have resulted in major economic gains for the Palestinians. Private funds were provided to maintain the greenhouses and transfer them to Gazans. Wolfensohn, a prodigious fund-raiser for the project, even gave $500,000 of his own money. Yet, shortly after the Israelis departed, some of the greenhouses were scavenged and looted by Palestinians. They were never able to function effectively after the Israelis left because of enduring internal instability and, Palestinians would argue, continued Israeli border restrictions.[10]

The Deal for Palestinian Movement and Access

Although crucial weeks were lost, the administration did recognize relatively early that the Gaza withdrawal would unravel without the United States stepping in after the Israelis left. In the fall, Secretary Rice devoted efforts to seeking an Israeli-Palestinian accord on Gaza crossings to Israel, Egypt, and the West Bank.[11] Drawing on her close relationship with Bush and the trust she had established with Sharon and his advisers, Rice was willing to bring pressure to bear in order to reach a deal. The Palestinians also needed an agreement on movement and access ahead of elections that were fast approaching.

Rice tried to iron out a deal, but dysfunction soon set in. During a mid-November trip, an agreement seemed within reach. The secretary was preparing to leave for the next stop on a multi-country itinerary, until Quartet envoy James Wolfensohn convinced her to delay her departure from the region. He argued that leaving behind lower-level officials would not be enough to finish the negotiations.

Rice leaned heavily on Israeli officials to overcome several last minute snags and be more forthcoming on terms for moving goods and people in and out of Gaza. She told the parties she needed a deal, and she personally steered an all-night session to cement an agreement. It was touch and go at times, according to all accounts. At one point, Mohammad Dahlan told Rice, "If I sign this I'll be a dead man."[12] Much to Wolfensohn's chagrin, he was initially left out of the closing negotiation, but he found his way back in.[13] The deal, the Agreement on Movement and Access (AMA), contained elaborate provisions for managing Gaza's access to Israel, Egypt, and the West Bank.[14] It established a system of bus convoys that would shuttle Palestinians between Gaza and the West Bank and produced a first ever arrangement where about seventy European Union personnel would monitor the Palestinian security forces operating at the Rafah crossing at the Egyptian border.[15]

The AMA was seen as vital to ensuring that Gaza did not become isolated and sink further into poverty and radicalism. But as soon as Rice departed, the deal began to fall apart. One of Rice's signature achievements in her first year as secretary of state would be stillborn. Virtually none of the provisions was effectively implemented.[16]

In a sense, the failed AMA was symbolic of the administration's lost opportunities of the previous two years. The Israeli intention to withdraw from Gaza, the death of Arafat and replacement by the moderate Abbas, and the Israeli withdrawal from Gaza were not translated into concrete, lasting achievements by the United States. But in many ways, the doomed crossings agreement was the worst of all these outcomes. Here was a case where the secretary of state did become involved center stage, and did negotiate an agreement (the only Arab-Israeli deal Bush can claim), but it still resulted in a collapse because of weak follow-through and no plan to assure implementation. The parties, especially Israel, now knew they could humor the new secretary, and then ignore her work once she left the region. That was a highly detrimental experience that would help to undermine her efforts in the coming three years.

In retrospect, the effort to coordinate the withdrawal—once Arafat was out and Abbas was in—was never adequate. Without visible, effective steps at coordination, there was no way to empower Abbas; this left Hamas able to argue that its resistance, not Abbas's diplomacy, forced Israel's withdrawal from Gaza.

Most importantly, the United States and Israel were too concentrated on whether the Israelis would withdraw and insufficiently focused on the functioning of the regime that would develop in Gaza afterward. Attention was paid to the crossings in and out of Gaza on both the Israeli and Egyptian frontiers, but even when looting of the greenhouses began one day after the last Israeli troop left Gaza in mid-September, there were insufficient arrangements for security and for the prevention of violence internally. The basis for the eventual Hamas takeover of Gaza was established even before the Israelis withdrew. Without an adequate plan for a functioning and prosperous Gaza under Palestinian Authority rule, which might become the basis for a future Palestinian state, serious trouble was likely. Yet, the administration tarried, as it had in Iraq, without interest in coordinating stability operations; the Israelis were ready to withdraw, but they too did not see the importance of handling the departure from Gaza in a way that would protect their interests and security afterward.

Abbas himself may have hesitated on resuming direct talks with Israel, but Sharon was equally if not more unwilling to talk with the Palestinians about disengagement. "He wanted the withdrawal defined entirely as an Israeli move made for Israeli interests" without the Palestinians being compensated, says former American ambassador Daniel Kurtzer. "He was absolutely adamant on that." Kurtzer continued, "Only by pulling teeth did we get him to agree to allow some technical discussions that took place 3 or 4 months before on things that needed to be done, 'where's the key to the barn?' type stuff. Certainly, he was opposed to any serious negotiations."[17] Initially Sharon had talked with the Palestinians about disengagement, meeting with them and discussing Israeli plans to some extent. The shortcoming was that he simply remained unwilling to then take steps in coordination with the PA, to take interest in supporting PA efforts, or to modify his plans at all to take consideration of their concerns. To Sharon, the Palestinians would not be allowed to influence how and when Israel would withdraw. Sharon preferred to take unilateral steps.

In the weeks after the Gaza pullout, the Israeli prime minister had cut off contact with Abbas, accusing him of failing to act against armed Palestinian groups.[18] Instead, he began planning a new political party, Kadima, given his inability to gain support from Likud on the Gaza withdrawal or on any future plans on which he might embark. There were rumors that further withdrawals from the West Bank might be possible. But in December Sharon suffered a mild stroke, and in early January a massive stroke, which permanently sidelined him in a coma. The White House had talked after Gaza about finding a new way to resume Israeli-Palestinian negotiations, but as so frequently happened with this administration, it had been just talk. The next developments would be determined by the outcome of the Israeli and Palestinian elections that were scheduled for early 2006.

The Palestinians Elect Hamas

With all its focus on disengagement and the AMA, not to mention growing crises in Iraq and Lebanon, little attention had been paid to the looming question of Palestinian elections. They had been held only once in January 1996, and not since, having been postponed by Arafat for some time, and again postponed by Abbas in July.

By the fall, following the Gaza disengagement and with the legislative elections set for January, Hamas was expressing its desire to compete, so the key question was whether Hamas should be allowed to run and, if so, under what conditions. A few voices in the administration and the international community argued for strict conditions on Hamas' participation—including ideas like signed pledges foreswearing violence, commitments to disarm, accepting past agreements on the peace process, or other stringent benchmarks. These arguments drew on Abbas's own "one authority, one law, one gun" mantra, which he had adopted, as well as international norms. Prominent organizations, like the National Democratic Institute (NDI), were telling the administration privately that stricter conditions needed to be placed on Hamas, as had been the case for elections in other conflict settings.[19]

"As our international observer delegation noted at the time, participation by an organization that advocates violence, including the killing of civilians, and the destruction of a United Nations member state, violates a fundamental principle of a democratic election," said NDI President Kenneth Wollack. "Therefore, I was more concerned with the electoral rules that allowed Hamas to compete without paying an admissions price than the Administration's refusal (afterward) to accept a Hamas victory."[20] Outside experts were saying the same in the public discourse.[21] However, this view was a minority opinion within the administration.

"I made the case for why I thought it was important that Hamas not be allowed to run without there being a price, an entry price paid," said Robert Danin, at the time a deputy assistant secretary of state, "that the elections should be used as a way to either force Hamas to subscribe to basic principles and change its stripes, or not participate." He added, "To allow them in for free was a mistake." Nonetheless, Danin describes a policy process largely shaped by a view that the elections should not be postponed a second time and that the administration should not second-guess Abbas, who was telling the administration that it would legitimize Fatah to run against and defeat Hamas. At one interagency meeting in the fall, chaired by Rice and Hadley, virtually no dissent was voiced.[22]

The conventional wisdom is that Abbas and his aides (not to mention opinion surveys) were predicting a Fatah victory. Confident of winning, Abbas consistently lobbied the administration against setting strict conditions on Hamas. "He said that no election that excluded Hamas would be legitimate," said Secretary Rice, "and he even seemed to have a sense that it could help to start to either moderate Hamas' behavior or expose them as not capable of moderation."[23] But for an administration so shaped by 9/11, its self-described "war on terrorism," and the agenda laid out in Bush's Second Inaugural, it was notable that such a relaxed approach would be adopted. Given the emphasis on ending violence during Arafat's last years and the outsized leverage the United States enjoyed in the wake of the PA's near-total dependence on outside support, a stricter approach might have seemed more likely.

What explains the anomaly? The president's worldview is the likeliest justification. "For [Bush] the elections were an issue of principle," said former national security advisor Stephen Hadley. "He was also influenced by the success of the elections in Iraq previously in 2005, which everybody had discouraged but which went well."[24] It is also the case that Bush had been promising Palestinian elections publicly since the June 24, 2002, speech. In his memoir, Bush says, "I supported the elections. America could not be in the position of endorsing elections only when we liked the projected outcome. I knew the election would be just one step on the journey to democracy. Whoever won would inherit the responsibilities of governing—building roads and schools, enforcing the rule of law, and developing the institutions of a civil society. If they performed well, they would be reelected. If not, the people would have a chance to change their minds. Whatever the outcome, free and fair elections reveal the truth."[25]

Therefore, there was a strong commitment—coming from the president—to encourage the Palestinians to hold the long-delayed vote. "We believed there should be a parliamentary election there," said White House adviser Elliott Abrams, adding that the administration also firmly believed that Fatah and Abbas's allies would win. "[Fatah] did not believe they were going to lose, [and] the Shin Bet did not believe they were going to lose," said Abrams.[26]

Despite Abrams's comment, it was widely known that the Israeli government had major misgivings about Hamas' participation, but ultimately backed off in the face of Bush and Rice's support for the election. A former Palestinian official says he disagreed with Abbas's decision at the time—and that Fatah leaders also wanted the elections postponed. He also criticized American assessments. "Every American was pressing [for a vote]." "They know zero," he says. "Americans cannot get a real assessment . . . Their sources of information were unreliable. That's why they thought the Fatah was going to win, but there was no chance. It was a big mistake." The former official thought the elections should have been postponed by two years. When asked in an interview for this book how he explained the discrepancy between what he was saying and what Abbas told the Americans, the former official hesitated and then said that he did not know what the Fatah leader had said to American representatives. He could only explain that the Fatah leadership was opposed to the election occurring then, and thought they would lose.[27]

In 2011 Abrams told the *Jerusalem Post* that just weeks before the elections were scheduled to take place, the PA had asked Sharon to scuttle the balloting as a way to allow Abbas a plausible excuse to delay the vote.[28] According to Abrams, Sharon responded, "If you want to call off the elections, call off the election, I don't care . . . But you do it—I'm not taking the blame for it."[29] Subsequent appeals to the United States were also unsuccessful, and in fact, the Americans did the opposite, pressing a reluctant Israel to facilitate the elections.

Thus, Abbas and the Bush administration were in effect colluding to make the elections happen with Hamas included because Bush believed in the value of elections per se and because Abbas thought the elections would strengthen his leadership when Fatah won. This alliance was able to defeat both the skeptical Israelis and worried Fatah officials because of the intensity of the president's belief in the salutary impact of elections.

During a late October visit to Washington, Abbas met first with Rice and Hadley and then with President Bush. "[Abbas argued] forcefully that we should let Hamas participate, in order that Fatah could defeat them politically," said a former senior American official, in an account that has been verified by other Bush officials. Abbas argued that "if you don't let them into the process, they're going to be a spoiler; you have to bring them in, defeat them politically, and then you're stronger."[30]

By December, ominous signs began to emerge. Hamas was continuing to attack Israel with rockets, which were countered with tough retaliation measures.

The AMA brokered by Rice in November had all but collapsed, and Hamas was claiming a victory for driving Israel out of Gaza. In December, Hamas also scored major gains in Palestinian municipal elections.

At a Quartet meeting in December, Rice and others proposed that a statement be issued with strong language "that anybody who participated in the elections had to be willing to give up their arms and put them in the hands of the (Authority)."[31] But the strong language never made it into the declaration. While everyone at the meeting agreed to issue the statement, Rice suggested running it past Abbas, who reacted negatively, fearing the language would appear to forbid Hamas' participation. It was dropped in favor of a softer declaration that would not be construed as setting preconditions.

Ultimately, the Quartet stated that "a future Palestinian Authority Cabinet should include no member who has not committed to the principles of Israel's right to exist in peace and security and an unequivocal end to violence and terrorism."[32] Tougher criteria would have undoubtedly constrained Hamas. Although the enforcement of stricter conditions might not have prevented a Palestinian political crisis on the eve of the elections, it certainly would have denied Hamas what they effectively enjoyed—that is, clear sailing heading into the election. Instead, the administration went so far as to pressure Israel to let the election unfold without interference, even pressuring the Israeli government to back off its threats to curtail voting in Jerusalem.[33]

On the eve of the elections, the *Washington Post* reported that a $2 million U.S. government fund—administered by the United States Agency for International Development (USAID)—was being used to bolster political support for Fatah. Although a small amount of money in the vast ocean of U.S. and international economic assistance to Palestinians, the revelation had the opposite effect: painting Abbas as a tool of Washington and giving Hamas an easy public relations victory.[34]

When the results of the January 25 election were tallied, the Bush administration was in a state of shock. According to Rice, American intelligence consistently thought Fatah would win. Although warning high-ranking American officials shortly before the elections that it would be closer than anticipated, intelligence agencies still predicted a Fatah victory. During an early morning workout on the 26th, Rice was astounded to see a newsflash on television that Hamas had won.[35] This unexpected turn of events took place at the beginning of 2006, which former assistant secretary of state David Welch has referred to as the administration's *annus horribilis*.[36]

It appeared that the administration had no "day after" plan in place should Fatah lose. Initially, the president praised the conduct of the vote. "We're watching liberty begin to spread across the Middle East," Bush said the next day, trying to put a positive spin on the balloting. But given the administration's stake in Abbas, it was an unmistakable defeat. Bush reflects on the election in his memoir, "Some interpreted the results as a setback for peace. I wasn't so sure. Hamas had run on a platform of clean government and efficient public services, not war with Israel." Instead, he relates, in referring to later events, "the militant wing of Hamas intervened," and "the extremists responded to the advance of freedom with violence."[37] Bush's reflections in his memoir are both self-serving and puzzling. He seems to be positing a good Hamas that won the elections, only to have them hijacked by the bad Hamas. Yet we have seen little evidence to support his spin on these events, either in developments on the ground or in how the administration approached the debacle.

The election had indeed been judged "free and fair" by scores of international observers. President Abbas's Fatah movement, saddled with a history of corruption, mismanagement, and failed peace negotiations, lost its monopoly on power. Although U.S. officials preferred to point to the corruption issue in explaining the outcome, there were some suggestions that the election was also a referendum on the Western-backed PLO leadership and its failure to make progress toward peace.[38] "America and Israel say no to Hamas," read a widely used Hamas campaign slogan plastered throughout the territories, "What do you say?"[39]

One wonders why no one—not U.S. intelligence and not the Washington bureaucracy—noticed that too many Fatah candidates were arrayed against a unified Hamas lineup in district after district. And we can question why the faith in elections trumped concerns about a party being allowed to run that was committed to the use of violence, that maintained its own militia, that was closely aligned with Iran, and that was not expected to meet conditions for recognition of Israel before the balloting that it would face afterward. Hamas technically ran as the Change and Reform Party, but it was always clear who stood behind the banner— and while the United States did not own the process, it should not be forgotten that the entire structure of the PA was kept afloat with outside political and financial support. Certainly, more so than Lebanon, or even more so than Iraq, this was a setting in which Washington had tremendous influence over outcomes.

The response from Israel was swift. Sharon's successor, acting prime minister Ehud Olmert, announced that Israel would again freeze revenue transfers to the PA and said Israel would not negotiate until Hamas disarmed. Rice took a hard line, implicitly threatening to freeze all economic assistance to the PA.[40] Meeting in London, the Quartet laid out three conditions for a new Palestinian government. At stake was billions of dollars in international economic assistance. "Future assistance to any new government would be reviewed by donors against that government's commitment to the principles of nonviolence, recognition of Israel, and acceptance of previous agreements and obligations, including the Road Map. The Quartet calls upon the newly elected Palestinian Legislative Council (PLC) to support the formation of a government committed to these principles as well as the rule of law, tolerance, reform and sound fiscal management," the Quartet said on January 31.[41]

According to Secretary Rice, there was unanimity within the Quartet on these principles, even with Russia. There were also no advocates in the administration for engaging Hamas or for taking a wait-and-see approach. "The mood was pretty hard line against Hamas," said Danin.[42] Although some Bush administration officials suggest in retrospect that the United States would have responded positively if Hamas had advanced even partway toward the Quartet conditions, the clear message from day one can only be described as a punitive strategy. The consensus within the administration, according to one senior official, was that "if Hamas runs [the new government], they have to meet the conditions or we turn [everything] off."[43] Moreover, there was a working assumption that Hamas was unlikely to change its stripes and that the task for the United States would be to isolate the group and strengthen Abbas and other moderate forces. And the administration also had to worry about the elections in Israel, two months away, when Olmert could be attacked by more conservative parties for looking weak on Hamas.

Thus, the idea of giving a Hamas government an opportunity to change, without relinquishing the possibility of isolation later on should it refuse, was never given serious consideration.[44] This option would have been greeted with some skepticism at home from conservatives and with push-back from Israel as well. Still, it would have been far more consistent with the administration's freedom agenda than the policy adopted. There was concrete internal and international consensus that Hamas should be isolated. Thus, for two months, while Hamas formed a new government, the U.S. position hardened and the Quartet conditions took on the status of nonnegotiable ultimatums.

The administration also reportedly considered far more aggressive tactics against Hamas. A *New York Times* story at the time reported that the Bush administration "and Israel are discussing ways to destabilize the Palestinian government so that new elected Hamas officials will fail and elections will be called again."[45] Although it fell short of what might be construed as a concerted "plan" to bring down the new government, there is no doubt the Bush administration understood how impactful an aid cutoff would be. Without tax revenues and external budget support, the PA would be unable to pay salaries for its 140,000 employees, including security forces, which would have crippling effects on Palestinian society as a whole.

Funds were pledged for the PA caretaker government, but when the Hamas government was installed in late March without explicitly endorsing the Quartet conditions, Western donors acted quickly to cut off economic assistance.[46] Direct transfers to the PA for budget support were halted, as were many development projects, given the administration's "no contact" policy that was adopted in an atmosphere of increasing congressional scrutiny.[47] Other than humanitarian assistance, which was largely channeled through the UN, the pipeline of U.S. and Western economic aid—which had kept the PA afloat in recent years and which supported a host of development projects—simply dried up.[48]

After the first shock of the Hamas victory wore off and the new government was in place, the initial Bush approach developed into a bolder (and therefore riskier) strategy of actively undermining the Hamas government and pressuring Abbas to dissolve the government and call for new elections. The United States also once again courted Mohammed Dahlan, Arafat and Abbas's former security chief in Gaza and someone viewed as a next generation Palestinian leader who had "street" support. Dahlan, however, was a controversial figure, with accusations linking his security forces to torture and corruption. The courting of Dahlan followed a pattern first set by Bill Clinton, who sought to appeal to the younger members of Arafat's team at the aborted Camp David summit in 2000. Bush himself had been impressed by Dahlan when they met at the Aqaba summit in 2003, reportedly remarking that "he's our guy."[49]

Meanwhile, the Israeli elections were held on March 28, which confirmed Olmert as the prime minister and Kadima as the largest party in Israel, though by a smaller margin than anticipated. Olmert ran on a peace platform, including the possibility, if negotiations failed, of unilateral withdrawal from the West Bank similar to the Gaza withdrawal, which he announced as a "convergence" plan: Israel would withdraw from some outer settlements and reinforce Israel's hold on the larger settlement blocs, establishing a new boundary between Israelis and Palestinians. But it was not until late in his prime ministership, in 2008, that he had the opportunity to advance his peace agenda through negotiations. In the interim, he was forced to confront two crises forced on him by Hamas and Hezbollah, respectively.

Hamas and Hezbollah Confront Israel

The first crisis erupted on June 25, 2006, when a Hamas team crossed the border into Israel, ambushed an Israeli border patrol operating on its own side of the border, killed two soldiers, kidnapped a young corporal Gilad Shalit, and took him back into Gaza. There he languished until October 2011, when he was released by

Hamas in return for 1,027 Palestinian prisoners of Israel, many of whom had been responsible for terrorist attacks on Israelis. In the meantime, the Shalit issue became highly emotional in Israel, distorting politics toward the right and making serious negotiations even more difficult.

The second crisis began in July 2006, when war suddenly broke out on the Israel-Lebanese border. The Bush administration, like most of the world, was astonished at this sudden turn of events. Syria, whose troops had been an occupying force in Lebanon since 1976, had been something of a backwater in the administration's first term. On the one hand, the young leader of Syria, Bashar al-Asad, seemed at times a reformist who, for example, wanted to aid the United States with intelligence sharing in the wake of 9/11.[50] On the other hand, his forces remained in Lebanon despite Israeli withdrawal in May 2000, and his government was far too supportive of Iraqi insurgents for any improvement to be serious in relations between Washington and Damascus. The efforts of Secretary Powell to achieve some sort of improvement in relations between the two countries came to naught, even when al-Asad in a December 1, 2003, interview with the *New York Times* said he would be willing to resume negotiations with Israel without preconditions.[51] But Sharon was uninterested, as was Bush. The White House wanted to see serious behavior change on a range of issues before it would consider renewed negotiations over the Golan. By early November 2003, both the House and Senate had passed, by wide margins, a new set of tough economic sanctions against Syria.[52] Bush signed the measure into law in December.

A year later, the new congressional sanctions had been intensified to the point where most American exports to Syria were prohibited.[53] The United States had also been critical in gaining the passage of UN Security Council Resolution 1559 that increased pressure on Syria to withdraw its military from Lebanon. In November and December 2004, when there were again signals of a possible resumption of Israeli-Syrian peace talks, the Bush administration remained uninterested.

The turning point that intensified the administration's antagonism to Syria emerged early in the second term when Rafik Hariri, the former Lebanese prime minister who had rebuilt Lebanon after the end of its civil war in 1990, was assassinated on February 14, 2005. Syria was widely regarded as the culprit, although in 2011 a UN investigative tribunal would blame Hezbollah operatives. The immediate impact of the assassination was to intensify the administration's opposition to Syrian actions and the Bush team's determination to isolate what it saw as an offending regime. After weeks of mounting international pressure, and facing an unprecedented protest movement in Lebanon, Syria abruptly withdrew its military forces by the end of April, ending what had been a twenty-nine-year occupation. Washington termed the events the "Cedar Revolution," in an attempt to evoke the uprisings in Central and Eastern Europe, though the Lebanese preferred the "March 14" branding, the date of the revolution. Administration officials felt a sense of vindication, though it would be short-lived.

Over the next several months the administration remained concentrated on making sure that "the Syrians don't creep back in (to Lebanon) through the back door," according to one former American official.[54] The focus was on behavior change, not "regime change."[55] But the impact in Lebanon itself was to create a freer rein for Hezbollah with the Syrians now able to claim diminished involvement.[56] All of this came to a head on July 12, 2006, when an Israeli border patrol on the Lebanese border was ambushed by Hezbollah forces that killed two Israeli soldiers and captured two wounded men, who were then taken back into Lebanon. These types of incidents had occurred before in recent years, but two conditions had changed: Syrian forces were no longer in Lebanon, and Sharon, with his checkered past and previous severe actions in Lebanon in the early 1980s, was no longer prime minister. The inexperienced Olmert government believed it had no choice but to react strongly against the Hezbollah attack because of past Hezbollah actions, because it believed that they must be stopped for purposes of deterrence, because of the capture of Shalit on the Gaza border just a couple of weeks earlier, and in part, because of its dovish stance on the West Bank. The result was a severe Israeli attack on Hezbollah-controlled areas of Beirut, accompanied by wide-scale destruction and civilian casualties. The Hezbollah War of summer 2006 had begun.

By the time the war was over, sections of newly rebuilt Beirut lay in ruins, with at least 1,110 Lebanese dead and 3,700 wounded. At the same time, a further shocking development during the war was Hezbollah's ability to rain missiles over northern Israel, causing civilian and military casualties in the process.[57]

Bush Fails the Test of War

The outbreak of the Hezbollah War, also known as the Israel-Lebanon War, found Bush in St. Petersburg, Russia, for a summit meeting. Rice received an urgent call from Israeli foreign minister Tzipi Livni on July 12, telling her of the Hezbollah border raid and anticipating a tough Israeli response. Before leaving Russia, Bush suggested to Rice that she go to the region, but Rice hesitated, unsure of what she could do at that point.[58]

Within Bush's national security team there was strong support for giving Israel a free hand and not intervening to stop the fighting. The war was viewed as a proxy of America's own "war on terrorism" and its confrontation with Iran. Israel's stated goal of destroying Hezbollah, therefore, was strongly embraced by figures such as Vice President Cheney. "Israel's war against Hezbollah in Lebanon was another defining moment in the ideological struggle," Bush reflects in his memoir.[59] Describing an NSC meeting during the war, Bush recalls the infighting "within the team" as "heated." "We need to let the Israelis finish off Hezbollah," Bush recalls Dick Cheney saying. 'If you do that,' Condi replied, 'America will be dead in the Middle East.' "[60] Rice recalls the infighting as one of only two instances when the split within the administration was "strategic," rather than "tactical."[61] Both American and Israeli leaders believed moderate Arab states were quietly supportive of Israel's offensive against Hezbollah. "Early on, everyone wanted Hezbollah to be bloodied, including the Arabs," Rice said.[62]

The United States wanted to end the conflict, White House spokesman Tony Snow stated, but only in a way that addressed the underlying causes.[63] "What we're seeing (are the) birth pangs of a new Middle East," Secretary Rice said in the second week of the Israel-Lebanon War.[64] The quote quickly became the source of heated debate, much of it disparaging toward Rice and the administration. Nevertheless, few public remarks better represent the Bush approach, with its unapologetic emphasis on breaking with the past, remaking U.S. Middle East policy, and transforming the region. Certain in their convictions, Bush and his inner circle interpreted even the most glaring setbacks as merely bumps in the road. There was little capacity for self-assessment, preferring instead to rationalize short-term setbacks as affirmation of their approach.

In late July, after scores of Lebanese civilians were killed at Qana, Bush's spokesman, Tony Snow, spoke of the president's "determination that it is really important to remove the conditions" that caused the war.[65] Rice had a similar message. "We also seek to address the root causes (of the war) so that a real and endurable (sic) peace can be established," Rice told reporters in an often testy exchange nearly ten days into the war, where she was pressed on why she had not visited the region sooner. "A cease-fire would be a false promise if it simply returns us to the status quo, allowing terrorists to launch attacks at the time and terms of their choosing and to threat (sic) innocent people, Arab and Israeli, throughout the region. That would be a guarantee of future violence."[66]

Throughout the war, Bush officials disdained traditional diplomatic approaches. "You're not going to solve this problem merely by passing another (UN) resolution," a senior official told the *Washington Post* at the end of July.[67] In pledging to use the war to address the "root causes," the White House raised expectations almost as high as Israel was doing in its declarations that it would defeat Hezbollah. Bush himself set expectations the highest. "The experience of September the 11th made it clear that we could no longer tolerate the status quo in the Middle East," Bush said. "This moment of conflict in the Middle East is painful and tragic . . . yet it is also a moment of opportunity for broader change in the region."[68] Transformation would indeed come, but it would leave Washington's adversaries in the region in a stronger position, not the other way around.

It was a dangerous mix of the Bush team's ideological predispositions and its view of the conflict as a proxy battleground, combined with Israel's own lack of a strategy in its rush to war. The two dynamics became mutually reinforcing. Rice finally traveled to the region, but Syria was not on her agenda. In his biography of Rice, Kessler reports that Welch had misgivings about ignoring Syria, but ultimately he and other advisers to Rice agreed that Damascus could be skipped. The decision not to travel to Damascus raised little debate within an administration only too keen to keep adversaries at arm's length.[69] The president himself would later affirm Rice's decision.

Asked subsequently on why the United States had not engaged Damascus, Bush dismissed the question. "We have been in touch with Syria. Colin Powell sent a message to Syria in person. Dick Armitage [Powell's deputy] traveled to Syria. Bill Burns traveled to Syria," said the president, referring to previous American encounters, some—as in the case of Powell—over three years before. "We've got a consulate office in Syria. Syria knows what we think. The problem isn't us telling Syria what's on our mind, which is to stop harboring terror and to help the Iraqi democracy evolve. They know exactly what our position is. The problem is," Bush continued, "that their response hasn't been very positive. As a matter of fact, it hasn't been positive at all."[70]

At a critical juncture, during an international meeting on the Lebanese crisis in Rome on July 26, the United States was virtually isolated in its refusal to call for an "immediate" cease-fire. Rice recalls the episode with apparent regret, calling it one of the most difficult moments of her tenure. "I had to stand there next to Fuad Siniora, who I adored, who's one of my favorite people," she said. "His country's being pounded and I have to stand there and say (the United States is) not in favor of an immediate cease-fire."[71]

The deaths of Lebanese civilians in Qana seemed to set off an unraveling of the administration's hands-off approach. Born of an eagerness for Israel to deal a decisive blow to Hezbollah, a belief that moderate Arab leaders were quietly supporting the Israeli assault, and a disregard for past attempts to restore calm in Lebanon, the initial U.S. approach was becoming less and less sustainable. By the second week of August, the administration found itself precisely where it pledged not to go: pressing for an end to the fighting based on a UN resolution that held little prospect for addressing the same root causes Bush and Rice spoke against so forcefully.

For his part, Bush would go on vacation in Texas in the midst of the war, not unlike a number of Europeans who also kept to their annual August vacation rituals.

But for Bush, it was also characteristic of his detached style and disinclination to get too involved in the nitty-gritty of an issue, even during a major foreign policy crisis. For example, he reportedly did not speak once to Olmert on the phone throughout the war.[72]

Despite the appearance of close coordination, the administration could not and did not try to influence Israel's actions. Washington failed to convince Israel to avoid certain steps that would undermine Siniora—including attacks against the Lebanese army and civilian infrastructure. "Unfortunately, Israel made matters worse," Bush writes in his memoirs. "I started to worry that Israel's offensive might topple Prime Minister Siniora's democratic government." Bush also felt Olmert was too lenient on Syria, and that Israel should not have ruled out wartime attacks against its regime, given al-Asad's support for Hezbollah.

"The Israelis had a chance to deliver a major blow against Hezbollah and their sponsors in Iran and Syria," Bush writes. "Unfortunately, they mishandled their opportunity. To compound matters, Prime Minister Olmert announced that Syria would not be a target. I thought it was a mistake. Removing the threat of retaliation let Syria off the hook and emboldened them to continue their support for Hezbollah."[73]

Israel's last-minute attempt to initiate a ground war floundered, and the administration turned to the UN after all. On August 12, the Security Council passed Resolution 1701, which called for an immediate cease-fire, an expanded role for the United Nations Interim Force in Lebanon (UNIFIL), and an Israeli withdrawal. The resolution also reiterated past demands, as in UN Security Council Resolution (UNSCR) 1559, for the "disarmament of all armed groups"—code for Hezbollah. It also contained a provision calling for a "long-term" solution that would include an end to all arms transfers, except those authorized by the Lebanon government.[74] But there were few illusions that these more expansive provisions had any teeth. The major benefit of 1701 was that it finally returned the Lebanese army to Israel's border, replacing the prime Hezbollah presence, and thereby bringing a measure of stability to the area. However, the resolution did not provide for the deployment of an international border force that could stop Syria's smuggling of weapons to Hezbollah, enabling the organization to rebuild its capacity within a short matter of time to beyond pre-war levels. With hindsight, these limited benefits did not make the war worth the costs that were incurred on both sides.

The outcome of the 2006 Israel-Lebanon War was a setback for Washington, whether defined in terms of support for Siniora's elected government and the March 14 movement broadly, the ever-diminishing prospect of renewed Arab-Israeli peacemaking, or the larger confrontation with Iran. Each of these American objectives suffered in the aftermath of the thirty-four-day war. "While it remains fragile and still faces pressure from Syria," Bush writes later in his memoir, "Lebanon's young democracy emerged stronger for having endured the test."[75] But nothing would be further from the truth.

"I have no interest in diplomacy for the sake of returning Lebanon and Israel to the status quo ante," Rice had said earlier in the war, when criticized for not intervening.[76] As events would later show, the administration did just that—though only after a costly delay that eclipsed the possibility of using the conflict to mount an American peace initiative and decisively shape the post-war setting.

Indeed, the Bush team's effort to once again pursue a different American policy than the United States had followed in similar situations was a dismal failure and demonstrated extremely poor judgment. However provocative and aggressive the initial Hezbollah foray into Israel was, and however necessary it was to reconfirm Israeli deterrence, weakening the Lebanese polity by severe air strikes on central Beirut and then a dismal Israeli ground attack late in the war did not produce effective results.[77] Further, the United States put its faith in an Israeli war plan that would be revealed as half-baked and unable to chart a realistic path to victory.

Although the leader of Hezbollah, Hassan Nasrallah, later stated he would not have attacked initially if he had had any inkling of the Israeli response, the ultimate outcome of the war was a gradual strengthening of the Hezbollah role in Lebanon.[78] The war's frustrations and Hezbollah's ability to attack northern Israel with missiles at will not only demonstrated a significant weakness in Israel's defensive capability but helped to turn the Israeli populace rightward against peace, which would be reflected in the next elections.[79]

Ironically, if Bush and Rice had stepped in earlier to end the war, Israel would have appeared stronger, its deterrence in better shape, and the American reputation would have been enhanced. Because Israel's demonstration of unchallenged strength came early, during the initial phase of the war, staying in the conflict longer only made the Jewish state look weaker. In a bizarre paradox, the administration's continued efforts to isolate Syria—before, during, and after the war—were quickly challenged from an unlikely source: Israel. Shortly after the war ended, former security chiefs Avi Dichter and Danny Yatom began calling for new peace talks with Syria. The debate didn't go very far, as Olmert was careful not to break from his erstwhile ally and wartime patron. Al-Asad's hard-line public statements after the war undercut the case for engagement, but so did American coldness to the idea.[80]

Bush's self-assured, even boastful statements the day the Israel-Lebanon War ended appeared far-fetched as best. "Most objective observers would give the United States credit for helping to lead the effort to get a resolution that addressed the root cause of the problem," he said.[81] "How can you claim victory," he told Hezbollah, "when at one time you were a state within a state, safe within southern

Lebanon, and now you're going to be replaced with a Lebanese Army and an international force?"[82] The effort he hailed not only failed, as Hezbollah rearmed and further entrenched its presence in the south, but Washington's allies in Lebanon grew weaker and weaker, forced to turn to other regional players when Bush's ineffective approach left them no option.

The U.S. and Israel Split on Syria

The administration was unable to maintain a tight diplomatic blockade of Syria for very long. The release of the Iraq Study Group Report, following the 2006 midterm elections, opened the door for political figures to speak out against the Bush approach. The Congressionally-sponsored report, co-authored by former secretary of state James Baker and former congressman Lee Hamilton, included a prominent recommendation for renewed engagement with Syria.[83] Foreign officials increasingly began returning to Damascus. Leading members of Congress, including Nancy Pelosi, Tom Lantos, Arlen Specter, John Kerry, Chris Dodd, and Bill Nelson, visited Syria despite protests from the White House.

The visits were cast in terms of implementation of the Baker-Hamilton report, but they also came against a background of growing unease in the United States over Bush's handling of the Iraq War and Middle East policy more broadly.[84] Signals from Damascus in late 2006 and early 2007 about renewing peace talks, which generated strong interest in Israel, provided even greater rationale for those willing to buck a determined president.

Still, administration admonitions to Israel against reviving peace talks with Syria became more unequivocal. Against the backdrop of reports that Syria was facilitating Hezbollah's rearming and desperate to support Washington's allies in Lebanon, Rice was adamant in advising Israeli leaders against embarking on "exploratory talks" with Damascus. A Syrian-Israeli peace process, in the administration's view, would be a "prize" for Damascus.[85] Olmert complied, at least for a time. Former national security advisor Stephen Hadley describes the approach in vivid terms:

> So the Israelis say, "we want to engage the Syrians, and we want to see if we can flip them, and we're willing to dangle Golan as part of that deal." We are skeptical as to whether Asad could be flipped, we've had a lot of dealings with him, and it had not worked out very well. We were very worried that by engaging Asad it would look like . . . an Israeli-Syrian peace was an alternative to a Palestinian peace, which would undermine Abbas and Abu Ala'a, and secondly if Israel did a peace with Syria before they did a peace with

Lebanon, before we had resolved the remaining Shebaa Farms issue, it would have undermined . . . Siniora.[86]

The administration's skepticism about promoting Syrian-Israeli peace talks was deeply rooted. It was inextricably tied to its goals of transforming the Middle East and the conviction that adversaries such as Syria needed to be isolated. It was a classic neoconservative perspective, as well as a mirror image of hard-line Israeli attitudes against territorial compromise—although to the right of attitudes in the Israeli government at the time.

The discovery of a suspected Syrian nuclear facility in the spring of 2007 did little to assuage U.S. concerns and restore trust in al-Asad. Bush writes in his memoir that Olmert asked him to order an American attack against the suspected site, which the president declined to do.[87] Instead, Israel destroyed the facility in an early September raid. By agreement, Israel and the United States kept silent about the Israeli attack, in an effort to avoid escalation.[88] However, it was American sources who first hinted and then revealed that it had been Israel, not the United States, that had executed the efficient attack.

The administration seemed satisfied with Israel's actions, with no public or private criticisms. The Olmert goverment had handled what could have been a situation that easily escalated out of control. Syria did not retaliate, perhaps because it had been caught red-handed and perhaps because of American backing for Israel. Whereas other administrations might have been displeased that Israel had not pursued the diplomatic track, the Bush team applauded this sort of activity by allies. An ongoing International Atomic Energy Agency (IAEA) investigation of Syria, launched in the wake of the Israeli raid, would become yet another irritant in a strained U.S.-Syrian relationship, especially because all evidence found by the IAEA confirmed that the Israelis had indeed attacked a secret nuclear facility.[89]

However, when Rice organized the November 2007 Annapolis meeting, she broke with the pattern and invited Syria.[90] Al-Asad sent Feysal Mekdad, his deputy foreign minister and former UN ambassador. He was not prepared to send his foreign minister, as the Saudis and several other Arab countries did. After Annapolis, Olmert therefore felt freer to entertain renewed discussions with Damascus.

The Israelis soon began indirect talks with Syria under the auspices of the Turks as mediators. It was ironic indeed. The United States had been the traditional intermediaries for any negotiations between the Israelis and their Arab neighbors. Unless dialogues were held directly and secretly between the two sides, as in Oslo, it was very unusual for major consultations to occur with another mediator besides the United States. But given the opposition of Bush and Cheney to engaging with Syria in any manner, the Israeli government—despite its extremely close ties to the United States—nevertheless pressed on with Turkish mediation.

Five rounds of indirect discussions took place in 2008. Once the Olmert administration entered the talks, the Bush team no longer actively discouraged Israel, but neither did it rush to give its support. What had been a "red light," in 2006–7 became a "yellow" light in 2008. Rice offered tepid backing in public, but in private the administration kept its distance, leaving Turkey to manage the mediation.[91] Regional dynamics were shifting, but the Bush administration chose to remain on the sidelines, unwilling to budge from its principled positions.

The effort culminated in Olmert's visit to Ankara in December 2008, where he met for several hours with Turkish prime minister Recep Teyyep Erdoğan—who then, with Olmert at his side, spoke with al-Asad by phone. Despite the absence of direct talks, the parties reportedly came quite close to a major breakthrough and had already begun discussions of demarcating a border. But when the Israeli military offensive in Gaza began a few days later, Erdoğan felt betrayed because he had not been informed beforehand and pulled out of the mediation effort. The bitterness would grow and Turkish-Israeli relations would spiral downward thereafter.

As Israel and Syria were engaged in a secret effort to restart peace talks, Washington's allies in Lebanon were coming under an assault at home. Locked in a continuing stalemate with its March 14 rivals, Hezbollah forces took to the streets of Beirut in May 2008—bringing Lebanon to the brink of civil war. In short order, all the major Lebanese factions—with Syrian and Saudi support—struck a deal, mediated by Qatar, which avoided war but enlarged Hezbollah's position in Lebanese politics. Hezbollah would not only have a role in a unity government, but it would effectively hold veto power. Its militia dominated Lebanese security affairs.

After the Doha Agreement, Hezbollah was poised to emerge paramount in Lebanon's politics as well. With its Lebanese allies already out in front on the Doha Agreement, the administration had few options other than to publicly welcome the accord. Rice called it "a positive step." Positive or not, the Doha Agreement made clear that the United States had ceded much of the diplomatic space to others.[92] The gap between American power and influence was widening. Future events would demonstrate how badly American influence had deteriorated and how much additional power Hezbollah had gained.

The saga of the Bush era in the Levant is markedly disappointing. Everything failed; the attempted isolation of Syria drove it closer than ever to Iran. The attempt to use Israel in 2006 to defeat Hezbollah and strengthen the Lebanese government did not work. The attempted ouster of Syrian influence from Lebanon caused Hezbollah to grow stronger after the 2006 Israel-Lebanon War. The attempt to prevent Syrian-Israeli talks frittered away a window of opportunity and failed because Israel eventually went on anyway through Turkish mediation. Looking back, the Bush administration's Syrian and Lebanese expedition was a microcosm of the inadequacy of applying inappropriate ideological preconceptions to a region that would not bend to Bush's whims.

Palestinian Unification?

The aftermath of the Hezbollah War deeply affected Palestinian developments as well. In September and October 2006, Abbas nearly brokered a unity government with Hamas that could have led to an easing of tensions and kept key portfolios, including negotiations, in Abbas's hands. Washington rejected the political arrangement because the administration opposed any kind of unity government despite the fact that it lacked a viable alternative strategy for handling Palestinian politics; it knew what it opposed but did not have a reasonable vision for what it wanted in its place. Violence continued with occasional spikes, including a particularly deadly series of clashes in the Gaza town of Beit Hanoun.

The administration pressured Abbas to act more decisively to resolve the government crisis, even encouraging him to dismiss the Hamas government if it continued to refuse to meet international conditions and instead install his own emergency government.[93] "We fully support President Abbas," said Rice at a Palestinian-American political event in Washington in October, "and the growing number of his fellow citizens, who are urging Hamas to put the interests of the Palestinian people ahead of their own rejectionist agenda." The subtle message in public was delivered not so subtly in private, where U.S. officials urged Abbas to effectively take over from the Hamas government then in place.[94]

The administration also began to pursue more aggressively a plan to strengthen Palestinian security forces, with nonlethal funding from the United States and weapons coming from the Arab neighbors. They were under the control of Abbas as president and not the Hamas government. A senior American military official, General Keith Dayton, who was already on the ground, was charged with overseeing the stepped-up effort. Yet, although the United States intended to strengthen Abbas and those loyal to him, in many respects its aid cutoff made matters worse. In Gaza, for example, the inability to pay salaries and to maintain adequate operational support for the Fatah-affiliated PA security service weakened Abbas's control and created opportunities for Hamas to step into the void. Also, Dayton's program took time to execute. Some of the new cadres of security personnel did not arrive in Gaza—for example—until well into 2007.[95] "We were trying to strengthen people, strengthen Abu Mazen [Abbas] working through people that he had designated to strengthen his position," said a senior U.S. official.[96]

Meanwhile, following the Israel-Lebanon War, a low point for the administration, Rice told her top advisers it was time to craft a new diplomatic initiative. With Ehud Olmert leading Israel and promising to set Israel's permanent borders—unilaterally if necessary—there was hope but also serious concern that a diplomatic process was needed in order to head off another Gaza-style disappointment that was not coordinated between Israel and the Palestinians.[97] Unfortunately, the landscape had become rougher; the Hamas victory, the capture of Shalit, and the Israel-Lebanon War made the possibility of a major breakthrough more challenging. Olmert had run on a platform to withdraw from most of the West Bank, with a high probability of unilateralism, but Shalit and Lebanon had undermined his program. Rice did not need just a diplomatic process; she would need a major and sustained effort, which until now the administration had not attempted and had not shown itself capable of pursuing.

Yet, on the broader level, there was a growing appreciation within the administration that in order to deal with threats across the region—Iran, Lebanon, and Iraq—a more robust peace process was essential to gather support from moderate Arab governments. It was classic linkage, the kind many conservatives—as well as Israelis—long opposed.

"What would bind that coalition and help keep them together," said Philip Zelikow, Rice's counselor at State, "is a sense that the Arab-Israeli issues are being addressed, that they see a common determination to sustain an active policy that tries to deal with the problems of Israel and the Palestinians." Zelikow's remarks captured this new frame for the administration.[98]

For the Arab moderates and for the Europeans, some sense of progress and momentum on the Arab-Israeli dispute is a sine qua non for their ability and willingness to cooperate actively with the United States. Zelikow acknowledged and reaffirmed a policy approach that had long been accepted by previous administrations, but which Bush had resisted—that Arab-Israeli peacemaking was an essential ingredient for dealing with other vital issues. He would leave the administration soon after.[99]

Thus, by late 2006, the State Department desired to rejuvenate the peace process, but the administration lacked both a concrete plan and a "Palestinian entity . . . we could work with," as one official put it.[100] Nonetheless, Rice tried to kick-start a process by setting up a trilateral mechanism—Rice-Olmert-Abbas—to resume negotiations, based on drawing a distinction between Abbas as president and the Hamas-controlled government. But Olmert resisted, particularly if final-status issues were on the agenda, arguing that Israel could not negotiate with Hamas in the government.

The administration's ability to mount a diplomatic initiative was effectively held hostage to the Palestinian governmental crisis—even the Arab League's reiteration of its peace initiative in early 2007 did not lead to serious consideration.[101] The problem was that when Abbas or Sharon or Olmert said they would not accept something, it was the administration's style to accept them at their word. No one in the Bush entourage seems to have raised the possibility that Olmert's position on Hamas was his opening salvo or subject to reconsideration. Abbas was the president of the Palestinian Authority and chairman of the PLO, the entity empowered by the Oslo Accords to negotiate with Israel (and also recognized by Israel). His position was politically and legally separate from the Hamas government. The United States was making that distinction; why couldn't Israel? Instead, the administration simply moved on, accepting Olmert's stance. Had it convinced the Israeli government to engage then, the Mecca crisis and Gaza coup that would soon follow might have been averted.

The United States Resists the Mecca Accords

In yet another blow to the peace process and Bush policy, Saudi Arabia brokered a power-sharing deal at Mecca in early February 2007 that set out a national unity government and temporarily ended the year-long internal Palestinian crisis. Asked months earlier about the possibility of Abbas calling early elections—and whether Washington would support the outcome—Rice said, "We always are going to accept democratic results of democratic elections."[102] Nevertheless, another chance would not come. Abbas resisted Washington's entreaties and instead chose a coalition arrangement and the regional support that came with it. The Saudis reportedly promised Abbas that they would line up U.S. support, which did not happen.

For Rice, the Hamas-Fatah Mecca Agreement was devastating. The deal was announced just days before she was to arrive in the region and preside over a trilateral meeting with Abbas and Olmert. "We get this all set up and then Mecca happens and Olmert doesn't want to come," Rice recalled. Bush weighed in with Olmert, who relented, but the meeting was a bust. In retrospect, Rice described this meeting as "the worst meeting . . . in my entire time." Olmert was incensed by the Mecca arrangement. Since the United States could not convince the parties to initiate peace talks on "final status," to which Olmert was adamantly opposed after the Mecca agreement, Rice developed the idea of a "political horizon" as a substitute that offered Palestinians at least a hint that endgame issues were on the table. She used this mechanism as a way to keep the leaders talking during the four tense months in which Hamas and Fatah shared power.[103]

At the same time as the United States was pushing the leaders to engage regularly, Washington sought ways to overturn the Mecca arrangement. In effect, Bush and Rice were pulling Abbas to the negotiating table and at the same time looking for ways to undermine the deal he struck in Mecca. The message was he should engage with Olmert but had to disengage from Hamas.

The administration redoubled its earlier efforts to refashion the Palestinian government—either by obtaining Hamas' explicit acceptance of the Quartet principles, which no one in the administration seriously pursued or believed was possible, or by Abbas disbanding the government. "The endgame should produce a (PA) government," read a leaked State Department document from this period, "through democratic means that accepts Quartet principles."[104] A key component of the strategy was the previously mentioned program to further bolster the security forces loyal to Abbas with nonlethal funding from the United States and arms from Arab neighbors.[105] The plan itself was questionable, given the risk of instigating a full-blown Hamas-Fatah arms race or even a civil war, but the administration failed to execute its own plan.[106]

The Bush administration's working assumption—like Olmert's—was that a basic accommodation among Palestinians would be an obstacle, rather than an enabler of a renewed diplomatic process. Although resistance to the Mecca Agreement was backed by American conservatives, the administration's policy still had its critics. "The United States is exacerbating this internal Palestinian power struggle by enticing Fatah with delusions of regaining power, along with shipments of equipment and cash," wrote an analyst at a prominent Washington think tank. "It is a dangerous game that can only lead to more bloodshed for both Palestinians and Israelis."[107]

In opposing the Hamas-Fatah Mecca Agreement, the Bush administration misjudged not only the Palestinian and wider Arab desire for accommodation and unity, but also the repercussions of an open confrontation. Moreover, the U.S. strategy undermined the very reform agenda that Bush himself set as a priority in his 2002 Rose Garden speech. "What we were doing at that time was trying to jury rig things in the Muqata [Abbas's headquarters in Ramallah]," said a former U.S. official, referring to the 2006–7 period, "so we could try to work with them. But that was not institution building at all . . . that was sort of anti-institution building because we were not helping the Authority."[108]

The Mecca arrangement did not hold up for long and intra-Palestinian violence in Gaza continued through the spring in addition to ongoing Gaza-Israel violence. Despite the setback of the Mecca Agreement, Rice persisted in her attempt to maintain a dialogue between Olmert and Abbas (although, again, without any U.S. pressure to produce results). In late March, a second Rice-Olmert-Abbas trilateral was held in Jerusalem. They announced plans for "parallel peace talks."

The two leaders agreed to meet regularly, but Olmert declined Rice's offer for her to serve as mediator.[109] A second track would involve a dozen bilateral com-

mittees led by Israeli foreign minister Tzipi Livni and longtime Palestinian negotiator and former prime minister Ahmed Qurie (Abu Ala'a). Olmert not only
sought direct and private talks with Abbas, but by now some Israelis had begun to
see Rice in a different light. They perceived her as tilting more and more toward
the Palestinian side.[110] With an administration still divided, Olmert could work a
separate channel with the White House and try his best to exploit differences between Rice and Bush.[111]

At the same time, the administration also asked Congress for another aid package to bolster Palestinian security forces loyal to Abbas.[112] By mid-June 2007, as the
U.S. security assistance program was still gearing up, factional fighting in Gaza
turned into a full-scale confrontation between Hamas and Fatah-affiliated PA
forces. Hamas had fewer fighters and less firepower, but they quickly overwhelmed
the Fatah-affiliated fighters. Fatah's poor performance is largely attributed to internal quarreling, corruption, and Abbas's lack of decisive leadership; Hamas appeared far more motivated and better organized.[113] The fighting was intense and, at
times, gruesome. PA security forces were completely routed and their facilities either abandoned or taken over by Hamas. The obvious embarrassment of U.S.- and
Arab-supplied equipment and weapons falling into Hamas' hands was overshad-
owed by the larger strategic setback of a deepening split in the Palestinian camp and
a victory for a movement backed by Washington's adversaries, Iran and Syria.

Who Lost Gaza?

The sudden military coup was not only controversial at the time, but its origins
would remain bitterly disputed for years. Three general explanations are offered
for the Hamas takeover:

1. The Bush administration explanation is clear and simple: blame Hamas.
   "In June 2007 the militant wing of Hamas intervened," Bush writes in his
   memoir. "In a familiar pattern in the ideological struggle, the extremists
   responded to the advance of freedom with violence. Hamas terrorists
   backed by Iran and Syria mounted a coup and seized control of Gaza.
   Fighters in black masks ransacked Fatah headquarters, threw party leaders off rooftops, and targeted moderate members of Hamas's political
   wing."[114]
2. David Rose, in a *Vanity Fair* expose, presents a very different explanation, one supported to some degree by the pre-coup reporting of the *New
   York Times* and other news outlets, as well as pre-coup predictions by
   analysts.[115] In Rose's account, Hamas acted to preempt the growing

strength of Fatah as it prepared—with American and Arab assistance—to defeat Hamas and seize complete power in Gaza. The implication is that Hamas would never have attacked if the United States and others had not armed and encouraged Fatah to assert itself.[116]

3. Another interpretation is offered by a former senior Palestinian official, who argues that the real problem was that the Mecca Agreement failed. As one of the negotiators who joined Abbas in Saudi Arabia to negotiate the deal, he claimed that "The Americans didn't realize that Mecca was a big step for Hamas . . . Mecca was a great achievement, but the Americans were not aboard." He suggested that Prince Bandar, then secretary-general of the Saudi National Security Council, tried but failed to get U.S. buy-in. "Hamas accepted Mecca and would have abided by the agreement if the U.S. had gone along, in particular because it was running out of the funds it required," said the former Palestinian negotiator, who also blamed Israel for weakening Fatah-affiliated forces during the Second Intifada.[117]

These three schools of thought assign blame to different actors: Bush faults Hamas; Rose and others blame the United States; and the former senior Palestinian official—perhaps reflecting the view from Ramallah—faults both the United States and Israel. Rose criticizes the arming of Dahlan's Fatah forces in Gaza and America's faith in him; the former senior Palestinian official blames the Bush administration for not backing the Mecca Agreement and Israel for destroying much of Fatah's infrastructure during the Intifada.[118]

There is more than enough blame to apportion. The basic explanation for the Gaza coup lies in a combination of factors: first and foremost, Hamas' militancy and its drive to dominate Palestinian politics; second, Fatah's own unwillingness to come to terms with its electoral defeat; and third, an American administration that had long since settled on a confrontational policy of isolating and undermining Hamas.

After the Hamas takeover, Israel, with Washington's concurrence, acted swiftly to try to seal Gaza from the outside world, allowing delivery of basic humanitarian assistance only. Abbas, incensed by what he termed a "coup," dismissed the government and declared a state of emergency. Salam Fayyad, an independent member of parliament and former finance minister who enjoyed strong support in the Bush administration and among Western donors, was quickly installed as head of an emergency government. The administration acted swiftly to recognize Fayyad's government and to pledge a large infusion of economic assistance.

For the first time since the January 2006 election, Washington had a Palestinian government with which it felt comfortable, although the price—Palestine divided—was steep. A "West Bank First" policy was adopted. The U.S. and Western aid spigot was quickly turned back on in an effort to bolster Abbas and Fayyad. By late June, the Quartet named former British prime minister Tony Blair as its new envoy and charged him with overseeing Palestinian economic recovery efforts. Bush had good ties with Blair, and the parties welcomed his appointment as well. With Hamas now firmly in control in Gaza and with fears of Hamas gaining strength in the West Bank, the effort to bolster Abbas became all the more urgent. The administration now turned its energies to improving conditions on the West Bank (encouraging Israel to do the same) and to intensifying the still embryonic Olmert-Abbas talks. *"West Bank First* is inevitable once you are where you are with Gaza after the coup," Elliott Abrams would later argue.[119]

In mid-July, President Bush called for an international meeting between Israeli, Palestinian, and Arab leaders, echoing Rice's goal of establishing a "political horizon" and moving "forward on a successful path to a Palestinian state."[120] From July forward, Rice set about launching a new American peace effort.

The United States signed a Memorandum of Understanding with Israel on August 13, 2007, to maintain Israel's "qualitative military edge," calling for a $30 billion aid package to be dispersed over ten years. Of that aid, however, 73.7 percent was to be spent on U.S. arms.[121] This decision seems to be a logical outcome of a variety of factors: the Gaza takeover by Hamas, the worsening tensions also epitomized by the Hezbollah War a year earlier, the inability to stop Iran's growing power and attempt to develop nuclear weapons, the strong feelings of sympathy for Israel at the highest levels of the administration, and the attempt to bolster Israeli confidence in the lead-up to the international peace process meeting.

Bush Initiates a Peace Process at Annapolis

The effort launched at Annapolis in November 2007 came as a surprise to many observers—as well as many administration skeptics, who had long lobbied the president against active mediation. The Middle East peace process, a second-tier priority since Clinton left office, would move toward, but not quite occupy center stage on Bush's foreign policy agenda for most of his last year in office.

Where did the new impulse come from? How did the administration craft its approach and define the U.S. role? What was the net impact of Annapolis? Was it an achievement, as veterans of the Bush administration and some negotiators on both sides suggest, that built on earlier American peace drives? The Annapolis negotiations, said one U.S. negotiator, were "the best that we'd ever seen," a sentiment echoed by Israeli and Palestinian insiders.[122]

Alternatively, did Annapolis amount to a lackluster experiment in diplomacy, burdened from the outset by internal administration divides ("Condi's peace process"), crippled by disdain for previous American initiatives, and hamstrung by a self-conception of the U.S. role that effectively left Washington on the sidelines?

The Hamas takeover in Gaza in June 2007 presented a dramatic setback on the ground, but it also offered an opportunity on the diplomatic track. With Abbas naming an emergency government under Prime Minister Salam Fayyad and the Mecca Agreement effectively dead, the United States could go back to promoting a more traditional, direct negotiation on final status. By the summer of 2007, with the surge taking hold in Iraq and the Hamas takeover in Gaza dramatizing the need for more active American diplomacy, Bush and Rice presided over their own type of surge in Arab-Israeli diplomacy—a new approach to peacemaking that looked very different from past attempts.

"It hasn't worked," said Secretary Rice in early November 2007, when asked about previous American attempts at Arab-Israeli peacemaking. "So, with all due respect, I'll try it my way."[123] Rice's comment neatly ignored the successes during the Nixon, Ford, Carter, first Bush, and Clinton presidencies. She presumably was referring to the last days of the Clinton administration. Indeed, every American administration since Nixon's had at one time or another devoted itself to the pursuit of Middle East peace through the stewardship of negotiations, and this Bush administration—it turns out—by its seventh year would make an attempt as well. But there was a catch. When Bush finally decided to engage in an intensive negotiating process—launched at Annapolis—his still divided administration designed an approach unlike any other that had come before.

The unique Bush-Rice style—which could be described as "facilitation from afar"—emerged from several building blocks, including the president's own limited view about the American role; his emphasis on Palestinian political reform; Rice's personal commitment to achieving a peace deal; and skepticism within the administration that served to limit Rice's options. It was also shaped by entreaties from the parties. Neither Olmert nor Abbas wanted the Americans to take an active mediation role. "The Americans do not have to bridge the gap," Abbas said in late 2008, reflecting back on the negotiations, "we have asked them to observe."[124]

In mid-July, 2007, the Administration called for a renewed peace effort that would be inaugurated with an international "meeting." And yet, the Bush team had to fuse its new diplomatic effort to its earlier emphasis on reform and its continued preference for ad hoc coalition building. "By supporting the reforms of President Abbas and Prime Minister Fayyad," Bush announced on July 16,

We can help them show the world what a Palestinian state would look like—and act like. We can help them prove to the world, the region, and Israel that a Palestinian state would be a partner—not a danger. We can help them make clear to all Palestinians that rejecting violence is the surest path to security and a better life. And we can help them demonstrate to the extremists once and for all that terror will have no place in a Palestinian state . . . First, we are strengthening our financial commitment.[125]

Bush reiterated his and Rice's earlier support for a "political horizon" for Palestinians, as well as his new intention to convene a multilateral gathering. "I will call together an international meeting this fall of representatives from nations that support a two-state solution, reject violence, recognize Israel's right to exist, and commit to all previous agreements between the parties."[126] He said Rice would lead the effort, and he offered Olmert a carrot that was becoming increasingly relevant in Israeli politics: recognition of Israel as a "Jewish state," which Bush would repeat later at Annapolis.

Skepticism was strong among several of the principals, particularly Vice President Cheney. The initiative, according to a Cheney adviser, was viewed as "something generated out of the State Department. The Secretary had a different view of the priority of the peace process . . . she seemed to believe that it was something that a lot of the Arab states really wanted and that it would assist our efforts on several other issues." But by the time of the July announcement, the president had made up his mind, and the skeptics essentially took a backseat. "Once the President decided that he needed to do something," said the Cheney adviser, "the debate was essentially over."[127]

And Bush did decide. He recounts in his memoirs that after the Gaza coup he was determined to create a situation in which the people of Gaza would see how much better off the West Bank was "under the democratic leader, Abbas," because "over time I was confident they would demand change." But what to do next?

Condi and I talked about a way to restart momentum for a democratic Palestinian state. She suggested an international conference to lay the ground work for negotiations between Abbas's government and the Israelis. At first I was skeptical. The aftermath of a terrorist coup didn't seem the most opportune time for a peace summit. But I came to like the idea. If wavering Palestinians could see that a state was a realistic possibility, they would have an incentive to reject violence and support reform.[128]

From the start of the Annapolis event, there was a hint of skepticism toward traditional diplomatic approaches. Bush was careful to propose a "meeting" rather than a "conference," so as not to evoke earlier American initiatives built around high-profile conferences—Geneva or Madrid, for example.[129] The emphasis was also squarely on the parties engaging face-to-face. Bush left little room for the United States to shuttle between the parties with its own bridging proposals or negotiating principles. The president emphasized the parties' own "bilateral discussions and negotiations."[130]

This approach had the added benefit of aligning squarely with Olmert's preference for direct talks without a heavy American role. Bush also made clear that it was Rice who would steer the process—simultaneously empowering her and signaling some degree of distance between himself and the new effort. Long before Annapolis was even proposed as a venue, there were clear signs that the administration would be taking a limited approach, even as its level of activity intensified.

In advance of Annapolis, Rice pushed Abbas and Olmert to meet as often as possible, but gridlock developed early on. At one point, Abbas called the exercise of planning an international meeting "a waste of time" unless the core issues were on the agenda.[131] Olmert wanted to produce a declaration of principles but avoid putting final-status issues on the agenda at the conference. Israel strongly resisted what it viewed as too activist an approach by Rice. As in earlier periods, White House–State Department differences were noticeable—despite the close relationship between President Bush and Secretary Rice. Olmert and his advisers preferred dealing with the White House, but his foreign minister, Tzipi Livni—a political rival of Olmert—developed a close bond with Rice. "Olmert's people did business with the White House, [Livni's] with the State Department," said a former Israeli official, "and they didn't always gel."[132]

Abbas and Olmert allowed their respective negotiators to try to sketch out a declaration before Annapolis, but the attempt failed, largely because Israel was reluctant to address substantive issues in an international gathering. "It quickly turned into more of a procedural document," said an Israeli official, and Livni "essentially convinced Condi that a procedural document" was all that could be achieved. Livni feared a more substantive document would lack public support in Israel. The Israelis relied on a narrow reading of Bush's own announcement in July in order to whittle down American and Palestinian expectations. An Israeli said Rice was at a disadvantage, unaccustomed to Israeli and Arab bargaining. The Secretary "wasn't used to the kind of brinkmanship and last minute games we play, Israelis and Palestinians" and "was pretty nervous and happy to have any results."[133] "Palestinians wanted and demanded that this conference would produce the launching of permanent-status negotiations," recalls an American official, "which will include the traditional issues: Jerusalem, borders, refugees, etc. . . . [but] we had to squeeze Abu Mazen to accept [the absence of] language on core issues . . . because we could not deliver from Olmert."[134]

As the administration came closer to pulling off its "meeting," internal divisions again came to the fore. Rice said the infighting was intense over Annapolis.[135] White House advisers such as Elliott Abrams were skeptical that negotiations could produce anything and felt the U.S. priority should be building up Fayyad, economic conditions, and public institutions on the West Bank. In an attempt to satisfy these competing pressures, Rice backed off from pressuring the parties to produce a declaration of principles. Moreover, by broadening the guest list—ultimately dozens of countries would participate—administration skeptics were kept at bay. The larger the event, said a senior U.S. official, the less important it might seem to some, and thus the easier it was to deflect internal administration opposition.[136]

"Annapolis . . . was designed to try to address one of the shortcomings of the Oslo process, which was to (1) bring in a regional dimension up front, and (2) to bring in the kind of ground-up institutional building, economic development track so that conditions improve and there's public support for the process," said Robert Danin.[137] Just days before the meeting, formal invitations were issued and the administration made it clear that it expected "yes or no" responses. Unlike Madrid, for example, the terms would not be open to negotiation.

As the meeting drew closer, and prospects for a substantive breakthrough dimmed, Rice focused almost entirely on putting together the strongest possible lineup of participants. To the surprise of doubters, it was a stellar group that the administration had brought to the conference, including representatives of sixteen Arab states. Bush reflected, "It was a historic moment to see the foreign minister of Saudi Arabia listen respectfully to the prime minister of Israel and applaud his words. The Annapolis conference was hailed as a surprise success."[138] The meeting itself had all the trappings of an impressive international gathering, with the picturesque, secluded setting of the U.S. Naval Academy providing an elegant backdrop—without being too evocative of summits past.

Bush tells the story of traveling to Annapolis with Rice on Marine One. When he asked her for a copy of the joint statement to open the meeting, "she said they had made a lot of progress but hadn't finished. 'You're going to have to deliver this one yourself,' she said." Bush accepted the lackluster situation, and he says, "I pulled Abbas and Olmert aside individually. I told them the summit would be viewed as a failure and embolden the extremists if we couldn't agree on a statement." According to Bush, the two leaders instructed their negotiators to work with the secretary. "A few minutes before we were due in front of the cameras, she brought me the document," Bush recalls. "There was no time to enlarge the font, so I pulled out my reading glasses and read from the page."[139] And so the Annapolis meeting began with a rather vague commitment by both sides to try to reach an agreement on a peace treaty by the end of 2008. On the core issues—including Jerusalem and refugees—which the parties had publicly acknowledged were part of the negotiating process as far back as 1993, there was virtual silence.

The joint declaration was a mix of declaratory statements (i.e., shared commitment to a two-state solution, ending violence, and incitement, etc.) and procedural agreements (i.e., to engage in "vigorous, ongoing, and continuous negotiations," formation of committees, etc.).[140] The only hint of progress was Bush's statement that "the United States will monitor and judge" each side's commitment to implementing the Road Map—though even this promise turned out to be a relatively empty pledge, similar to Bush's pledge in 2003 to "ride herd" on the parties to implement the Road Map.[141]

For his part, Olmert could claim some important gains. Bush spoke of America's commitment to Israel as a "Jewish state," and a "homeland for the Jewish people." Olmert could not claim Palestinian agreement on this point (it was not addressed in the Joint Understanding), but having Bush's unequivocal support was still something to bring back home. Moreover, the statement left out any mention of Jerusalem or other difficult issues for Israeli leaders. Olmert could also claim that Palestinians had to fulfill their Road Map obligations on reform and security before any deal on final status was implemented. "Unless otherwise agreed by the parties, implementation of the future peace treaty will be subject to the implementation of the road map, as judged by the United States."[142]

Four-and-a-half years after the launch of the Road Map, the reiteration of each side's commitment to this document seemed an empty pledge at best, and at worst an incredulous statement that became fair game for critics. Though the vague statements with which Annapolis began were not what Abbas genuinely preferred, the Palestinians did gain something they had not had for nearly seven years: a return to direct negotiations with Israel on all the core issues, backed by the U.S. and key Arab states. In any case, Palestinians had little influence in defining Annapolis, given the Hamas challenge and the failure of the Mecca gambit earlier in the year. Abbas's dependency on Washington was probably at its peak.

Although the meeting itself produced little in the way of a breakthrough, it launched a process in which Israelis and Palestinians began to engage intensively on permanent-status questions, going well beyond the earlier talks about a "political horizon" and certainly jumping well ahead of the process envisioned by the Road Map. When the latter document debuted in 2003, Sharon insisted on the parties meeting their "phase one" benchmarks before moving into negotiations on either a "provisional state" ("phase two") or a permanent deal ("phase three"). In effect, Annapolis allowed the parties to jump straight into "phase three." But the process faced myriad challenges with the Americans on the sidelines, Israel's

leadership divided, Olmert under the accelerating pressure of criminal indict-
ments, and the ever-cautious Palestinian leaders still reeling from the loss of Arafat and Gaza.

At a dinner the night before Annapolis, Bush pledged his "personal commitment" to realizing the goal of two states, but the impression he left was one of detachment and reserve. His White House spokesperson, Dana Perino, told reporters
the day after Annapolis that "he's only a phone call away." Adopting a self-justified
rationale similar to Clinton's on the eve of Camp David, Bush said "it is worth it
to try," even if failure might embolden extremists.[143] The United States would
provide the platform and preside over the process, but the parties would have to
do all the heavy lifting.

"So much effort was put into just getting to Annapolis, and trying to get Annapolis to come out right, that [the administration] never thought a lot about what
happened afterward. We also ran into the typical Israeli position of 'it's bilateral negotiations, we don't want you in the room . . . which the administration accepted,"
said a senior U.S. official.[144] Another U.S. official was even more critical, "This is a
conference about doing everything and doing nothing at the same time."[145]

Thus, unlike the lead-up to the 1991 Madrid conference, this Bush administration had no game plan for translating the Annapolis "meeting" into a successful
negotiation. "We have said from the very beginning, and the president made clear,
that it is the parties themselves that have to make peace," said National Security
Advisor Stephen Hadley on the eve of Annapolis, signaling a less than active
U.S. role.[146]

Yet it would be overly simplistic to declare Madrid a complete success and Annapolis a total failure. Madrid broke major new ground by bringing the regional
parties together for the first time, and it began major and promising bilateral and
multilateral discussions. But all of this petered out under new American leadership, replaced by Oslo and Syrian-Israeli negotiations led by the United States.

By contrast, Annapolis began with a minimal U.S. strategy and continued with
no participation on the Syrian-Israeli front and limited American involvement
between the Israelis and Palestinians. Yet the talks on both tracks went further than
ever before. They too collapsed under new American and Israeli leadership. Unlike Madrid, however, which begot new hopeful processes, Annapolis died when
the incumbents in Washington and Jerusalem departed.

Negotiations Heat Up, Flame Out

Surprisingly, despite the weaknesses of American diplomacy, the negotiations did
heat up after Annapolis. In January 2008, Bush paid his first visit to Israel and the

West Bank as president. During the trip he called for an end to Israel's "occupa-tion" of Palestinian territories and urged both sides to make painful concessions in order to secure a peace treaty before he left office. But the talks were not pro-gressing quickly, and Rice returned the following month to try to inject some momentum. Large-scale violence in Gaza in early March complicated the atmo-sphere and led to a suspension of the talks.

Fissures in the administration continued to appear. Rice spoke out against con-tinued settlement activity. But when Vice President Cheney—who had long led the administration's more conservative camp—visited the region later in March, he offered unambiguous support for Israel and signaled that the administration would not go beyond facilitating the negotiations. "It is not America's role to dictate the outcome," said Cheney in an appearance with Olmert, adding that the United States will never "pressure Israel to take steps that threaten its security."[147]

Rice returned to the region in late March and was able to organize a trilateral meeting with Israeli and Palestinian negotiators—and also to convince Abbas to resume meetings with Olmert, suspended in early March over violence in Gaza. Throughout this period, Rice was continuously pressing Olmert's government to do more to improve conditions in the West Bank, particularly in terms of move-ment and access, but with only modest results.[148]

Secretary Rice maintained a hectic travel schedule, visiting the region almost monthly, usually convening the top negotiators for trilateral meetings. But partici-pants testify that these meetings were largely an opportunity for Rice to hear from the parties. She did not bring new ideas or bridging proposals. "[The trilateral meetings] were basically small and not negotiating sessions," said a U.S. official. "She would sometimes try to steer them in a certain direction, but it was not a very hands-on U.S. role."[149] Moreover, the parties felt they were making progress and didn't want the United States at the table. "[Rice], in effect, forced the parties to meet with her in a trilateral setting to talk about the negotiations," said the for-mer administration official; "they did not want U.S. officials in the room or man-aging their agenda."[150] This official's comments are another indication that the Palestinians as well as the Israelis wanted to deal directly, without the U.S. presence.

As the negotiations began to intensify in the spring, the United States was not always fully informed. "The Israelis . . . wouldn't give us readouts of their meet-ings with the Palestinians," said the U.S. official. Olmert and Livni would do this only when seeing Rice. Back in Washington, Rice kept a close hold on information about the negotiations, often circumventing the traditional "cable" traffic, accord-ing to the same official.[151]

Of course, Olmert and Livni each had their own version of the talks, leading to two parallel, but often uncoordinated, tracks. Olmert wanted a deal as a capstone to his term, which was increasingly marked by corruption scandals and the after-effects of the costly war with Hezbollah. Livni had other considerations and was positioning herself domestically to vie for the prime ministership—leading to a more careful, calculated approach to the negotiations. Abbas remained willing to participate even though the process was initiated without any meaningful terms of reference, but he had long proved an overly cautious negotiator—and throughout this period he always had to contend with the looming questions of unity and reconciliation within the Palestinian camp, an internal agenda that constrained rather than expanded his choices in peace talks. Both sides, for different reasons, were not eager for the U.S. role to intensify.

Olmert and Abbas continued talks sporadically but steadily during mid-2008, the high-water mark of the Annapolis process, often meeting at the Israeli prime minister's residence in Jerusalem—sometimes with no one else in the room. On the other track, Livni and Qurie (the former Palestinian prime minister, also called Abu Ala) presided over a complex process in which twelve committees worked through a wide range of issues. This intensive, elaborate process was steered day-to-day by Saeb Erekat and Tal Becker.[152] These talks have been described by all sides as thorough, deliberate, and highly detailed, though little was known about them at the time.[153]

The parties in the Livni-Qurie track began drafting various elements of a peace deal, relying on bracketed language where disagreements remained.[154] They moved forward without U.S. involvement. Neither side wanted a "third party" at the table, said a former U.S. official, though Abbas would say later that he had waited for American bridging proposals that never came.[155] Participants in each of the two sets of talks thought they held the answer to success, creating a certain inner conflict and competition, which the United States was unable to manage and channel positively.

By early May, in anticipation of Bush's return to Israel to mark the Jewish state's 60th anniversary, Rice pressed the parties to at least reach an initial agreement on borders—but she did so without offering any new ideas and without any attempt to bridge the remaining divide. As the cloud of scandal began to envelop Olmert, expectations suddenly began to diminish. Ahead of the president's visit, White House officials said Bush would not be bringing any new ideas.[156]

Bush's speech to the Israeli parliament expressed a total and complete identification with Israel and its threat perceptions. The speech was devoted to condemnations of the UN, "moral relativism," and diplomatic "appeasement."[157] Bush focused heavily on democracy promotion and was silent on the very peace process over which he was presiding.

"Our alliance will be guided by clear principles—shared convictions rooted in moral clarity and unswayed by popularity polls or the shifting opinions of international elites," Bush told the rapt audience of Israeli lawmakers and political elite. "We also believe that nations have a right to defend themselves and that no nation should ever be forced to negotiate with killers pledged to its destruction."[158]

Three days later, at a regional business conference in Egypt, he reiterated his support for the Palestinians and for the Annapolis process, but this did little to quell Arab and Palestinian anger and disappointment. The day after hosting Bush for dinner, Abbas said he was "angered" by the Knesset speech. The Palestinian leader added that "we do not want the Americans to negotiate on our behalf."[159]

Six months after Annapolis, and after numerous visits by Rice and two visits by Bush, the level of activity was high and progress had been achieved, but there was no indication yet of willingness to bridge the final gaps to an agreement. The parties were supposedly negotiating the core issues that defined their nearly one hundred-year conflict, yet the leaders gave little or no indication in public. Moreover, the negotiating space was fractured on the Israeli side via the two parallel tracks and weighed down on the Palestinian side because of the internal split between Fatah and Hamas. On top of it all was a sponsor of the process, the United States, that remained unwilling and unable to drive the process toward a conclusion in part because of lingering, internal administration divides, as well as a conscious attempt to define a different, less intrusive style of American mediation.

Given that the United States was unable to bridge the lasting differences between the parties, a more reasonable strategy would have been to switch gears and try to codify the common ground that did exist between this particular set of Israeli and Palestinian leaders. However, such an effort was not forthcoming.

What the Talks Achieved

Of the core issues, progress was most advanced on the question of security.[160] There was heavy reliance on work done by the administration's envoy, General James Jones, who had been charged by Bush and Rice after Annapolis with developing a regional security architecture in support of a two-state solution. Abbas agreed to limitations on Palestinian arms and shared arrangements on airspace. He also agreed that a U.S.-led international security force, rather than an Israeli deployment, would be stationed in the Jordan Valley, which satisfied Olmert. In separate accounts, published after Olmert left office, both leaders repeatedly said they reached agreement on security provisions, and that the remaining disagreements were on other issues. Olmert writes that he agreed to the concept of a "non-militarized" Palestinian state. Like Olmert, Abbas has said the security provisions aligned with Jones's ideas. The Palestinian leader has said since that in the talks he accepted the idea of a "demilitarized" Palestinian state.[161] "The file on security was closed," Abbas told an interviewer in early 2011. "We do not claim it was an agreement, but the file was finalized.[162]

In addition to security, progress was also achieved on the question of territory. For the first time, according to various accounts—and confirmed by Rice—the two sides agreed on a definition of a "baseline" for the 1967 boundary, spelling out in detail that this meant all territories occupied in 1967—including East Jerusalem, which had been annexed by Israel in 1967. With an understanding that modifications would be subject to negotiation, the parties could now calculate proposed "swaps" and territorial adjustments to the line based on a common understanding. "The Palestinians were ecstatic," Rice said, "because they'd never gotten the Israelis" to say this.[163]

On the point of the 1967 baseline, an administration insider said, "At the end of that process . . . Condi Rice did achieve what I think no other administration did achieve, and that is to get the Israelis to define what they mean by occupied territories in 1967. And that, in my judgment, is a major breakthrough."[164] Abbas also confirms the agreement on the definition of the "baseline."[165] But an Israeli negotiator at the time told the authors that what the Israelis meant by the baseline was the gross size of the West Bank pre-1967, and not particular areas of the West Bank. This interpretation gives much more latitude for land swapping.[166]

The talks went well beyond the question of the "baseline" and the principle of "swaps." The parties discussed in detail various options for drawing a border—though without reaching an agreement on the size or location of the "swaps." Palestinians proposed a 1.9 percent West Bank swap, with Israel suggesting between 5.8 and 6.3 percent. Israel's offer included evacuation of many settlements, including all those in the Jordan Valley.[167] One of the stickiest points in the negotiations over territory was not abstract percentages, but a specific location on the map: the Jewish settlement of Ariel, located in the heart of the northern West Bank. Olmert wanted to keep it, but Abbas raised it repeatedly, arguing that it had to go. Palestinian negotiators even offered Israel more time to evacuate, but the issue remained unresolved.[168] It was a fraught issue and a perfect opportunity for an American bridging proposal, but none would come. In not-for-attribution interviews with the authors, senior Bush officials said they saw no way around the issue of Ariel, and explained they favored moving the settlement back from where it protruded into the West Bank. It is unclear how hard they pushed Olmert and his negotiators on this issue, if at all.

"[Olmert] said that he would give me 100 percent," said Abbas; "he presented maps to me [reflecting Israel retaining] settlement blocs in exchange for territories in the north, west, and south of the West Bank, in addition to territories to the east of Gaza."[169]

The territorial question still needed fine-tuning. Despite her usual reluctance in this situation, Rice was apparently willing to broach in private what had previously been taboo issues for American mediators. Bill Clinton only went so far as to talk about percentages; Rice cut to the heart of the matter. "I told the Palestinians, you're going to have to accept Maale Adumim in ways you don't like, and they're going to have to fix Ariel, and that's going to be the deal."[170] But this notion never became a formal American bridging proposal, and neither Olmert nor Abbas indicated in negotiations that they would accept a compromise akin to what Rice claims she said. Israelis put forward ideas that the Palestinians rejected, like getting credit for a West Bank-Gaza corridor in calculations over "swaps," even though the corridor would not be sovereign territory of the Palestinian state. But despite being close, nothing was ever agreed on the demarcation of a border.

Progress on the other files was more difficult. Rice reports that Livni did not want to broach the question of Jerusalem, and Rice appears to have refrained as well, in deference to her Israeli counterpart.[171] It would be Olmert, not Livni, who would broach the Jerusalem question in a major way.

One Israeli negotiator said when Americans joined the discussions the Palestinian position hardened, on territory and other issues.[172] On the other hand, one Palestinian negotiator, when asked whether Rice wanted to stay out of the negotiations and keep them bilateral, answered, "No. We had trilateral and bilateral [negotiations]. She sat with us, it was very consistent. After Annapolis, the Bush administration did a good job. Rice did a good job. But they are gone." In explaining why they did a good job, he proceeds to maintain that "they brought negotiations back to the table for the first time in several years. They had the parties stay the course of negotiations, . . . they worked consistently with institution building and security reform, economic development. The truth of the matter was that what prevented us for [sic] getting an agreement wasn't Abu Mazen or Bush, it was the scandal of Olmert. We were close to peace, and they crippled Olmert with this scandal."[173]

Through the late summer and early fall, Olmert's political troubles grew as corruption investigations intensified, culminating in his formal resignation after the mid-September Kadima Party primary. He stayed on as acting prime minister until Netanyahu was elected and took office on March 31, 2009. Still, for Olmert, peace talks would not slow. "The more he got into trouble, the more he laid out," according to a former senior American official.[174] But the impending Kadima Party vote did distract Livni, with Qurie complaining to Rice that his counterpart was not focused on negotiations. "I do not see any progress since [the] Washington meeting [late July]," he told Rice in Jerusalem.[175]

As time passed, Olmert decided to accelerate his channel with Abbas—making bold, yet general proposals for ending the conflict. At one point, during their

September 16, 2008 meeting at Olmert's residence, the Israeli leader laid out his most detailed proposal. Olmert even included a map in his presentation, which Israeli leaders had long avoided doing, detailing which territories Israel would annex, which settlements would be evacuated, and what lands in pre-1967 Israel would be transferred to the Palestinian state as part of the proposed swap.

However, Olmert would not leave a copy of the map with Abbas. After the meeting, Abbas was forced to make a rough sketch of Olmert's map on a napkin, which later became known as the "napkin map."[176] Secretary Rice reports that Olmert also showed her maps to illustrate his last and final "offer," and as with Abbas, he would not leave a copy with her. Still, Rice recalls having aides reconstruct the maps immediately afterward based on her recollections.[177]

On the eve of his party's vote for a new leader, Olmert's offer to Abbas on September 16, 2008, included the following:[178]

- "The 1967 borders" would serve as the baseline for swaps.
- A shared arrangement in Jerusalem—with "Jewish neighborhoods" built after 1967 remaining in Israel, and "Arab neighborhoods" part of a Palestinian state. "This part of the city," writes Olmert in his memoir, "would be considered, if they desired, as the capital of the Palestinian state."[179]
- The "holy basin"—including the Old City—would come under the "trusteeship" of Saudi Arabia, Jordan, the United States, Israel, and the Palestinian state.[180]
- Israel would accept one thousand Palestinian refugees a year, for five years, on an "individual and humanitarian" basis.[181]

Olmert said his offer was based on obtaining a written Palestinian commitment that no further demands would be made of Israel and that an agreement would constitute an "end of the conflict."[182]

At the September negotiating session, Olmert says Abbas found his presentation "very interesting" and asked "many questions" about the map. Abbas also told Olmert that annexing Ariel would be a major problem. The meeting ended abruptly, according to Olmert. "Give me the map so that I can consult with my colleagues," he quotes Abbas saying. "No," Olmert replied, "take the pen and sign now." Abbas instead proposed that aides meet the next day for more detailed discussions, to which Olmert agreed. But the Palestinians called later and cancelled.[183] The September session at Olmert's residence was the high-water mark for Annapolis.

Referring to Abbas simply walking away from a major proposal, one former official, Robert Danin, suggests, "It's slightly inaccurate to say that Abu Mazen rejected (Olmert's offer)"; "I think what was driving Olmert crazy was that Abu Mazen simply wouldn't react to it."[184] "He never tabled a counter to Olmert's offer," said Hadley.[185] Abbas's passivity probably was due partly to suspicions bred by Olmert's own negotiating tactics, partly to Olmert's dwindling political fortunes, and partly to Abbas's inherent caution.[186]

Olmert became more and more desperate to reach a peace deal, continuing to negotiate as a lame duck even after his resignation and the Kadima Party election of Livni as Olmert's successor. The Israeli leader also began to speak more boldly in public. In a late September interview, Olmert said Israel must cede the West Bank and Gaza Strip to the Palestinians, and he dismissed talk of an Israeli military attack on Iran as "megalomania."[187]

In a paper dated December 2009, Saeb Erekat, recounts that Abbas traveled to Washington in mid-December 2008. He met with President Bush and presented a "briefing note," which included a summary of where the negotiations stood at that juncture from the Palestinian perspective. At this meeting Abbas promised to provide further information on maps and positions at a then scheduled but later canceled meeting. At this time the Palestinians were trying to document everything possible so the entire process would not start again from zero after Obama assumed office. They were particularly interested in what Olmert meant by his percentages of territory to be returned and his details about Jerusalem.[188]

The closest to a definitive account of the continuing negotiations after Annapolis may be Rice's own internal summation that she prepared before leaving office, including her own recreations of the maps offered by Olmert. This account has not been released by the United States—nor is there any evidence that it was shared with the parties. It is also not clear whether Obama officials took Rice's report seriously or understood, at the time, the potential of what had transpired between Olmert and Abbas. Moreover, the presumption that the Bush administration's approach was inferior certainly colored the Obama team's early reaction to the reports left by the outgoing administration on the Olmert plan. Hanging over the negotiations was the principle of "nothing is agreed until everything is agreed," an escape clause to which both sides subscribed, and which was intended to link the core issues in a way that conditioned a deal on comprehensiveness.[189] It was intended to give negotiators flexibility, but it also served as an impediment, preventing "closure" on settled issues and leading American negotiators toward a self-imposed silence that was carried on well into the Obama administration.[190]

Meanwhile, at the urging of both sides, the Quartet stated in late September 2008 it "recognized that a meaningful and results-oriented process was underway." It urged all parties to maintain "confidentiality" in order to maintain the "integrity" of the process. In a call that would be echoed again in mid-December in UNSCR 1850, the Quartet declared the "irreversibility" of the bilateral negotiations.[191]

In effect, the United States caused the international community to sideline itself, putting all of its faith in the parties' own ability to complete the task even after it was clear that Olmert would be unable to continue in office. The United States and its Quartet partners refrained from taking any action to memorialize or preserve progress as a hedge should the talks fail, thereby proving that the process could indeed be reversible.[192]

Once Olmert had resigned and become a caretaker prime minister, there should have been a policy review in Washington and a decision about how to approach the Israeli political transition, especially since the administration itself had limited time. But this review did not occur. Instead, the U.S. approach was to watch, wait, and listen—and hope for the best, against quickly diminishing odds.

Meanwhile, "[Bush's] message to Tzipi and to Abbas was exactly the same, 'you guys should conclude a peace agreement and then each of you should run in your respective elections based on it,'" said Hadley. "The President's solution to Hamas in Gaza is for Abbas to have a peace agreement creating a Palestinian state and then run on that platform."[193] But Livni, who was still foreign minister, believed that she would be stronger after defeating Likud in the forthcoming election. The always cautious Abbas also preferred to wait to see who would be the new leader in Israel and what the new president would do in the United States. At the equivalent point in the Clinton administration, the president had offered a belated set of parameters. For Bush and Rice, bridging proposals were not a part of their diplomatic arsenal, and they were left, as was typical for them, to try to convince both sides to act on their own. As had happened so many times in the past, this approach failed and no agreement was reached on their watch.

The End of the Bush Administration

Rice continued to hope until the very end that there was still a chance of salvaging some type of agreement, yet time was running out, and as always, violence between the Israelis and the Palestinians intervened to make the situation tougher, as had happened at the end of the last three administrations.

When an informal six-month truce between Israel and Hamas ended in mid-December 2008, violence flared, including renewed Palestinian rocket attacks on Israel. Concerns were widespread that Israel was planning a major military offensive in Gaza, which the Administration—in its final days—appeared to do nothing to stop.

Over the course of three weeks in late December and early January, Israel launched a massive air and ground campaign on Gaza designed to end the violent missile attacks on southern Israel. Beyond the widespread destruction to buildings and infrastructure, over one thousand Palestinians, including many civilians, were killed. Despite an unprecedented international outcry, Israel remained confident in its justification because after the Gaza War, the debilitating missile attacks against Israeli civilians almost entirely disappeared. Its lockstep support from Washington continued.[194]

As an example, Olmert said publicly on January 12 that he had persuaded President Bush to overrule Secretary Rice and abstain on a UN Security Council vote on Gaza instead of voting for it as all other members of the Council did. The secretary of state had been strongly supportive of the resolution, which called for "an immediate, durable and fully respected cease-fire leading to the full withdrawal of Israeli forces from Gaza." Rice had been heavily involved in this initiative, but the president shared Olmert's nervousness that Israel would not accomplish its objective of ending attacks from Gaza if the resolution was implemented immediately. The secretary did not respond directly to Olmert's statement, but said the United States "fully supports" the resolution, but abstained because of a pending French-Egyptian ceasefire initiative. The sporadic confusion in the administration's positions continued to its last days.[195]

The fighting in Gaza ended any remaining hope for the Annapolis process. Abbas claims that in December Rice invited negotiators from both sides to come to Washington on January 3 for a "last attempt," and that despite the beginning of the Gaza War, "until 3 January we were ready to continue to negotiate." Olmert would not send his designated aide, Shalom Turgeman, but Abbas was apparently prepared to send Saeb Erekat.[196] A U.S. official interviewed by the authors said that once the war began it was understood that the January 3 meeting would not take place.[197]

The Gaza War also precipitated an abrupt end to the behind-the-scenes negotiations mediated by Turkey between Israel and Syria. It also led to a major decline in Turkish-Israeli relations because during his trip to Ankara a few days before the Israeli attack, Olmert did not inform Prime Minister Erdoğan of the impending Israeli action in Gaza. The military campaign infuriated Erdoğan, and bilateral relations went into a tailspin afterward.

In another final act, during the last days of the administration, Israelis came to the White House with requests to formalize a variety of understandings about how Israel and the United States operated under the Bush administration. But the White House refused.[198] Israel ended its military operation just before Obama's inauguration, effectively handing off to the new administration a political crisis in the peace process and a humanitarian crisis in Gaza.

In a last ditch effort, according to one American official, the secretary of state spent her last day in office "finalizing an agreement with Tzipi Livni that they hoped would help Tzipi win the coming election." It was another sad failure and the official concludes, "In retrospect, it seems like an appropriate way for the Bush Administration's Middle East efforts to come to an end."[199]

Conclusion

Bush 43 had strong views, and he frequently laid down red lines beyond which he would not allow his feuding aides to go. Democratic states could be trusted; autocrats could not. Those who used terrorism as an instrument of policy were to be isolated and confronted. For Bush, the world was divided into those who were "with us or against us." Bush identified with Israel, its doctrines of preemption and deterrence, and its vibrant democracy, even if he did not always fully agree with Israeli actions, such as settlement building. But when the question revolved around issues of terrorism or radical regimes—as with the security barrier, the 2006 Israel-Lebanon War, the attack on a Syrian nuclear installation, and the Gaza War—Bush was ready to give Israel far more leeway than his predecessors.

His was an administration that intentionally broke ranks with both its activist predecessor, Bill Clinton, and the traditional peacemaking role pursued by all U.S. administrations since Nixon (other than Reagan). Bush sought to sideline leaders he did not favor, he offered unprecedented assurances to Israel, and he supported Palestinian institution-building as an alternative to peace negotiations. When negotiations did resume in his last year, again he broke with precedent by limiting the United States to a convening role, without ever giving serious consideration to putting forward U.S. ideas or bridging proposals, even when the parties had substantially narrowed the gaps on major issues. Moreover, unlike his predecessors, George W. Bush went beyond the traditional pattern of reassuring and defending the Israelis in the face of threats or even pressing them to accept compromise. By the end of the administration, Bush and his key aides strongly identified with Israel and its strategic dilemmas. This identification conditioned Israelis and their advocates to expect from Washington a new and unprecedented level of American support. Even under Bush, however, there would be limits. For example, Bush reluctantly acquiesced in, but did not approve of, Israel's back-channel talks with Syria in 2008 and did not approve the sale of certain "bunker-busting" munitions, viewed as a way to restrain Israel from launching a preventive attack on Iran.

The administration quickly moved to the sidelines after every milestone, whether it was Bush's June 2002 Rose Garden speech, the 2003 Road Map, the 2005 AMA, or even the Annapolis meeting in 2007. The Bush team did not believe in active peacemaking. They focused on the idea that you could not want peace more than the parties, and thus decreased the ability of the parties to actualize the desire for peace.

In the case of Annapolis, the administration promoted a new opportunity to negotiate a conflict-ending agreement, and set a one-year deadline, but then assumed a noninterventionist posture. There was considerable activity, including several trips by Secretary Rice and two trips by President Bush, and some of the most far-reaching and intensive bilateral negotiations ever to take place by the parties themselves—yet in the end nothing was consummated.

The Annapolis saga demonstrates that an administration cannot easily change course late in the game, after years of moving in another direction. After encouraging the peace process, the Clinton administration swerved without success into intensive engagement in the latter part of the president's second term. Even more dramatic, the Bush presidency, with Secretary Rice leading the way, became active proponents of linkage and American mediation, but adopted a style that would prove ineffective. The administration also remained divided and less than fully committed.

In the end, the self-styled transformation of George W. Bush—as witnessed by his Annapolis denouement—was limited and inconsistent, as the president made clear in his speech to the Israeli parliament in May 2008. His was an administration that did not "do diplomacy," certainly not as it had been practiced in the Middle East since Richard Nixon. In his speech, Bush essentially equated diplomacy with appeasement, a jab that seemed aimed squarely at candidate Obama but nonetheless was quite revealing of his own views on diplomacy.

In the Middle East, President Bush's emphasis was on trying to transform the regional landscape—both through war (Iraq and Afghanistan) and by supporting democratic change—rather than the traditional transactional approach of assertive diplomacy and peacemaking. He was not the first president to deploy military forces in the support of American foreign policy aims in the region. But he was the first to topple a regime and then initiate a wholesale occupation of an Arab state. Bush favored coercive diplomacy and confrontation. He tended to shy away from give-and-take negotiations, particularly when it inevitably involved U.S. adversaries in some way. When Bush did engage in peacemaking, it was with little effect, halfhearted effort, and limited follow-through. His administration represents a detour from the American model of negotiating Arab-Israeli peace.

Yet, despite being often criticized for "disengaging" from Arab-Israeli peacemaking, the administration of George W. Bush was in fact quite involved, particularly in its final two years. Rather than abandonment, then, a more apt description is of an administration dominated by neoconservative ideas and personalities that viewed the conflict through the prism of its "global war on terror" and later its "freedom agenda." Those who sought a negotiations-driven process from the vantage of the State Department either lacked the White House's backing (as in the first term) or shared its point of view that America could not want peace more than the parties.

From the outset, the Bush administration did not assess resolving the Arab-Israeli conflict as central to American interests in the Middle East, a view that was only reinforced by 9/11 and its aftermath. The conflict held second-tier status for most of Bush's two terms in office. The fight against al-Qaeda, the war in Afghanistan, and democracy promotion and political reform—particularly in the Arab world—took center stage. The 2003 invasion of Iraq—followed by a costly and debilitating U.S. occupation—cemented the Arab-Israeli conflict's status as a relative sideshow to Bush's foreign policy.

When the administration did take initiatives, as with the 2003 Road Map peace plan, it was typically in response to exogenous factors and rarely led to sustained engagement. In a dramatic contrast to the Nixon, Ford, Carter, Bush 41, and Clinton legacies, the peace process became derivative of broader American goals, rather than a driving force behind Washington's approach to peace and stability in the region. The one departure from this pattern, Annapolis, appears as a major exception, but in the end the administration let the initiative peter out.

Even when the strategic and diplomatic environment shifted, as with the Arab Peace Initiative in 2002, Arafat's death in 2004, or Ariel Sharon's unilateral Gaza disengagement, the administration failed to adapt adequately, and sometimes it did not react at all. When faced with war, whether Israel's reoccupation of the West Bank in 2002, the Israel-Lebanon War in 2006, or the Gaza War in 2008, the administration was unable or unwilling to stop the fighting, to shape the post-war environment, or to address adequately the fundamental political issues at stake. On the contrary, in regard to the wars in Lebanon and in Gaza, the administration appeared to encourage the Israelis once military action began, although its hopes that these engagements would advance the process by marginalizing extremist forces proved unrealistic.

When it did engage, the Bush administration displayed a poor ability to execute its policies. Bush failed to recognize or to create opportunities as conditions on the ground shifted. His administration had a poor track record in following through on his own initiatives—whether it was sending out emissaries, only to have them undermined (Powell, Zinni, Wolf, Ward, Dayton, Wolfensohn, Jones); launching peace plans with inadequate and often little follow-up (Road Map and Annapolis); and even brokering deals, such as the 2005 AMA for Gaza, which fell apart the moment the involved senior American, Secretary Rice, left the scene.

When there has been success in negotiating Arab-Israeli peace, progress has often hinged on opportunism and steely determination, rather than ideological rigidity or deference to the parties. Examples are abundant, including Kissinger's active role in achieving the Egyptian-Israeli and Syrian-Israeli disengagement agreements (1974) and Sinai II (1975), Carter's concluding of the Israel-Egypt Peace Treaty (1979), Bush 41's drive to Madrid (1991), or Bill Clinton at Wye (1998).[200]

Far too often, however, under Bush 43 the United States seemed to lurch from defeat to defeat. If the Hamas victory in January 2006 was not bad enough, a year later Palestinian president Mahmoud Abbas in Mecca formed a coalition government with Hamas at the urging of Saudi Arabia, only to be opposed by the United States. In the previous summer, amid the deepening Palestinian divide, war erupted between Israel and Lebanon, which the Bush administration proved unable and even unwilling to stop. This conflict improved Hezbollah's standing in the region and would end in a devastating stalemate for all sides. By mid-2007, the fallout on the Palestinian track became all the starker with Hamas' violent takeover of the Gaza Strip, swiftly defeating the Fatah-allied, Western- and Arab-backed PA security forces.

But as a result of this string of diplomatic defeats, the Bush administration regrouped around two urgent objectives. The first was the need to strengthen President Abbas and security forces loyal to him and, in the process, to gain support for strong Palestinian public institutions and to generate economic progress in the West Bank. The idea was that improvements under the PA would thereby increase pressure on Hamas and Gaza.

The second objective was to restart the Israeli-Palestinian peace process and resume direct negotiations—Bush and Rice's antidote to the troubles of 2006. The administration would ultimately achieve limited success on both fronts. Some progress was indeed made on the peace process, even as the prospects for a substantial agreement between the Israelis and Palestinians slipped away.

Left to their own devices, Israelis and Palestinians had long proven incapable of reaching sustainable solutions, as the Oslo process so profoundly demonstrated. When Annapolis stumbled over Mahmoud Abbas's hesitations and Ehud Olmert's political troubles, Washington was unable to step in and to salvage anything of lasting value—even unwilling to publicly affirm that the negotiations had made substantial progress. Thus the outgoing Bush administration essentially left the incoming Obama administration with a blank slate, which enabled the parties to create their own narratives about what took place in the talks.

Where George W. Bush did leave his mark is on the question of the "nature," rather than of the "contours" of a future Palestinian state.[201] The emphasis on good governance produced greater transparency of PA finances, a reformed and more effective internal Palestinian security force, and a strong international consensus among Western donors that Palestinians would now be held to certain standards of accountability, whether or not the peace process was moving forward. This approach garnered support in Israel and across the international community and was later adopted by Barack Obama. It was certainly an achievement in keeping with the administration's emphasis on political reform, and it can only be sustained if an eventual peace agreement is reached. Thus, it still left the historic frustration of what might have been if the Bush team had matched its reform convictions with greater emphasis on implementation and diplomatic achievement.

A public battle to define the Bush legacy in the Middle East quickly emerged after Bush left office. The Bush years, its advocates and alumni argue, set in motion a "bottom-up" process of Palestinian state-building, facilitated Israel's withdrawal from Gaza, brought down Saddam Hussein, and isolated regimes such as Syria that sponsor terrorism. Most prominent among its accomplishments, advocates argue, is that democracy was bolstered in Lebanon, Iraq, and the Palestinian territories; terrorism was defeated; and weapons proliferation was either contained (Iran) or rolled back (Libya, Syria). Yet in all of these areas, including democracy promotion, the outcome of Bush's policies was highly problematic. The U.S. strategic position in the region was weaker at the end of his eight years in office. Under Bush, American influence did not match Washington's previous near hegemonic power and unrivaled economic and military power.[202] Moreover, the overall claims of Mideast success obscure the reality of an administration that redefined American involvement with decidedly poor results.[203]

Not surprisingly, George W. Bush comes to a different conclusion in his memoir. While acknowledging that no Arab-Israeli peace agreements were reached under his watch, he argues that he took "office during a raging intifada, with Yasir Arafat running the Palestinian Authority, Israeli leaders committed to a Greater Israel policy, and Arab nations complaining from the sidelines. By the time I left, the Palestinians had a president and prime minister who rejected terrorism. The Israelis had withdrawn from some settlements and supported a two-state solution. And Arab nations were playing an active role in the peace process."[204]

In Chapters 4 and 5, we have offered a far more critical and complex assessment, terming the Bush administration's record on the peace process an overall failure. The story of the Bush administration's approach to the peace process in the Middle East is fundamentally a saga of missed opportunities and inadequate preconceptions that left the prospects for peace far weaker when Bush left office. There is no doubt that his government came to office facing a less hospitable set of circumstances in the region than had his immediate predecessor. Bush surely presided over a tumultuous period, epitomized by the September 11 terrorist attacks and shaped by wars in Afghanistan, Iraq, Israel, the Palestinian territories, and Lebanon. But these events do not explain the failures of George W. Bush in the Middle East. His administration's lack of interest in promoting the peace process and weak follow-up when it did get involved made a bad situation worse. For their inability to mesh power with diplomacy effectively, the president and his administration bear significant responsibility. The challenge for future presidents, policymakers, and negotiators is to draw the appropriate lessons and to chart a different course.

CHAPTER SIX

OBAMA

An Early Assessment

Few American presidents have assumed office with expectations as great as those that greeted Barack Obama in January 2009. Panicked by financial crisis and disillusioned by a decade of war, Americans elected Obama with high hopes that he could transform critical domestic and foreign policy problems. Promising a new style of politics, Obama pledged to turn around issues such as Iraq and the collapsed Arab-Israeli peace process. On the international stage, Obama's rise to power was greeted with almost universal enthusiasm, including in almost all Arab and Muslim countries.

Obama entered office with a strong desire to differentiate himself from what he viewed as the failed Middle East policies of George W. Bush. He was also acutely aware of the failures of earlier administrations, such as the Clinton experience in 2000. Obama was determined and committed, and he started strong and fast.

Yet he proved unable to generate significant movement in Arab-Israeli peace-making during his first three years in office. On the Arab-Israeli front, the new American president would encounter numerous obstacles. Despite, and in part on account of, his desire to distinguish his policies from those of his predecessors, his administration ironically fell into some of the same troubling patterns that beset U.S. policy in the past.

Because of these setbacks and because of the pressing domestic political agenda of the administration, the pursuit of Middle East peace waned in priority over time, despite the president's early devotion. Lingering economic woes at home, the war in Afghanistan, and the explosion of the political transformations that swept across the Arab world in 2011 combined to push this issue to second-tier status.

It is exceptionally difficult to define a coherent Obama administration approach during the 2009–11 time frame. On the one hand, the president seemed intent on assuring Israel of its security and defense needs and in deepening strategic consultation, especially with respect to Iran. But on the other hand, Obama acted aloof when it came to the trust-building aspects of personal diplomacy— not visiting Israel or speaking directly to the Israeli people. On the peace process, as seen from the outside, the administration appeared to career from tactic to tactic, without a sense of strategy or larger purpose. Tough words would be addressed to Israel, for example on settlements, but follow-up was weak. And Palestinian interests seemed to matter very little. Indeed, the administration did not seem to understand that its tactics (e.g., on settlements) often left the Palestinians exposed and weakened before the court of their own public opinion.

What makes this absence of a coherent strategy hard to understand is that Barack Obama was the first president since Jimmy Carter to enter office with determination to advance the Arab-Israel peace process at the outset of his presidency. Obama had not shied away from the issue during the campaign, and the fact that he had garnered the support of a very large majority of Jewish voters seemed to breathe air into his peace process sails. But this was to be an adventure on the high seas with little sense of direction and even less staying power.[1] The administration chose not to repeat past commitments important to either Palestinians or Israelis. For example, the Netanyahu government complained strongly when the Obama administration would not reaffirm Bush's April 14, 2004, letter to Ariel Sharon with its language on settlements and refugees. The administration also did not pursue systematically the idea of picking up the negotiations from where Ehud Olmert and Mahmoud Abbas had left off in 2008. Rather, the administration accepted Benjamin Netanyahu's (and Tzipi Livni's) opposition to doing so, and left it at that. It is also unclear why the Obama team chose some of its tactics: the administration must have known how challenging it would be for Netanyahu and his right-wing coalition to accept a settlement freeze, especially after it was clear that the Palestinians and the Arab states would not reciprocate with confidence-building measures of their own. Yet the president pursued this approach. However promising the Israeli-Palestinian peace process appeared when last seen in 2008, it was to falter and ultimately grind to a halt by the middle of 2011.

Equally curious was the absence of any discernible movement on the Israeli-Syrian track of negotiations. Turkish mediation had produced substantial progress by December 2008 when the talks broke down—and Turkish relations with Israel soured—over the Gaza War between Israel and Hamas. That war ended just as the Obama administration entered office. The new president had campaigned on a platform of diplomatic engagement even with hostile states, such as Iran and Syria.

To this end Robert Ford, a career diplomat and former ambassador to Algeria, was eventually (after an inexplicably long search process in the State Department) nominated by the president to go to Damascus. Yet Ford's ambassadorial prospects hit an immediate roadblock as twelve Republican senators, arguing that engagement with al-Asad equaled endorsement of his policies, placed individual "holds" on the nomination, thereby obliging the president eventually to post Ford to Damascus in December 2010 via a recess appointment. For most of 2009 and nearly all of 2010, therefore, the bulk of diplomatic engagement with Syria fell to George Mitchell and his deputy for the Israel-Syria (and Israel-Lebanon) track, Frederic Hof. Mitchell and Hof visited Damascus several times for talks with al-Asad and his key deputies: discussions that covered the full range of sensitive bilateral issues as well as potential terms of reference for renewed peace talks.

Hof, meanwhile, engaged in additional talks on peace prospects through numerous extended visits to both Israel and Syria. In September 2010, Hof launched an extended round of focused discussions in Damascus and Jerusalem, shuttling between the two cities and engaging senior officials in both places in intensive talks aimed at finding a formula for a framework agreement or, ideally, a treaty of peace. These discussions did not bring Syrians and Israelis to the same table; Hof engaged them separately on substantive issues. Neither did the talks produce irrevocable commitments; everything was kept informal and ad referendum pending complete agreement. This potentially promising initiative came to a total halt in March 2011, when al-Asad elected to use deadly force against peaceful protesters in the southern city of Dara'a and elsewhere, a choice that would, in the view of the Obama administration, fatally undermine his legitimacy and render him radioactive as a potential interlocutor for peace with Israel.

This chapter examines the critical phases of Obama's policies on the Middle East peace process from his inauguration until May 2011, with an emphasis on the Israeli-Palestinian track. It is organized around the following sections: Obama's candidacy, the transition and first days in office, the long and ultimately unsuccessful road to negotiations, and the lead-up to and rollout of the May 2011 U.S. initiative on permanent status.[2]

The Presidential Campaign of 2008

Barack Obama entered the race for the presidency facing enormous challenges—a black man with little legislative and no executive experience, untested in foreign and national security affairs, and with persistent questions about character, ranging from his choice of pastor to whether he was a Muslim. No amount of reasoned discourse or presentation of facts seemed to satisfy some of those determined to denigrate candidate Obama. In a hard-fought Democratic Party primary campaign against then senator Hillary Clinton, Obama adopted some foreign policy positions substantially to the left of his opponent: a commitment to the withdrawal timetable in Iraq; a willingness to "engage" diplomatically even with adversaries, such as Iran; and a strong interest in advancing Israeli-Palestinian peace, which Obama characterized as an American national interest.

Obama's positions and the questions about his background raised significant concerns within some segments of the pro-Israel community of voters. This prompted Obama to demonstrate the connection between the peace process and his pro-Israel credentials. In a May 2008 essay in the Israeli daily *Yediot Ahronot*, marking Israel's 60th anniversary, Obama wrote that the U.S. commitment to Israel's security is inseparable from the goal of Arab-Israeli peace. "There is no greater gift America can give to Israel—no better way we can salute our Israeli friends on this important anniversary—than to redouble our commitment to help Israel achieve its goal of true security through lasting peace with its neighbors. . . . The United States does Israel no favors," Obama wrote, "when it neglects opportunities for progress in Arab Israeli peacemaking."[3]

In a speech to the American-Israel Public Affairs Committee (AIPAC) on June 4, 2008—one day after securing the Democratic nomination over Hillary Clinton—Obama emphasized his commitment to Israel's security, which he described as non-negotiable, and to American-Israeli strategic partnership. But that speech, designed to calm the waters politically as his campaign began against Senator John McCain, created a minor flap when Obama said "Jerusalem will remain the capital of Israel, and it must remain undivided,"[4] but then hurried to refine that line the next day to make clear that Palestinians would also have a share in the city's political future.[5]

During the campaign, Obama faced pressure on the question of his commitment to Israel not only from McCain, but also from President Bush. During a visit to Israel in May 2008, Bush delivered a speech to the Knesset that focused on the promotion of democracy, was curiously almost silent on the peace process that the Bush administration had launched at Annapolis, and defended strongly Israel's right of self-defense. "Our alliance will be guided by clear principles—shared convictions rooted in moral clarity and unswayed by popularity polls or the shifting opinions of international elites," Bush told the audience of Israeli lawmakers and political elites. "We also believe that nations have a right to defend themselves and that no nation should ever be forced to negotiate with killers pledged to its destruction."[6] In a message clearly directed at Obama, Bush also condemned what he called diplomatic "appeasement," placing himself squarely at odds with Obama's intent to strengthen diplomatic engagement and injecting himself into the presidential campaign in front of a foreign audience.[7]

During the campaign, in July 2008, Obama went overseas to visit Israel, the West Bank, Jordan, and Iraq. In Israel, he toured the border town of Sderot, which had been under indiscriminate rocket fire from Palestinian militants in Gaza. He made strong statements about Israel's right to defend itself, and he met with the full spectrum of Israeli and Palestinian leaders. Obama repeatedly pledged to get involved in Arab-Israeli diplomacy from the outset of his administration—again, partly framed as a critique of Bush, who was seen as getting involved only in his seventh year as president with the Annapolis process.

Despite early reservations about his commitment to Israel, in the election, Obama received 78 percent of the Jewish vote, according to exit polls, a strong recovery from the 60 percent that early polls had given the new president. Entering office with this kind of support and a Democrat-controlled Congress, Obama appeared poised to launch his ambitious agenda, including on the Arab-Israel peace process.

The Transition and Day One

As the Obama transition team organized, events in the region would shape the new administration's attitude and latitude for action. As noted in chapter 5, on December 27, 2008, Israel launched Operation Cast Lead, designed to stop rocket fire from Gaza and, if possible, to deal a mortal blow to Hamas. As a result, the peace negotiations between Israel and the Palestinians, which had begun to show much promise, came to a halt, as did the Turkish-sponsored proximity talks between Israel and Syria. Prior to the outbreak of the Gaza War, the Bush administration pressed for a joint Israeli-Palestinian paper on the status of the talks as they were suspended in 2008, but the Israeli government opposed the idea. Israel also did not provide its own paper to the Americans. Israel feared that the attempt to put the progress achieved thus far in writing would only push the Palestinians to harden their negotiating position. In any event, Livni believed that if she would win the Israeli election, the talks would continue anyway from where they left off, and if she didn't, the new Israeli government would likely back away from the Annapolis talks regardless of what was recorded on paper about their status. As a result, the Bush administration provided its own summary of the talks to the Obama team, but without a "stamp of approval" from either the Palestinians or the Israelis.[8]

To the relief of the Obama transition team, the Israeli operation in Gaza came to end just before the U.S. presidential inauguration, but not before leaving behind a residue of damaged lives and peace prospects. The war afforded Obama an opportunity to reinforce his determination to push forward the peace process. Commenting on the rising toll of casualties and destruction, Obama said, "It makes me much more determined to try to break a deadlock that has gone on for decades now."[9]

The first days of Barack Obama's presidency witnessed the usual jockeying for political appointments in the new administration but also saw a significant departure in the Middle East peace process. Obama took the unprecedented step of highlighting his commitment to Arab-Israeli peace on the second day of his presidency by appointing former senate majority leader George Mitchell as special envoy for the peace process. Mitchell decided against forming a large staff, instead relying on a few new aides and the State Department's Near East Bureau. Mitchell appointed Frederic Hof as his deputy for negotiations with Syria; David Hale as his representative on the ground in the region; and Mara Rudman as his deputy for Palestinian institution-building and economic development. At the State Department, the new secretary of state, Hillary Clinton, appointed career foreign service officer Jeffrey Feltman as the assistant secretary for Near East affairs. Rounding out the Middle East team, Obama appointed General James Jones, who had served in the Bush administration as a security adviser for the Middle East, as national security advisor, and one of his campaign advisers, Dan Shapiro, as the senior official on the National Security Council responsible for the peace process. Over time, it appeared that the real policy of the administration would be developed in the Oval Office, by Obama himself and a small coterie of close, longtime aides with little knowledge or experience related to the Middle East, such as Rahm Emanuel, David Axelrod, Denis McDonough, Valerie Jarrett, and Robert Gibbs.[10] The speed with which this Middle East group was formed further underscored Obama's intention to begin working on Middle East peace "from day one."[11]

One of the key unknowns from this period is whether and how much the new administration knew about the progress that was registered in the Olmert-Abbas negotiations in the second half of 2008.[12] In her memoir, former secretary of state Condoleezza Rice says, "In the end, the Palestinians walked away from the negotiations. . . ." She says she turned over the "negotiating file" to Secretary Clinton, noting that the conditions for a deal were "almost ripe" during her tenure. But Rice is silent on what exactly she passed on to the Obama administration: Was it a file of the ins and outs and ups and downs of the peace process, or was it a manicured document that showed how close the parties had come to an agreement and what remained to be done?[13] From the Palestinian-drafted minutes of meetings held between the Palestinians and George Mitchell, it appears that the Obama administration had a full Palestinian file dealing with the 2008 negotiations, but this has not yet been verified from other (American) sources.[14] Since then, much has been learned about how close the parties had gotten in their negotiations.[15]

Obama's Inaugural Address gave few hints about his approach to the peace process. Later that week, when he announced the appointment of George Mitchell as special envoy, Obama promised that his administration would "actively and aggressively" pursue the peace process but provided no indication of his substantive approach. He repeated familiar refrains such as commitment to Israel's security and support of a two-state solution, and he made specific mention of the Arab Peace Initiative (API), saying it contained "constructive elements" and calling on the Arabs to take steps toward normalizing relations with Israel.[16]

Within days, Mitchell traveled to Israel and the region. With Israel in the throes of its own election campaign, Mitchell used this first visit to listen and to learn, to assess the impact of the Gaza conflict, and also to project the president's commitment to activism. Mitchell was warmly received, notwithstanding the right-wing critiques of Obama during the American election. Both Israelis and Palestinians lost no time in advancing their views to the new administration. During this visit, Mitchell was briefed by former prime minister Olmert on the Israeli version of what transpired in the 2008 negotiations with the Palestinians; the day after meeting Mitchell, Olmert provided the same readout to the Israeli press. In subsequent meetings with Netanyahu and Livni, Mitchell asked whether they supported reviving negotiations from the point where they left off. He received a firm no from both Israelis: Netanyahu strongly repudiated what Olmert had put forward and said those positions could not serve as the basis of future talks.[17]

Even in this earliest stage of Mitchell's mission, the sour atmosphere between Israelis and Palestinians colored his talks. The idea began to gel that a first step should be "to try to find some way, some basis, some course of action, that could bring the temperature down, that could create a context in which negotiations could proceed."[18] In an early February letter to Obama, Palestinian president Mahmoud Abbas warned against Israeli settlement expansion, especially in the E-1 area between Jerusalem and the Maale Adumim settlement to the east. "As you know," Abbas wrote, "Israeli settlement activity constitutes the single greatest threat to the two-state solution. And nowhere is the threat to the viability of a future Palestinian state and our shared vision of two states living side by side in peace and security more serious than in and around East Jerusalem."[19] According to one former official, Abbas told Mitchell, "Just give me like three or four months of just quiet; I don't need anything formal."[20]

At almost the same time, Netanyahu—soon to be elected prime minister—delivered a speech in which he assessed that "extremists" would seize any territory yielded by Israel. Netanyahu said, "I will not keep Olmert's commitments to withdraw and I won't evacuate settlements . . . Those understandings are invalid and unimportant."[21] For Mitchell, these Palestinian and Israeli shots across the bow were to test his resolve and to call into sharp relief a statement he had made on the day of his appointment that was to shadow his Middle East mission: "In the negotiations which led to that [Northern Ireland] agreement, we had 700 days of failure and one day of success."[22]

On this first visit to the region, Mitchell did not visit Syria, despite Obama's campaign pledge to engage diplomatically even with regimes with which the United States had profound differences. Instead the administration deferred to the particular sensitivities of engaging with Syria in the run-up to elections in Lebanon and the ongoing UN investigation into the assassination of Lebanese prime minister Rafik Hariri.[23]

During these early weeks, the administration found its policy development constrained by the lengthy process of elections and government formation in Israel and by the return of Benjamin Netanyahu to power. Indeed, Netanyahu told Mitchell he would need about six weeks after being installed as prime minister to conduct a "strategic review" before being ready to engage in serious peace process discussions. The administration thus knew it needed a new approach but could not start serious engagement until mid-May at the earliest.[24] Secretary Clinton traveled to the region to participate in a Palestinian donors' conference and used the occasion of her visit to Israel to criticize settlement activity. This issue would increasingly become the policy focus of the Obama administration.

Elusive Quest for a Settlement Freeze

In April 2009 (Netanyahu became prime minister formally on March 31), Obama engaged in a round of personal diplomacy to advance the prospects for negotiations. In Ankara on April 6, Obama delivered the first of two messages to the Muslim world that promised a new relationship with the United States. Obama welcomed the Saudi and Jordanian monarchs in Washington, using those occasions to underscore the priority he had assigned to the peace process. The administration understanding the challenge of working with Netanyahu as prime minister, hoped these early messages would drive home the need in Israel for rapid movement toward negotiations.

Mitchell used this time to solicit the views of the Washington policy community. Think-tank roundtables and blue-ribbon panels of senior statesmen forwarded ideas to Mitchell, many of them focused on the need to address permanent-status issues through the issuance of American "parameters" or terms of reference to guide the negotiations. Rejecting these approaches, Mitchell and the administration opted for a more incremental approach and crafted a peace policy designed around confidence-building measures (CBMs) that would be sought from Israel, the Palestinians, and the Arab states. Comprehensive Arab-Israeli peace remained the goal, but the administration considered CBMs as the best way to encourage the parties to renew negotiations and to repair the atmosphere that had soured so as a result of the 2008 Gaza War.

Netanyahu visited Washington in May. He and Obama had met twice before and had established what appeared to be a cordial relationship. Netanyahu's visit had been preceded by the visit of Israeli president Shimon Peres, who left the impression in Washington that Netanyahu would be bringing some ideas for moving the peace process forward. In the event, however, Netanyahu did not present any new ideas. Rather, he reportedly told Obama that he rejected what Olmert had done in the 2008 negotiations and wanted to review the entire Annapolis process. The Obama team accepted Netanyahu's answer and did not press to resume negotiations from the point where they had stopped in 2008.

The administration began moving toward a complete settlement freeze as a means of jump-starting negotiations. Mitchell was already invested in this idea, having chaired the Sharm el-Sheikh fact-finding commission in 2000–2001 that had advocated a complete Israeli settlement freeze including natural growth.[25] At President Obama's first meeting with Prime Minister Netanyahu in May, the American leader laid out his approach, including the settlement freeze. The demand was not new—a freeze was a prominent feature of the 2003 Road Map, for example. Netanyahu pushed back and tried to counter by focusing attention on the Iran nuclear file. But the administration responded with determined rhetoric. "[President Obama] wants to see a stop to settlements," said Secretary Clinton on May 27, "not some settlements, not outposts, not natural growth exceptions." "We think it is in the best interests of the effort that we are engaged in that settlement expansion cease. That is our position . . . and we intend to press that point."[26]

Palestinian Authority (PA) president Abbas visited Washington in late May, and President Obama pressed him on continued security cooperation with Israel and anti-incitement. The administration had made no headway in bringing about Palestinian or Arab confidence-building measures, but continued to focus on settlements.[27] In an early June interview on National Public Radio, Obama strongly defended his administration's call for a settlement freeze,

> I don't think that we have to change strong U.S. support for Israel. I think that we do have to retain a constant belief in the possibilities of negotiations that will lead to peace. And that's going to require, from my view, a two-state

solution that is going to require that each side—the Israelis and Palestinians—meet their obligations.

I've said very clearly to the Israelis both privately and publicly that a freeze on settlements, including natural growth, is part of those obligations. I've said to the Palestinians that their continued progress on security and ending the incitement that, I think, understandably makes the Israelis so concerned, that that has to be—those obligations have to be met. So the key is to just believe that that process can move forward and that all sides are going to have to give. And it's not going to be an easy path, but one that I think we can achieve.[28]

Obama addressed the issue head-on in his speech in Cairo on June 4, when he laid out the core trade-off in his thinking,

Palestinians must abandon violence. Resistance through violence and killing is wrong and it does not succeed. . . . Now is the time for Palestinians to focus on what they can build. The Palestinian Authority must develop its capacity to govern, with institutions that serve the needs of its people. . . . At the same time, Israelis must acknowledge that just as Israel's right to exist cannot be denied, neither can Palestine's. The United States does not accept the legitimacy of continued Israeli settlements. This construction violates previous agreements and undermines efforts to achieve peace. It is time for these settlements to stop.[29]

The speech in Cairo broke no new substantive ground in the peace process, but it was framed by unprecedented expressions of American empathy with the Palestinians. "They endure the daily humiliations—large and small—that come with occupation," Obama said.

In Cairo, Obama again noted the importance of the Arab Peace Initiative: "The Arab states must recognize that the Arab Peace Initiative was an important beginning, but not the end of their responsibilities." But the president already knew that it would be hard, if not impossible, to get traction on this point, for en route to Cairo, the president had stopped in Saudi Arabia and had asked King Abdullah for a Saudi confidence-building measure to allow Israeli civilian overflights of the kingdom. But he was rebuffed.[30] Curiously, the API did not again figure prominently in the administration's calculations during this period.

The Palestinians clearly understood that things had changed in Washington. In an internal briefing following Abbas's visit to Washington, chief Palestinian negotiator Saeb Erekat told his staff, "The Washington I went to last week isn't the

Washington I knew before. . . . There is a growing sense in the United States that something must be done soon."[31] The Palestinians said they were led to believe that Washington had demanded Netanyahu's response to their peace process demands before July 1, that is, before Obama's scheduled trip to Moscow.

Adding further drama and pressure to the situation, on June 1, Al Hayat newspaper published an interview with General David Petraeus, commander of the U.S. Central Command.[32] Petraeus argued that resolving the Palestinian issue would defuse Arab anger and thus reduce the threat against American forces in the region. Israel and its supporters in the United States reacted bitterly, charging Petraeus and the administration with falsely linking the safety of Americans with the conflict.

During this emerging divergence of U.S. and Israeli views on how to proceed, Netanyahu spoke next, delivering a major speech at Bar Ilan University on June 14, 2009. For the first time, a Likud prime minister accepted the two-state paradigm, a significant change in Israeli positions. Netanyahu conditioned this acceptance with emphasis on two principles: First, "a fundamental prerequisite for ending the conflict is a public, binding and unequivocal Palestinian recognition of Israel as the nation state of the Jewish people. To vest this declaration with practical meaning, there must also be a clear understanding that the Palestinian refugee problem will be resolved outside Israel's borders." Second, Netanyahu said, "The territory under Palestinian control must be demilitarized with ironclad security provisions for Israel."[33]

Israeli spokesmen and their supporters in the United States also took aim at Obama's call for a settlement freeze, arguing that Israel and the Bush administration had reached understandings on settlements that Obama was now ignoring. This claim was strongly rebutted in what amounted to a public U.S. debate on the issue of a settlement freeze.[34]

As Mitchell set out to negotiate the terms of a settlement freeze, Obama got some heat from supporters of Israel. Obama, however, did not back down. As reported in the *New York Times,*

> During the July meeting [with supporters of Israel], . . . Malcolm Hoenlein, executive vice chairman of the Conference of Presidents of Major American Jewish Organizations, told Obama that "public disharmony between Israel and the U.S. is beneficial to neither" and that differences "should be dealt with directly by the parties." The president, according to Hoenlein, leaned back in his chair and said: "I disagree. We had eight years of no daylight"—between George W. Bush and successive Israeli governments—"and no progress."[35]

In September, Obama convened a trilateral meeting in New York with Abbas and Netanyahu, the first direct contact between the parties at a senior level since the talks had broken down in 2008. No ground was broken, and neither trilateral nor bilateral talks continued. Mitchell, meanwhile, was continuing a twofold effort to secure as much of a settlement freeze as possible and to construct the terms of reference for negotiations. Because Mitchell understood that he could accomplish far less than the complete freeze including natural growth that the administration had talked about several months before, he reportedly offered to "compensate" the Palestinians by drafting terms of reference that specified all the core issues to be negotiated. But, the United States and the Palestinians differed over the terms of reference—the Palestinians wanted to start negotiations from where they had left off—and they differed over the concept of "nothing is agreed until everything is agreed."[36] The Palestinians also insisted that the Obama administration reiterate former secretary Rice's statement that the parties should use the 1967 lines as a baseline for negotiations, but Mitchell demurred.[37] Mitchell advised the Palestinians to stop asking the administration to endorse positions from the previous negotiations.[38]

In September, the report of a UN Human Rights Council investigation into alleged war crimes during the 2008–9 Gaza War—conducted by the Goldstone Commission—was released. The report found "evidence indicating serious violations of international human rights and humanitarian law . . . committed by Israel during the Gaza conflict, and that Israel committed actions amounting to war crimes, and possibly crimes against humanity." The UN report also cited "evidence that Palestinian armed groups committed war crimes, as well as possibly crimes against humanity, in their repeated launching of rockets and mortars into Southern Israel."[39]

Israeli leaders launched a fierce campaign to discredit the investigation, and they appealed to the Obama administration to confront and to undermine the Goldstone report. Israeli leaders tied the report to a broader campaign to delegitimize Israel. The administration decided to try to discredit the report and pressured others to do the same. Speaking at an October 27 J Street conference, National Security Advisor James Jones criticized the Goldstone report while also urging Israel to undertake its own investigation.[40] However, pressuring Abbas to downplay the report made it harder for him to go back to talks. The report poisoned the Israeli-Palestinian atmosphere at a critical moment when the talks were in limbo. And Goldstone himself refuted part of his report in fall 2011.

By late October, the United States and Israel agreed on a formula for a ten-month moratorium on new housing starts in settlements. Palestinians expressed immediate opposition to anything less than the promised full freeze including natural growth. In an October 31 press conference with Secretary Clinton, Netanyahu said that while he rejected a complete freeze, he was willing to adopt a policy of restraint. "The fact of the matter is that we—I said we would not build new settlements, not expropriate land for addition for the existing settlements, and that we were prepared to adopt a policy of restraint on the existing settlements, but also one that would still enable normal life for the residents who are living there."[41]

Netanyahu did not explain his rationale for agreeing to the moratorium on new housing starts, although it could be attributed both to U.S. pressure on the settlement issue and U.S. support on such issues as the Goldstone report. Netanyahu did make clear in his talks with Clinton and Mitchell that this restraint would not apply to East Jerusalem or to the settlement blocs, as defined by Israel. In response, Secretary Clinton termed Netanyahu's announcement "unprecedented," thereby giving U.S. blessing to the limited-duration moratorium. Clinton's embrace of the very partial moratorium was hard to explain, as was her view that it was unprecedented. On the ground, there was little difference seen, as ongoing construction in settlements and outposts continued as before. It appeared the administration, desperate to get something started, grabbed what was available and tried to play it as a major breakthrough on settlements.

In an effort to capitalize on this Israeli move, Secretary Clinton issued a statement on November 25 that introduced a formula designed to frame negotiations. Although it fell short of declaring a U.S. position on the 1967 lines, Clinton came close by linking negotiations "based on the 1967 lines" with Israeli security requirements:

> Today's announcement by the Government of Israel helps move forward toward resolving the Israeli-Palestinian conflict. We believe that through good-faith negotiations the parties can mutually agree on an outcome which ends the conflict and reconciles the Palestinian goal of an independent and viable state based on the 1967 lines, with agreed swaps, and the Israeli goal of a Jewish state with secure and recognized borders that reflect subsequent developments and meet Israeli security requirements. Let me say to all the people of the region and world: our commitment to achieving a solution with two states living side by side in peace and security is unwavering.[42]

This statement on the 1967 lines was made in the context of praise for Israel and received no complaints or protests from the Netanyahu government. Some eighteen months later, Obama would return to this formula with negative results. But then it was made in the context of a surprise announcement without prior consultation with Israel on the eve of a major trip to Washington by the prime minister. American governments have repeatedly found that the context in which major statements are made affecting Israel often prejudge the reaction, even if Israel disagrees.

The partial settlement freeze did not ease the administration's burden. The Palestinians rejected the Israeli decision and expressed profound disappointment that the United States had abandoned its earlier insistence on a full freeze. The Palestinians decided that a settlement freeze would be a precondition for restarting negotiations. Mitchell and the U.S. team faced equally challenging problems in the effort to negotiate agreed terms of reference for negotiations. Palestinians demanded specificity and insisted on resuming negotiations from where they had left off. Rather than work with an essentially sympathetic American administration, Palestinians held out for demands that were unrealizable, and thus frittered away almost nine months of the ten-month settlement moratorium on new housing starts. And the Israelis seemed content to allow time to pass, demanding very loose, largely procedural terms of reference and insisting that negotiations start without preconditions.[43] The administration decided to change course as it entered its second year.

Indirect Talks as the Goal

On top of all the other challenges faced by President Obama during his first year in office, the Middle East peace process took a toll. "This is just really hard," Obama told *Time* magazine in January, "this is as intractable a problem as you get." "I think we overestimated our ability to persuade them to [resume negotiations] when their politics ran contrary to that."[44]

The administration had expended the better part of a year to achieve a partial settlement moratorium that had left the Israelis angered and the Palestinians dissatisfied. Rather than a freeze becoming a confidence builder and a catalyst to negotiations, the Palestinian demand for a complete freeze had become a precondition for negotiations for the first time. And they claimed that they were only taking this tough stance because the Obama administration had demanded the total freeze in the first place. Instead, the Palestinian stance eventually permitted the Netanyahu government to proceed with settlement construction in any case, though at a somewhat slower pace than in previous Israeli governments.

Therefore, although the administration by and large assessed Netanyahu to have been the recalcitrant party until that point, Netanyahu effectively had maneuvered himself into a more favorable light—partly responsive to American demands and ready to restart negotiations without preconditions. Palestinians, with pressure coming from Saudi Arabia, started talking about reconciliation with

Hamas, further signaling their conviction that peace talks with Netanyahu were unlikely to get started.

The administration felt compelled to repair the bilateral relationship with Israel, frayed as a result of the settlements interaction and exacerbated by charges from the pro-Israel community in the United States that Obama was insensitive to Israel's needs. High-level foreign policy and national security visits to Israel increased in 2010, as did military assistance, strategic cooperation, and coordination of policies vis-à-vis Iran. The Palestinians, although impatient with what they saw as Obama's coddling of Israel, chose not to escalate differences. Chief Palestinian negotiator Saeb Erekat leaked a paper, purported to be a record of the process, to demonstrate Palestinian unhappiness that the administration had chosen not to hold Netanyahu to positions put forward by Olmert in 2008, or to affirm understandings they asserted were reached with Rice, such as the notion of a 1967 "baseline."[45]

Mindful of the need to achieve some measure of progress before the expiration of the ten-month settlement moratorium, the administration appeared to backpedal from the goal of restarting talks on the basis of agreed terms of reference and settled on a more modest objective—proximity talks. The administration reasoned it might be easier to shuttle between the parties and start to negotiate in earnest on the core issues. The administration asked the two parties to present their substantive views to Mitchell, who would move between the two sides. Not everyone in the administration agreed with this approach. "I was deeply troubled by the idea of proximity talks because I felt we turned the clock back twenty years," argued one official at the time.[46]

The Palestinians responded to the invitation to proximity talks with a number of conditions, for example, that the agenda include all core issues, that the period of negotiations not exceed two years, and that the United States should confirm that the baseline for the negotiations on borders would be the June 1967 line with agreed swaps of equal size and value.[47]

The settlement issue, however, would not go away. A March 2010 visit to Israel by Vice President Joseph Biden, part of the administration's effort to rebuild ties with Israel, was upended by an announcement of new construction in a contested East Jerusalem neighborhood. The Americans were caught off guard and did not accept Netanyahu's explanation that East Jerusalem had not been part of the moratorium or that he too had been surprised by the timing of the announcement. An angry Biden condemned the Israeli move, saying "the decision by the government of Israel to advance planning for new housing units in East Jerusalem . . . is precisely the kind of step that undermines the trust we need right now."[48] Secretary Clinton reportedly excoriated Prime Minister Netanyahu in an angry phone call—and then again in a public interview: "But we have to make clear to our Israeli friends and partners that the two-state solution—which we support, which the prime minister himself says he supports—requires confidence-building measures on both sides," said Clinton in an interview with CNN, "and the announcement of the settlements the very day that the vice president was there was insulting."[49]

Around the same time, General Petraeus, in testimony to the Senate Armed Services Committee, linked the Israeli-Palestinian conflict with broader problems facing the Middle East. "The conflict foments anti-American sentiment, due to a perception of U.S. favoritism for Israel," he said in his prepared testimony. "Arab anger over the Palestinian question limits the strength and depth of U.S. partnerships with governments and peoples . . . and weakens the legitimacy of moderate regimes in the Arab world."[50] As with Petraeus's previous comments on the Arab-Israeli conflict, this statement angered Israel and its supporters.

Israeli-American tensions continued to simmer. Netanyahu told an AIPAC conference in Washington, "Jerusalem is not a settlement, it's our capital."[51] Obama and Netanyahu met at that time, but Israeli media charged that the president had treated the prime minister poorly—Netanyahu reportedly was not received with proper protocol, and photographers were kept from the meeting. After the meeting reportedly started poorly, Obama asked the Israeli delegation to consult while he absented himself for an hour. Clearly, things were not going well between the two leaders.[52]

The dispute over settlements in Jerusalem lingered for several weeks. Although some in the administration sought to broker an agreement with the Israelis that would satisfy the complaints that Clinton had registered with Netanyahu, Mitchell, on the other hand, did not want to get sidetracked and preferred returning to the objective of proximity talks. As time passed, Mitchell's view prevailed. The Palestinians reportedly provided Mitchell with a substantive set of proposals, largely reflecting their positions from the 2008 Annapolis talks—for example, offering a 1.9 percent land swap. Israel reportedly did not reciprocate, arguing that the best way to make progress was through direct talks without preconditions. Mitchell tried to portray the glass as half-full. In a late May speech to the United States Institute of Peace, he defended the administration's approach, citing the following accomplishments:

Limited as it is, there has been some progress.
1. A right of center government in Israel has endorsed the creation of a Palestinian state in the West Bank and Gaza as the way to resolve the conflict.
2. Israel has frozen new housing construction starts in the West Bank for 10 months.

3. The Palestinian Authority is aggressively working to prevent violent attacks against Israel based on its publicly stated belief that violence does not advance the Palestinian cause.

4. There has been substantial and continuing improvement in security, in law and order and in economic development on the West Bank. This is the result of an effort to build, from the bottom up, the capacity to function effectively as a state from the moment of establishment. This involves extensive cooperation between Israel and the Palestinian Authority, with strong support from the United States, the Europeans, the United Nations, and other of our allies.

5. In circumstances that are very difficult for both, Israel and the Palestinian Authority are working to combat incitement and to refrain from taking actions that are provocative and that undermine further trust and confidence.

6. The Arab League has expressed its support for the negotiations. As a result, the Arab states have an important interest in a positive outcome, and they can play an important role in achieving it.

7. And finally, we have consequently begun proximity talks with Israeli and Palestinian leaders in an environment that is more constructive than has existed in the immediate past.[53]

Mitchell concluded his address with optimism, "There's no such thing as a conflict that can't be ended." Conflicts are "created, conducted, and sustained by human beings. They can be ended by human beings. No matter how hateful, no matter how hurtful, peace can prevail."

As is often the case in the Middle East, a spark on the ground served to quickly reshape the agenda. In late May 2010, Israeli naval commandos confronted a flotilla organized by a Turkish nongovernmental organization (NGO) that aimed to break the blockade of Gaza. The Israeli restrictions on Gaza had grown more severe over time, particularly in the wake of the 2008–9 Gaza War. Building materials, for example, were largely off-limits as the Israelis were concerned these would be used for military construction. Egypt largely cooperated and kept its border with Gaza sealed.

The sudden clash in open seas sparked a major crisis. The Israeli raid, which left nine activists dead (eight Turks and one Turkish-American), and scores injured, severely strained Turkish-Israeli relations. International condemnation of Israel was fierce, and the incident quickly turned into a major political and public relations liability for Israel.

The Obama administration, sensing an opportunity to restore credibility with the Netanyahu government, defended Israel against much of the diplomatic onslaught by highlighting Israel's right of self-defense and at the same time pressed Israel hard to ease restrictions on access and movement for Gaza. In the weeks and months after the flotilla incident, there were measurable improvements on Gaza access, though the overall situation remained bleak given the area's endemic poverty, the Israeli blockade, and the lingering and bitter division between Hamas-ruled Gaza and Palestinian Authority–controlled West Bank.

On a positive note, Israeli-Palestinian security cooperation improved markedly in the West Bank. The U.S. Security Coordinator, General Keith Dayton, a hold-over from the Bush 43 administration, managed the large security assistance and training program. The Obama administration actively sought to maintain and increase congressional support for funding the program. Palestinian prime minister Salam Fayyad, ostensibly head of an emergency government, continued to lead PA efforts to build the institutions of a future state and to improve service delivery. American funding for the security program totaled $392 million from 2007 to 2010, including more than $160 million to train the PA's National Security Force (NSF), approximately $89 million to provide nonlethal equipment, about $99 million to renovate or construct PA installations, and $22 million to build the capacity of the Interior Ministry and its Strategic Planning Directorate.[54] The Palestinians appeared bent on meeting the international community's demands for accountable government, civilian control over security forces and institution-building—all of this leading Fayyad to argue that Palestine would be ready for independent statehood by the middle of 2011.

With the proximity talks going nowhere, in a July 2010 visit to Washington, Netanyahu took a fresh approach with Obama. He sought to convince the president that he was serious about peacemaking and that he was willing to make major concessions, including concessions on territory. However, Netanyahu argued, he could not spell out such details until Israel received assurances on security and until face-to-face negotiations started. Obama accepted Netanyahu's commitment, no doubt stimulated in part by the imminent expiration of the settlement moratorium at the end of September. On August 20, Secretary Clinton extended an invitation to Netanyahu and Abbas to meet in Washington on September 2 to launch direct negotiations, with a proposed deadline of one year to complete the negotiations.[55] Two days later, Netanyahu accepted, noting that any agreement between the sides will reflect three principles:

> This agreement will be based on three initial components: First of all, on real and sustainable security arrangements on the ground; secondly, upon recognition of Israel as the national state of the Jewish people, and this means that the solution of a problem like the demand for return will be real-

ized in the territory of the Palestinian state; and the third component, the end to the conflict. We are discussing a peace agreement between Israel and a demilitarized Palestinian state. This state, if it should be established after this process, is due to end the conflict and not to be a façade for its continuation by other means.[56]

Palestinians also accepted the invitation to direct negotiations in Washington.

The launch of direct negotiations in Washington, September 1–2, attended by Egyptian president Hosni Mubarak and Jordan's king Abdullah II, had all the trappings of a summit meeting. President Obama orchestrated the proceedings and joined Netanyahu and Abbas for a trilateral session. Quartet envoy Tony Blair was also included.

The terms of reference for the negotiations were minimal, as Netanyahu had demanded and notwithstanding Palestinian entreaties. Obama summarized the purpose of these talks in a statement following his bilateral meetings with each of the attendees: "The purpose of these talks is clear. These will be direct negotiations between Israelis and Palestinians. These negotiations are intended to resolve all final status issues. The goal is a settlement, negotiated between the parties, that ends the occupation which began in 1967 and results in the emergence of an independent, democratic and viable Palestinian state, living side by side in peace and security with a Jewish state of Israel and its other neighbors. That's the vision we are pursuing." The president also described the American role, repeating some time-worn mantras: "The United States will put our full weight behind this effort. We will be an active and sustained participant We will support those who make difficult choices in pursuit of peace. But let me be very clear. Ultimately the United States cannot impose a solution, and we cannot want it more than the parties themselves."[57]

Following the talks, Mitchell briefed the press and said the parties had agreed to reach a "framework" peace agreement within one year. They would meet again in two weeks and every two weeks thereafter. A framework agreement, he said, "is not an interim agreement. It's more detailed than a declaration of principles, but is less than a full-fledged treaty. Its purpose is to establish the fundamental compromises necessary to enable the parties to then flesh out and complete a comprehensive agreement that will end the conflict and establish a lasting peace."[58]

Secretary Clinton and Mitchell traveled to the region in mid-September to preside over the next set of meetings in Sharm el-Sheikh, Egypt. However, the looming expiration of the settlement moratorium and renewed terrorism against Israelis brought the talks to a halt. The Israelis declined to put much substance on the table, insisting on the need to discuss security first. The direct

Palestinian-Israeli negotiations gave way to a frantic effort by the administration to extend the settlement freeze and thus prevent a collapse of the negotiations. Washington reportedly offered an expansive set of incentives to Israel to continue the moratorium, including a squadron of sophisticated military aircraft and political guarantees about opposing certain measures at the United Nations—in exchange for a three-month extension of the partial freeze.[59] The terms under consideration soon became publicly known and provoked considerable skepticism and opposition in U.S. policy circles for offering the Israelis such a huge package of aid and assurances for so little in return.[60] The more that came to be known about the bilateral discussions between the United States and Israel over an extension, the more questions were raised—both in Israel, where some cabinet ministers opposed the moratorium in principle while others were inclined to distrust U.S. assurances, and in the United States, where serious questions were raised about the high price being offered for a very short extension of the moratorium. Netanyahu was closing in on a likely razor-thin inner Cabinet vote in favor of accepting the American offer and extending the moratorium for a couple of months. But the Palestinians insisted that any extension of the moratorium needed to include East Jerusalem. At that point, the administration withdrew the offer of a deal, the moratorium came to an end, and negotiations did not resume.

November also ushered in a new Congress, with a Republican majority in the House. President Obama, who had enjoyed two years of a solid Democratic majority in both the Senate and the House, now would face partisan opposition to his Middle East policies. In an unprecedented private meeting in New York before Netanyahu met the president, incoming House Republican Whip Eric Cantor (R-Virginia) assured the Israeli leader that the Republicans would stand behind him. "Eric stressed that the new Republican majority will serve as a check on the administration and what has been, up until this point, one-party rule in Washington," according to a description of the meeting released by Cantor's office. "He made clear that the Republican majority understands the special relationship between Israel and the United States, and that the security of each nation is reliant upon the other."[61]

In December, Secretary Clinton signaled U.S. interest in framing negotiations around the core issues of borders, security, settlements, water, refugees, and Jerusalem. The objective, she said, would be a framework agreement, and the United States would be active in urging the parties toward agreement.[62] But this approach also did not stimulate the resumption of negotiations. By the end of 2010, the peace process was stuck. Mitchell stopped traveling to the region, and the United States still had no durable peace process strategy.

Stalemate and No Strategy

In early 2011, a trove of internal Palestinian negotiating documents—the so-called Palestine Papers—was leaked. The documents revealed, for the first time in public, a number of concessions and peace proposals that Palestinian negotiators had offered over many years of on-again, off-again negotiations. Palestinian leaders were caught off guard. The Palestine Papers became a source of deep embarrassment for an already weak and cautious Palestinian leadership and inhibited their inclination to take further steps toward negotiations with Israel.[63]

With the peace process in stalemate, action moved elsewhere. Regional leaders and their publics, and the administration, became absorbed in the profound changes that were under way in the Middle East—the "Arab Spring." Even as the attention shifted to the prospects for democratic change in the region, Palestinian supporters brought a resolution to the UN Security Council condemning settlements, with language drawn primarily from U.S. statements as a tactic to prevent an American veto. But on February 18, the United States did in fact veto the draft resolution. In explaining the U.S. veto, Ambassador to the UN Susan Rice said,

> Our opposition to the resolution should therefore not be misunderstood to mean we support settlement activity. On the contrary, we reject in the strongest terms the legitimacy of continued Israeli settlement activity. For more than four decades, Israeli settlement activity in territories occupied in 1967 has undermined Israel's security and corroded hopes for peace and stability in the region. Continued settlement activity violates Israel's international commitments, devastates trust between the parties, and threatens the prospects for peace.[64]

Rice further told reporters,

> The United States has said on many, many occasions for many years, we reject in the strongest terms the legitimacy of continued Israeli settlement activity. . . .
> No outside country has invested more effort and energy and resources in pursuit of that peace than the United States has, and we will continue to do so. But the only way that that goal can be reached, the common goal of a two-state solution, is, as a practical matter, through direct negotiations between the parties. . . . And our judgment was that this resolution would not have advanced the goal of getting the parties closer to negotiations and agreement. On the contrary, it would have hardened the positions of one or both sides.[65]

While the Israelis celebrated the American decision, the Palestinians—for reasons associated with frustration over the stalemate in the peace process, anger over the U.S. veto, and the impetus that the Arab uprisings gave to change in the region—started down a road that would take them further away from negotiations. Talks on reconciliation between the Palestinian Authority and Hamas, which had stalled consistently in the past, were renewed in Cairo and the framework of a deal was signed in Cairo in early May.[66] The Palestinians also started plotting a strategy to seek full membership of the State of Palestine in the United Nations. Both the United States and Israel opposed these Palestinian moves in the strongest terms.

Then, on May 13, George Mitchell resigned as special envoy, providing no hint of policy differences in a terse letter to the President,

> When I accepted your request to serve as U.S. Special Envoy for Middle East Peace my intention was to serve for two years. More than two years having passed I hereby resign effective May 20, 2011. I trust this will provide sufficient time for an effective transition.
>
> I strongly support your vision of comprehensive peace in the Middle East and thank you for giving me the opportunity to be part of your administration. It has been an honor for me to again serve our country.[67]

Mitchell's resignation reflected a significant debate within the administration and in Washington policy circles about the direction of peace process efforts. Some analysts argued that the process was not "ripe" for resolution, and that the leaders in the region were either too weak or unwilling to offer necessary concessions and trade-offs. Others argued that the administration had too many other competing priorities and that the peace process simply did not matter as much as it once did. Still others argued that the Arab Spring had relegated the peace process to second-tier status even in the Middle East. And, finally, some argued the contrary case, that the United States needed a strong strategy and a serious commitment to move the parties toward an agreement. The timing of Mitchell's resignation, just days before a major presidential address on U.S. policy in the region and toward the peace process, suggests that Mitchell was not at one with the peace process approach adopted by the president. Later reports suggest there was tense discord at the time within the administration, including deep divisions between Mitchell and Ross.[68]

On May 19, President Obama addressed a State Department audience on "A Moment of Opportunity," referring to the Arab Spring and the possibilities of peace in the Middle East. The thrust of the president's message centered on U.S. policy toward change in the Arab world. But he also advanced a new proposal for structuring Israeli-Palestinian negotiations,

> A lasting peace will involve two states for two peoples. Israel as a Jewish state and the homeland for the Jewish people, and the state of Palestine as the homeland for the Palestinian people; each state enjoying self-determination, mutual recognition, and peace.
>
> So while the core issues of the conflict must be negotiated, the basis of those negotiations is clear: a viable Palestine, and a secure Israel. The United States believes that negotiations should result in two states, with permanent Palestinian borders with Israel, Jordan, and Egypt, and permanent Israeli borders with Palestine. The borders of Israel and Palestine should be based on the 1967 lines with mutually agreed swaps, so that secure and recognized borders are established for both states. The Palestinian people must have the right to govern themselves, and reach their potential, in a sovereign and contiguous state.
>
> As for security, every state has the right to self-defense, and Israel must be able to defend itself—by itself—against any threat. Provisions must also be robust enough to prevent a resurgence of terrorism; to stop the infiltration of weapons; and to provide effective border security. The full and phased withdrawal of Israeli military forces should be coordinated with the assumption of Palestinian security responsibility in a sovereign, non-militarized state. The duration of this transition period must be agreed, and the effectiveness of security arrangements must be demonstrated.
>
> These principles provide a foundation for negotiations. Palestinians should know the territorial outlines of their state; Israelis should know that their basic security concerns will be met. I know that these steps alone will not resolve this conflict. Two wrenching and emotional issues remain: the future of Jerusalem, and the fate of Palestinian refugees. But moving forward now on the basis of territory and security provides a foundation to resolve those two issues in a way that is just and fair, and that respects the rights and aspirations of Israelis and Palestinians.[69]

The speech sparked a frenzy in Israel. Netanyahu was preparing to depart for Washington, where he was scheduled to meet Obama, address an AIPAC conference, and speak to a joint session of Congress, an invitation arranged directly with the Republican leadership on the Hill. In a statement released even before boarding his plane, Netanyahu pushed back hard against Obama's approach,

Prime Minister Netanyahu expects to hear a reaffirmation from President Obama of U.S. commitments made to Israel in 2004, which were overwhelmingly supported by both Houses of Congress. Among other things, those commitments relate to Israel not having to withdraw to the 1967 lines which are both indefensible and which would leave major Israeli population centers in Judea and Samaria beyond those lines. Those commitments also ensure Israel's well-being as a Jewish state by making clear that Palestinian refugees will settle in a future Palestinian state rather than in Israel. Without a solution to the Palestinian refugee problem outside the borders of Israel, no territorial concession will bring peace. Equally, the Palestinians, and not just the United States, must recognize Israel as the nation state of the Jewish people, and any peace agreement with them must end all claims against Israel. Prime Minister Netanyahu will make clear that the defense of Israel requires an Israeli military presence along the Jordan River.[70]

After more than two years of wrestling over settlements and the terms for resuming peace negotiations, Obama and Netanyahu now locked horns over the core issues in the negotiations, more specifically, whether to start negotiations on the issues of borders and security. Obama, probably annoyed at both Netanyahu and the Republicans for arranging the speech at the joint session of Congress, preempted Netanyahu's arrival with a peace process proposal that was not new but, according to previous U.S.-Israeli practice, would have been discussed first privately with the Israelis before making the proposal public.[71] Netanyahu, equally annoyed at Obama for springing the idea on him just before his arrival in Washington, took the unusual step of conveying his displeasure in a public message that would arrive on the president's desk just as the prime minister was taking off.

But things got even worse. After their private meeting in the Oval Office on May 20, Obama made a perfunctory statement that referred only to "some differences between us in the precise formulation and language." Netanyahu would have none of these diplomatic niceties. In a pointed lecture to the press, with the president sitting at his side, Netanyahu went on at length about the principles that were required for Israel to accept a peace process, emphasizing the indefensibility of the 1967 lines—an issue that Obama had not even raised.

Obama blinked first. In his speech to AIPAC on Sunday, May 22, the president clarified what he meant with reference to the 1967 lines and "swaps,"

By definition, it means that the parties themselves—Israelis and Palestinians —will negotiate a border that is different than the one that existed on June 4, 1967. That's what mutually agreed-upon swaps means. It is a well-known formula to all who have worked on this issue for a generation. It allows the parties themselves to account for the changes that have taken place over the last 44 years. It allows the parties themselves to take account of those changes, including the new demographic realities on the ground, and the needs of both sides. The ultimate goal is two states for two people: Israel as a Jewish state and the homeland for the Jewish people and the State of Palestine as the homeland for the Palestinian people—each state enjoying self-determination, mutual recognition, and peace.[72]

It made little difference that the Palestinians also did not embrace the president's speech. While they welcomed his initiative to start talks on borders and security, they insisted that a settlements freeze was still a precondition for negotiations, and they expressed unhappiness that the president had not associated U.S. policy with the 1967 borders. Neither party appeared willing to start talking on the basis of Obama's speech.

*   *   *

In many respects, this phase of the peace process ended the way the previous phases of the administration's approach had ended. Choosing tactics over strategy, the administration had sought at the outset to entice the parties to the negotiating table through confidence-building measures—a settlement freeze and gestures from the Arabs. When the partial moratorium on new housing starts left the Palestinians unenthusiastic, the administration tried crafting terms of reference, ultimately abandoning that effort in favor of indirect or proximity talks. When those failed to produce progress, the administration accepted Netanyahu's commitment to negotiate seriously if direct talks were convened, and the president arranged a trilateral summit and direct negotiations. And when those collapsed—under the weight of renewed settlement activity, renewed terrorism emanating from Gaza (not under the authority of the Palestinian Authority), and Israel's reluctance to put forward its views on territory until security had been discussed—the president tried the gambit of launching negotiations that would start with borders and security, two issues that had been linked during the preceding several years of peace process engagement. This, too, did not succeed.

By mid-2011, President Obama's peace process policy had failed, falling far short of the expectations that the president himself had raised at the outset of his term in office. Should he be reelected in 2012, Obama may use this new electoral mandate to put forward more substantive ideas to shape negotiations. Should a moment occur when the administration does reengage energetically, it would benefit from an assessment of what went right and wrong during the 2009–11 time frame:[73]

- The decision to seek a settlement freeze was misguided and had no chance of success as a confidence-building measure disconnected from negotiations. This is even more serious in light of the administration's inability to get the Palestinians or Arab states to reciprocate with CBMs of their own. Netanyahu faced little concrete pressure beyond rhetoric, and the administration accepted far less than what it sought, leaving Netanyahu with an important political victory over the president.
- Palestinian President Abbas became convinced that this decision left the Palestinians out on a limb for, as they said, they could demand no less than the Americans on settlements. But the administration then had no strategy for preventing the Palestinians from making a settlement freeze a precondition for negotiations. The wrong tactical choice mushroomed into a problem from which the administration could not extricate itself.
- This tactic gave way to another tactic (proximity talks), which gave way to yet another tactic (direct talks), all without a clear U.S. strategy. The administration elevated the methodology of seeking agreement to the level of a major policy goal, rather than seeing it as a means to an end and thereby retaining tactical flexibility.
- In every case—most notably after the president's speech of May 2011—the administration backed away at the first sign of resistance from Israel. No administration wants to engage Israel in a squabble over the peace process, and thus it is understandable to devote some attention to understanding Israel's concerns and trying to address those that are reasonable. But the Obama administration made no such distinction between reasonable and unreasonable Israeli demands. There was no reason for the president to essentially walk away from his May 2011 suggestion to start negotiations with borders and security, basing the borders negotiations on the 1967 lines with swaps. This concept had been discussed for some time and represented a sound basis on which to try to restart negotiations.
- The president's policy also lacked a strong alter ego to manage the peace process, and the policy-making process appeared uncoordinated and lacking direction. Mitchell was the envoy, but policy meetings in Washington were held without him, and contacts between the administration and Israeli officials were conducted without being coordinated with Mitchell.[74] It never was clear who had the lead in formulating policy recommendations for the president. And the policies decided on always had

the appearance of half-baked tactics, rather than elements in a fully formed strategy. The president did make clear his strong interest in advancing the prospects for peace, but that interest did not translate into a sustainable and salable strategy.

Thus, as of the summer of 2011, the peace process was derailed, with Palestinian energies concentrated on gaining UN membership and on finalizing the reconciliation deal with Hamas; and with Israeli energies concentrated on defeating the Palestinians' diplomatic moves and continuing to build housing in settlements in the West Bank and East Jerusalem. For its part, the administration had all but admitted that a combination of fatigue, the recalcitrance of the parties, and the need to shore up the president's electoral support among American Jews and the pro-Israel community had come together to push the peace process off even the back burner. The leading personalities of the president's peace team—Mitchell, Ross, and Jones, as well as Emanuel, Axelrod, and Gibbs–had all departed, leaving a void in the senior ranks. As the twenty-year anniversary of the Madrid Peace Conference was celebrated in 2011, the peace process launched at Madrid lay moribund.

EPILOGUE

LESSONS LEARNED
AND UNLEARNED

The United States does not bear sole responsibility for the persistence of the Arab-Israeli conflict or for the inability of the parties to resolve their differences through a negotiated peace settlement. This conflict is rooted deeply in history, both ancient and modern. Arabs and Israelis must assume the burden of explaining to their own people why they have not yet made the requisite compromises necessary for peace.

In his speech to the UN General Assembly on September 21, 2011, President Obama emphasized the importance of bridging the narratives that separate the parties.[1] He said, "Each side has legitimate aspirations—and that's part of what makes peace so hard. And the deadlock will only be broken when each side learns to stand in the other's shoes; each side can see the world through the other's eyes." Interestingly, the historical narratives of the Israelis and the Palestinians—the main protagonists in this drama—are in essence mirror images of each other.

Both peoples' national stories have been shaped by exile, as refugees from their homeland. Both believe they have been victimized, and both have suffered as a result of victimization. Both seek vindication and apologies for past suffering, and both seek recognition of the legitimacy of their historical experience. Both want justice for themselves. Both have deeply rooted security needs and fears. Both are attached to the same homeland, and both hold the land as a significant value in and of itself. Both are ethnic and national communities that place a high value on unity, even when it seems like an unobtainable dream. Each has a positive self-image and a negative image of the other.

Thus, notwithstanding Obama's hope that the two sides can somehow place themselves in the shoes of the other, the reality is that narratives will separate these parties until the proximate issues of conflict have been addressed—territory and borders, security, water, refugees and settlements, and Jerusalem. It is for this reason that the peace process has become such a consuming obsession with the world's diplomats; and it is for this reason that the parties themselves have turned so often to the United States for help in addressing the tangible and inherently resolvable issues that divide them. The centrality of the American role and its successes and failures have constituted the main subject of this volume.

As noted in the introduction and as detailed in our earlier volume,[2] there are serious and far-reaching lessons to be learned from the past twenty years of American diplomacy, lessons that might help future U.S. administrations assist the parties to reach peace settlements. Despite the mantra repeated by too many Washington insiders, the United States can and should want peace at least as much, if not more, than the parties themselves; without peace, and with recurring conflict, American resources are drained and our diplomatic strengths are dissipated by chasing cease-fires and temporary fixes. The challenge for the United States is to craft a policy and a strategy—not simply a succession of tactics—that speak to the core issues in dispute, are sensitive to the domestic politics and constraints of the parties, and stay within the narrowing confines of American political views about the Middle East. To craft such a policy and a strategy is no small challenge, as attested to by successive American administrations that have not succeeded in doing so.

To accomplish these purposes, presidents and the empowered aides they select to manage the policy on a day-to-day basis need to be agile and sensitive to the narrow openings that sometimes present themselves to be exploited for diplomacy to advance. We are firmly of the view that opportunities do not "knock," but rather that political leaders and diplomats must create them, often with the smallest of leads and threads. The more diverse and experienced a team selected by the president, the better the chance that such openings will not be missed. Indeed, experienced diplomats, familiar with the cultures and nuances of the Middle East, will serve the president wisely, judiciously advising when presidential involvement is necessary and when it is better not undertaken. Experienced hands will also ensure that a president will be prepared well for those moments when his involvement is most critical, especially at meetings or summits with other leaders.

However, the ingredients for possible success go well beyond diplomatic technique and timing. The Middle East peace process motivates Europe and Asia, and thus American diplomacy must integrate better the qualifications and assets that groups such as the Quartet can bring to the table. The peace process also evokes very strong emotions at home, and thus any administration must strive hard to recapture the sense of bipartisan resolve that once underpinned our diplomacy on the conflict. No American politician will favor pressure on Israel in the abstract; but politicians from both sides of the aisle can be brought to support an approach that asks both sides in the conflict, including Israel, to reach beyond current positions and to consider the kinds of concessions that are required for a deal to be made. American bipartisan support for Israel must not become a tool for immobilizing the Israeli political system, but rather an incentive for Israel to think beyond its current positions, confident that American support will be unwavering as it takes risks for peace. And historic Palestinian—and Arab—reluctance to make concessions and take advantage of Israeli offers when they emerge must be discouraged as strongly as possible.

The rise of the Arab Spring in 2011 presented new challenges for American peace diplomacy even beyond the broader tension that is often present in American foreign policy between supporting democracy and human rights on the one hand, and protecting important American interests in the Middle East on the other. Certainly, the Arab Spring placed more emphasis on Arab public attitudes that could no longer be ignored by Arab rulers or by the outside world. And these attitudes were far more hostile toward the United States and its diplomacy than the traditional positions of Arab governments. Looking ahead, there are at least two issues with which the United States will have to contend in designing its future approach to Arab-Israeli peace.

The first issue is the revolutionary changes taking place in Egypt that have some short-term consequences but also have the potential of even more important long-term consequences. Egypt, its relations with the United States, and its peace treaty with Israel have been anchors of the American approach to the Middle East for over three decades. Even aside from the unpredictability of the long-term consequences of the revolutionary upheavals in Egypt, the fall of Hosni Mubarak had immediate consequences. Beyond the Egyptian-Israeli Peace Treaty, which was not immediately in jeopardy, Mubarak's Egypt had become Israel's chief ally in the Middle East, especially after the decline of the Israeli-Turkish relationship. And Mubarak and his aides had been highly instrumental in selling American diplomacy in the Arab world, in mediating between Israel and the Palestinians, and in keeping in check Hamas' (and Hezbollah's) influence. For years, Israelis had grown so comfortable with the relationship with official Egypt—even as they were concerned about the lack of warmth at the public level—that these relations were taken for granted. All this changed with the fall of Mubarak.

To be sure, the Egyptian military has continued to coordinate with Israelis as both sides have mutual interests and long-standing cooperative relations. The Egyptian military also has understood the importance of the Egyptian-Israeli treaty to Egypt and to the United States, from whom they hope to continue receiving military, economic, and political support. But the military is now weakened in its ability to go against public sentiments, particularly with the rising power of Islamist groups, from the Muslim Brotherhood to the Salafis who together have gained a substantial majority of parliamentary seats. Fighting for its own legitimacy,[3] the military leadership has become less able to go against prevailing Egyptian sentiments. This is one reason why Egyptian mediators moved quickly after the revolution to clinch a reconciliation deal between Hamas and Fatah that they were reluctant to clinch in the past in deference to Israel and the United States.

Israelis will be particularly worried about the change in Cairo and the loss of Mubarak as a key ally. But they also will be considering the long-term consequences, including implications for the Egyptian-Israeli treaty. Although the peace treaty is in the interests of both countries—and even the Islamist groups, including some of the Salafis, have made reassuring statements about the future of the Israeli-Egyptian treaty—there are also signs that many Egyptians are at least inclined to want to renegotiate its terms.

From the Obama administration's point of view, the net result of the Arab Spring has been to reduce its ability to utilize Egypt in its diplomatic efforts and to provide the Israeli government another argument—with considerable sympathy in the U.S. Congress—for its reluctance to be more forthcoming on the peace process. Certainly, the ongoing efforts at Hamas-Fatah reconciliation have complicated American diplomacy in an election year where the American mainstream—and official American policy—view Hamas as a terrorist organization.

A second issue is the impact of the Arab Spring on Palestinian politics. Palestinian Authority president Mahmoud Abbas has made it clear in signing the deal with Hamas that, in the era of the Arab Spring, he feels he must respond to the sentiments of the Palestinians and other Arabs, the majority of whom want to see the Palestinians unified. Among the Arabs who support one Palestinian faction or another, support for Hamas is strong.[4] At the same time, the picture has become more complicated for Hamas. On the one hand, it has found more sympathy in Egypt, particularly with the election of an Islamist majority in the parliament. On the other hand, the instability in Syria has left Hamas more vulnerable and has forced it to seek a new home. Hamas leader, Khaled Meshaal, has even touted the utility of peaceful, as opposed to militant, protests. The net result has been a new mood that has pressured both Fatah and Hamas to find a way to coexist politically, which can only be accommodated through a major shift in the Israeli and American approaches to the peace process.

Notwithstanding all the negatives and unanswered questions, there are also opportunities for American diplomacy if there is a will to move forward. Israeli concerns about the Egyptian-Israeli relationship present one opportunity. In the short term, no Egyptian rulers, including the Muslim Brotherhood, are likely to seek foreign policy confrontation or war as their need to address the pressing economic and political problems will trump all else. The potential danger thus arises from possible escalation and bloodshed on the Israeli-Palestinian front, which could draw Egypt into a conflict, as there would be no one to defend the relations with Israel as aggressively as the Mubarak regime did. Thus some kind of accommodation in the Palestinian-Israeli front will not disrupt Egyptian priorities. And Israel, to the extent that protecting its treaty with Egypt remains a priority, has an equal interest in avoiding an environment in which the treaty is seriously challenged.

One can also envision a potential benefit down the road for which American diplomacy can prepare, even if the timing will depend somewhat on the outcome of events in Egypt: on a broader scale, the value of the Egyptian-Israeli treaty—which can no longer be taken for granted—has the potential of substantially enhancing the value of the Arab Peace Initiative, which offers Israel peace and security with the Arab states in exchange for a comprehensive peace settlement with the Palestinians.

The point is that diplomatic initiatives cannot simply be held back until "events" settle down. Diplomacy is part and parcel of the dynamics of unfolding regional events and plays a part in shaping the outcome. There are choices available to the Obama administration on how to proceed on the Palestinian-Israeli peace front in the face of the Arab Spring. This is the sort of internal debate that took place in the early months of 2011 on whether to move aggressively in pursuit of Middle East peace and put forth bold ideas, such as "Obama Parameters."[5] It is a debate that needs to continue, especially in the immediate aftermath of the 2012 American presidential election.

*   *   *

In this volume, we have paid particular attention to the dynamics of presidential transitions, especially the discontinuities and their impact on policy. Newly elected presidents expect to put their own stamp on policies and personnel, often seeing these changes as necessary immediately to demonstrate why voters supported them in the first place. The issue, then, is not to contemplate a change in the "spoils" system of politics—which is a reality that will not change—but to introduce a moment of policy reflection during transitions when a new administration can consider whether to continue or to change an inherited policy. Such a policy pause might have persuaded President Clinton in 1993 that the tough line adopted by his predecessor—tough toward both Israel and the Arabs—might have been reframed in a more positive way without throwing out the baby with the bathwater. Such a policy pause in 2001 might have persuaded President George W. Bush not to turn his back on the peace process, notwithstanding the challenges posed by the ongoing Intifada. And such a policy pause in 2009 might have led President Obama to determine at the outset that the Annapolis negotiations had progressed substantially enough to warrant throwing American weight behind their resumption from the point where they stopped. We are sensitive to the need for presidential administrations to put their own stamp on policy, but this need not require the wholesale disavowal of what went on before.

Finally, we would agree with those who argue that the peace process is hard and thus the United States can be excused somewhat for having tried without success to reach a negotiated settlement. It is hard. But we believe firmly that the United States can conduct diplomacy with as much strength, will, determination, backbone, and intensity as we conduct military operations. Policies, like military strategies, often collapse once the first bullet—rhetorical or physical—is fired. That is no reason to walk away from the fray or to run after an alternative approach. Flexibility and diplomatic agility can sustain an effective policy while our political leaders and diplomats work the issue. It would have been easy for Kissinger to take no for an answer in 1975 when the Sinai II negotiations stalemated; it would have been easy for Carter to abandon the Egyptian-Israeli talks in 1978 when they foundered; it would have been easy for Bush 41 to accept the Syrian and Israeli initial rejections in 1991. Each of these administrations persisted, however, and turned imminent failure into diplomatic success. Although persistence is no guarantee of future results, it should teach us something about the power of American diplomacy when employed wisely and with determination.

As attentive as we may be about the cost of this conflict regarding human suffering on all sides—and this should be a serious consideration—our conclusions are based on more calculated reasons. There is no alternative to a two-state solution to the Israeli-Palestinian conflict—if there is to be a negotiated agreement at all—but the ability of the parties to reach such a settlement is becoming harder every day, the problem being exacerbated by violence, rejectionism, settlements, and leaders unwilling to face up to the compromises that are necessary. The substantive pathway to the two-state solution is no longer a mystery, even if it will be very hard to hammer out the details.

This challenge puts a premium on leadership, both in the region and in Washington. We are under no illusions about the incredibly important issues that compete for the president's attention. We are also persuaded that determined American leadership on the peace process will yield tremendous benefit in many other areas of our foreign policy, especially during this extended period of upheaval in the Middle East. If there is one lesson among many that stands out from the cases studies in this volume, it is the diplomatic weight and bearing that an American president and his team can bring to the Arab-Israeli peace process.

A number of conclusions and lessons can be drawn from the case studies in this volume. They are not exhaustive, but rather suggestive of ways that American diplomacy can be strengthened in the search for Arab-Israeli peace.

1. **Taking sides.** Given the realities of American politics, there will always be deeper coordination of policy with Israel than with the Palestinians, and the Palestinians will always believe the United States is biased in Israel's favor. The challenge for policymakers is to make this work in favor of peace process progress, that is, to select the right combination of pressures and incentives for both sides that keeps the focus on moving forward. There are numerous examples of the effective use of such tactics, for example, the letters of assurance that accompanied the Madrid terms of reference and the U.S. withholding of loan guarantees to gain assurances that the funds would not go to settlements.

2. **Both Israelis and Palestinians need coddling.** Israel, still surrounded by some Arab states formally at war with it, needs continuous reassurance that the United States is a constant ally; and the Palestinians, stateless and dispersed, need reassurance that their basic interests will not be sacrificed. The United States cannot provide such assurances alone, but it remains the most important international actor in this regard. U.S. policies predicated solely on either pressure or incentives alone do not work.

3. **Transitions.** Presidential transitions during the past twenty years have proven to be problematic and discontinuous with respect to the peace process. Each transition has been marked by an attitude of "anything but my predecessor," and each has devalued peace process progress that bears the mark of the preceding administration. Although incoming administrations will rightfully want to put their own mark on policy and will want to install their own personnel, a better job must be done in ensuring the continuity of policies that are working and ongoing. A prime example is the Bush 43–Obama transition, where all of the progress registered in the Olmert-Abbas negotiations in 2008 was seemingly lost.

4. **Seize the moment.** We have emphasized that opportunities normally do not just happen, but need to be developed. When such opportunities do open up, the United States needs to be agile and determined to exploit whatever opening is provided. It remains unclear to us why Secretary of State Warren Christopher and the U.S. team went on vacation in August 1993, just when Rabin had offered his breathtaking "deposit" vis-à-vis Syria and just when the Oslo negotiations were nearing completion. It remains equally unclear why President Bush (43) did not throw his weight behind the Olmert-Abbas negotiations in September 2008. Examples abound of opportunities missed.

5. **Slogans.** Slogans associated with the peace process are usually inadequate or even plain wrong: thus we are not "Israel's lawyer," we do want peace as much as the parties do, a deal doesn't have to wait until everything is agreed, and the Palestinians do not miss opportunities. In the Middle East, at least, the situation is always more complex than can be captured in a simple slogan.

6. **Surprises do not work.** Other than holiday gifts, no one likes a surprise, especially when it involves issues of vital national interest. The Reagan Plan in 1982 contained many important elements, but it was stillborn in part because it was sprung on Israel and Arab countries with no advance consultation. Among Israel's complaints about Obama's May 19, 2011, speech was that he announced his ideas—which had been discussed among the parties for some time—without prior coordination with Israel and just on the eve of Israeli prime minister Benjamin Netanyahu's meeting with the president. The United States can still own its policy even if it consults with the parties in advance.

7. **Prepare, prepare, prepare.** Inadequate preparation contributed significantly to American peace process failures including the Geneva Summit with Hafez al-Asad in 2000, the Camp David Summit in 2000, and elsewhere. The peace process cannot be dealt with casually, individually, or off the cuff; substantial interagency homework can make the difference between success and failure.

8. **Difficult leaders' positions can be influenced.** The United States has dealt with hard-line, difficult leaders and sometimes produced results, for example, with Begin at Camp David I and Asad and Shamir at Madrid. Building trust and confidence is critical, as is a determination not to take an initial "no" as a final answer.

9. **There is no avoiding the Arab-Israeli dispute, so do not pretend it can be outsourced.** Every administration in the past twenty years has become

deeply involved in the Arab-Israeli conflict, notwithstanding an initial disposition to remain on the sidelines. As such, it makes sense to choose senior personnel early on who can shepherd U.S. policy in the right direction. The choice of secretary of state, national security advisor, and the three or four senior bureaucratic appointees is most critical. The U.S. team needs to understand the region and be seen as diverse in its thinking.

10. **Israelis and Palestinians are tough negotiators, and thus the United States must be equally tough.** The United States must be tough in negotiations, even as it maintains the confidence of the parties. It is imperative not to confuse tough negotiating style with anger or resentment over the policies of others. In particular, the United States needs to refine its approach in dealing with Israel's Likud Party prime ministers. They will always be harder to deal with than their left-wing colleagues, but a peace deal in Israel must secure substantial support from the right in order to be viable. With Palestinians, there is a historic unwillingness to go the last mile, to make the concessions necessary to seal the deal. Arafat exemplified this at Camp David; Abbas followed this pattern in the Annapolis process. Thus, the end game of negotiations—always the hardest part—is where the greatest amount of U.S. resolve and determination will be necessary with both sides.

11. **Congress and public opinion.** Until the 1990s Congress was likely to support a president's policy if it made sense; today, partisanship has become the watchword in Washington and has infected foreign, as well as domestic, policy. Presidents cannot ride roughshod over congressional or public opinion on issues relating to Israel and the peace process. Bush 41's success in Congress on loan guarantees that prevailed over Shamir's position is unlikely to be repeated; consider the tumultuous welcome given to Prime Minister Netanyahu in May 2011 just after he stiffed the president in the Oval Office. An administration's peace process policy needs to be understandable and perceived as fair. And administrations need to keep Congress and the American public informed regarding strategy and tactics.

NOTES

Introduction

1. To be sure, both Kissinger and Carter ultimately were to coordinate diplomatically much more closely with Sadat, who thought in strategic terms and often left details to the Americans to negotiate, than with Rabin or Begin, who focused much more closely on the details of the negotiations.

2. See Lawrence Freedman, *A Choice of Enemies: America Confronts the Middle East* (New York: Public Affairs, 2008), Kindle ed., 1174; "The Iranian Revolution: An Oral History with Henry Precht, Then State Department Desk Officer," *Middle East Journal* 58, no. 1 (Winter 2004): 12; Gary Sick, *All Fall Down: America's Tragic Encounter with Iran* (New York: Penguin, 1985), 60–61

3. George H.W. Bush, "Address before a Joint Session of the Congress on the Cessation of the Persian Gulf Conflict," March 6, 1991, George Bush Presidential Library and Museum, http://bushlibrary .tamu.edu/research/public_papers.php?id=2767.

4. Interview with Scott Lasensky, December 21, 2004.

5. President Clinton, in a 2001 speech to the Israel Policy Forum that laid out the so-called "Clinton Parameters," referred to a Palestinian state, saying, "[Jerusalem] should encompass the internationally recognized capitals of two states, Israel and Palestine." "Text: Clinton Speech on Mideast Peace Parameters," U.S. Embassy, Tel Aviv, January 7, 2001, http://usembassy-israel.org.il/publish/ peace/archives/2001/january/me0108b.html. However, it was not until Bush 43 that U.S. support for Palestinian statehood became officially stated U.S. policy.

Chapter One

1. George H.W. Bush, "Address before a Joint Session of the Congress on the Cessation of the Persian Gulf Conflict," March 6, 1991, George Bush Presidential Library and Museum, http://bushlibrary .tamu.edu/research/public_papers.php?id=2767.

2. Some of the events in this chapter are ones with which one of the authors had direct experience. We have drawn on his memory, as well as interviews with other participants, to reconstruct events.

3. The phrase "sole legitimate representative of the Palestinian people" was incorporated in a resolution of the Seventh Arab League Summit Conference, "Resolution on Palestine," Rabat, Morocco, October 28, 1974.

4. United Nations, "Resolution 242 (1967) of 22 November 1967," http://daccess-ods.un.org/TMP /4613271.65365219.html.

5. "The Khartoum Resolutions, September 1, 1967," The Avalon Project, Yale Law School, http://avalon.law.yale.edu/20th_century/khartoum.asp.

6. William Rogers, "Statement by Secretary of State Rogers, 9 December 1969," Israel Ministry of Foreign Affairs, www.mfa.gov.il/MFA/Foreign+Relations/Israels+Foreign+Relations+since+1947 /1947-1974/9+Statement+by+Secretary+of+State+Rogers-+9+Decemb.htm.

7. Henry Kissinger, *White House Years* (Boston: Little, Brown, 1969), 374–76.

8. Anwar Sadat, *The Public Diary of President Sadat: The Road of Pragmatism* (London: Leiden Brill, 1979), 1019.

9. Ezer Weizman, *Battle for Peace* (New York: Bantam, 1981), 18.

10. George P. Shultz, *Turmoil and Triumph: My Years as Secretary of State* (New York: Scribner's, 1993), 1016.

11. See Mahmoud Abbas (Abu Mazen), *Through Secret Channels: The Road to Oslo* (Reading, UK: Garnet, 1995); Moshe Arens, *Broken Covenant: American Foreign Policy and the Crisis between the U.S. and Israel* (New York: Simon & Schuster, 1995); Hanan Ashrawi, *This Side of Peace: A Personal Account* (New York: Simon & Schuster, 1995); James A. Baker III and Thomas M. DeFrank, *The Politics of Diplomacy: Revolution, War & Peace, 1989–1992* (New York: Putnam, 1995); Yossi Beilin, *Touching Peace: From the Oslo Accord to a Final Agreement* (London: Weidenfeld & Nicolson, 1999); Eytan Bentsur, *Making Peace: A First-Hand Account of the Arab-Israeli Peace Process* (New York: Praeger, 2000); Bill Clinton, *My Life* (New York: Vintage, 2005); Warren Christopher, *In the Stream of History: Shaping Foreign Policy for a New Era* (Stanford, CA: Stanford University Press, 1998); Martin Indyk, *Innocent Abroad: An Intimate Account of American Peace Diplomacy in the Middle East* (New York: Simon & Schuster, 2009); Aaron David Miller, *The Much Too Promised Land: America's Elusive Search for Arab-Israeli Peace* (New York: Bantam, 2008); Ahmed Qurie, *From Oslo to Jerusalem: The Palestinian Story of the Secret Negotiations* (London: Tauris, 2006); Dennis Ross, *The Missing Peace: The Inside Story of the Fight for Middle East Peace* (New York: Farrar, Straus and Giroux, 2004).

12. See Jane Corbin, *The Norway Channel: The Secret Talks That Led to the Middle East Peace Accord* (New York: Atlantic Monthly, 1994); Laura Zittrain Eisenberg and Neil Caplan, *Negotiating Arab-Israeli Peace: Patterns, Problems, Possibilities* (Bloomington: Indiana University Press, 1998); Charles Enderlin and Susan Fairfield, *Shattered Dreams: The Failure of the Middle East Peace Process, 1995–2002* (New York: Other Press, 2003); Galia Golan, *Israel and Palestine: Peace Plans from Oslo to Disengagement* (Princeton, NJ: Markus Wiener, 2007); Daniel C. Kurtzer and Scott Lasensky, *Negotiating Arab-Israeli Peace: American Leadership in the Middle East* (Washington, DC: United States Institute of Peace Press, 2008); David Makovsky, *Making Peace with the PLO: The Rabin Government's Road to the Oslo Accord* (Boulder, CO: Westview, 1996); Itamar Rabinovich, *Waging Peace: Israel and the Arabs, 1948–2003* (Princeton, NJ: Princeton University Press, 2004); Ofira Seliktar, *Doomed to Failure? The Politics and Intelligence of the Oslo Peace Process* (New York: Praeger, 2009); Mark Tessler, *A History of the Israeli-Palestinian Conflict* (Bloomington: Indiana University Press, 2009).

13. See especially William B. Quandt, *Peace Process: American Diplomacy and the Arab-Israeli Conflict since 1967*, 3rd ed. (Washington, DC: Brookings Institution Press, University of California Press, 2005).

14. Avishai Margalit, "The Violent Life of Yitzhak Shamir," *New York Review of Books* 39, no. 9 (May 14, 1992): 18–24.

15. "Memorandum of Conversation, Meeting with Foreign Minister Arens of Israel," The White House, March 13, 1989.

16. "Memorandum of Conversation, One-on-One Meeting with Prime Minister Shamir of Israel," The White House, April 6, 1989.

17. "Memorandum of Conversation, Meeting with Prime Minister Shamir of Israel," The White House, November 15, 1989.

18. Yitzhak Shamir and Yitzhak Rabin, "Israel's Peace Initiative," *Israel Ministry of Foreign Affairs*, May 14, 1989, www.mfa.gov.il/MFA/Peace%20Process/Guide%20to%20the%20Peace%20Process/Israel-s%20Peace%20Initiative%20-%20May%2014-%201989.

19. Yossi Ben-Aharon (former director-general of the Israeli Prime Minister's Office), interview with one of the authors, July 14, 2009, Jerusalem.

20. James A. Baker III, "Baker's Five Points," Knesset Website, December 6, 1989, www.knesset.gov.il/process/docs/baker_eng.htm.

21. See Baker and DeFrank, *The Politics of Diplomacy*, p. 115.

22. "Principles and Pragmatism: American Policy toward the Arab-Israeli Conflict, Address before the American-Israel Public Affairs Committee," Department of State, May 22, 1989, www.archive.org/details/departmentofstatc89unit.

23. Baker and DeFrank, *The Politics of Diplomacy*, 128.

24. Al Kamen, "Administration Attempts to Blunt Israeli Criticism: Bush Remark on Settlements Created Uproar," *Washington Post*, March 6, 1990.

25. See Baker and DeFrank, *The Politics of Diplomacy*, 411–29, 443–69, 487–513, 540–57.

26. Faisal Husseini, "Palestinian Politics after the Gulf War," *Journal of Palestine Studies* 20, no. 4 (Summer 1991): 106.

27. See Camille Mansour, "The Palestinian-Israeli Peace Negotiations: An Overview and an Assessment," *Journal of Palestine Studies* 22, no. 3 (Spring 1993): 5–31.

28. Secretary of State James A. Baker III, "Testimony to House Appropriations Subcommittee on Middle East Peace Mission, May 22, 1991," *Journal of Palestine Studies* 20, no. 4 (Summer 1991): 181.

29. John Kelly, "Loan Guarantees for Israel: The Clock Is Ticking," Memorandum to the Secretary, June 24, 1991; Dennis Ross, "Loan Guarantees, Settlements and the Peace Process," Memorandum to the Secretary, June 27, 1991.

30. "Secretary Baker's Meeting with Palestinians, July 21, 1991: Draft Memorandum of Conversation," Department of State.

31. "Middle East Mirror," *Journal of Palestine Studies* 21, no. 2 (Winter 1992): 169.

32. The U.S. Letter of Assurances said the following about Palestinian representation: "Only Palestinians can choose their delegation members, which are not subject to veto from anyone. The United States understands that members of the delegation will be Palestinians from the territories who agree to negotiations on two tracks, in phases, and who are willing to live in peace with Israel. No party can be forced to sit with anyone it does not want to sit with. Palestinians will be free to announce their component of the joint delegation and to make a statement during the opening of the conference. They may also raise any issue pertaining to the substance of the negotiations during the negotiations." "Letter of Assurances to the Palestinians, October 18, 1991," in Quandt, *Peace Process*, app. M, www.brookings.edu/~/media/Files/Press/Books/2005/peaceprocess3/peaceprocess_appendixM.pdf.

33. See Ghassan Khatib, *Palestinian Politics and the Middle East Peace Process: Consensus and Competition in the Palestinian Negotiating Team* (London: Routledge, 2010), 61. Also cf. Hanan Ashrawi, *This Side of Peace* (New York: Simon & Schuster, 1995).

34. "Letter of Assurances to Palestinians," in Quandt, *Peace Process*, app. M.

35. Baker and DeFrank, *The Politics of Diplomacy*, 540–44.

36. Clyde Haberman, "Shamir Again Criticizes U.S. on Loan Guarantees," *The New York Times*, October 8, 1991.

37. Ross, *The Missing Peace*, 82.

38. "Israeli Politics and the Madrid Conference," National Intelligence Council Executive Brief, October 23, 1991.

39. Yediot Ahronot poll in Jackson Diehl, "Peace Rally in Israel Attracts Tens of Thousands," *Washington Post*, October 27, 1991.

40. Yitzhak Shamir interview with Joseph Harif, *Maariv*, June 26, 1992, in Clyde Haberman, "Arens Faults Minister's 'Greater Israel' Concept," *New York Times*, June 29, 1992.

41. Shlomo Ben-Ami, *Scars of War, Wounds of Peace: The Israeli-Arab Tragedy* (Oxford: Oxford University Press, 2006), 198. Yossi Ben-Aharon said the same thing in an interview, that Shamir went

to Madrid only because of U.S. pressure and in order to protect U.S. relations with Israel. One senior Israeli official was quoted as saying, "We feel we're being pushed into a political killing field." Clyde Haberman, "Israelis Suggest Talks on Peace Could Falter," *New York Times*, October 20, 1991.

42. Kurtzer and Lasensky, *Negotiating Arab-Israeli Peace*, 15–17.

43. Eisenberg and Caplan, *Negotiating Arab-Israeli Peace*, 83.

44. Makovsky, *Making Peace with the PLO*, 108.

45. Kurtzer and Lasensky, *Negotiating Arab-Israeli Peace*, 25–74.

46. "Palestinian Interim Self-Governing Authority—'PISGA'—Plan," Jerusalem Media and Communication Centre, March 3, 1992, www.jmcc.org/Documentsandmaps.aspx?id=348. Throughout the negotiations, Palestinians referred to their model as "PISGA" to emphasize the centrality of the Palestinian role in the interim arrangements, whereas the Israelis referred to their model as "ISGA," dropping the word "Palestinian" from the definition of the interim self-governing arrangements.

47. Khatib, *Palestinian Politics*, 70.

48. "Israel's Ideas for Self-Government: Presented to the Palestinian Delegation," reprinted in Ami Ayalon, ed., *Middle East Contemporary Survey*, vol. 16 (Boulder, CO: Westview Press, 1992), 143, http://books.google.com/books?id=87hLBZJNkhUC&lpg=PA67&ots=YCV_WvFNqu&dq=middle%20east%20contemporary%20survey%20xvi%201992&pg=PA143#v=onepage&q=middle%20east%20contemporary%20survey%20xvi%201992&f=false.

49. David A. Weinberg, "American Intervention in Israeli Politics: Past Experience, Future Prospects," *Strategic Assessment* 14, no. 3 (October 2011): 96.

50. Quandt, *Peace Process*, 327.

51. Yair Hirschfeld, unpublished manuscript, chap. 2, pp. 3–4.

52. Edward Djerejian and Dennis Ross, "Untitled Memorandum to Secretary Baker," July 31, 1992.

53. Avi Gil (former director general of the Israeli Foreign Ministry), interview with the authors, August 12, 2009, Jerusalem.

54. Marwan Muasher, *The Arab Center: The Promise of Moderation* (New Haven, CT: Yale University Press, 2008), 105. See also Mahmoud Abbas, interview by *Voice of the Arabs*, September 12, 1993, in which Abbas points to the absence of progress in Washington attributable to the open nature of the negotiations.

55. Qurie, *From Oslo to Jerusalem*, 36–37.

56. Ron Pundak (Israeli academic and Oslo negotiator), interview with one of the authors, August 3, 2009, Tel Aviv, Israel.

57. Former American official, interview with one of the authors.

58. Makovsky, *Making Peace with the PLO*, 112.

59. "Memorandum of Conversation, Meeting with Yitzhak Rabin of Israel," The White House, December 4, 1991.

60. Rabinovich, *Waging Peace*, 46–47; Indyk, *Innocent Abroad*, 18.

61. Although this agreement paved the way for the loan guarantees to be disbursed, it did not deliver on its promise of restraining the growth of settlements. See Daniel Kurtzer, "Do Settlements Matter? An American Perspective," *Israel Journal of Foreign Affairs* 3, no. 2 (2009).

62. President-elect Clinton, in *Mideast Monitor*, November 3, 1992.

63. According to a senior AIPAC staffer at the time, Indyk wanted not to be seen as AIPAC's candidate for the position, to which Clinton reportedly replied, "Are you kidding us? It benefits me to have him as AIPAC's candidate." Senior AIPAC staffer, in a private conversation with one of the authors.

64. Martin Indyk and Robert Satloff, "Issues Paper: Middle East Peace Talks," transition paper, n.d., p. 2. Provided to the authors by Robert Satloff. The full text of the transition paper can be found in the online appendix to this volume at: www.thepeacepuzzle.org.

65. Indyk, *Innocent Abroad*, 19.

66. From the outset of the Oslo process, Norwegian officials and the Israeli academics (Yair Hirschfeld and Ron Pundak) briefed Kurtzer on the progress of the Oslo talks, and Kurtzer briefed the secretary of state and the peace team. The Israeli and Norwegian briefings stopped when the Israelis made the Oslo channel official, fearing that the United States might leak the existence of the secret talks

inadvertently. The Israeli briefings of the United States resumed at the end of July 1993. It is clear that many U.S. officials working on the peace process knew about the Oslo talks—in particular, they were aware of how far Oslo had come at the time of Rabin's "deposit" initiative with the Syrians—but it is equally clear that they paid little attention and ascribed little importance to this initiative.

67. The issue of whether the United States played any role in the Oslo process on the issue of mutual recognition is in dispute. Ross, *Missing Peace*, 117–18, claims that with Christopher's concurrence, he persuaded a reluctant Shimon Peres to conclude a mutual recognition deal with the PLO before the Oslo Accords were signed. However, Uri Savir, one of the key architects of the Oslo Accords and Israel's chief negotiator, argues that this was not the case, "After the PLO secretly agreed to our conditions for mutual recognition, it was agreed to postpone the negotiations on it till after the conclusion of the DOP. They took place in Paris with Norwegian mediation and Arafat, Rabin and Peres on the phone with AA [Ahmed Qurie] and me. Washington consented to this move, as it consequently would oblige it, but did not have to push for it. Mutual recognition was signed in Jerusalem and Tunis, before the DOP." Uri Savir (former director general of the Israeli Foreign Ministry), private correspondence with the authors, October 19, 2011.

68. Hirschfeld (ms., chap. 2, 17–18) and Qurie (*From Oslo to Jerusalem*, 43–44) agree that the two sides wanted Oslo to feed into Washington, as does Terje Roed-Larsen, the Norwegian nongovernmental activist who shepherded the Oslo talks. Terje Roed-Larsen (former UN Middle East envoy), interview with the authors, December 4, 2006, New York, NY. The Draft Declaration of Principles and the Israeli and Palestinian comments on the draft can be found in the online appendix to this volume at: www.thepeacepuzzle.org.

69. Hirschfeld ms., chap. 2, 17–18.

70. Throughout the process, it appears that Shimon Peres argued against keeping Washington informed. Peres was resentful that the United States had failed to support the "London Agreement" he had reached privately with Jordan's king Hussein in 1987. Roed-Larsen, interview; and Makovsky, *Making Peace with the PLO*, 74.

71. Hirschfeld ms., chap. 2, 17–18.

72. Corbin, *The Norway Channel*, 175.

73. Makovsky, *Making Peace with the PLO*, 28–29.

74. Abbas, *Through Secret Channels*, 194.

75. Indyk (*Innocent Abroad*, 80) says that the United States "had no knowledge of what was transpiring in Oslo" at the time that Rabin delivered the "deposit" to Christopher. This is not accurate. Kurtzer notes that Yossi Beilin briefed him in detail about the official talks in Oslo the evening before the "deposit" was delivered, and that Kurtzer informed Christopher and the peace team about Beilin's briefing before the fateful meeting with Rabin. Daniel Kurtzer (former ambassador to Egypt and Israel), interview with the authors, May 3, 2007, Washington, DC. It is also factually incorrect to say the U.S. team was uninformed of the Oslo back channel before August. For example, see the April 5, 1993, memorandum from Assistant Secretary Edward Djerejian to Secretary Christopher that provided a detailed description of what was transpiring in the Oslo talks, and appended several of the documents being discussed, including a draft Declaration of Principles. Edward Djerejian, "Peace Process Israeli/PLO Back Channel," memorandum to Secretary Christopher, April 5, 1993.

76. Uri Savir, *The Process: 1,100 Days That Changed the Middle East* (New York: Random House, 1998), 4; and Hirschfeld ms., chap. 2, 4.

77. "The Oslo Agreement: An Interview with Nabil Shaath," *Journal of Palestine Studies* 23, no.1 (Autumn 1993): 9.

78. Uri Savir (former director general of the Israeli Foreign Ministry), interview with the authors, August 19, 2009, Tel Aviv, Israel.

79. Gil, interview.

80. "Oslo Agreement: An Interview with Nabil Shaath," 7.

81. "The Oslo Agreement: An Interview with Haydar 'Abd Al-Shafi," *Journal of Palestine Studies* 23, no. 1 (Autumn 1993): 14–18.

82. Ibid., 14–15.

83. Makovsky, *Making Peace with the PLO*, 77.

84. Pundak, interview.

85. Yair Hirschfeld (Israeli academic, Oslo negotiator), interview with the authors, August 3, 2009, Tel Aviv, Israel. In the interview, Hirschfeld says the issues of settlements, prisoners, and freedom of movement were not even secondary issues, but rather "tertiary" issues for Israel.

86. Savir, *The Process*, 177, 189.

87. Qurie, *From Oslo to Jerusalem*, 45; and Savir, interview.

88. Roed-Larsen, interview.

89. Former Israeli official, interview with the authors.

90. Amnon Lipkin-Shahak (former Israeli IDF chief of staff), interview with the authors, August 11, 2009, Maccabim-Reut, Israel.

91. Savir, interview.

92. Ben-Aharon, interview.

93. Osama El Baz (former senior adviser to President Hosni Mubarak), interview with the authors, January 14, 2007, Cairo, Egypt.

94. "Oslo Agreement: An Interview with Nabil Shaath," 6.

95. Yossi Beilin (former Israeli deputy foreign minister), interview with the authors, August 3, 2009, Tel Aviv, Israel.

96. Khalil Shikaki (Palestinian pollster), interview with the authors, November 6, 2006, Washington, DC.

97. Ashrawi, *This Side of Peace*, 230, 116, 171.

98. Miller, *The Much Too Promised Land*, 75.

99. Ross, *The Missing Peace,* 55.

100. Kurtzer and Lasensky, *Negotiating Arab-Israeli Peace*, 45.

101. For a critique of the substance of the Oslo Accords from a source sympathetic to the Palestinians, see Laura Drake, "Between the Lines: A Textual Analysis of the Gaza-Jericho agreement," *Arab Studies Quarterly* 16, no. 4 (Fall 1994): 1–34, http://findarticles.com/p/articles/mi_m2501/is_n4_v16/ai_17041252/?tag=content;col1.

102. *Al-Dustur*, September 19, 1993.

103. Savir, *The Process*, 180.

104. Makovsky, *Making Peace*, 47.

105. Pundak, interview.

106. Ibid. The Altalena reference recalls a confrontation that took place in June 1948 between the new Israeli army and the Irgun, a militant Jewish underground group that was attempting to bring weapons for its members aboard the vessel Altalena. Prime Minister David Ben Gurion ordered the army to fire on the ship in order to assert the state's supremacy over former militias. After that incident, Israeli leaders argued that at some point, Arafat would have to take a similar step to curb the independent actions of factions outside the PLO.

107. Khatib, *Palestinian Politics,* 171–72.

108. "By every reasonable barometer, Madrid was a resounding success. Its enduring legacy was simply that it happened at all." Baker and DeFrank, *The Politics of Diplomacy*, 510.

109. Edward Djerejian (former U.S. ambassador to Syria and Israel), interview with the authors, March 6, 2006, Washington, DC.

110. Yossi Beilin has said that he pressed Rabin to move directly to a permanent agreement, but Rabin demurred, arguing that a failed interim agreement would not mean the end of the process, whereas a failed permanent agreement could not be followed by any further interim steps. Beilin admits the argument sounded convincing, but in retrospect thinks it was "a big mistake." Beilin, interview.

111. See "Letter of Assurances to Palestinians," in Quandt, *Peace Process,* app. M.; also cf. Mansour, "The Palestinian-Israeli Peace Negotiations."

112. James A. Baker III (former secretary of state), interview with the authors, March 6, 2007, Houston, TX.

113. Indyk went on to say, "Rabin had shown how effectively the Israeli tail could wag the American dog." The chief Syrian negotiator, Ambassador Walid al-Moualem (Syrian foreign minister), in an interview, expressed astonishment that the Americans had taken vacations during August 1993, when a Syrian-Israeli breakthrough loomed. Indyk, *Innocent Abroad*, 83, 89.

114. Gil, interview.

115. Prime Minister Rabin, interview, IDF Radio, September 15, 1993.

Chapter Two

1. Elliott Abrams (former senior director for Near East and North African Affairs, National Security Council), interview with the authors, October 19, 2006, Washington, DC.

2. I. William Zartman and Maureen Berman, *The Practical Negotiator* (New Haven, CT: Yale University Press, 1982), 66–78.

3. See Ze'ev Schiff, "Not Less Than $65 Billion," *Ha'aretz*, January 7, 2000.

4. Madeleine Albright and Bill Woodward, *Madam Secretary* (New York: Miramax, 2003); James A. Baker III and Thomas M. DeFrank, *The Politics of Diplomacy: Revolution, War & Peace, 1989–1992* (New York: Putnam, 1995); Shlomo Ben-Ami, *Scars of War, Wounds of Peace* (New York: Oxford University Press, 2006); Warren Christopher, *Chances of a Lifetime* (New York: Scribner's, 2001); Bill Clinton, *My Life* (New York: Knopf, 2004); Edward P. Djerejian, *Danger and Opportunity: An American Ambassador's Journey through the Middle East* (New York: Threshold, 2008); Martin Indyk, *Innocent Abroad: An Intimate Account of American Peace Diplomacy in the Middle East* (New York: Simon & Schuster, 2009); Henry Kissinger, *Years of Upheaval* (Boston: Little, Brown, 1982); Itamar Rabinovich, *The Brink of Peace: The Israeli-Syrian Negotiations* (Princeton, NJ: Princeton University Press, 1998); Itamar Rabinovich, "How to Talk and How Not to Talk to Syria," *Middle East Memo* 18 (Washington, DC: Saban Center at The Brookings Institution, May 2010); Itamar Rabinovich, *Waging Peace: Israel and the Arabs at the End of the Century* (New York: Farrar, Straus and Giroux, 1999); Dennis Ross, *The Missing Peace: The Inside Story of the Fight for Middle East Peace* (New York: Farrar, Straus and Giroux, 2004); Uri Savir, *The Process: 1,100 Days That Changed the Middle East* (New York: Random House, 1998); Linda Butler, "Fresh Light on the Syrian-Israeli Peace Negotiations: An Interview with Ambassador Walid Al-Moualem," *Journal of Palestine Studies* 26, no. 2 (Winter 1997): 81–94; Danny Yatom, *Sod* (in Hebrew) (Tel Aviv: Yedioth Ahranoth, 2009); Riad Daoudi, presentation at "Madrid + 15. Madrid Fifteen Years Later: Toward Peace in the Middle East: Addressing Concerns and Expectations," January, 10–12, 2007, www.toledopax.org; Uri Saguy, in Uri Misgav, *Yediot Friday Political Supplement*, June 11, 2010, trans. Didi Remez, http://coteret.com/2010/06/17/uri-saguy-tells-all-ctd-provides-an-insiders-account-of-baraks-missed-opportunity-with-syria-in-2000/. In addition, the following people have been interviewed as part of a United States Institute of Peace project, mostly on a not-for-attribution basis: Dennis Ross, Martin Indyk, Robert Malley, Sandy Berger, Madeleine Albright, Edward Djerejian, James Baker, Toni Verstandig, Gamal Helal, Itamar Rabinovich, Farouq Sharaa, Walid al-Moualem, Riad Daoudi, Uri Saguy, Bruce Riedel, Butheina Shaaban, Elliott Abrams, Aaron Miller, and Rihab Messaoud. For full transcripts of on-the-record interviews with many of these same participants, see Clayton Swisher, "Investigating Blame: US Mediation of the Arab-Israeli Conflict from 1999 to 2001" (MA thesis, Georgetown University, 2003), 146–463; Clayton Swisher, *The Truth about Camp David: The Untold Story about the Collapse of the Middle East Peace Process* (New York: Nation Books, 2004). For particularly good secondary accounts, see Ahron Bregman, *Elusive Peace: How the Holy Land Defeated America* (New York: Penguin, 2005); Helena Cobban, *The Israeli-Syrian Peace Talks: 1991–96 and Beyond* (Washington, DC: United States Institute of Peace, 1999); Charles Enderlin, *Shattered Dreams: The Failure of the Peace Process in the Middle East, 1995–2002* (New York: Other Press, 2002); Jeremy Pressman, "Mediation, Domestic Politics, and the Israeli-Syrian Negotiations, 1991–2000," *Security Studies* 16, no. 2 (July–September 2007): 350–81; Patrick Seale, "The Syria-Israel Negotiations: Who Is Telling the Truth?" Special Document, *Journal of Palestine Studies* 29, no. 2 (Winter 2000): 65; Eyal Zisser, "The Israeli-Syrian Negotiations: What Went Wrong?" *Orient* 42 (June 2, 2001): 225–51; Radwan Ziadeh "The Syrian-Israeli Peace Negotiations: The Track of Lost Opportunities," in

The Middle East—Peace by Piece: The Quest for a Solution to the Arab-Israeli Conflict, ed. Hassan Barari (Bonn, Germany: Friedrich Ebert Foundation, 2009), 121–37; Jerome Slater, "Lost Opportunities for Peace in the Arab-Israeli Conflict: Israel and Syria, 1948–2001,"*International Security* 27, no. 1 (Summer 2002): 79–106.

5. This calculus changed in the course of 2011 when the Syrian regime responded to mass protests with bloody repression. Even if the al-Asad regime were to survive, there would be no enthusiasm in Washington for trying to revive negotiations between Syria and Israel. And if the al-Asad regime were to be replaced, it would probably take time before Syria's new leaders would be ready to deal with Israel.

6. Tom Segev, *1967: Israel, the War, and the Year That Transformed the Middle East* (New York: Henry Holt, 2005), 501.

7. Zisser, who is one of Israel's leading experts on Syria, says: "For the Syrians, or at least for al-Asad, the position of the 4 June line was a matter of principle. . . . The entire area up to that line became sacred Syrian territory, on which there would be no compromise. This was, incidentally, much the same as the position adopted by President Sadat and King Husayn. . . ." Zisser, "The Israeli-Syrian Negotiations: What Went Wrong?" 239.

8. For the full text of the letter, see "Letter from President Ford to Prime Minister Rabin, September 1, 1975," in William B. Quandt, *Peace Process: American Diplomacy and the Arab-Israeli Conflict since 1967,* 3rd ed. (Washington, DC: Brookings Institution Press / Berkeley: University of California Press, 2005), app. C, www.brookings.edu/~/media/Files/Press/Books/2005/peaceprocess3/peaceprocess_appendixC.ashx.

9. Indyk, *Innocent Abroad,* 18.

10. In a meeting with al-Asad in spring 1991, Baker said that "he would propose to President Bush that the U.S. guarantee the border between Israel and Syria in both directions after peace. . . ." When the Syrians responded about the pending Madrid conference, they made their acceptance conditional upon the promised U.S. guarantee of the eventual border. Ross, *Missing Peace,* 73.

11. For examples, see Daniel Pipes and Laurie Mylroie, "Back Iraq: It's Time for a U.S. 'Tilt,'" *New Republic,* April 27, 1987; Daniel Pipes, "Isolate Syria," *New York Times,* October 29, 1986.

12. Baker, *Politics of Diplomacy,* 295. Baker notes that Dennis Ross "was vehemently opposed" to Baker's visiting Damascus, since he thought that al-Asad was prepared to send troops against Iraq for his own reasons and did not need to be rewarded by a visit from the secretary of state. Baker disagreed, seeing in Syria's participation an important symbolic step. But he was already thinking about drawing al-Asad into the post-war peace diplomacy (296). Bush 41 strongly supported Baker's trip to Damascus.

13. Ibid., 294

14. Ibid., 425–29. Former Israeli defense minister Yitzhak Rabin had told Baker that al-Asad was tough but also a man of his word. Baker tested that proposition for the first time on September 14, 1990, and then in another eleven meetings over the next year. In this initial meeting, al-Asad said that peace would require the "full return of Golan." Al-Asad accepted the invitation to Madrid before anyone else, on July 14, 1991 (487).

15. George H.W. Bush, *All the Best: My Life in Letters and Other Writings* (New York: Scribner's, 1999), 523–24.

16. Baker, *Politics of Diplomacy,* 443–69.

17. For an example of how Baker operated, see Djerejian's account of the secretary's meeting with al-Asad in April 1991where, after al-Asad seemed to be retreating from points he had agreed to, "Baker looked hard at him across the table, slammed his leather portfolio shut, and said, 'Mr. President, I don't think we can do business together.'" Djerejian, *Danger and Opportunity,* 96–97.

18. Quandt, *Peace Process,* 312–14.

19. Rabinovich, *Brink of Peace,* 47. Baker met with Rabin on July 21–22, 1992, and told him that al-Asad was interested in moving forward with peace negotiations. Rabin had been inclined to start with the Palestinian front, but in light of Baker's urging, he decided to explore both tracks. Rabinovich was asked by Rabin to take charge of the Syrian file, in addition to becoming ambassador to the United States. On August 31, 1992, the Syrian negotiators provided their Israeli counterparts with a draft declaration of principles, to which the Israelis responded on April 29, 1993. In short, early in the Clinton

period, there was some real momentum in the Syrian-Israeli track, which is no doubt one reason that Clinton chose to accord it priority. The full text of the Syriah Draft Declaration of Principles and the Israeli response can be found in the online appendix to this volume at: www.thepeacepuzzle.org.

20. The full text of the transition paper can be found in the online appendix to this volume at: www.thepeacepuzzle.org.

21. Indyk states that on March 3, 1993, Clinton met with his advisers to assess the results of Christopher's first trip to the Middle East. Christopher had met al-Asad who made it clear that Israel would have to fully withdraw from the Golan Heights, but in return al-Asad was prepared for full peace and security. Rabin had reportedly been encouraged when he heard this. Colin Powell, still serving as chairman of the Joint Chiefs, opined that the United States would need to be prepared to put a brigade of troops on the Golan to provide security. Clinton said it would be worth it. Indyk, *Innocent Abroad,* 16–18.

22. Ibid., 28–29.

23. Rabinovich, *Brink of Peace,* 97.

24. Rabin made clear that he was not fond of the structure of negotiations stemming from Madrid. "Prime Minister Yitzhak Rabin today criticized the basic format of the Middle East peace talks as 'not a successful one' but said it would be 'a waste of time' for Israel to try changing it." See "Rabin Doesn't Like Format of Talks," *New York Times,* January 26, 1993.

25. Djerejian made a secret visit to Damascus in April 1993. He had a letter from Clinton for al-Asad. His goal was to find out, among other things, if al-Asad would agree to a discreet military or civilian channel of communication outside the formal talks in Washington, and whether he would engage in some form of public diplomacy. The eventual answer was not encouraging. Rabinovich, *Brink of Peace,* 93 and 97.

26. Ross, *Missing Peace,* 107–9. On July 10, 1993, Ross informed al-Asad that "Prime Minister Rabin asked me to say that he is aware of your requirements on full withdrawal and he is aware that you will not conclude an agreement, that there will be no agreement, without full withdrawal. But before he can consider additional steps, he needs to know if you are aware of his needs." Al-Asad's response was "Of course these meanings are important. My understanding is that they [Israel] want real peace. We want real peace . . . As I said, full peace for full withdrawal. I don't want to get into detailed steps. But I believe they clarified their position in a good way and we clarified our position in a good way. That's why I say when the co-sponsor [the United States] moves between the two he can reach results probably quickly."

27. Ross, *Missing Peace,* 108. In his meeting with Rabin, the Israeli prime minister showed Ross a letter he had received from Arafat. It became apparent to Ross that progress was being made toward an interim agreement between Israelis and Palestinians.

28. Ibid., 109.

29. Ibid., 111. Rabinovich, *Brink of Peace,* 105–6, provides a longer version of the meeting, making it clear that Rabin insisted on certain "tangibles" from al-Asad before any significant withdrawal would take place.

30. Itamar Rabinovich, "From Deposit to Commitment: The Evolution of US-Israeli-Syrian Peace Negotiations, 1993–2000," in Elie Podeh and Asher Kaufman, *Arab-Jewish Relations: From Conflict to Resolution? Essays in Honour of Professor Moshe Ma'oz* (Portland, OR: Sussex Academic Press, 2006), 278–79.

31. Christopher describes the deposit as "what should have been the ultimate winning hand on the Syrian track." He even says he "was barely able to contain my usually very containable self. Rabin had put in my hand the promise that al-Asad had been demanding for years." Christopher, *Chances of a Lifetime,* 221.

32. Ross, *Missing Peace,* 111–12.

33. Christopher, *Chances of a Lifetime,* 221. Indyk was less directly involved in these exchanges but remembers the atmosphere as more positive. Indyk, *Innocent Abroad,* 83.

34. Rabinovich, *Brink of Peace,* 106–7, says that Christopher and Ross presented al-Asad's reply in positive terms, but "Rabin saw it as disappointing." He was not ready for a "long process of bargaining." According to Seale, "On 4 October 1999, Eytan Haber, who was Rabin's office director in 1993,

was interviewed on Israeli television about Rabin's offer of full withdrawal. Haber recounted that when Rabin heard that Christopher had delivered the offer to al-Asad as an Israeli commitment, he 'shouted at Warren Christopher so loudly that the walls of the Prime Minister's office in Jerusalem actually shook.' Christopher, he claimed, 'screwed up' by presenting the offer to al-Asad as an Israeli proposal rather than as an American 'inference' from what Rabin had said." Seale, "Who Is Telling the Truth?"

35. Ross, *Missing Peace*, 113. This was the meeting where al-Asad was told that the Rabin "deposit" would remain in the American "pocket." In subsequent rounds of diplomacy, the Syrians would usually start by asking if the deposit was still in the pocket, and if later prime ministers had reaffirmed it.

36. Walid al-Moualem, a key Syrian negotiator during most of this period, said that he pleaded with Christopher to engage in shuttle diplomacy, but Christopher preferred to return to the United States for vacation. Swisher, *The Truth about Camp David*, 265. This was confirmed by Moualem (former Syrian ambassador to the United States), interview with the authors, January 16, 2007, Damascus, Syria.

37. Indyk, *Innocent Abroad*, 83–91. This is also the view of Patrick Seale, who says the Rabin deposit was "a political deception, a ruse of war." See Seale, "Who is Telling the Truth?"

38. Rabinovich, *Brink of Peace*, 107, 113, says that Rabin had not been ready in August to see his hypothetical offer turned into a commitment. The way Christopher presented the deposit had gotten things off on the wrong footing. In ensuing bargaining, Rabin feared, he would no longer control the withdrawal card, and all the pressure would be on him to make concessions in the other areas.

39. In an interview, Rabinovich said "Rabin was utterly disappointed by the way it [the deposit] was handled by the U.S. team. . . . I imagine that certainly Kissinger, probably also Baker, Holbrooke, that kind of negotiator who also knows bargaining, would have said to al-Asad, you know I was in Jerusalem the other day and I think I heard a whiff of something new, and I may be able to get something from Rabin, but I need something from you. And he would have gone back and forth five times. But in this case, I suspect, Christopher just laid it on the table and al-Asad said, 'OK, I accept Israeli withdrawal, but here is what I want.'" Itamar Rabinovich (former Israeli ambassador to the United States), interview with the authors, January 18, 2007, Tel Aviv, Israel.

40. Rabinovich, *Brink of Peace*, 235, where he argues that at no time in the 1992–96 period were Israel and Syria on the brink of a breakthrough, but that the "potential" did exist in August 1993 and again in November–December 1995 just after Rabin's assassination. In an interview with Clayton Swisher, Rabinovich was much more critical of Christopher. He stated that Rabin was disappointed with the way in which Christopher had handled the deposit. Rabin, he said, had a high regard for Clinton, but not for Christopher, who seemed poorly informed compared to previous secretaries of state (Kissinger and Baker in particular). See Clayton Swisher, *The Truth about Camp David*, 308–9. In an interview with the authors, Rabinovich went on to say, "I think that to me the critical moment, the one moment in which a deal could have been made and was missed, is August 1993. . . . I would have expected a much more assertive and persistent U.S. conduct at that time. . . . Rabin, by the way, expected to be coerced at some point. . . . An Israeli prime minister sometimes needs to go public, 'I would not have made that concession, but did you want me to jeopardize our relations with Washington?' It's part of the game." Rabinovich, interview.

41. Ross, *Missing Peace*, 140; Indyk, *Innocent Abroad*, 106–8, says that Clinton was able to reaffirm the Rabin deposit for al-Asad, but it was still in the U.S. pocket, not on the bargaining table. Rabin apparently complained to Indyk that the United States was undermining his bargaining position by committing Israel to full withdrawal. See also Djerejian, *Danger and Opportunity*, 116–21, on Rabin's unhappiness with the way the United States was playing its role and why Rabin was skeptical about al-Asad. Djerejian, who was U.S. ambassador to Israel at this time and had previously been ambassador to Syria, also provides some details on the Clinton-al-Asad meeting.

42. Rabinovich, *Brink of Peace*, 141. Indyk, *Innocent Abroad*, 124, notes that Christopher had not been aware of the difference between the June 4 line and the 1923 border until al-Asad had told him about it.

43. Rabinovich, *Brink of Peace*, 145–47. Ross, *Missing Peace*, 147–48, gives the date of the crucial meeting with Rabin as July 18. In his version, Christopher told al-Asad the next day that Israeli withdrawal would be to the June 4 line if all else was agreed upon, but the Israeli commitment remained in

the American pocket. Rabinovich, *Waging Peace*, 61, says that "a formula had been found for grafting the lines of June 4 onto the original hypothetical, conditional suggestion made in 1993."

44. Ross, *Missing Peace*, 150. Al-Asad apparently agreed to lengthen the timetable for full withdrawal and to accept an Israeli diplomatic presence four months before the withdrawal would be completed. But he did not deliver on his promise to condemn terrorism.

45. Cobban, *Israeli-Syrian Peace Talks*, 66–67.

46. In an addendum to paragraph 2 of the "aims and principles" paper, the notion of equality in security arrangements was further defined to address the Israeli argument that, because Israel and Syria were not geographically symmetrical, some flexibility would be required: "Equality, particularly insofar as geography and difficulties with geography are concerned, being as follows: The purpose of the security arrangements is to ensure equality in overall security in the context of a state of peace between Syria and Israel. If, during the negotiations on security arrangements, it appears that the implementation of equality in principle insofar as geography is concerned with regard to a particular arrangement is impossible or too difficult, the experts of the two sides will discuss the difficulty of this particular arrangement and resolve it either by modifying it (which includes supplementing or subtracting from) or by mutually agreeing to a satisfactory solution."

47. See Seale, "Who Is Telling the Truth?"; Yatom, *Sod*, 447. A copy of the actual document with handwritten corrections is found in Yatom. Seale provides the same text, without indicating a source.

48. Ross, *Missing Peace*, 158, called the "nonpaper" a "high point" of the talks that had now been going on for more than thirty months.

49. Cobban, *Israeli-Syrian Peace Talks*, 86–95, covers this period, including the leak of the so-called "Shtauber document." Rabinovich, *Brink of Peace*, 175–79, covers this same period, adding the intriguing detail that Baker and Djerejian made a secret visit to Damascus to persuade al-Asad to show flexibility on the "symmetry" of security arrangements. Rabinovich also says that Rabin was annoyed with the way the negotiations were going and felt that he would not be able to conclude both the second Oslo agreement and a deal with Syria.

50. Ross, *Missing Peace*, 159.

51. Senior Syrian official, in an interview with the authors

52. Rabin at times seemed afflicted by the diplomatic equivalent of "buyer's remorse." At such moments, he would back away from the conditional offer that he had made on full withdrawal and would complain that the Americans had mishandled his "hypothetical" offer, but he would always reaffirm the "deposit" after these brief moments of irritation.

53. For an informative account of how Peres differed with Rabin on dealing with Syria, see Aluf Benn, "The Orderly Golan Paper," *Ha'aretz*, November 24, 1995, B3.

54. Ross, *Missing Peace*, 230–31. Al-Asad referred to Peres as a "leader with vision, imagination and creativity."

55. Daoudi, "Madrid + 15," described the Israeli delegation as "very, very forthcoming."

56. Ross, *Missing Peace*, 243.

57. For a discussion of the issues dealt with at Wye, see Savir, *The Process*, 173–79; Butler, "An Interview with Ambassador Walid Al-Moualem," 92.

58. Indyk, *Innocent Abroad*, 176–77, blames Iran for instigating the terrorist bombings of spring 1996.

59. Savir, *The Process*, 279–80.

60. Israeli political scientist Zeev Maoz, draws on presentations by Israeli and Syrian officials at a conference at the Baker Institute in 1998 as follows: "Yet both sides agree that the United States (US) envoys also failed to capitalize on major opportunities. The fact that the Clinton administration refrained from playing a more assertive role at crucial junctures of negotiation may have been as decisive a factor for the failure to reach an agreement as any error, hesitation, or misperception on the side of the Israeli and Syrian decision makers." See Zeev Maoz, "Syria and Israel: From the Brink of Peace to the Brink of War," *Cambridge Review of International Affairs* 12, no. 1 (Summer/Fall 1998): 266–67.

61. For reasons that are still not clear, Christopher wrote to Netanyahu on September 18, 1996, asserting that Netanyahu would not be bound under international law by the "aims and principles"

paper. See Ze'ev Schiff, "U.S. Letter Says Israel Not Bound by Israel-Syria Non-Paper," *Ha'aretz*, January 19, 1997. The full text of the letter was eventually published in Eli Kamir, "The Secret Negotiations between Netanyahu and al-Asad," *Maariv*, December 31, 1999.

62. Advisers to Netanyahu later claimed that their boss never agreed to the June 4, 1967, lines. But American officials involved in the controversy believe that he did. See "Defending the Golan Heights," *Foreign Affairs*, March–April 2009, notes by Dore Gold and Shimon Shapira; and Richard N. Haass and Martin Indyk. Uri Saguy also maintains that Netanyahu did confirm the Rabin deposit. See Interview with Uri Saguy by Misgav, *Yediot Friday Political Supp.*

63. Ross, *Missing Peace*, 511–15, includes a summary of the ten points. The actual text is accessible online at www.imra.org.il/story.php3?id=6061. Ross, *Missing Peace*, 527–28, notes that later Lauder did show them the eight-point paper that Syria had accepted. Lauder did insist, however, that Netanyahu had been ready to withdraw to the June 4, 1967, line. Sharaa told Ross that the eight-point paper had been acceptable to Syria. Also see Indyk, *Innocent Abroad*, 246–47.

64. On November 12, 1999, Lauder wrote to Clinton explaining the "misunderstanding," this time including the text of the eight points (dated September 12, 1998) that the Syrians had reportedly agreed to. On the issue of the border, point one, the text says: "Israel will withdraw from the Syrian land taken in 1967, in accordance with Security Council Resolutions 242 and 338, which established the right of all states to secure and recognized borders in the 'land for peace' formula, to a commonly agreed border based on the line of June 4, 1967. The withdrawal will be effected in three stages and completed over a period of 18 months with normalization implemented during the third stage and declaring an end to the state of war during the first phase of withdrawal." Lauder claimed in his letter that both sides accepted the eight points, but that some work needs to be done "by defining the security zones on both sides of the border." It has also been reported that the talks broke down when Netanyahu refused to provide a map showing his understanding of the location of the June 4, 1967, line. A copy of Lauder's letter to Clinton, as well as the text of the eight points, can be found in Yatom, *Sod*, 448–50.

65. Ross, *Missing Peace*, 515. The full texts of the Seale interviews may be found in Patrick Seale, "Assad and Barak Prepare to Negotiate," *Mideast Mirror*, June 23, 1999; "Syrian Leader Trades Compliments with Israeli," *New York Times*, June 24, 1999.

66. Ehud Barak, "The Myths Spread about Camp David Are Baseless," in *The Camp David Summit–What Went Wrong?* ed. Shimon Shamir and Bruce Maddy-Weitzman (Brighton, UK: Sussex, 2005), 133.

67. Ross, *Missing Peace*, 515. Ross notes that al-Asad by this time did not view him, Ross, as having "been positive to us." He also covers the Bern talks in this section (515–20).

68. In an interview with the authors, an Israeli official confirmed that he told the Syrians that Israel was prepared to discuss the June 4 line, but that he needed to know first what they meant by it. He argued at some length that no one knew exactly where it was. In any event, one could distinguish between sovereignty and control–meaning, it seems, that Israel might be willing to recognize Syrian sovereignty up to the June 4 line, provided that Israel could arrange to pass through the area near the lake, perhaps within a "peace park" of some sort. Saguy agrees that Barak got cold feet at Shepherdstown but has no explanation to offer. As in Saguy's interview with *Yediot Friday Political Supp.*, he indicated that an agreement was possible but required that the Israelis understand the "ethos," which seems to mean the issue of principle, that June 4 represented for the Syrians.

69. Ross, *Missing Peace*, 516–17. Saguy gives his own somewhat confusing version of the Bern meeting, as well as others in his interview with Misgav, *Yediot Friday Political Supp.*

70. Ross, *Missing Peace*, 518–19. At this time, Ross showed Daoudi the Lauder ten points and was told that they were not the final version.

71. Ibid., 521, and the map on page 522.

72. Indyk, *Innocent Abroad*, 248–49, adds that Saguy said that Israel respected the Syrian claim to the June 4 line, but "we need to find a way to draw the line to satisfy your principle and yet meet our needs." Daoudi reportedly responded, "We recognize Israel has needs and we are prepared to meet the needs that are based on objective principles. I fully understand the relationship between the line and the water and the vitality of water to the Israelis."

73. Ross, *The Missing Peace,* 525–26.

74. Indyk, *Innocent Abroad,* 249, has Daoudi telling Saguy that "I am authorized to tell you that the June 4 line sticks to the 1923 line," presumably referring to the northeast corner of the lake.

75. Ross, *Missing Peace,* 526. Indyk, *Innocent Abroad,* 249, says that Daoudi told Ross in private that Syria could accept a 30- to 50-meter strip around the lake as long as Syrian farmers had the right to use the water for irrigation. In interviews with Syrian officials in Damascus, June 2009, this was denied outright or treated as a misrepresentation of what may have been said.

76. Ross, *Missing Peace,* 527. Saguy, in his Yediot interview, enigmatically notes that "Israel played very cleverly with the solution proposed by the Americans, of the difference between sovereignty and control, and I will not elaborate so as not to cause damage." Interview with Saguy in, *Yediot Friday Political Supp.*

77. Ross, *Missing Peace,* 528.

78. Ibid., 528–29.

79. Sandy Berger (a Clinton adviser), interview with the authors, November 16, 2006, Washington, DC.

80. Ross, *Missing Peace,* 530. Indyk, *Innocent Abroad,* 249, says that Clinton's letter contained a confirmation that the Rabin deposit "remains in my pocket and has not been withdrawn." If that is the case, it is not clear why Barak wanted the president to make a trip to Damascus to confirm to al-Asad face-to-face Barak's commitment to the deposit as the quid pro quo for resuming political-level negotiations. One cannot endlessly resell the same point and expect to get a good price for it each time.

81. Indyk, *Innocent Abroad,* 250, says that the al-Asad letter argued that a summit could only be held after the issues identified by Clinton had been resolved in lower level talks. He also cautioned against the idea of using "territorial swaps" to solve the problem of the strip around the lake. In al-Asad's words, cited by Indyk in a note, "I am sure that you appreciate that the Syrian Arab citizens, especially those who were uprooted from the areas and the villages on the coast of the lake, will not consider that the Golan has been returned to their country unless they make sure that the areas on the lake have been returned to them as a result of a peace agreement."

82. Ross, *Missing Peace,* 532.

83. Ibid., 556–57. Al-Asad's uncharacteristically positive attitude in this meeting convinced Ross that an agreement would be reached.

84. Indyk, *Innocent Abroad,* 251–52. Barak told Indyk, "I cannot look like a *freier* (sucker) in front of my people. . . . We won't agree to give without receiving anything."

85. Ross, *Missing Peace,* 539. Ross professes to have been "incredulous," but earlier on the same page he cites himself as urging Barak not to look too eager for an agreement. "I worried that politically it was a mistake for him to look like he was rushing to give up the Golan Heights. Later that day I asked him if he didn't have need, for political reasons, to demonstrate that in an extremely tough process he had managed to produce peace with Syrian on the best possible terms?" This would seem to go beyond reflecting a sensitivity to Israeli domestic politics to actually advising the prime minister on how to play the game.

86. Ibid., 542.

87. Ibid., 543. Indyk places this comment earlier in the talks but also gives it prominent attention. "Sharaa's admission that the [June 4] line did not exist on a map opened up the possibility of drawing an Israeli-Syrian borderline that suited Barak's needs. That simple idea saved the Blair House talks." Indyk, *Innocent Abroad,* 255–56.

88. Ross, *Missing Peace,* 550–51, says that Barak wanted the United States to serve as Israel's surrogate.

89. Ibid., 551.

90. Indyk, *Innocent Abroad,* 258, says that Barak's wish list also included large-scale American military assistance ($23 billion, "strategic ally" status, and intelligence sharing), as well as Arab state recognition. On the issue of aid, the well-informed Israeli journalist, Ze'ev Schiff, has given a much higher figure than Indyk. See Schiff, "Not Less Than $65 Billion."

91. Ross, *Missing Peace,* 553.

92. Ibid., 554. Ross recorded Sharaa's statement in italics, but not in quotes, so whether Sharaa explicitly mentioned the ten-meter strip is unclear. Indyk's version, *Innocent Abroad,* 259, of this point is that Israel would withdraw to "a line based on the line of June 4, 1967," with no mention of a ten-meter strip for Israel. Sharaa reportedly went on to say "sovereignty on the lake is Israel's; sovereignty on the land is ours." Indyk adds that Sharaa stated that on the northeast shoreline the June 4 line was the same as the 1923 boundary, which would mean that the Israelis could keep a ten-meter strip off the waterline. The Syrians deny that Sharaa ever said this explicitly. Syrian official, interview with the authors. Clinton, *My Life,* 885–86, states that the Syrian position was to allow Israel a narrow strip of land off the shoreline of the lake—ten to fifty meters wide—but does not give the precise source or language, and says the offer was conditional upon Barak confirming the June 4 line as the basis for the future border.

93. Ross, *Missing Peace,* 553, states that the Syrian position "was full withdrawal to the June 4 lines, which in the northeast part of the lake were defined by putting the border 10 meters off the shoreline."

94. Seale, "What Went Wrong?" provides considerable evidence that al-Asad was unwavering in his insistence on the June 4 line, and he cites a number of communications from Clinton that acknowledge that point.

95. Ross, *Missing Peace,* 557.

96. For the full text of the draft treaty, see Indyk, *Innocent Abroad,* 434–40.

97. Ibid., 262. Interview with a Syrian official, where he states that Ross "snatched" a specific and misleading meaning from something Sharaa had said. He claims that there was no ambiguity on the importance of the June 4, 1967, line, only an issue of its precise demarcation.

98. Ross, *Missing Peace,* 561.

99. Ibid., 565. Indyk, *Innocent Abroad,* 262–63, quotes Clinton as exploding on the last night, saying "God damn it! I convened this meeting now against my better judgment and Barak is gaming Sharaa and me." In a private meeting with Barak, Clinton tried to persuade him to put the Rabin deposit on the table. Barak apparently told him that he would be ready to do so "if the next meeting was in a completely leakproof environment and al-Asad agreed to allow the Lebanese negotiations to recommence at the same time."

100. Ibrahim Humaydi, "Damascus Considers US Document Positive Step; Border Committee Expected to Meet; Clinton to Receive Barak and Sharaa Notes Today," *Al-Hayat* (London, Arabic), January 9, 2000, 16.

101. See "IDF to Tell Sharon to Show Restraint This Month," *Ha'aretz,* March 9, 2001. This article claimed that "IDF officers now feel at liberty to state explicitly a conclusion at which they only hinted prior to the end of the Barak government's term. As they see it, responsibility for the failure of negotiations with Syria last year is borne by Barak, not the late Syrian ruler Hafez Assad. General Staff officers were willing to assent to Assad's demand that Israel withdraw from the north-east shoreline of Lake Kinneret [Sea of Galilee]; and they believed that Barak's intransigent refusal to comply with the Syrian demand reflected a triumph of passing domestic political considerations over permanent security needs."

102. Senior American official, in an interview with the authors.

103. Indyk, *Innocent Abroad,* 264.

104. Ibid., 265. It is worth noting that Indyk was the most consistent "Syria-first" voice on the American team. Years later, the Syrians singled him out as the one who seemed most sincere in wanting Israeli-Syrian peace. Senior Syrian official, in an interview with the authors.

105. Bruce Riedel (former special assistant to the president and senior director for Near East Affairs on the National Security Council), interview with the authors, December 14, 2006, Washington, DC. "If I were to say one place in the Clinton administration where we really made a monumental error, it was in buying that redline [Israel's need for a sliver of land off the water in the northeast quadrant of the Sea of Galilee], because I believe that in the late part of 1999, early part of 2000, Hafez al-Asad was ready to make a deal, and the deal was very, very simple, it was the line of the 4th of June 1967. . . . He [Barak] persuaded the President at Shepherdstown that he needed time, that it wasn't the right place, that Sharaa was the wrong person to give it to, and we left and it fell apart. I still think had we gone back at Geneva with something with the essence of the June 4 line, al-Asad would have said yes."

106. Pressman, "Mediation," 378–79, argues that ambiguity may be acceptable in the early phase of negotiations but should be replaced with clarity as one approaches the endgame.

107. For example, Ross, *Missing Peace*, 567, says that when Clinton called al-Asad after Shepherdstown he told him that "if the Lebanon talks resumed, Barak would not only reaffirm Rabin but also agree to demarcate the border based on the Rabin deposit." This position was well beyond what Barak had agreed to at this point.

108. Saguy describes Sharaa's speech as follows: "He [Shara'a] attacked the Israeli approach that couldn't decide. He said to Barak: 'You said we were going to talk here about borders and water, that is what I reported to my president. It did not happen. What am I going to tell him now, that I deceived him?' Barak tried to explain that he had political issues. . . ." Interview with Saguy, in, *Yediot Friday Political Supp.*

109. Swisher, *The Truth about Camp David*, 154. According to Gamal Helal in Swisher, 119–20, "For the Syrians, all the land must be returned in exchange for peace. This is the basis for all agreements, it was applied in Egypt, it worked for Jordan also. . . . This theory was applied by Syria at Geneva. Syria wanted all the way to the water line on the Sea of Galilee. But Barak offered all the territories minus a few hundred yards of shore on the lake. In the Syrian mind, this was not a 100 percent portion. No matter how small it was, it was very strategic because it gave Syria a foothold to water, which the Syrians had before June 5, 1967. . . . On the eve of the 1967 war, the Syrians had control of the water line. They would fish and swim there. Barak was taking away a few hundred yards. . . . The Syrians wanted to go back to the lake, because they perceived it as their right. . . . The water itself was an international issue, and the Syrians would be willing to work around it—but not the territories. The territorial aspects never changed from day one with the Syrians—You want a peace agreement? You have to go to the lake." A high-level American official added in an interview with the authors, "You either go to the water, or you can't [get an agreement]. For the Syrians, the last five feet are the most important ones."

110. Ross, *Missing Peace*, 568. This conversation is confirmed by Bandar's assistant, Rihab Messaoud, in Swisher, *The Truth about Camp David*, 412–15. Also, see the article on Bandar by Elsa Walsh "The Prince," *New Yorker*, March 24, 2003. "'I know what President Assad wants,' Clinton said; according to Bandar's version, Assad wanted Israel to withdraw from the Golan Heights, and to the borders that were taken in the 1967 war. As Bandar recalled, Clinton planned to pressure Barak to satisfy Assad's demands; if he succeeded, he would call for a summit. Bandar asked Clinton to repeat all this, and told Messaoud to write it down and repeat it to Clinton."

111. Ross, *The Missing Peace*, 569.

112. Ibid., 570.

113. Ibid., 574–75.

114. Butheina Shaaban says that Clinton called al-Asad at least three times before Geneva. She served as interpreter. In the last call, al-Asad asked what they were going to do in Geneva. Clinton said, in her account, "Your requests are met; you will be very happy. . . . The [Rabin] deposit is in my pocket." Clayton Swisher, *The Truth about Camp David*, 94. Clinton had called al-Asad before Geneva and told him "I know what you want and I have what you want." al-Asad was reportedly not confident. He had a high regard for Clinton, but felt that he was being misled by his staff, especially Ross. Butheina Shaaban (senior Syrian official), interview with the authors, January 16, 2007, Damascus, Syria. See also Bregman, *Elusive Peace*, 56.

115. Ross, *The Missing Peace*, 582, describes himself as "highly skeptical. . . . I doubted that al-Asad would accept what Barak was offering and requiring, especially on the border and on an Israeli presence in the Mount Hermon early-warning station."

116. "Always the micromanager, Barak produced a complete script for the President's use with al-Asad. In a manner I thought patronizing, he said it would be fine for the President to improvise the opening generalities, but the description of Israel's needs had to be recited word for word." Albright, *Madam Secretary*, 480.

117. Ibid., 481. This version also is given by one other American present at the meeting, but this person is relying only on memory. Senior American official, interview with the authors. A former American official recollected that Clinton said, "Barak is prepared for full withdrawal to a

commonly agreed border based on the June 4 line. Al-Asad reacted negatively to 'commonly agreed' and then Dennis showed him the map. Al-Asad got angrier when Clinton said that Israel wanted sovereignty over the lake and the Jordan River." Former American official, interview with the authors.

118. Bregman, *Elusive Peace*, 59.

119. Indyk, *Innocent Abroad*, 273, says that he "knew that Barak had developed a 'bottom, bottom' line in case al-Asad refused anything more than the ten meters from the shoreline allowed by the international border."

120. Butheina Shaaban, who was present at the Geneva meeting as interpreter for al-Asad, said in an exchange with Clayton Swisher on July 31, 2003, that "the issue was access to the water. Al-Asad insisted on going back to the line of June 4 in which Syria had access to the water and the [Barak] offer was to move Syria away from the water; the thing that al-Asad rejected. The territory that was offered [in the swap] instead of water was a useless and rocky territory, and al-Asad knew it inch by inch." Swisher, *The Truth about Camp David*, 101. For a detailed and seemingly accurate version, based on many interviews, of the Clinton-al-Asad meeting, see Bregman, *Elusive Peace*, 59–63.

121. Robert Malley provides an anecdote that suggests Clinton was not quite so happy with the way Barak set him up at Geneva: "And, in an extraordinary moment at Camp David, when Barak retracted some of his positions, the President confronted him, expressing all his accumulated frustrations. 'I can't go see Arafat with a retrenchment! You can sell it; there is no way I can. This is not real. This is not serious. I went to Shepherdstown [for the Israeli-Syrian negotiations] and was told nothing by you for four days. I went to Geneva [for the summit with Assad] and felt like a wooden Indian doing your bidding. I will not let it happen here!'" Hussein Agha and Robert Malley, "Camp David: The Tragedy of Errors," *New York Review of Books*, August 9, 2001.

122. Clinton, *My Life*, 903.

123. Ross, *The Missing Peace*, 589. In an interview with Dennis Ross on November 12, 2002, Clayton Swisher was told that "we let Barak dictate too much of what was going to be possible and what we could do." In the same interview, Ross says that he had no expectation that Geneva would be successful. Swisher, *The Truth about Camp David*, 82.

124. Senior Syrian official, interview with the authors. In this person's recollection, on the way to Geneva al-Asad was not very hopeful. He had concluded from Shepherdstown that Barak did not want peace.

125. Albright, *Madam Secretary*, 480.

126. Djerejian, *Danger and Opportunity*, 167, says bluntly that "Clinton's negotiating team mismanaged this summit, with insufficient preparation and without bringing to the table a U.S. position or bridging proposal that addressed the key requirements of both sides. . . . Some [such as Ross] have argued that because of al-Asad's terminal illness he was not really interested in concluding a deal at Geneva, but was preoccupied with assuring the succession of his son, Bashar, to the presidency. There is serious reason to believe that the opposite is the case."

127. One member of Clinton's team said that "if we had gone to Geneva with something with the essence of the June 4 line, al-Asad would have said yes. Dennis thinks that by that point he would not have taken it, but my reading of the Syrians when they got to Geneva was that they expected that's what they were going to get and that was what was supposed to happen, and when they didn't get it, they were shocked." Riedel, interview.

128. Indyk, *Innocent Abroad*, 278–84, where he lays out all the reasons to blame al-Asad, and even suggests that the United States would have had more leverage with both sides if it had threatened to walk away from the negotiations.

129. Ibid., 286–87.

130. In not-for-attribution interviews with Clayton Swisher, some in the Clinton circle expressed the belief that Ross in particular did not believe that Geneva would succeed and made little effort to craft a proposal that al-Asad might accept, since his goal by this time was to end the Israeli-Syrian track and move on to the more important Palestinian negotiations. We find little concrete evidence for this view, although Ross argues in his memoir that he did not think Geneva would succeed. Ross, *Missing*

Peace, 588; Swisher, Confidential Sources 4, "A Senior Diplomat Who Participated in the Israeli-Syrian Negotiations," and 5, "A Former State Department Political Appointee," "Investigating Blame: US Mediation of the Arab-Israeli Conflict from 1999 to 2001" (M.A. Thesis, Georgetown University, December 3, 2003).

Chapter Three

1. Hussein Agha and Robert Malley, "Camp David: The Tragedy of Errors," *New York Review of Books* 48, no. 13 (August 9, 2001); Yossi Beilin, *The Path to Geneva* (New York: RDV Books/Akashic Books, 2004); Shlomo Ben-Ami, *Scars of War, Wounds of Peace* (Cambridge: Oxford University Press, 2006); Bill Clinton, "Proposals for a Final Settlement," *Journal of Palestine Studies* 30, no. 3 (Spring 2001): 171–73; Raviv Drucker, *Harakiri* (Tel Aviv: Yedioth Ahronoth Books, 2002); Charles Enderlin, *Shattered Dreams: The Failure of the Peace Process in the Middle East, 1995–2002* (New York: Other Press, 2003); Akram Haniyeh, "The Camp David Papers," *Journal of Palestine Studies* 30, no. 2 (Winter 2001): 75–97; Martin Indyk, *Innocent Abroad: An Intimate Account of American Peace Diplomacy in the Middle East* (New York: Simon & Schuster, 2009); Arie M. Kacowicz, "Rashomon in Jerusalem: Mapping the Israeli Negotiators' Positions on the Israeli-Palestinian Peace Process, 1993–2001," *International Studies Perspectives* 6 (2005): 252–73; Hebert C. Kelman, "Acknowledging the Other's Nationhood: How to Create a Momentum for the Israeli-Palestinian Negotiations," *Journal of Palestine Studies* 22, no. 1 (Autumn 1992): 18–38; Menachem Klein, *The Jerusalem Problem: The Struggle for Permanent Status* (Gainesville: University Press of Florida, 2003); Daniel C. Kurtzer and Scott B. Lasensky, *Negotiating Arab-Israeli Peace* (Washington, DC: United States Institute of Peace, 2008); Robert Malley, "Camp David: An Exchange," *New York Review of Books* 48, no. 14 (September 20, 2001); Robert L. Rothstein, Moshe Maoz and Khalil Shikaki, eds., *The Israeli-Palestinian Peace Process: Oslo and the Lessons of Failure* (Portland, OR: Sussex Academic Press, 2002); Aaron David Miller, *The Much Too Promised Land* (New York: Bantam, 2008); Benny Morris, "Camp David and After: An Exchange," *New York Review of Books* 49, no. 10 (June 13, 2002); Jeremy Pressman, "Visions in Collision: What Happened at Camp David and Taba?" *International Security* 28, no. 2 (Autumn 2003): 5–43; William B. Quandt, *Peace Process: American Diplomacy and the Arab-Israeli Conflict since 1967* (Washington, DC: Brookings Institution Press / Berkeley: University of California Press, 2005); Dennis Ross and Gidi Grinstein, "Camp David: An Exchange," *New York Review of Books* 48, no. 14 (September 20, 2001); Dennis Ross, *The Missing Peace: The Inside Story of the Fight for Middle East Peace* (New York: Farrar, Straus and Giroux, 2004); Jerome Slater, "What Went Wrong? The Collapse of the Israeli-Palestinian Peace Process," *Political Science Quarterly* 116, no. 2 (Summer 2001): 171–99; Clayton E. Swisher, *The Truth about Camp David: The Untold Story about the Collapse of the Middle East Peace Process* (New York: Nation Books, 2004); Tamara C. Wittes, ed., *How Israelis and Palestinians Negotiate* (Washington, DC: United States Institute of Peace Press, 2005).

2. Ezer Weizman, *Battle for Peace* (New York: Bantam Books, 1981), 18.

3. Of particular significance in losing the trust of President Bush was the Israeli interception of a weapons shipment on the ship *Karine A,* which was destined for the occupied territories, in January 2002.

4. For an account of dual containment, see Indyk, *Innocent Abroad,* 149–67. Indyk notes that he was not the inventor of the concept, only its articulation.

5. Hillary Rodham Clinton, "Remarks at the Dedication of the S. Daniel Abraham Center for Middle East Peace," April 15, 2010, Washington, DC, www.state.gov/secretary/rm/2010/04/140297.htm.

6. Former senior American official, interview with the authors.

7. It is worth noting here the highly instrumental work by Herbert C. Kelman and his colleagues that has contributed to the evolution and acceptance of the ideas that served as the building stones of the Oslo agreement. Herbert C. Kelman, "Interactive Problem Solving in the Israeli-Palestinian Case: Past Contributions and Present Challenges," in Roger Fisher, ed., *Paving the Way: Contributions of Interactive Conflict Resolution to Peacemaking* (Lanham, MD: Lexington Books, 2005). For examples of other influential studies and articles by Kelman on the Israeli-Palestinian peace negotiations, see Kelman,

"Acknowledging the Other's Nationhood," 18–38, and "A One-Country/Two-State Solution to the Israeli-Palestinian Conflict," *Middle East Policy* 18, no. 1 (Spring 2011): 27–41.

8. While the Israeli-Jordanian peace agreement is not the subject of analysis in this chapter, it is noteworthy that Israelis and Jordanians needed minimal American efforts to cement the agreement, and that the deal was enabled by the Oslo Accords, without which the king of Jordan would not have been able to sell it to his people and to the rest of the Arab world. It also helped that there was no significant dispute over territory.

9. Quoted in the Associated Press, "Bill Clinton in Israel: There Would Be Peace if Rabin were still alive," *Haaretz*, November 14, 2009, www.haaretz.com/news/bill-clinton-in-israel-there-would-be -peace-if-rabin-were-still-alive-1.4184. Note that the implication of Clinton's assessment is that had Rabin lived, Arafat was capable of making a deal with him. Coming nine years after the failure at Camp David, the assessment goes against the view put forward by Dennis Ross that Arafat was incapable of making a peace deal.

10. Bruce Riedel (former National Security Council official), interview with the authors, December 14, 2006, Washington, DC.

11. "Protocol Concerning the Redeployment in Hebron: January 17, 1997," Israel Ministry of Foreign Affairs, www.mfa.gov.il/MFA/Peace+Process/Guide+to+the+Peace+Process/Protocol+Concer ning+the+Redeployment+in+Hebron.htm.

12. "The Sharm el-Sheikh Memorandum: September 4, 1999," Israel Ministry of Foreign Affairs, www.mfa.gov.il/MFA/Peace+Process/Guide+to+the+Peace+Process/The+Sharm+el-Sheikh+Memo- randum-+Main+Points.htm.

13. Agha and Malley put it this way, "The Prime Minister's [Barak's] insistence on holding a summit and the timing of the Camp David talks followed naturally. . . . Only by insisting on a single, high-level summit could all the necessary ingredients of success be present: the drama of a stark, all-or-nothing proposal; the prospect that Arafat might lose US support; the exposure of the ineffectiveness of Palestinian salami-tactics (pocketing Israeli concessions that become the starting point at the next round); and, ultimately, the capacity to unveil to the Israeli people all the achievements and concessions of the deal in one fell swoop. . . . For these reasons, Camp David seemed to Arafat to encapsulate his worst nightmares. It was high-wire summitry, designed to increase the pressure on the Palestinians to reach a quick agreement while heightening the political and symbolic costs if they did not. And it clearly was a Clinton/Barak idea both in concept and timing, and for that reason alone highly suspect. That the US issued the invitations despite Israel's refusal to carry out its earlier commitments and despite Arafat's plea for additional time to prepare only reinforced in his mind the sense of a US-Israeli conspiracy." Agha and Malley, "Camp David," 1.

14. Arie M. Kacowicz, "Rashomon in Jerusalem: Mapping the Israeli Negotiators' Positions on the Israeli-Palestinian Peace Process, 1993–2001," *International Studies Perspectives* 6 (2005): 252–73.

15. Agha and Malley, "Camp David," 3; Beilin, *The Path to Geneva*, 148; Ben-Ami, *Scars of War*, 255– 56; Ross, *The Missing Peace*, 625–27, 631–40; Swisher, *The Truth about Camp David*, 222–25, 286–87.

16. Kurtzer and Lasensky, *Negotiating Arab-Israeli Peace*.

17. Former senior government official, interview with the authors.

18. Haniyeh, "The Camp David Papers," 75–97; Moshe Maoz, "The Oslo Peace Process: From Breakthrough to Breakdown," in Rothstein, Maoz, and Shikaki, chap. 9; Miller, *The Much Too Promised Land*, 304–5.

19. Former senior American official, interview with the authors.

20. Former senior administration official, interview with the authors.

21. Agha and Malley, "Camp David," 1; Indyk, *Innocent Abroad*, 282, 295; Beilin, *The Path to Geneva*, 148–51; Manuel Hassassian, "Why Did Oslo Fail? Lessons for the Future," in Rothstein, Maoz, and Shikaki, eds., 126–27; Ross, *The Missing Peace*, 710–11; Swisher, *The Truth about Camp David*, 223, 241–42.

22. Samuel Berger (Clinton adviser), interview with the authors, July 7, 2010, Washington, DC.

23. The quotation refers to a session of the committee on borders and security when Clinton angrily lectured Palestinian negotiator Ahmad Qurie (Abu Ala'a) when the latter insisted that the Is-

raelis first accept the principle of territorial exchange and that point of reference is the 1967 border. Clinton reportedly shouted, "This isn't the Security Council here. . . . If you want to lecture, go over there and don't make me waste my time. I'm President of the United States. I'm ready to pack and go . . . You're obstructing the negotiations." Enderlin, *Shattered Dreams*, 202.

24. Berger, interview.

25. Former senior administration official, interview with the authors.

26. Beilin, *The Path to Geneva*, 158; Bill Clinton, *My Life* (New York: Knopf, 2004), 915; Deborah Sontag, "And Yet So Far: A Special Report: Quest for Mideast Peace: How and Why It Failed, *New York Times*, July 26, 2001, www.nytimes.com/2001/07/26/world/and-yet-so-far-a-special-report-quest-for-mideast-peace-how-and-why-it-failed.html?pagewanted=all&src=pm; Swisher, *The Truth about Camp David*, 277–79, 327–31.

27. Ben-Ami, *Scars of War*, 261–64; Clinton, *My Life*, 913; Quandt, *Peace Process*, 362–63; Ross, *The Missing Peace*, 622–24.

28. Ben-Ami, *Scars of War*, 255–56.

29. Agha and Malley, "Camp David," 1; Ben-Ami, *Scars of War*, 253; Clinton, *My Life*, 911–12.

30. Yasir Abed Rabbo (PLO Executive Committee member), interview with the authors, November 16, 2006, Washington, DC; Akram Haniyeh (Palestinian newspaper editor), interview with the authors, January 21, 2007, Ramallah, West Bank.

31. Enderlin, *Shattered Dreams*, 186–87.

32. Ibid., 178.

33. Former senior administration official, interview with the authors.

34. Ross, *The Missing Peace*, 721–22.

35. Berger, interview.

36. Former senior administration official, interview with the authors.

37. Edward Abington (former American consulate general in Jerusalem), interview with the authors, November 16, 2006, Washington, DC; Haniyeh, interview

38. Former American official, interview with the authors.

39. Ibid.

40. Berger, interview.

41. Former senior American official, interview with the authors.

42. Edward Djerejian (former ambassador to Syria and Israel), interviews with the authors, March 6, 2006, and March 6, 2007, Houston, TX. A striking example of the American team's failure to understand Palestinian and Israeli domestic politics is the assumption at the end of the Camp David that blaming Arafat for failure would help Ehud Barak and his Labor Party win the elections. Instead, the message sent was that Barak offered so much and Arafat offered so little that Barak appeared as a sucker. So much so that Barak's team scrambled to pretend that he knew that Arafat could not compromise and just wanted to reveal that to the United States and the world. He badly lost the elections by a wide margin.

43. Berger, interview.

44. One scholar who has delved deep into the issue of grievances on both sides is Herbert C. Kelman. Kelman argued that "creating momentum requires a commitment to certain basic principles that inspire hope in the two bodies politic. . . . This commitment might take the form of mutual acknowledgment of each other's nationhood-an acknowledgment that is based on principle, that is phrased in some way that the other side finds meaningful, that goes beyond the half-hearted and ambiguous statements made heretofore, but that does so without threatening the vital interests of the party offering the acknowledgment." Kelman, "Acknowledging the Other's Nationhood," 18–38.

45. Former senior administration official, interview with the authors.

46. Former American adviser, interview with the authors.

47. Ross, *The Missing Peace*, 635, 640, 667, 673–75, 724–25, 768.

48. Former American adviser, interview with the authors.

49. Ibid.

50. Rabbo, interview.

51. Abington, interview.

52. Former senior American official, interview with the authors.

53. Berger, interview.

54. Kurtzer and Lasensky, *Negotiating Arab-Israeli Peace*, 48, 52–54, 60–61.

55. Edward (Ned) Walker, interview with the authors, October 19, 2006, Washington DC.

56. Former senior administration official, interview with the authors.

57. Former senior administration official, interview with the authors.

58. Toni Verstandig, interview with the authors, November 16, 2006, Washington, DC.

59. Martin Indyk, interview with the authors, October 19, 2006, Washington, DC.

60. Riedel, interview.

61. Abington, interview.

62. Marwan Muasher, interview with the authors, January 10, 2007, Madrid, Spain.

63. Gilad Sher, interview with the authors, June 2, 2011, Washington, DC.

64. Ibid.

65. Amnon Lipkin-Shahak, interview with one of the authors, Maccabim-Reut, Israel, August 11, 2009.

66. Former American official, in an interview with the authors.

67. Aaron David Miller put it this way: "Far too often the small group with whom I had worked in the Clinton administration, myself included, had acted as a lawyer for only one side, Israel" (*The Much Too Promised Land*, 75).

68. For example, Ross writes of Barak's hardening his position, "When I left the meeting, I said to Martin [Indyk]: [Barak] is hardening but I think it is just tactics. He wants us to push the Palestinians and get Arafat to move before he will do anything" (*The Missing Peace*, 667). In contrast, when George Tenet came out of a meeting with Arafat feeling positive about Arafat's position, Ross reacted in this way, "George Tenet had seen Arafat and felt that he had gotten a qualified yes from him on the President's ideas. But when he described what Arafat had said, I could see the 'qualification,' but had a harder time seeing the 'yes.' Arafat was saying yes provided he got several additions: the Armenian Quarter in the Old City and contiguity with sovereignty in all the inner neighborhoods. Barak would certainly interpret this as a 'no'" (Ibid., 702).

69. Former senior administration official, interview with the authors.

70. Beilin, *The Path to Geneva*, 147; Clinton, *My Life*, 911–12; Miller, *The Much Too Promised Land*, 289–94; Ross, *The Missing Peace*, 599–649.

71. Beilin, *The Path to Geneva*, 148–56; Miller, *The Much Too Promised Land*, 280–96; Swisher, *The Truth about Camp David*, 223–43; Indyk, interview.

72. Former American adviser, interview with the authors.

73. Ibid.

74. Berger, interview.

75. Miller, *The Much Too Promised Land*, 294–96.

76. Former senior administration official, interview with the authors; Pressman, "Visions in Collision," 5–43.

77. Miller, *The Much Too Promised Land*, 296–308.

78. Former American adviser, interview with the authors.

79. Ross, *The Missing Peace*, 657; Enderlin, *Shattered Dreams*, 187.

80. Ross, *The Missing Peace*, 657.

81. Ibid., 658.

82. Ibid.

83. Enderlin, *Shattered Dreams*, 181–82.

84. Ross, *The Missing Peace*, 659; Enderlin, *Shattered Dreams*, 190–91.

85. Ross, *The Missing Peace*, 659.

86. Ibid., 660.

87. Ross writes that Helal reported that Palestinian adviser Saeb Erekat "was very destructive. He is stoking Arafat; misleading him about the paper." Ross, *The Missing Peace*, 662.

88. Ibid., 663; Enderlin, *Shattered Dreams*, 196–200.

89. Indyk, *Innocent Abroad*, 308.

90. The territory and security committee included Ahmed Qurie, Hassan Asfour, Mohammad Rashid, and Mohammad Dahlan from the Palestinian side, and Shlomo Ben Ami, Yossi Ginossar, and Amnon Lipkin-Shahak from the Israeli side. The refugee committee included Mahmoud Abbas, Nabil Aburdeineh, and Nabil Shaath from the Palestinian side, and Eli Rubinstein, Dan Meridor, and Oded Eran from the Israeli side. The Jerusalem committee included Yasir Abed Rabbo and Saeb Erekat from the Palestinian side, and Gilad Sher, Shlomo Yanai, and Shlomo Ben Ami from the Israeli side.

91. On refugees, the Israelis were prepared to specify an agreement that would allow a small number of the refugees to move to Israel in the framework of family reunification, but they continued to have major reservations about compensation and did not want to take any responsibility for the creation of the refugee problem; the Palestinians insisted on the moral right of return and made specific proposals on compensation. But the gap was wide, and more importantly, the negotiations on this issue were superseded by the Jerusalem issue.

92. On territory, Barak's final offer was Israeli annexation of 9 percent of the West Bank with a 1 percent swap opposite Gaza and the Palestinians would get 85 percent of the border with Jordan (Ross, *The Missing Peace*, 688). On July 18, Clinton proposed to Arafat a deal that included Palestinian control of 91 percent of the West Bank (Indyk, *Innocent Abroad*, 323). But the Palestinian position from the outset was that the terms of reference had to be the 1967 lines. This was a good example of the different starting points of Israelis and Palestinians and the American position coming closer to the Israeli one: For Palestinians, any territory Israel annexes, no matter how small, constituted a Palestinian concession; for the Israelis, any territory that they agreed to come under Palestinian control constituted an Israeli concession. These differences made agreement more difficult, but even more so because of a lack of agreement on the central issue of Jerusalem.

93. On the security issues, there appeared to be early consensus on a set of issues including Israeli early-warning stations in the West Bank, airspace, and joint and cooperative responses to terrorism. On other issues, including demilitarization of the Palestinian state and an Israeli and international presence in the Jordan Valley, progress proved to be much more difficult. The Palestinians rejected the Israeli insistence on a military presence in the West Bank, but they accepted joint Jordanian-American Palestinian patrols along both Palestinian and Jordanian sides of the border area. Martin Indyk described the situation this way, "We made some progress on security issues. I remember drafting a security protocol of what we agreed, but it got swamped in on the Jerusalem issue" (Indyk, in Swisher, *The Truth about Camp David*, 321).

94. David Matz, "Reconstructing Camp David," *Negotiation Journal* 22, no. 1 (January 2006): 89–103. However, Matz also notes: "Much of the battle over what went wrong turns on different interpretations of motive [of Barak and Arafat]. Some say that Arafat used rigidity about Jerusalem as a means of avoiding agreement on anything . . . Others say that Arafat was a deeply religious man for whom Jerusalem was holy and not negotiable . . . . .After years of experience and twelve days at the [Camp David] summit, observers of Arafat still found his motives to be a puzzle."

95. At the outset of the Camp David negotiations on July 14, 2000, Shibley Telhami wrote in the *Los Angeles Times*: "By 'Jerusalem,' both Israelis and Palestinians refer largely to the Old City within the ancient walls that houses the most significant holy sites for Jews, Muslims and Christians. The symbolism evoked by these sites cannot be overcome by creative ideas of expanding the city's boundaries. This symbolism is, in some ways, bigger than the Palestinian-Israeli conflict because it ultimately mobilizes Jewish and Muslim groups from outside the areas controlled by Arafat and Barak . . . In the Arab and Muslim worlds, no issue with Israel mobilizes more people." A week later, July 21, 2000, in another article in the *Washington Post* he wrote: "It is no secret that many people on the U.S. and Israeli negotiating teams arrived at Camp David assuming this about the Jerusalem issue: If Yasir Arafat was offered a state in more than 90 percent of the West Bank and all of Gaza and some control over Muslim

holy sites and Arab neighborhoods in Jerusalem, he would be willing to accept Israeli legal sovereignty over the old city. It is hard to know how this impression was formed when conventional wisdom among most students of Arab and Palestinian politics was to the contrary. It is certainly the case that one never truly knows the absolute bottom line of the other party until it is tested in negotiations, and it is always worth trying to push the limits. But the likelihood that there was much Palestinian flexibility on this issue of Jerusalem was always small, if one listened attentively to both sides."

96. Berger, interview.

97. Haniyeh, "The Camp David Papers."

98. Quoted in Marwan Kanafani, *Sanawat al-Amal* (Cairo: Dar al-Shorouk, 2007), 419.

99. Former senior administration official, interview with the authors.

100. Berger, interview.

101. The report, *Changing Minds, Winning Peace: A New Strategic Direction for U.S. Public*, was prepared by a committee chaired by Ambassador Edward Djerejian and was submitted to the Committee on Appropriations of the House of Representatives on October 1, 2003.

102. Beside Albright, Ross, Miller, Gamal Helal, John Herbst, Martin Indyk (U.S. ambassador to Israel), Toni Verstandig (U.S. deputy assistant secretary of state), and legal adviser Jonathan Schwartz also attended.

103. According to Schwartz, "I think when the leadership, you know Sandy Berger and the President recognized that this question of sovereignty actually was a serious impediment to a solution, I was asked to educate them about sovereignty under international law. I did a paper with 10 different gradations of sovereignty and different models, including some that later were the butt of many jokes. It was a brainstorming exercise to look at the full range, and some of the ideas actually were of interest to some of the Israeli negotiators. I can't say anything short of what the Palestinians describe as 19th century sovereignty was ever of interest to them, because they felt their public would not understand. So I think the Palestinians, maybe, on a united basis were much more interested in a bright-line traditional-sovereignty allocation of territory. Whereas some of the Israeli officials were willing to consider much more exotic things, all the way to the point of both sides renouncing sovereignty, either renouncing or suspending, like the Antarctica treaty. There are countries that have claimed sovereignty in Antarctica, but under the multilateral convention, they're obliged to suspend the claim during the duration of the treaty. In any event, there were many variations. But I don't think the Palestinians were prepared to negotiate on that basis." Schwartz, interview with the authors.

104. Ibid.

105. Ross, *The Missing Peace*, 655. "On Jerusalem, we (*Americans*) took a more conceptual tack. Jerusalem would be described as being three cities in one. It was a practical city that had to be governed and managed on a day-to-day basis; it was a holy city, holy to the world, holy to the three monotheistic religions, home to more than fifty-seven holy sites in the Old City alone; and it was a political city. We had eleven points that formed a basis for discussion and were tied to each of the three cities; many of the points—e.g., having one undivided city for municipal services, free, unimpeded access to religious sites—were not contentious and represented building blocks for agreement. The most sensitive points were on political control, not functional responsibility. Here, initially, questions would be posed rather than solutions suggested. The logic was to forge understandings on practical and functional ways to manage the city before tackling the harder questions."

106. Enderlin, *Shattered Dreams*, 181.

107. According to Enderlin, Erekat replied, "The American position has always been *corpus separatum*. With no solution on Jerusalem, it will be impossible to reach an accord" (ibid., 182).

108. "I was in Togo for the Arab summit. I spoke in Arabic, and when I mentioned the Haram al-Sharif, everyone understood and all the Muslim delegates applauded," Arafat reportedly told Clinton (ibid).

109. Ibid.

110. Ross, *The Missing Peace*, 666–67.

111. Ibid., 671.

112. Ibid., 672.

113. Ibid., 673.

114. Ibid.

115. "On Jerusalem, the northern Arab neighborhoods of Kafr Aqab, Kalandia, and Bayt Hanina would become sovereign; the inner neighborhoods (Shaykh Jarrah, Wadi al-Jawz) would have services provided by the Palestinian capital of Al-Quds while being under Israeli sovereignty; in the Old City, there would be a special regime in which there would be shared responsibilities in the Muslim and Christian Quarters—the special regime and the shared responsibilities would need to be worked out jointly" (ibid., 674).

116. Ibid., 679.

117. Ibid.

118. Ibid.

119. According to Ross, Barak walked back on some of the proposals Shlomo Ben Ami had made. "Now, instead of at least three villages in the current municipal boundaries of East Jerusalem to become part of sovereign Al-Quds, it was one village. On almost every issue there was a retreat. This is what Barak had put us on hold for thirteen hours to do so" (ibid., 684).

120. Ibid., 685.

121. Ibid., 689–90.

122. Ibid., 689.

123. Ibid., 702.

124. Enderlin, *Shattered Dreams*, 258.

125. Miller, *The Much Too Promised Land*, 301; Ross, *The Missing Peace*, 666–67, 674–77; Ron Pundak argued that Arafat's timeline was not July but September or even November—he requested a series of summits, preferring tactically that the concluding one would be held after U.S. elections, so as to free Clinton from the influence of domestic Jewish pressure; and that Arafat needed time to build a domestic coalition (Ron Pundak, "From Oslo to Taba What Went Wrong?," in Rothstein, Maoz, and Shikaki, 108–9).

126. Former American official, interview with the authors.

127. Berger, interview.

128. American official, interview with the authors.

129. Berger, interview. On Clinton's promise to Arafat, see also; Indyk, *Innocent Abroad*, 293; Kurtzer and Lasensky, *Negotiating Arab-Israeli Peace*, 31; Sontag, "And Yet So Far"; Swisher, *The Truth about Camp David*, 225–26, 242–43; Swisher interview with Beth Jones; Swisher interview with Aaron Miller; Swisher interview with Rob Malley; Swisher interview with Muhammad Dahlan.

130. Former senior administration official, interview with the authors.

131. Note that the Hebrew term "friar" or "freier" for "sucker" is far more negative in its connotation in Israeli culture. "'Don't be a freier' is practically the 11th commandment of the Israeli," wrote Haaretz's Benny Ziffer in 2006, and Israeli scholars have debated how such a great fear of being a freier has developed in Israel, www.haaretz.com/print-edition/opinion/thou-shalt-not-be-a-freier-1.211247.

132. Eran Halperin and Daniel Bar-Tal, "The Fall of the Peace Camp in Israel: The Influence of Prime Minister Ehud Barak on Israeli Public Opinion: July 2000–February 2001," in *Conflict and Communications Online* 6, no. 2 (2007).

133. In a meeting with a group of the American Academy of Arts and Sciences in Tunis in spring 1992, Arafat was asked what his options were given his weakened position after the Iraq War and the reduction of Arab support for the PLO. After disagreeing with the analysis that his options were limited, he concluded with his typical wave of the finger, "Don't forget, I still have Jerusalem."

134. Indyk, *Innocent Abroad*, 336.

135. One high-level American official who usually attended meetings between Clinton and Arafat put it this way, "[Clinton] got used to that, because he heard it from Arafat over the previous seven years. . . . He [Arafat] challenged it with the Israelis! I remember he told Peres that when they were doing the Jericho agreement, Jericho first. And I remember a story that was really a great story, that Arafat was arguing with Shimon Peres that there was no temple, that 'no one can believe that there is a temple under the Haram, it is just unbelievable, nobody can believe this.' So Shimon Peres looked at Arafat

and said 'okay, you are not going to believe that there is a temple under the Haram. But you want me to believe that there was a horse with wings with a prophet that got on top of it and flew from Mecca to Jerusalem and ascended to heaven and back, and you want me to believe this, and you don't want to believe that there is a temple under the Haram?'" Former American adviser, interview with the authors.

136. Ben-Ami, *Scars of War*, 246.

137. Sontag, "And Yet So Far."

138. Riedel, interview.

139. Enderlin, *Shattered Dreams*, 251.

140. Berger, interview.

141. Former senior American official, interview with the authors.

142. The full text of the Clinton Parameters can be found in the online appendix to this volume at: www.thepeacepuzzle.org.

143. Indyk, *Innocent Abroad*, 366.

144. Ross, *The Missing Peace*, 753.

145. The full text of Gilad Sher's letter can be found in the online appendix to this volume at: www.thepeacepuzzle.org.

146. On the same day, "Barak informed Clinton that the country was so shaken by Palestinian violence that he was now beyond the point where he could participate in the negotiations without causing fatal damage to his candidacy." Indyk, *Innocent Abroad*, 369.

147. Ibid., 370.

148. Beilin, *The Path to Geneva*, 224. Ross identifies only three reservations raised by Arafat—the Western Wall versus the Wailing Wall, airspace, and refugees, of which the latter is arguably been most significant.

149. Ross, *The Missing Peace*, 755.

150. It is important to keep in mind the bloody environment in which the Clinton ideas and the Israeli and Palestinian reactions take place. By year's end, there were already 279 Palestinians and 41 Israelis killed in the violence that started with the al-Aqsa Intifada (Enderlin, *Shattered Dreams*, 182).

151. After the meeting in which Clinton articulated his ideas on December 23, 2000, one Israeli participant, Israeli Hasson, reportedly asked the peace team, "Why so late? Everything would have been different if you'd submitted this proposal in September or at Camp David!" (ibid., 339).

152. Nabil Fahmy, interview with the authors, September 21, 2010, Washington, DC.

153. "The real purpose was not to reach agreement, but on the Israeli side to try to constrain what Sharon could do and on the Palestinian side to try to get the Bush administration to buy into the Clinton ideas" (Ross, *The Missing Peace*, 756).

154. The following is a short description of the outcome of the negotiations on the permanent-status issues at Taba, as portrayed by the unofficial EU paper: On territory, both sides agreed that in accordance with the UN Security Council Resolution 242, the June 4, 1967, lines would be the basis for the borders between Israel and the state of Palestine. On Jerusalem, both sides accepted in principle the Clinton suggestion of having a Palestinian sovereignty over Arab neighborhoods and an Israeli sovereignty over Jewish neighborhoods. Both sides also favored the idea of an Open City, whose geographical scope, according to the Israelis, would encompass the Old City of Jerusalem plus an area defined as the Holy Basin or Historical Basin. The Palestinian side was in favor of an Open City provided that continuity and contiguity were preserved. The Israeli side accepted that the City of Jerusalem would be the capital of the two states: Yerushalaim, capital of Israel and Al-Quds, capital of the state of Palestine. The Palestinian side expressed its only concern, namely that East Jerusalem is the capital of the state of Palestine. Both parties also accepted the principle of respective control over each side's respective holy sites (religious control and management). Both sides agreed that the question of Haram al-Sharif/Temple Mount has not been resolved. However, both sides were close to accepting Clinton's ideas regarding Palestinian sovereignty over Haram al-Sharif notwithstanding Palestinian and Israeli reservations. On refugees, both sides suggested, as a basis, that the parties should agree that a just settlement of the refugee problem in accordance with the UN Security Council Resolution 242 must lead to the

implementation of UN General Assembly Resolution 194. On security, the Israeli side requested, among other security-related issues, to have three early warning stations on Palestinian territory. The Palestinian side was prepared to accept the continued operations of early warning stations but subject to certain conditions. The two sides disagreed over a timetable for withdrawal from the West Bank and Jordan Valley, with the Israelis agreeing to a thirty-six-month period while the Palestinians proposing an eighteen-month period. The full text of the EU non-paper can be found in the online appendix to this volume at: www.thepeacepuzzle.org.

155. The limits of American influence in Israeli politics as well as the failure to fully understand these politics were painfully demonstrated after the assassination of Yitzhak Rabin, when President Clinton's appeal to Israelis failed to influence the outcome of the elections despite the President's almost unprecedented personal popularity among Israelis.

156. Washington's failings during and immediately preceding the early Oslo years included (a) having a lack of "focus and follow-through"; (b) not investing in multilateral negotiations, which had proven fruitful in getting Arab state involvement in the peace process; (c) largely ignoring the Oslo negotiations prior to their conclusion and so losing an opportunity to shape them; (d) prioritizing Israel's negotiations with Syria over those with the Palestinians; (e) not engaging in a sustained diplomatic effort with Syria and "squandering" Rabin's willingness to withdraw from the Golan in exchange for peace; (f) waiting almost two years after the Oslo signing ceremony to get deeply involved in Israeli-Palestinian negotiations; and (g) avoiding regular and serious high-level engagement on the Israeli-Palestinian track until late in the second Clinton administration. See Kurtzer and Lasensky, *Negotiating Arab-Israeli Peace*, 16–19; Matz, "Reconstructing Camp David," 89–103.

157. Former senior administration official, interview with the authors.

158. Bruce Riedel, interview with the authors, January 11, 2009, Washington DC.

159. Former Israeli foreign minister, Shlomo Ben-Ami, who was critical of Arafat's behavior in his book, nonetheless noted, "Admittedly, however, Camp David might not have been the deal the Palestinians could have accepted. The real lost opportunities came later on" (Ben-Ami, *Scars of War*, 270).

Chapter Four

1. James Mann, *Rise of the Vulcans* (New York: Viking Penguin, 2004).

2. Former senior American official, interview with the authors.

3. "Bush Gore Debate Transcript," *CBS News*, accessed February 11, 2009, www.cbsnews.com/stories/2000/10/11/politics/main240442.shtml.

4. See George W. Bush, "A Distinctly American Internationalism," Ronald Reagan Presidential Library, November 19, 1999; Condoleezza Rice, "Campaign 2000: Promoting the National Interest," *Foreign Affairs* 79, no. 1 (2000).

5. See Elliott Abrams, "Israel and the 'Peace Process,'" in Robert Kagan and William Kristol, eds., *Present Dangers: Crisis and Opportunity in American Foreign Policy* (San Francisco: Encounter Books, 2000), 239. Some in the administration even tried to strike use of the term "peace process." See also Ron Kampeas, "In the Mideast, Both Sides Doubt Bush's Detachment," *Associated Press*, February 10, 2001. On June 25, 2001, Abrams was appointed the NSC senior director for Democracy, Human Rights, and International Operations. On December 2, 2002, he became the NSC senior director for Near East and North African Affairs; and on February 2, 2005, he became the deputy national security advisor for Global Democracy Strategy.

6. See Dennis Ross and David Makovsky, *Myths, Illusions, and Peace* (New York: Viking, 2009), 91–113.

7. For full polling results, see www.people-press.org/2004/12/06/religion-and-the-presidential-vote/.

8. For the full study, see www.pewforum.org/Christian/American-Evangelicals-and-Israel.aspx.

9. Since 2001, the view that linkage does not exist between the Arab-Israeli conflict and other problems in the region has become dominant within national Republican circles, particularly in terms of presidential politics. In Democratic circles, the linkage argument is more prevalent.

10. Bruce Riedel (former special assistant to the president and senior director for Near East Affairs on the National Security Council), December 14, 2006, Washington, DC.

11. Dick Cheney, Los Angeles World Affairs Council, Beverly Hills, CA, January 14, 2004. Clinton gave a similar briefing to Powell. See Clayton Swisher, *The Truth about Camp David: The Untold Story of the Collapse of the Middle East Peace Process* (New York: Nation Books, 2004), 404.

12. Ron Suskind, *The Price of Loyalty* (New York: Simon & Schuster, 2004), 71. A year later White House press adviser Ari Fleischer went so far as to blame Clinton for the outbreak of the second Intifada, comments he would later be forced to take back, but that nonetheless reflected the president's own views about Clinton and what Bush saw as the perils of overreaching.

13. See William B. Quandt, *Peace Process: American Diplomacy and the Arab-Israeli Conflict since 1967,* 3rd ed. (Washington, DC: Brookings Institution Press/Berkeley: University of California Press, 2005), 390.

14. Suskind, *The Price of Loyalty,* 71–72. See also George W. Bush, *Decision Points* (New York: Crown, 2010), 401–2.

15. Jane Perlez, "Bush Officials Pronounce Clinton Mideast Plan Dead," *New York Times*, February 9, 2001.

16. Condoleezza Rice (former secretary of state), interview with the authors, January 7, 2010.

17. Bush, *Decision Points,* 400.

18. Norman Kempster, "Bush Warns Israel's Sharon to Avoid Adding Fuel to Fire," *Los Angeles Times*, March 21, 2001.

19. See Nahum Barnea and Ariel Kastner, "Backchannel: Bush, Sharon and the Uses of Unilateralism," *Saban Center Monograph Series*, no. 2 (December 2006): 15. Shortly after this meeting, Sharon also initiated his own, private "back-channel" in order to consolidate dealings with Washington. Initially he relied on an Israeli émigré, Arieh Genger, who was a close associate. Genger maintained a direct line to Sharon, and initially conferred with both the White House and the State Department, but increasingly came to deal exclusively with the White House. Under pressure from the Israeli attorney general because of alleged shady business dealings by Genger, Sharon replaced him the following year with lawyer Dov Weissglas. For further details, see Barnea and Kastner, 8–13. According to a former senior Israeli official in a confidential interview, "(Sharon) did come (to office) with an extremely important notion that to succeed you have got to have the best relationship possible with the U.S. . . . (therefore) it was critically important to have this channel . . . operational, almost on a daily basis via phone calls. That is why Ambassador Kurtzer had an open door to the prime minister's office."

20. Martin Indyk, *Innocent Abroad: An Intimate Account of American Peace Diplomacy in the Middle East* (New York: Simon & Schuster, 2009), 387.

21. Ibid., 379. Indyk, who was Clinton's ambassador to Israel, remained in Tel Aviv through the first several months of the Bush administration and was replaced by Daniel Kurtzer in 2001.

22. Ibid., 379.

23. Sheryl Gay Stolberg, "Bush and Israel: Unlike His Father—Americas—International Herald Tribune," *New York Times*, August 2, 2006.

24. Ibid.

25. Powell described the incursion as "excessive and disproportionate," and he stated, "We call on both sides to respect the agreements they have signed"; "For the Israelis this includes respecting their commitment to withdraw from Gaza, according to the terms of the agreement signed by Israel and the Palestinians. There can be no military solution to this conflict." Jane Perlez, "Powell Assails Israel for Gaza Incursion," *New York Times*, April 18, 2001.

26. David Satterfield (former deputy secretary of state), interview with the authors, August 3, 2010, Rome, Italy.

27. Committee members included George Mitchell, Warren B. Rudman, Suleyman Demirel, Javier Solana, and Thorbjørn Jagland.

28. George Mitchell, chairman, "Sharm El-Sheikh Fact-Finding Committee Report," Department of State, April 30, 2001.

29. Condoleezza Rice (former secretary of state), interview with the authors, April 29, 2010, Palo Alto, CA. Rice recalls mostly pessimism in this period. "I don't think we believed that there was any real possibility," she told the authors. "We tried to do what we could about the violence—you remember there was the Mitchell plan—George Tenet got very active—I can remember trying to arrange a meeting between the Israelis and the Palestinians on the QT and [Palestinian security official Mohamed] Dahlan got shot at on his way there and never made it to the meeting. That period, really through the Israeli occupation—reoccupation of the West Bank in 2002—just didn't lend itself to any kind of peace overtures."

30. Jane Perlez, "U.S. Widens Role in Mideast Crisis, Sending an Envoy," *New York Times*, May 21, 2010.

31. Sharon's view was in stark contrast to that of former prime minister Yitzhak Rabin, who responded to the first wave of suicide terrorism in the mid-1990s by declaring that Israel could negotiate and fight terrorism at the same time.

32. Edwin Chen, "For Israel, the Road to Peace Requires '10 Days of Quiet,'" *Los Angeles Times*, June 27, 2001; Jane Perlez, "Powell Arrives in Israel to Push Peace Effort," *New York Times*, June 28, 2001.

33. Perlez, "Powell Arrives in Israel."

34. Jane Perlez, "Bush Senior, on His Son's Behalf, Reassures Saudi Leader," *New York Times*, July 15, 2001.

35. Jane Perlez, "U.S. Says Killings by Israel Inflame Mideast Conflict," *New York Times*, August 28, 2001.

36. Robert G. Kaiser and David B. Ottaway, "Saudi Leader's Anger Revealed Shaky Ties; Bush's Response Eased a Deep Rift on Mideast Policy; Then Came Sept. 11," *Washington Post*, February 10, 2002.

37. Bob Woodward, *State of Denial* (New York: Simon & Schuster, 2006), 76.

38. Hadley admits that the Bush administration missed signals of disquiet that the Saudis were sending early on. The Bush team was getting "behind the ball," he said, acknowledging the impact of Abdullah's letter. Stephen Hadley, interview with the authors, June 8, 2009, Washington, DC. See also Kaiser and Ottaway, "Saudi Leader's Anger Revealed Shaky Ties." *The New Yorker* quotes the Bush letter as follows: "I firmly believe that the Palestinian people have a right to self-determination and to live peacefully and securely in their own state in their own homeland." Elsa Walsh, "The Prince," *New Yorker*, March 24, 2003.

39. Senior State Department official, interview with the authors.

40. Richard Armitage (former deputy secretary of state), interview with the authors, May 17, 2007, Washington, DC; Daniel C. Kurtzer (former ambassador to Egypt and Israel), interview with the authors, September 15, 2010, Washington, DC; Syrian diplomat, interview with the authors. Later, at the height of the Bush administration's confrontation with Syria after Rafik Hariri's assassination, al-Asad would suspend cooperating with Washington on counter-terrorism.

41. See Tracy Wilkinson, "After the Attack: The Middle East; Arafat, Sharon Answer U.S. Plea," *Los Angeles Times*, September 19, 2001.

42. Ariel Sharon, "Statement on October 4, 2001," Israel Ministry of Foreign Affairs, www.mfa .gov.il/MFA/Government/Speeches%20by%20Israeli%20leaders/2001/Statement%20by%20Israeli %20PM%20Ariel%20Sharon%20-%204-Oct-2001.

43. Kurtzer, interview, September 15, 2010. See also James Reynolds, "Sharon's Appeasement Warning," *BBC*, October 6, 2001, http://news.bbc.co.uk/2/hi/middle_east/1581280.stm; Barnea and Kastner, "Backchannel," 20–22.

44. Daniel C. Kurtzer, telephone interview with the authors, March 9, 2011.

45. Ibid. The episode is reported incorrectly in Ahron Bregman, *Elusive Peace: How the Holy Land Defeated America* (New York: Penguin, 2005), 161. In the book, Kurtzer is misquoted. Elusive Peace has two formats: A book written by Ahron Bregman and a DVD produced by Norma Percy.

46. According to Kurtzer, the Latrun speech opened the door for the U.S. endorsement weeks later. Kurtzer, interview, March 9, 2011.

47. Former senior American official, interview with the authors.

48. George W. Bush, "Address at the United Nations General Assembly," United Nations, November 10, 2001, www.pbs.org/newshour/terrorism/international/bush_11-10.html.

49. Andrea Koppel and Elise Labbot, "Bush: Palestinian State 'Part of a Vision' if Israel Respected," CNN.com, October 2, 2001, http://articles.cnn.com/2001-10-02/us/gen.mideast.us_1_palestinian-state-israeli-palestinian-conflict-arab-support?_s=PM:US. Bush first stated that he supported a Palestinian state in a congressional meeting on October 2, 2001, and formally reiterated his support in a speech to the UN in November. See Glenn Kessler, "Talking Points Aside, Bush Stance on Palestinian State Is Not a First," *Washington Post*, October 5, 2005. In her memoir, Rice reports that on informing Sharon's office, Israel initially sought to forestall the president's endorsement of a Palestinian state. See Condoleezza Rice, *No Higher Honor: A Memoir of My Years in Washington* (New York: Crown, 2011), 131–47.

50. Gil Hoffman, "Likud Angry at Sharon Support for Palestinian State," *Jerusalem Post*, September 25, 2001.

51. Colin Powell, "Speech at the University of Louisville in Louisville, KY," November 19, 2001, www.usembassy-israel.org.il/publish/peace/archives/2001/november/111901.html.

52. Former senior American official, interview with the authors.

53. Aaron David Miller, *The Much Too Promised Land* (New York: Bantam Books, 2008), 337.

54. For example, General Zinni did not carry the title of presidential envoy, but rather was a "special adviser" to the secretary of state. A former senior administration official discovered that Sharon went around Zinni's (and Powell's) back via his special emissary (Genger) who maintained a back channel with the White House. Powell brought Zinni to the Oval Office to get his marching orders directly from the president. Zinni recalls that Bush remarked to Powell on the way out, "Colin, this is your baby." Anthony Zinni (retired Marine Corps general, former CENTCOM commander, former security emissary and special envoy to Israel and the Palestinian Authority), interview with the authors, Washington, DC, December 14, 2006.

55. Miller, interview; Zinni, interview. See also The Zinni Paper, full text available online via the United States Institute of Peace, www.usip.org/files/file/resources/collections/peace_agreements/joint_goals.pdf.

56. Bregman, *Elusive Peace*, 168–73.

57. Zinni, interview.

58. Elliott Abrams (former National Security Council official), interview with the authors, June 24, 2010, Washington, DC.

59. Rice, *No Higher Honor*, 135.

60. Former senior American official, interview with the authors.

61. Dick Cheney, *In My Time* (New York: Threshold Editions, 2011), 373. See also Rice, *No Higher Honor*, 135.

62. Bush, *Decision Points*, 400–401.

63. Ibid.

64. Daniel C. Kurtzer, e-mail correspondence with the authors, March 18, 2011.

65. Norma Percy, producer, *Israel and the Arabs: Elusive Peace* (DVD), BBC, 2005.

66. Bush officials would later acknowledge that the Saudi offer was positive, but it lacked a vehicle for implementation. It told the administration where to go, and it offered a better region after peace agreements had been concluded, but it did not show them how to get there. It also came at a bad time, at the end of the worst month of violence of the Intifada. Rice, interview, April 29, 2010; Satterfield, interview.

67. Israeli official, interview with the authors.

68. Suzanne Goldenberg, "Cheney Calms Palestinian Anger with Arafat Offer," *The Guardian*, March 20, 2002; Cheney, *In My Time*, 378–79.

69. Zinni, interview.

70. Ibid.

71. Bush, *Decision Points*, 400.

72. George W. Bush, "Speech Announcing Secretary of State Colin Powell's Mission to the Middle East," April 4, 2002, www.pbs.org/newshour/updates/april02/bush_4-4.html.

73. Bush, "Speech Announcing Powell's Mission to the Middle East."

74. "Interview with Christopher Dodd, Henry Kissinger, George Mitchell, Condoleeza Rice, and Arlen Specter by Wolf Blitzer," *CNN Late Edition with Wolf Blitzer*, April 7, 2002, http://transcripts.cnn.com/TRANSCRIPTS/0204/07/le.00.html.

75. "Remarks by Spanish Foreign Minister Josep Pique, U.N. Secretary General Kofi Annan, Russian Foreign Minister Igor Ivanov, EU Senior Official Javier Solana, and Secretary Colin Powell in Madrid, Spain," United Nations, April 10, 2002, http://unispal.un.org/UNISPAL.NSF/0/4808D2E68A33B35385256B970062DEAF. Given the legacy of the 1991 Madrid Peace Conference, the venue for launching the Quartet appeared deliberate. The idea of the Quartet itself can be traced to an October 25, 2001, statement issued in Jerusalem by UN special coordinator Terje Roed-Larsen (in the name of UN, EU, Russian, and American diplomats on the ground).

76. Former senior American official, interview with the authors.

77. Ibid.

78. See Miller, *The Much Too Promised Land*, 344–45. See also Bregman, *Elusive Peace*, 202.

79. Cheney, *In My Time*, 381. Cheney adds, "I'm not sure what transpired between Condi and Colin, but the next day, when the Principals Committee—the NSC minus the president—met to discuss the Middle East, Colin apologized. . . . It was critically important that we not launch high-profile international conferences or summit meetings in futile pursuit of a final settlement agreement that Arafat showed no willingness to embrace on any reasonable terms. Bill Clinton had made that mistake at the end of his second term with a high-profile, high-expectations, and high-stakes maneuver that brought Arafat and Israeli prime minister Ehud Barak to Camp David for a series of talks that failed tragically and led to the renewed intifada. There was no way we could afford to repeat that train wreck if we wanted to successfully pursue the War on Terror."

80. Ambassador Kurtzer recalls being instructed "by high ranking officials to tell the Israelis, 'don't harm Arafat, don't kidnap him, don't create an accident.'" Kurtzer, interview, March 15, 2010. See also Barnea and Kastner, "Backchannel," 23. Throughout this tense period, Powell was frustrated with the way in which President Bush was communicating with Sharon. According to a former senior American official, "The one time [Powell] got Bush to say—you've got to tell Sharon, next time you talk to him, that there has to be relief at Muqata [Arafat's compound in Ramallah]. And [Powell] was in the Oval Office when he talked to Sharon, and it was kind of, 'Oh yeah, Arik, you've got to do something about that, right, okay, bye.' And he says, 'See, I told him.' Arik knew that he wasn't really being ordered. And you may recall that for, what, a week or so after that, Sharon still didn't do anything . . . It was the second time. The President said he was going to—you know, 'You've got to stop.' Sharon said, 'Okay.' And then what he meant was, 'When I'm finished.'" Former senior American official, interview with the authors.

81. Peter Slevin and Mike Allen, "Bush: Sharon A 'Man of Peace' Israel 'Responded' to Call for Pullout," *Washington Post*, April 19, 2002.

82. Sharon Samber and Matthew E. Berger, "Speakers Stick to Consensus Theme at National Solidarity Rally for Israel," *JTA*, April 15, 2002.

83. Bush, *Decision Points*, 404.

84. Rice, *No Higher Honor*, 141.

85. Bush, *Decision Points*, 404.

86. Bregman, *Elusive Peace*, 209.

87. Rice, interview, April 29, 2010.

88. Bush, *Decision Points*, 401–3.

89. Kurtzer, interview, September 15, 2010. U.S. diplomats in the Middle East and Europe solved a series of last-minute obstacles to end the standoff, including the disposition of Palestinian weapons the militants had brought into the Church of the Nativity.

90. Former senior Israeli official, interview with the authors. According to the official, Israel disagreed with Washington's appraisal of Arafat's standing in the Arab world, believing "his personal

weight was significantly less than they thought." Although Sharon heeded Bush and Rice's warnings on Arafat, he did not when it came to Sheikh Ahmad Yassin, the Hamas leader Israel assassinated in March 2004. The Israeli official added, "More than once [Rice] told me that if we will touch Sheikh Yassin the whole Middle East will burst into flames. I told her that nobody would cry about it for more than two hours. I was wrong it was less than one hour. . . . When we killed him, she called me hysterically at four in the morning Washington time and she was hysterical because she was convinced in the next ten minutes you would see now 15 US embassies across the Middle East in flames. If you remember the three days of mourning called in the West Bank, it didn't last not even a day."

91. Former senior Israeli official, interview with the authors.

92. In a bid to show international donors he was serious about financial reform, Arafat appointed Salam Fayyad as finance minister. Fayyad had been a respected World Bank and International Monetary Fund official for many years. Observers were skeptical, knowing how tightly Arafat controlled the PA, but Fayyad distinguished himself from the outset—and later he would assume a major role as Palestinian prime minister following the Hamas coup in Gaza in 2007.

93. Bush, *Decision Points*, 404.

94. Bregman, *Elusive Peace*, 226.

95. Dov Weissglas (senior adviser to Prime Minister Ariel Sharon), interview with the authors, January 19, 2007, Tel Aviv, Israel.

96. Cheney, *In My Time*, 384.

97. See Miller, *The Much Too Promised Land*, 350.

98. Robert Danin (former deputy assistant secretary of state and former National Security Council official), telephone interview with the authors, December 10, 2009. See also Rice, *No Higher Honor*, 142–44. Still, some who pushed for a more activist approach gave up trying after the Rose Garden speech. "After I lost the argument with Condi in 2002 about the speech, I just basically said this is not going to go anywhere," said one former senior administration official.

99. George W. Bush, "President Bush Calls for New Palestinian Leadership," The White House, June 24, 2002, http://georgewbush-whitehouse.archives.gov/news/releases/2002/06/20020624-3.html. Powell had previewed the speech to the Jordanians, as Marwan Muasher recalls, "Then Powell laid the line on Arafat. The speech would call for new leaders among the Palestinians, he said. This was exactly the kind of American policy statement that we had feared and that we felt would complicate efforts to move the process forward. Powell said that an international conference no longer made sense, and although he agreed that ultimately, there must be a comprehensive settlement with Syria and Lebanon, he was noncommittal on their immediate involvement." See Marwan Muasher, *The Arab Center: The Promise of Moderation* (New Haven, CT: Yale University Press, 2008), 153.

100. Bush, "Bush Calls for New Palestinian Leadership."

101. President Bush briefly mentions reading Sharansky's book in his memoir. See Bush, *Decision Points*, 398. See also Elisabeth Bumiller, "White House Letter: Bush Borrows a Page from Natan Sharansky," *New York Times*, January 31, 2005.

102. Rice, *No Higher Honor*, 144.

103. Bush, *Decision Points*, 404.

104. Ibid.

105. Ibid., 403–4.

106. Kurtzer, e-mail correspondence.

107. Flynt Leverett recalls that Rice angrily told Dov Weissglas and Israeli ambassador Danny Ayalon, "Israel has had no better friend in the White House than this Administration, and you've had no better friend in this Administration than me, but I am telling you, if you do not end this siege in Ramallah, if you don't withdraw your forces from the compound, you are going to have a public rift with this President. This needs to end now. If you and I are having this same conversation a week from now, you are going to have a serious problem in this building, and you're going to have that serious problem with me." See Bregman, *Elusive Peace*, 241. A former senior Israeli official confirms the episode, "I do not recall, before then or after then, that she was so upset like at that meeting." She told Weissglas the siege on Arafat had nothing to do with "security," that it was a political statement. Rice said the administration

was trying to put together a coalition against Iraq and that what Israel was doing was damaging U.S. ties with Arab states. "It isn't done between friends," the official recalls her saying, "you are hurting a friend for nothing." After reporting the conversation immediately to Sharon, as indicated in the text, it was not long before Israeli forces pulled back. Former senior Israeli official, interview with the authors.

108. Hadley, interview.

109. Ibid.

110. Muasher, *The Arab Center*, 159–62. Despite the president's refusal, Muasher reports that Rice pulled him aside afterward and said the United States would "work something out" with (Jordan) to translate the president's speech into practical steps, reversing her earlier position" (ibid., 163).

111. Ibid., 184–85.

112. Bush, "Bush Calls for New Palestinian Leadership."

113. At the time, David Satterfield was serving as deputy assistant secretary for the Department of State, Bureau of Near Eastern Affairs, and Terje Roed-Larsen was serving as UN special coordinator for the Middle East peace process. In her interview with the authors, Rice claims that: "[The Road Map] was produced by our Arab allies and Tony Blair," and she readily admits, "who wanted to have something on the peace process as we were dealing with Iraq." We have been able to confirm the concern of our Arab allies and Tony Blair that the road map be produced as soon as possible, in large measure because of Iraq, but we cannot find any evidence that they "produced" it unless the word is intended to suggest that they pushed for the document. Satterfield, interview; Rice, interview, April 29, 2010.

114. Danin, interview. See Miller, *The Much Too Promised Land*, 345–53.

115. On the eve of the war, Bush was also seeking an explicit guarantee from Israel that it would not retaliate if attacked by Iraq. According to a former senior Israeli official, Sharon promised restraint unless Israel suffered major casualties (unlike in 1991), or was attacked with nonconventional weapons. It was not enough for Bush, who asked Sharon to at least coordinate with the United States if he had to react—which Sharon interpreted as a "semi-approval." Weissglas, interview. See also Daniel C. Kurtzer, "Remarks at United States Institute of Peace Roundtable: U.S.-Israeli Relations and the Iranian Nuclear Crisis," March 2, 2010.

116. Muasher, *The Arab Center*, 173. See also Miller, *The Much Too Promised Land*, 352.

117. The full text of the Road Map can be found in the online appendix to this volume at: www.thepeacepuzzle.org.

118. Danin, interview. "Just accept it, you have enough," said the NSC staffer in recalling the administration's response to Israel's reservations, "There are enough tripwires in the Roadmap, . . . to address your concerns, so don't worry" was the message that was being conveyed, at least in Washington, in regards to the fourteen reservations that they were pushing.

119. Ibid.

120. Ibid.

121. See Barnea and Kastner, "Backchannel," 34.

122. "President Bush said to all of us, 'I'm driven with a mission from God. God would tell me George go and end this, fight those terrorists in Afghanistan, and I did. And then God would tell me George go and end the tyranny in Iraq, and I did. And now again I feel God's words coming to me, go and get the Palestinians their state and get Israelis security and get peace in the Middle East. And by God I am going to do it." Nabil Shaath, in Percy, *Elusive Peace* (DVD).

123. Former senior American official, interview with the authors. "I never felt 100 percent secure in American support," Quartet envoy James Wolfensohn told the authors. James Wolfensohn (former special envoy for the Quartet on the Middle East), interview with the authors, December 1, 2006, New York, NY.

124. Rice, *No Higher Honor*, 219.

125. Percy, *Elusive Peace* (DVD). Abbas said, "The Americans were giving me a bear hug but their words were hollow. The Israelis conceded nothing. My people were turning against me."

126. Zinni, interview.

127. Miller, *The Much Too Promised Land*, 351.

128. Former senior American official, interview with the authors.

129. For more background on how the "opportunities" of this period were viewed from Washington, see David Makovsky, Robert Malley, and Steven Spiegel, "Arab-Israeli Futures: Next Steps for the United States," United States Institute of Peace, March 2005, www.usip.org/publications/arab-israeli-futures-next-steps-united-states.

130. "He told me about it in November in Rome and he announced it publicly in December, and we got behind that. The President thought that was a very bold move," Abrams said. Abrams, interview.

131. Ariel Sharon, "Address by Prime Minister Ariel Sharon at the Fourth Herzliya Conference," Israel Ministry of Foreign Affairs, December 18, 2003, www.mfa.gov.il/MFA/Government/Speeches+by+Israeli+leaders/2003/Address+by+PM+Ariel+Sharon+at+the+Fourth+Herzliya.htm?DisplayMode=print.

132. Kurtzer, interview, September 15, 2010. See also Barnea and Kastner, "'Backchannel," 42–44.

133. In May 1999, Ehud Barak's government had withdrawn from southern Lebanon unilaterally, but under enormous domestic pressure.

134. Kurtzer, interview, March 9, 2011.

135. Ibid.

136. Abrams, interview.

137. Danin, interview.

138. The Israelis had specifically asked for language about "blocs," but here the administration refused, preferring language that was less definitive and consistent with the overarching principle that changes to the 1967 lines had to be agreed by both sides. Hadley, interview. See Rice, *No Higher Honor*, 281.

139. For the text of the letters exchanged by Bush and Sharon, see "Exchange of Letters between PM Sharon and President Bush," Israeli Foreign Ministry Online, April 14, 2004, www.mfa.gov.il/MFA/Peace+Process/Reference+Documents/Exchange+of+letters+Sharon-Bush+14-Apr-2004.htm.

140. Powell opposed the language that hinted at U.S. support for Israel retaining parts of the West Bank, as well as the refugee provisions—warning the president he was "touching two third rails." Percy, *Elusive Peace* (DVD). For Powell's own words, see note 142 below.

141. For the text of the letters, see "Exchange of Letters between PM Sharon and President Bush."

142. "I said to [the president] you're touching two third rails, electric rails: one right of return, and second the line. And for the president of the United States to say something about them in a way that was not going to be received kindly in the Arab world was going to create one heck of a ruckus." Powell, in Percy, *Elusive Peace* (DVD).

143. Dore Gold claims that Bush's letter was stronger on behalf of Israel than Clinton's Parameters. See Dore Gold, "Bush Erases the Clinton Parameters," *Jerusalem Issue Brief* 3, no. 21 (April 15, 2004), www.jcpa.org/brief/brief3-21.htm.

144. Senior American official, interview with the authors.

145. Ibid.

146. Dov Weissglas, "Letter to NSA Condoleezza Rice," *Ha'aretz*, April 19, 2004, www.haaretz.com/news/letter-from-dov-Weissglas-to-nsa-condoleezza-rice-1.119993.

147. Hadley, interview.

148. Ibid. According to Hadley, the tentative understandings faded from the scene for some time. Then, in spring of 2008, a top adviser to then prime minister Olmert—in discussions with the White House—claimed that Israel had been quietly complying with the 2003 understandings all along. However, independent assessments do not concur, and even Elliott Abrams grants that Israel did not fully comply with the tentative understandings. See Elliott Abrams, "The Settlement Freeze Fallacy," *Washington Post*, April 8, 2009.

149. Daniel C. Kurtzer, "The Settlement Facts," *Washington Post*, June 14, 2009.

150. Danin, interview. The entire episode was typical of the administration's conflicted operations on the peace process. The Israelis were supposed to take pictures and provide maps of the settlements, but they did not do it, and the administration did not follow up.

151. For the text of President Bush's letter to King Abdullah, see www.jordanembassyus.org/05072004002.htm.

152. Muasher, *The Arab Center*, 212–13.

153. Ari Shavit, "The Big Freeze," *Haaretz Magazine*, October 8, 2004. Weissglas continues, "And when you freeze that process, you prevent the establishment of a Palestinian state, and you prevent a discussion on the refugees, the borders and Jerusalem. Effectively, this whole package called the Palestinian state, with all that it entails, has been removed indefinitely from our agenda. And all this with authority and permission. All with a presidential blessing and the ratification of both Houses of Congress."

154. The question was from Senator Lincoln Chaffee at an open Senate Foreign Relations Committee hearing on the Road Map. Witnesses were Ambassador David Welch and Quartet envoy James Wolfensohn, June 30, 2005.

155. At a press conference in the Rose Garden with Abbas on July 25, Bush was asked about the barrier. He responded, "I think the wall is a problem . . . It is very difficult to develop confidence between the Palestinians and Israel with a wall snaking through the West Bank." That answer put the Palestinian delegation "on cloud nine. This was a huge success, a huge coup," according to one Abbas aide. See Bregman, *Elusive Peace*, 268. See transcripts of Bush's news conferences with Mahmoud Abbas, Washington, DC, July 25, 2003 and May 26, 2005.

Abbas: It's like teaching a child at school. You can't just tell him once. He has to see it, hear it, touch it so he can learn. I told him, "look at this wall. It's eating into Palestinian land . . ." . . . Mr. Bush said "This cuts like a snake through the West Bank." He looked at the map and threw it aside. He said to Dick Cheney "With this wall, we'll never have a Palestinian state." Percy, *Elusive Peace* (DVD).

156. Bush, *Decision Points*, 402.

157. Just as "fence" is the preferred term by the Israelis, so is "wall" preferred by the Palestinians. The most neutral terminology on this particular disputed action is "barrier"—which in fact consists of both a fence and a wall.

158. See Stephen Zunes, "The Implications of the U.S. Reaction to the World Court Ruling against Israel's 'Separation Barrier,'" *Middle East Policy* 9, no. 4 (Winter 2004).

159. Kurtzer, interview, September 15, 2010.

160. Using this approach, Kurtzer recalls meeting with Israeli officials frequently to discuss the barrier on behalf of many institutions, especially in and around Jerusalem, such as Christian churches, which claimed that their properties would be split or that they would be cut off from their congregants, or Al Quds University, which would have been potentially cut off from an athletic field. He received a sympathetic hearing and changes were made. Kurtzer, interview, September 15, 2010. Kurtzer's account of the Al Quds episode was verified by an Israeli official, who said that Rice herself contacted Israeli officials about the matter. For public statements that reflect this general U.S. approach, see the following Rice statements: Condoleezza Rice, interview with *LA Times*, March 24, 2005, which is also accessible online via Churches for Middle East Peace, www.cmep.org/documents/BushAdmin_Jerusalem.htm; conversation with Israeli foreign minister Silvan Shalom, as reported in *Ma'ariv*, June 26, 2005.

161. William Burns (former assistant secretary of state for Near Eastern Affairs and former ambassador to Russia), telephone interview with the authors, May 17, 2007, Washington, DC.

162. Daniel C. Kurtzer, interview with the authors, May 3, 2007, Washington, DC. Kurtzer said the Bureau of Near Eastern Affairs at the State Department, supported by American diplomats in the field, pushed for a series of peace process–related steps to bolster Abbas and moderate Palestinian leaders, but the ideas were not adopted by the administration.

163. Karen DeYoung, *Soldier: The Life of Colin Powell* (New York: Knopf, 2006), 6.

164. Jacob Weisberg, *The Bush Tragedy* (New York: Random House), 186–87.

165. Former senior American official, interview with the authors.

166. Ibid.

167. Burns, interview.

168. Satterfield, interview.

169. Former senior American official, interview with the authors. Secretary Rice makes this clear in her memoir as well. See Rice, *No Higher Honor*, 53–54.

170. Bush, *Decision Points*, 399.

171. Rice, *No Higher Honor*, 22. Rumsfeld blames the perceived dissension in the administration on Rice and her handling of the interagency process. For example, he states that on a number of issues, including Arab-Israeli peace talks, "Rice would craft policy briefings for the President that seemed to endorse conceptual points one department had advanced, but also would endorse proposals for the way ahead that came from a different department. . . . This bridging approach could temporarily mollify the NSC principals, but it also led to discontent, since fundamental differences remained unaddressed and unresolved by the President. . . . The aversion to decisions in favor of one course of action or another—and sometimes in favor of one department or agency over another—ironically led to more disharmony than would have been the case if the President had had an opportunity to make the decisions himself." Donald Rumsfeld, *Known and Unknown* (New York: Penguin, 2011), 326–29.

172. A senior administration official recalls bitter disagreements, including between Powell and Rice—who rebuffed requests for the president to become more deeply involved. Former senior administration official, interview with the authors. Overall, Rice's memoir is frank and candid about the infighting, though some specific fights are left out. Many of these are detailed throughout these two chapters on Bush 43, drawn from our oral history database and secondary sources. Though Rumsfeld is much less direct, he alludes to "issues" with Rice's management style in the National Security Council in his memoirs, as noted in note 171. See Rumsfeld, *Known and Unknown*, 324–30.

173. Nathan Guttman and Aluf Benn, "US Regards Ben-Eliezer 'Loose Talk' a Closed Matter," *Haaretz*, February 10, 2002. Ben-Eliezer claims Cheney said this to him during a visit to Washington.

Chapter Five

1. Anatoly Natan Sharansky with Ron Dermer, *The Case for Democracy: The Power of Freedom to Overcome Tyranny and Terror* (New York: Public Affairs, 2004).

2. George W. Bush, *Decision Points* (New York: Crown, 2010), 398.

3. Condoleezza Rice (former secretary of state), interview with the authors, April 29, 2010, Palo Alto, CA. See Condoleezza Rice, *No Higher Honor: A Memoir of My Years in Washington* (New York: Crown, 2011), 292–93.

4. Ariel Sharon, "Ceasefire Declaration," February 8, 2005, http://news.bbc.co.uk/2/hi/middle_east/4247233.stm. See also Greg Myre, "Abbas Fires 3 Security Chiefs after an Attack," *New York Times*, February 11, 2005.

5. Glenn Kessler, "Understanding Obama's Shift on Israel and the '1967 Lines,'" *Washington Post*, May 20, 2011.

6. Glenn Kessler and Scott Wilson, "Israel Agrees to Demolish Its Settlers' Gaza Homes," *Washington Post*, June 20, 2005.

7. See "Memorandum, Negotiations Affairs Department, Subject: Briefing Notes from the Abu Mazen/Sharon Summit Held on June 21 in Jerusalem," *Jewish Virtual Library*, the Palestine Papers, June 22, 2005, www.jewishvirtuallibrary.org/jsource/arabs/PalPaper062205.pdf.

8. A stinging critique of the international aid effort published at the same time can be found in Michael Keating, Anne Le More, and Robert Lowe, eds., *Aid, Diplomacy and Facts on the Ground: The Case of Palestine* (London: Chatham House, 2005).

9. Scott Wilson, "Israel Lowers Its Flag in Gaza as Last Troops Withdraw; Palestinians Enter Settlement Areas," *Washington Post*, September 12, 2005.

10. American official, interview with the authors. See Mohammed Samhouri, "Gaza Economic Predicament One Year after Disengagement: What Went Wrong?" *Middle East Brief*, no. 12 (November 2006), www.brandeis.edu/crown/publications/meb/MEB12.pdf.

11. According to a press report at the time, "Rice's aides attributed her decision to become directly and intensively involved to a memorandum from Wolfensohn that she received on arrival in Tel Aviv on Sunday and read as her motorcade made its way up the long and winding road to Jerusalem. One U.S. official who saw the document said it outlined the nature of the sticking points and made a concise case for an urgent solution." Tyler Marshall, "Diplomat Steps out of Character, into Spotlight:

A Special Envoy's Memo Persuaded Rice to See through an Accord on a Gaza Border Crossing," *Los Angeles Times*, November 16, 2005.

12. See Rice, *No Higher Honor*, 408–9.

13. According to Wolfensohn, it was only after he confronted Rice at her hotel that she relented to his involvement in the final negotiations "I put my hand on her shoulder and I said, but Condi, I'm 72 years old . . . I've been in negotiations longer than you have . . . I know when I'm in and I know when I'm out." James Wolfensohn (former special envoy for the Quartet on the Middle East and former president of the World Bank), interview with the authors, December 1, 2006, New York, NY. The former Quartet envoy is particularly critical of Abrams and David Welch, assistant secretary of state for Near Eastern Affairs at the time, "There was never a desire on the part of the Americans to give up control of the negotiations, and I would doubt that in the eyes of Elliot Abrams and the State Department team, I was ever anything but a nuisance," Wolfensohn told *Haaretz* a year after leaving his post. See Shahar Smooha, "All the Dreams We Had Are Now Gone," *Haaretz*, July 19, 2007.

14. The full text of the AMA can be found in the online appendix to this volume at: www.the peacepuzzle.org.

15. Wolfensohn, interview. See Robin Wright and Scott Wilson, "Rice Negotiates Deal to Open Gaza Crossings," *Washington Post*, November 16, 2005.

16. Rice reflects lightheartedly on the high-stakes final negotiations, saying, "The press loved the high drama and pure adrenaline of the eleventh hour agreement. So did I." She recalls telling the president about reaching the agreement. "They're going to expect this all the time," he said. "Then we'll just have to get it done," Rice replied. But in effect the United States did not "get it done," since the deal largely fell apart even before the ink was dry. See Rice, *No Higher Honor*, 410.

17. Daniel C. Kurtzer (former ambassador to Egypt and Israel), interview with the authors, September 15, 2010, Washington, DC.

18. Dan Ephron, "After Attack, Israel Cuts Abbas Contact," *Boston Globe*, January 15, 2005, www .boston.com/news/world/middleeast/articles/2005/01/15/after_attack_israel_cuts_abbas_contact.

19. See "Statement of the National Democratic Institute/Carter Center: Pre-Election Assessment of the Palestinian Legislative Council Elections," January 6, 2006, Jerusalem, Israel, www.cartercenter .org/documents/2269.pdf. From the statement: "Hamas' current political participation, while simultaneously advocating violence, undermines a fundamental principle of democratic elections." NDI and other institutes, such as the International Foundation for Electoral Systems (IFES) and the International Republican Institute (IRI), were voicing their concerns before this January 2006 paper was published; in fact, they had recommended more stringent candidacy requirements to the Bush administration as far back as 2002. See also Leslie Campbell (NDI senior associate and director of Middle East and North Africa programs), and NDI officials, interview with the authors, December 2005, Washington, DC. David Makovsky at the Washington Institute for Near East Policy, was vocal throughout this period with his concerns. See, for example, note 21 below.

20. Kenneth Wollack (NDI president), interview with the authors, March 23, 2011, Washington, DC.

21. See David Makovsky and Elizabeth Young, "Toward a Quartet Position on Hamas: European Rules on Banning Political Parties," Washington Institute for Near East Policy, *Peacewatch*, no. 515, September 12, 2005. They write "any party that could use force of arms as political leverage is a threat to the entire democratic process."

22. Robert Danin (former deputy assistant secretary of state for Near Eastern affairs and National Security Council official), telephone interview with the authors, December 10, 2009.

23. Rice, interview. See also Rice, *No Higher Honor*, 415.

24. Stephen Hadley (former national security advisor), interview with the authors, June 8, 2009, Washington, DC.

25. Bush, *Decision Points*, 406–7.

26. Elliott Abrams (former National Security Council official), interview with the authors, June 24, 2010, Washington, DC.

27. Former senior Palestinian official, interview with the authors.

28. Herb Keinon, "Fatah Asked Sharon to Prevent Voting in Jerusalem in 2006," *Jerusalem Post,* June 27, 2011, www.jpost.com/DiplomacyAndPolitics/Article.aspx?id=226682.

29. Ibid.

30. According to Walles, "The assumption all around was that Fatah would win, certainly at that point but even right up to the election." Jake Walles (former U.S. consul general and chief of mission in Jerusalem), interview with the authors, December 7, 2009, Washington, DC.

31. Rice, interview; Rice, *No Higher Honor,* 415.

32. "Quartet Statement on Palestinian Legislative Council Elections," December 28, 2005, United Nations, New York, NY, www.un.org/news/dh/infocus/middle_east/quartet-28dec2005.htm.

33. Before Abrams and Welch traveled to Israel to see Olmert on January 14, Israel relented on the administration's request to allow Palestinian residents of East Jerusalem to vote—announcing procedures laid out in the Oslo Accords. Olmert spoke with Rice by phone to let her know of the decision, instead of waiting for the administration's emissaries. See Aluf Benn, "Olmert Faces Reality," *Haaretz,* January 11, 2006. See also Aluf Benn, "Cabinet Expected to Approve East Jerusalem Proposal Today," *Haaretz,* January 15, 2006; Greg Myre, "Questions Raised about Sharon's Prospects for Recovery," *New York Times,* January 13, 2006.

34. Scott Wilson and Glenn Kessler, "U.S. Funds Enter Fray in Palestinian Elections: Bush Administration Uses USAID as Invisible Conduit," *Washington Post,* January 22, 2006.

35. Rice, interview. See also Rice, *No Higher Honor,* 416; Stephen Weisman, "Rice Admits U.S. Underestimated Hamas Strength," *New York Times,* January 30, 2006.

36. Term drawn from David Welch (former assistant secretary of state), interview with the authors, June 8, 2009, Washington, DC.

37. Bush, *Decision Points,* 407.

38. Saeb Erekat, "What the P.L.O. Has to Offer," *New York Times,* March 1, 2006, www.nytimes.com/2006/03/01/opinion/29erekat.html.

39. The administration repeatedly pointed to the "corruption" explanation. For two examples, see President Bush's White House press conference on January 26, 2006; and Condoleezza Rice, "Remarks en Route to London, United Kingdom," Department of State, January 29, 2006, http://2001-2009.state.gov/secretary/rm/2006/60016.htm. The Hamas slogan has been widely cited; in this case, the translation is drawn from Haim Malka, "Hamas: Resistance and Transformation of Palestinian Society," in Jonathan Alterman and Karin von Hippel, eds., *Understanding Islamic Charities* (Washington, DC: Center for Strategic and International Studies, 2007).

40. See Rice, "Remarks en Route to London, U.K."

41. "Quartet Statement," January 30, 2006, London, www.un.org/news/dh/infocus/middle_east/quartet-30jan2006.htmm.

42. Danin, interview.

43. Walles, interview.

44. An example of the argument for engagement can be found in General Shlomo Brom (Ret.), "A Hamas Government: Isolate or Engage?" *Peace Brief,* United States Institute of Peace, March 2006, www.usip.org/resources/hamas-government-isolate-or-engage.

45. Steven Erlanger, "U.S. and Israelis Said to Talk of Hamas' Ouster," *New York Times,* February 14, 2006.

46. Rice does report that in the first days after the election, Russia passed messages to Hamas in order to explore the possibility of engagement and whether the group could meet the Quartet's conditions. However, the only response was a belated and underwhelming letter from Hamas' putative leader, Ismail Haniyeh, to Rice, which did not address the Quartet's conditions. The Quartet did not receive any further communication from Hamas; Rice did not pursue the matter further. Rice, interview; see Rice, *No Higher Honor,* 419–20.

47. Ironically, funds that the administration had offered Abbas and the PA before the election, including a widely publicized $50 million package of direct assistance, had to be returned post-election in light of the aid cutoff. "It was really painful," said Walles about the process of ensuring that the PA returned the funds. Walles, interview. U.S. government officials around the world were told to have no

contact with Hamas members of the Palestinian Authority after Hamas refused to meet the above conditions established by the Quartet.

48. One "work-around" for the administration was to increase U.S. funding of UN relief programs, which allowed Washington to avoid cutting off all American assistance. Addressing Arab journalists ahead of a visit to the Middle East in mid-February, Rice pledged that "The United States of America is not going to stop giving money for the immunization of Palestinian children . . . It would be against our values to do that. So, for the most vulnerable and innocent populations, you know, we will find a way to respond to those humanitarian needs." But she also said, "Assistance that might help a government that is dedicated to the destruction of Israel, that's just not going to happen." See Ralph Dannheisser, "Rice Says No Direct U.S. Funding Now to Hamas," America.gov, February 18, 2006, www.america.gov/st/washfile-english/2006/February/20060218135111mbzemog0.4493524.html #ixzz1Gnk9KkHb. On the "no contact" policy, see Sean McCormack, "State Department Briefing, March 29: Iraq, Iran, Israel, Palestinian Authority, Sudan, Nigeria/Liberia, United Kingdom," Department of State, March 29, 2006, www.america.gov/st/washfile-english/2006/March/20060329184742 xjsnommiS0.6140406.html.

49. Norma Percy, *Israel and the Arabs: Elusive Peace* (DVD), BBC, 2005. See also David Rose, "The Gaza Bombshell," *Vanity Fair,* April 2008, www.vanityfair.com/politics/features/2008/04/gaza200804.

50. James Risen and Tim Weinter, "3 New Allies Help CIA in Its Fight against Terror," *New York Times*, October 30, 2001, www.nytimes.com/2001/10/30/international/30INTE.html.

51. Neil MacFarquhar, "Syrian Pressing for Israel Talks," *New York Times*, December 1, 2003. Some analysts saw Assad's statement as a positive sign, evidence that the young president was breaking free from regime hard-liners. But others viewed the statement with more skepticism, suggesting it was an insincere ploy designed to improve Syria's international standing.

52. See Helen Dewar, "Syria Sanctions Bill Easily Clears Senate," *Washington Post*, November 12, 2003; Glenn Kessler, "Support Grows for Sanctions on Syria; Bill Would Give Bush Six Options," *Washington Post*, October 8, 2003.

53. Carl Hulse, "Senate Follows House and Votes to Impose Sanctions against Syria," *New York Times*, November 12, 2003, www.nytimes.com/2003/11/12/politics/12SANC.html.

54. Former American official, interview with the authors.

55. See Scott Lasensky and Mona Yacoubian, "Dealing with Damascus," Council on Foreign Relations Special Report, 2008; see also Robin Wright, "U.S. Sees Opening for Change in Syria: Eroding Assad's Power s Short-term Goal," *Washington Post,* October 23, 2005.

56. Paul Salem, "The Future of Lebanon," *Foreign Affairs* (November–December 2006): 13–22, www.jstor.org/stable/20032139.

57. Anthony H. Cordesman, *Lessons of the 2006 Israel-Hezbollah War* (Washington DC: Center for Strategic and International Studies, 2007).

58. Glenn Kessler, *The Confidante: Condoleezza Rice and the Creation of the Bush Legacy* (New York: St. Martin's Press, 2007), 216; Rice, interview.

59. Bush, *Decision Points*, 414–15.

60. Ibid.

61. Rice, interview. The second dispute, according to Rice, would come a year later, over Annapolis.

62. Ibid.

63. Peter Baker, "U.S. Risks Backlash in Mideast," *Washington Post*, July 30, 2006.

64. CQ Transcripts Wire, "Secretary Rice Holds a News Conference," *Washington Post*, July 21, 2006, www.washingtonpost.com/wp-dyn/content/article/2006/07/21/AR2006072100889.html.

65. Baker, "U.S. Risks Backlash in Mideast." In his memoirs, Bush says "as the violence continued into its second week, many of the G8 leaders who started out supportive of Israel called for a cease-fire. I didn't join. A cease-fire might provide short-term relief, but it wouldn't resolve the root cause of the conflict. If a well-armed Hezbollah continued to threaten Israel from southern Lebanon, it would only be a matter of time before the fighting flared again. I wanted to buy time for Israel to weaken Hezbollah's forces. I also wanted to send a message to Iran and Syria: They would not be allowed to use terrorist organizations as proxy armies to attack democracies with impunity." Bush, *Decision Points*, 413–14.

66. CQ Transcripts Wire, "Secretary Rice Holds a News Conference."

67. Peter Baker, "Crisis Could Undercut Bush's Long-Term Goals," *Washington Post*, July 31, 2006.

68. "Bush Outlines Effort to Resolve Middle East Crisis," America.gov, July 29, 2006, www .america.gov/st/washfile-english/2006/July/20060729114946emohkcabhplar0.5075189.html. Richard Haass, a former senior State Department official who had left the Bush administration in 2003, ridiculed Bush's positive comments. "If this is an opportunity, what's Iraq? A once-in-a-lifetime chance." Peter Baker, "Crisis Could Undercut Bush's Long-term Goals."

69. Kessler, *The Confidante*, 221.

70. "President Bush and Secretary Rice Discuss the Middle East Crisis," The White House, August 7, 2007, http://georgewbush-whitehouse.archives.gov/news/releases/2006/08/20060807.html.

71. Rice, interview; Rice, *No Higher Honor*, 484–87.

72. Kessler, *The Confidante*, 227.

73. Bush, *Decision Points*, 413.

74. For the text of Security Council Resolution 1701, see www.un.org/News/Press/docs/2006/sc8808 .doc.htm.

75. Bush, *Decision Points*, 414–15.

76. Condoleezza Rice, "Special Briefing on Travel to the Middle East and Europe," Department of State, July 21, 2006. See also David S. Cloud, "U.S. Speeds Up Bomb Delivery for the Israelis," *New York Times*, July 22, 2006.

77. Rory McCarthy, "Fresh Ground Assault on Hizbullah Villages," *The Guardian*, July 31, 2006, www.guardian.co.uk/world/2006/jul/31/syria.israelandthepalestinians2.

78. "If someone had said July 11 that there was 'a one percent possibility' Israel's military response (to his organization's attack against an Israeli patrol inside Israeli territory, and the capture of two Israeli soldiers) would be as extensive as it turned out to be, 'I would say no, I would not have entered this for many reasons—military, social, political, economic,' said Nasrallah, speaking in Arabic." "Nasrallah: Soldiers' Abduction a Mistake," CNN.com, August 27, 2006, http://edition.cnn.com/2006/WORLD /meast/08/27/mideast.nasrallah.

79. The rise and success of the right wing in Israel's 2009 election has been tied to the wars in Lebanon and Gaza. See Jonathan Marcus, "The 2009 Israeli Election: A Bump in the Road to Peace?," *Washington Quarterly* (July 2009): 57, www.twq.com/09july/docs/09jul_Marcus.pdf; Mohanad Mustafa and As'ad Ghanem, "The Empowering of the Israeli Extreme Right in the 18th Knesset Elections," *Mediterranean Politics* 15, no. 1 (2010): 25–44, www.informaworld.com/smpp/section?content=a919980961& fulltext=713240928#references.

80. In addition to a growing number of Israelis advocating for an opening to Syria, prominent Democratic foreign policy figures, such as Richard Holbrooke, began to speak out against the Bush approach. See Nathanial Popper, "Calls for Talks with Syria Increase in U.S., Israel: Olmert Says Not Now, Bush Also Seen as Being Opposed," *Forward*, August 25, 2006, www.forward.com/articles/1443.

81. Jim Rutenberg, "Bush Defends U.S. Handling of Lebanese Conflict: Asserting that Hizbullah Is the Loser," *New York Times*, August 15, 2006.

82. Ibid.

83. See James A. Baker III and Lee Hamilton, *The Iraq Study Group Report* (New York: Vintage, 2006).

84. See Nathan Guttman , "Senators Visit Damascus, Push for Syrian Talks: Israeli Intelligence Branches Split over Assad Overture," *Forward*, December 29, 2006. Bush would ultimately reject most of the Baker-Hamilton recommendations, opting instead for a "surge" of military forces in Iraq, but he did partially accept the advice on outreach to Iraq's neighbors, agreeing to U.S. participation— alongside Iraq—in a series of "neighbors" conferences that included Syria and Iran.

85. See Zeev Schiff, Amos Harel, and Yoav Stern, "U.S. Hardens Line on Israel-Syria Talks, Jerusalem Obeys," *Haaretz*, February 23, 2007. Recalling this period, a former senior American official said, "I'm not sure anybody had a good idea of how you could be rid of al-Asad and what would follow him. Nobody ever answered those questions satisfactorily. But given his activities in Lebanon and Iraq, as well as in the territories with Hamas, the fear was that Olmert's negotiations with Syria would serve

as a get out of jail free card for al-Asad. Once the Israelis had an investment in al-Asad's regime and negotiations with Syria," the official said, it became "much more difficult" to mobilize "the rest of the international community to keep the screws on Assad." Former senior American official, interview with the authors.

86. Hadley, interview. Hadley continued, "What is it that Syria wants that Israel could give? The Golan—territory. Once you give it to him, he's got it. What is it that Israel wants? Support for the peace process, throwing out Hamas, stopping his support for Hezbollah, breaking his ties with Iran, stopping supporting bad guys going from Syria into Iraq. All things he can turn on and turn off. So, our part of the deal is irrevocable, and his part of the deal is eminently revocable."

87. See Bush, *Decision Points*, 420–22. See also David Sanger and Mark Mazzetti, "Israel Struck Syrian Nuclear Project, Analysts Say," *New York Times*, October 14, 2007.

88. See David Sanger and Mark Mazzetti, "Israel Struck Syrian Nuclear Project."

89. IAEA Board of Governors, "Implementation of the NPT Safeguards Agreement in the Syrian Arab Republic," November 19, 2008, www.isis-online.org/publications/syria/IAEA_Report_Syria_19Nov2008.pdf. See also Yitzhak Benhorin, "IAEA Examines Syria Bombing Site Photos," Ynetnews.com, October 19, 2007, www.ynetnews.com/articles/0,7340,L-3461758,00.html.

90. In his memoir, Cheney recalls, "It was my view that the Syrians needed to be held accountable, not sent a personal letter from Secretary Rice inviting them to the Annapolis Conference on Middle East peace." Dick Cheney, *In My Time* (New York,Threshold Editions, 2011), 479.

91. Rice may have been content to stand back, but not Vice President Cheney. President Abbas recalls Cheney asking him in early 2008 to boycott an Arab summit meeting in Damascus, though Abbas attended anyway. See "PA Pres. Mahmud Abbas, Interview with *Al-Sharq al-Awsat*, Ramallah, 22 December 2009 (excerpts)," *Journal of Palestine Studies* 39, no. 3 (Spring 2010): 192–97.

92. See Helene Cooper, "Advice from White House Not Always Followed," *New York Times*, May 28, 2008.

93. Rose, "The Gaza Bombshell."

94. Ibid. In the *Vanity Fair* essay by Rose, documents were revealed that describe how the United States pressured Abbas to act "decisively" and what was promised if he did, including on security sector assistance. Walles, reflecting on the expose in *Vanity Fair*, added, "In a sense, the article did accurately reflect the fact that we spent a lot of time during that period trying to work with Abu Mazen [Abbas] to develop alternate authorities, outside the Palestinian Authority, within the Mukata." Walles, interview. It appears that the National Support Unit (NSU) view also supported the overall *Vanity Fair* claims. For e-mail exchanges between Ziyad Clot, Andrew Kuhn, Zeinah Salahi, and Rami Dajani, see Al Jazeera, the Palestine Papers, www.ajtransparency.com/files/4311.pdf.

95. See Yezid Sayigh, "Fixing Broken Windows: Security Sector Reform in Palestine, Lebanon and Yemen," *Carnegie Papers*, no. 17 (October 2009).

96. Walles, interview.

97. Danin, interview.

98. Philip Zelikow, "Strategies for the Multifront War against Radical Islamists," Washington Institute for Near East Peace, Weinberg Founders Conference, September 15, 2006, www.washington institute.org/html/pdf/Zelikow091506.pdf.

99. There were many reports at the time about the controversy of Zelikow's remarks, inside and outside the administration. In an article in the New York Times some weeks later, it was reported that "The State Department quickly distanced itself from the speech, issuing a statement denying any linkage (between Iran and the Palestinian issue), and Israeli officials, flustered by Mr. Zelikow's remarks, said Ms. Rice later assured the Israeli foreign minister, Tzipi Livni, that the United States saw the Iranian and Palestinian issues as two separate matters." See Helene Cooper and David Sanger, "Rice's Counselor Gives Advice Others May Not Want to Hear," *New York Times*, October 28, 2006.

100. American official, interview with the authors.

101. According to an American official, the administration "didn't pay attention to (the API reaffirmation) . . . I don't think there was a serious discussion within the administration about 'can we use this in some way?'" American official, interview with the authors.

102. Condoleezza Rice, "Interview with Peter Mackler and Christophe de Roquefeuil of Agence France-Presse," Department of State, December 11, 2006, http://2001-2009.state.gov/secretary/rm/2005/46749.htm.

103. Rice, interview. See also Rice, *No Higher Honor*, 551–54.

104. Rose, "The Gaza Bombshell." The document Rose revealed is titled "An Arab Quartet Action Plan for the Palestinian Presidency in 2007 'Plan B.'" In addition to the "endgame" quote in the main text of this document, it defines another objective as "Undermine political strength of Hamas through continued international pressure and steps that accrue domestic political credit to Abbas, particularly in areas where Hamas cannot deliver (e.g. GOI [Government of Israel] deliverables)."

105. "Legal or not, arms shipments soon began to take place. In late December 2006, four Egyptian trucks passed through an Israeli-controlled crossing into Gaza, where their contents were handed over to Fatah. These included 2,000 Egyptian-made automatic rifles, 20,000 ammunition clips, and two million bullets. News of the shipment leaked, and Benjamin Ben-Eliezer, an Israeli Cabinet member, said on Israeli radio that the guns and ammunition would give Abbas 'the ability to cope with those organizations which are trying to ruin everything'—namely, Hamas. Avi Dichter points out that all weapons shipments had to be approved by Israel, which was understandably hesitant to allow state-of-the-art arms into Gaza. "One thing's for sure, we weren't talking about heavy weapons," says a State Department official. "It was small arms, light machine guns, ammunition." Rose, "The Gaza Bombshell."

106. Walles, interview.

107. Haim Malka, "The U.S. Should Support Palestinian Unity," Washingtonpost.com, Think Tank Town, February 13, 2007, www.washingtonpost.com/wp-dyn/content/article/2007/02/12/AR2007021201210.html.

108. Walles, interview.

109. "When asked about Miss Rice's offer to act as interlocutor, she [Miri Eisin, spokesperson for Olmert] said: 'That was just one idea.'" Glenn Kessler, "Arab Ministers Agree to Revive Initiative for Mideast Peace," *Washington Post*, March 27, 2007. See also "Israel Snubs Condoleezza Rice," *The Telegraph*, March 27, 2007, www.telegraph.co.uk/news/worldnews/1546835/Israel-snubs-Condoleezza-Rice.html. Olmert was reportedly "uncomfortable" with Rice serving as an intermediary, see "Rice Loses Support for Parallel Talks," *Washington Times*, March 26, 2007; Glenn Kessler, "Olmert, Abbas Agree to Hold Biweekly Talks," *Washington Post*, March 28, 2007, www.washingtonpost.com/wp-dyn/content/article/2007/03/27/AR2007032700542.html.

110. For more on Rice's efforts to get Israel to agree to include the three final-status issues (Jerusalem's fate, a Palestinian state's borders, and Palestinian refugees) in peace talks with the Palestinians, see Helene Cooper, "Look Who's Reboarding that Clintonian Shuttle," *New York Times*, April 1, 2007, www.nytimes.com/2007/04/01/weekinreview/01cooper.html?pagewanted=all.

111. See Nathan Guttman, "Olmert's Boasts of 'Shaming' Rice Provokes Diplomatic Furor," *Jewish Daily Forward*, January 15, 2009, www.forward.com/articles/14957.

112. According to a Congressional Research Services (CRS) report and the *Washington Post*, the United States originally proposed an aid package of $86.362 million, which it reprogrammed in March 2007 to approximately $50 million, intended to support forces loyal to PA president Mahmoud Abbas. See Jim Zanotti, "US Aid to the Palestinians," Congressional Research Services Report 12 (August 2010); Matthew Lee, "US Revises Aid Package to Palestinians," *Washington Post*, March 21, 2007, www.washingtonpost.com/wp-dyn/content/article/2007/03/21/AR2007032101002.html. See Connie Veillette et al., "FY2008 Emergency Supplemental Appropriations for International Affairs," Congressional Research Service (January 2008), www.au.af.mil/au/awc/awcgate/crs/rl34276.pdf. The Bush administration reportedly reprogrammed the package in order to ensure that Hamas did not receive any aid, stating in the CRS report from August 2010 that it hoped to ensure the money would go only to "non-lethal assistance." As part of the emergency supplemental appropriations for the International Narcotics and Law Enforcement fund, $25 million was allocated to train and equip members of the Palestinian Presidential Guard and the National Security Force.

113. See Karin Laub, "Poor Leadership Cited in Fatah's Failure," *Boston Globe*, June 15, 2007. See also Tim McGirk, "A Fight to the Death in Gaza," *Time Magazine*, June 12, 2007.

114. Bush, *Decision Points*, 407.

115. See Rose, "The Gaza Bombshell"; Malka, "Hamas: Resistance and Transformation of Palestinian Society." Bruce Riedel provides a very different account, arguing that Hamas was provoked both strategically and tactically, noting that General Keith Dayton was making an obvious attempt to build a force capable of overtaking Hamas with the help of Egypt and Jordan, and with explicit Israeli approval. He argues that this provided a spark for the conflict, aided by the actions of both Iran and al Qaeda. He attributes Hamas' decision to attack to the summation of U.S. and Israeli desires to reverse the 2006 election results, and pressure from both the Shi'ite (Iran) and Sunni jihadist (al Qaeda) communities. Both distrusted Saudi Arabia, and therefore disapproved of the Mecca Agreement because of its sponsorship by Riyadh. Moreover, according to Riedel, the Hamas military commanders were never enthusiastic about the Mecca agreements, and the planning for the takeover had been underway for months. Thus, this account has elements that agree with each of the other explanations in the text. Bruce Riedel, "Battle for Gaza: Hamas Duped, Provoked and Pushed," The Brookings Institution, August 16, 2007, www.brookings.edu/opinions/2007/0816middleeast_riedel.aspx.

116. Rose, "The Gaza Bombshell,"; former senior Palestinian officer.

117. Former senior Palestinian official, interview with the authors.

118. Rose, "The Gaza Bombshell."

119. Abrams, interview.

120. George W. Bush, "President Bush Discusses the Middle East," The White House, July 16, 2007, http://georgewbush-whitehouse.archives.gov/news/releases/2007/07/20070716-7.html.

121. See Carol Migdalovitz, "Israel: Background and Relations with the United States," Congressional Research Service, Report RL33476 (April 2, 2009), www.hsdl.org/?view&did=36943.

122. Jonathan Schwartz (U.S. State Department deputy legal adviser), interview with the authors, July 8, 2009, Washington, DC. Similar sentiments were expressed by an Israeli and a Palestinian negotiator, respectively.

123. Rice was speaking just ahead of the November 2007 Annapolis Conference. Helene Cooper, "Rice's Way: Restraint in Quest for Peace," *New York Times*, November 29, 2007.

124. Abbas, interview with *Al-Sharq al-Awsat*.

125. "President Bush Discusses the Middle East," White House speech, July 16, 2007, http://georgewbush-whitehouse.archives.gov/news/releases/2007/07/20070716-7.html.

126. Ibid.

127. John Hannah (former adviser to Vice President Cheney), interview with the authors, July 8, 2009, Washington, DC.

128. Bush, *Decision Points*, 408.

129. See William B. Quandt, *Peace Process: American Diplomacy and the Arab-Israeli Conflict since 1967*, 3rd ed. (Washington, DC: Brookings Institution Press / Berkeley: University of California Press, 2005), [Geneva] 138–41, 180–81, 184–91; [Madrid] 30612, 324–28. Ironically, Bush called it a "conference" in his memoirs (Bush, *Decision Points*, 408–9).

130. "President Bush Discusses the Middle East," July 16, 2007.

131. Scott Wilson, "Olmert, Abbas Discuss 'Core Issues' for Peace," *Washington Post*, August 29, 2007.

132. Former Israeli official, interview with the authors.

133. Ibid.

134. Walles, interview.

135. Rice, interview. See Rice, *No Higher Honor*, 613–18.

136. Welch, interview.

137. Danin, interview.

138. Bush, *Decision Points*, 409. Despite Bush's rosy portrait from his memoir, the atmospherics also reflected old divides. Saudi foreign minister Saud al-Faisal, for example, may have listened to Olmert, but reportedly refused to shake his hand, as did other Arab participants in shunning personal interactions with Israeli participants. By not sending their foreign minister, the Syrians made it clear that their difficult relations with the United States had not been resolved.

139. Ibid., 408. See also Rice, *No Higher Honor*, 614–15.

140. See "Joint Understanding Read by President Bush at the Annapolis Conference," U.S. Naval Academy, November 27, 2007, http://georgewbush-whitehouse.archives.gov/news/releases/2007/11 /20071127.html. The statement formally established the framework for the permanent-status talks. From a legal perspective, the document—termed the "Joint Understanding on Negotiations," carries some weight, given that it was the product of a trilateral negotiation. Admittedly short on substance, it did constitute one of the few formal agreements brokered by the Bush administration in its eight years, together with the Road Map (2003) and the Agreement on Movement and Access (2005). However, when Olmert's caretaker government was replaced by Netanyahu's in early 2009, it was clear that the Annapolis framework was a dead letter, in part because the Obama administration did not pursue it.

141. It had long been observed that the lack of an effective monitor throughout the many years of Israeli-Palestinian peacemaking was one of the major weaknesses of the peace process—given that the process was step-by-step, and given that Israelis and Palestinians had long failed to observe their mutual commitments on a wide range of issues. So, in that sense, Bush's announcement at Annapolis was new, though it would turn out to lack significance. The United States selected a military figure, General William Fraser, to act as monitor. But there were indications from the beginning that Israel put little stock in the effort. On March 14, when Fraser tried to hold his first trilateral, with Palestinian prime minister Fayyad attending, Israeli defense minister Barak did not bother to show up, instead sending a ministry official. Fraser's reports were private and went only to the secretary of state. His efforts never amounted to the kind of active and engaged monitoring that an effective peace process requires. "So we did monitor," said a U.S. official, "but we never judged, and we never briefed (the) parties on what we had monitored." Walles, interview. On the larger subject of monitoring, see Daniel C. Kurtzer and Scott B. Lasensky, *Negotiating Arab-Israeli Peace* (Washington, DC: United States Institute of Peace, 2008), 43–47.

142. See text of Joint Understanding, www.pij.org/documents/postAnnapolis.pdf.

143. Hilary Leila Krieger, "US to Be 'Actively Engaged' in Peace Process," *Jerusalem Post*, November 29, 2007.

144. Walles, interview. Walles summed up the approach as "okay, we'll launch it at Annapolis, we'll give it a big kickoff, and then you guys go and negotiate." That approach is not inherently negative, unless the parties hit a snag and were unable to recover. That, of course, is precisely what happened.

145. Former senior American official, interview with the authors.

146. Steven Lee Meyers, "Bush Offers a Nudge to Start Mideast Talks," *New York Times*, November 27, 2007.

147. Griff Witte, "Cheney Focuses on Mideast Talks," *Washington Post*, March 23, 2008.

148. Still, internal skeptics, such as Elliott Abrams at NSC, were unhappy with the balancing act. "My criticism of the administration's policy was we invested everything in the last couple years in negotiations and in Annapolis," and not on building Palestinian institutions and pressing for tangible quality of life improvements for Arabs in the West Bank. Abrams, interview

149. Walles, interview.

150. Ibid.

151. Ibid.

152. According to a senior Palestinian official, "[Erekat] led 12 committees under the radar—288 working sessions with each of these 12 working groups—totally under the radar." Senior Palestinian official, interview with the authors; and former Israeli officials, interviews with the authors.

153. Senior Palestinian official, interview with the authors; Schwartz, interview; senior Israeli official, interview with the authors.

154. Schwartz, interview.

155. Rice, interview. See also Abbas, in *Al-Sharq al-Awsat;* Bernard Avishai, "A Plan for Peace That Still Could Be," *New York Times,* February 7, 2011.

156. Nathan Guttman, "Expectations Low for President's Visit to Israel," *Forward,* May 8, 2008.

157. The mention of "appeasement" touched off a controversy in the U.S. presidential election, as many viewed Bush as taking a not-so-indirect swipe at candidate Barack Obama, who at the time was pushing for engagement with adversaries such as Iran. See Ron Kampeas, "Obama, Democrats Slam

Bush on His Speech to the Knesset," *JTA*, May 16, 2008, http://archive.jta.org/article/2008/05/16/2942024/obama-democrats-slam-bush-on-his-speech-to-the-knesset.

158. George W. Bush, "Address to the Knesset," May 14, 2008. In her memoirs, Rice wonders how she could have missed the absence of any mention of the peace process when she "reviewed and approved the speech." It is astonishing, however, that the White House speech writers did not automatically mention the Israeli Palestinian negotiations in the first place, reflecting again the divergent cultures in which Bush and Rice operated and their differing perspectives. Rice, *No Higher Honor*, 655.

159. Charles Levinson, "Bush Wraps Up Mideast Trip with a Thud, Analysts Say," *USA Today*, May 19, 2008.

160. In an apparent reference to the security negotiations and separate U.S.-Israeli discussions, in his memoir, Olmert claims that Bush "expressed his support" for the eight-point document drafted by Israel's defense establishment, including Israel's security interests, which Olmert presented during Bush's May 2008 visit. But in the memoir, he also distinguishes between those security requirements raised in negotiations with Abbas versus those for which Israel sought U.S. support (including control over Palestinian airspace and "the West Bank's electromagnetic space"). Olmert also says he "reached an agreement (with Washington) about the security principles we defined as essential," and says Bush reiterated "his support" for Israel's security requirements during their last meeting in November 2008. See Ehud Olmert, in *Yediot Ahronot, Weekend Supplement*, January 28, 2011.

161. Avishai, "A Plan for Peace That Still Could Be." On a "demilitarized" state, see "Abbas Meets with Leaders of the American Jewish Community," speech delivered at the S. Daniel Abraham Center for Middle East Peace, New York, NY, September 21, 2010.

162. See Avishai, "A Plan for Peace That Still Could Be."

163. Rice, interview.

164. Former senior American official, interview with the authors.

165. See Abbas, interview with *Al-Sharq al-Awsat*. In a paper released in December 2009, Palestinian negotiator Saeb Erekat said that at a trilateral meeting in Washington in July 2008—shortly before Olmert announced his intention to resign—the parties agreed that the 1967 baseline would include "East Jerusalem, the Dead Sea, Jordan Valley, the no man's land and the Gaza Strip," with the no-man's land to "be divided on a 50–50 percent basis between the two States [sic]." Erekat's paper was released a year into Obama's tenure. It was apparently disclosed because Palestinians were unhappy with the new president and his administration's unwillingness either to hold Netanyahu to positions put forward by Olmert, or even to affirm understandings reached with Bush and Rice, as with Rice's understanding about the 1967 "baseline." Akiva Eldar, "Palestinians Threaten to Adopt One-State Solution," *Haaretz*, February 26, 2010. See Gregg Carlstrom, "Deep Frustrations with Obama," *Al Jazeera*, the Palestine Papers, January 24, 2011, http://english.aljazeera.net/palestinepapers/2011/01/201112411395242.5385 .html. In 2008, during the meeting with Rice, the Israelis responded flexibly, though this was not the position of the Israeli government by late 2009. See Lorna Fitzsimons, "The Palestine Papers Revisited," *New Statesman*, January 31, 2011. According to internal Palestinian notes from the trilateral meeting with Rice, which took place the afternoon of July 29, 2008, there was indeed an understanding about the "baseline," but not whether the no-man's land would be included. See "Minutes from Bilateral and Trilateral US-PAL-ISR Sessions," *Al Jazeera*, the Palestine Papers, July 29, 2008. http://transparency.aljazeera.net/document/3048.

166. Senior Israeli official, interview with the authors. The Obama team either ignored or was not aware of the difference in preparing the president for his presentation of a 1967 baseline with mutual swaps in his speech of May 19, 2011, when the president (inadvertently or not) took the Palestinian side of the definition of a baseline. At the September 2008 Olmert-Abbas meeting, Olmert proposed a 50–50 split of the "demilitarized" areas (e.g., no-man's land); see Olmert, in *Yediot Ahronot*.

167. See Avishai, "A Plan for Peace That Still Could Be"; Eldar, "Palestinians Threaten to Adopt One-State Solution"; and Olmert, in *Yediot Ahronot, January 28, 2011, weekend supplement*. See also Dan Rothem, "Borders as a Core Issue," *Middle East Progress* (April 2010), http://middleeastprogress .org/2010/04/borders-as-a-core-issue. Also Hadley, interview. Small variations in percentages across different sources usually reflect differences in calculating territory. *Haaretz* published a map, also by

Rothem, purporting to represent Olmert's last offer on territory, as did *Yediot Ahronot* in an excerpt of Olmert's memoirs. For the *Haaretz* map, see www.haaretz.co.il/hasite/images/iht_daily/D171209/ olmertmap.pdf. In his interview with Avishai, 2011, Olmert was asked about his demand to annex 6.3% of Palestinian territory, and he replied, "I gave him reason to believe that I would go down to 5.9, but that would be final."

168. See Avishai, "A Plan for Peace That Still Could Be."

169. Mahmoud Abbas, interview with *Al-Sharq al-Awsat*, December 14, 2008.

170. Rice, interview. Although Rice's formulation on the 1967 "baseline" included East Jerusalem, she seemed unwilling to explicitly say so on every occasion. When asked by Palestinian negotiators in late August, during a bilateral meeting, if she would restate this formulation in the trilateral session, she said "leave it without saying this." This response was likely due to her sensitivity to Livni's unwillingness to raise the Jerusalem file. Nevertheless, Rice was comfortable discussing Jerusalem with Palestinians. At the same August meeting, she even went as far as to speak of Jerusalem as "a capital for two states." "Meeting Minutes, August 28, 2008," Al Jazeera, the Palestine Papers, 6–9. http://transparency.aljazeera .net/en/projects/thepalestinepapers/20121823171359468.html.

171. Rice, interview

172. An alternative view of Rice's involvement is provided by Udi Dekel, a top Israeli negotiator. "So long as the two sides negotiated, there was some progress. The minute (Secretary of State Condoleezza) Rice's teams went into the details the two sides barricaded themselves behind their basic positions, and instead of the negotiations progressing, they regressed," Dekel said. "The Palestinians understood that the Americans were closer to their position on the issues of Jerusalem, the borders and security, and opted to wait it out." Barak Ravid and Aluf Benn, "Olmert's Negotiator: Full Mideast Peace Impossible," *Haaretz*, January 25, 2010.

173. Senior Palestinian negotiator, interview with the authors. However, according to one former Israeli official, "Neither the Israeli side nor the Palestinian side wanted trilateral meetings . . . and quite frankly when Condi would come and we would have these meetings, she said she needed these meetings in order to convince other international players that the talks were credible and serious. . . . But I can't say that her contribution in the trilaterals was anything special." Former senior Israeli official, interview with the authors.

174. Former senior American official, interview with the authors.

175. See "Meeting Minutes, August 28, 2008."

176. See Gregg Carlstrom, "The 'Napkin Map' Revealed," Al Jazeera, January 23, 2011, www.al jazeera.com/palestinepapers/2011/01/2011122114239940577.html

177. Rice, interview.

178. Summary of Olmert's offer was included in an excerpt of his memoirs in *Yediot Ahronot*. In a July 17, 2009 op-ed in the *Washington Post*, Olmert claimed he made a "far-reaching and unprecedented" offer, including solutions for "all outstanding issues: territorial compromise, security arrangements, Jerusalem and refugees"—an offer "that the Palestinians rejected." But according to Olmert's later interviews, Abbas did not formally respond to the offer. See Greg Sheridan, "Ehud Olmert Still Dreams of Peace," *The Australian*, November 28, 2009, www.theaustralian.com.au/news/opinion/ ehud-olmert-still-dreams-of-peace/story-e6frg76f-1225804745744; and Olmert memoir excerpts. In a departure from his 2009 op-ed and charges of "rejection," Olmert told Avishai that Abbas "had never said no." See Avishai, "A Plan for Peace That Still Could Be."

179. See Olmert, in *Yediot Ahronot*.

180. According to Avishai, the two leaders agreed in principle to Olmert's idea, but differed over the size of the area, Abbas wanted Arab neighborhoods like Silwan outside so that they would clearly be part of the Palestinian state. Abbas also reportedly considered Egypt and the Vatican as additional custodians. See Avishai, "A Plan for Peace That Still Could Be."

181. Ibid. Accounts to date make clear the issue was discussed and numbers were bandied about, but some confusion remains about the precise figures and where the negotiations ended up. In his December 2009 paper, Erekat cites the Israeli offer of "1,000," as noted above, but in an interview he said the Israeli offer was "5,000." See Saeb Erekat, "The Political Situation in Light of Developments

with the US Administration and Israel Government and Hamas' Continued Coup d'etat: Recommendations and Options" December 2009, *Al Jazeera*, www.aljazeera.com/palestinepapers/2011/01 /2011122114239940577.html. Senior Palestinian official, interview with the authors. In his paper, Erekat says Abbas countered Olmert's offer with a demand for 15,000 refugees a year for ten years. In a not-for-attribution interview, a senior American said Olmert offered "10,000 per year, for five years." In September 2010, Olmert said Bush had agreed to accept 100,000 Palestinian refugees in the United States; see Olmert in *Haaretz*, September 19, 2010; Bush's deputy NSA Elliott Abrams denied that such an offer was made. See Gil Hoffman, "Abrams: Bush Never Agreed," *Jerusalem Post*, September 21, 2010. Additionally, according to Greg Sheridan, Olmert said he offered to accept 1,000 Palestinian refugees per year.

182. Avishai, "A Plan for Peace That Still Could Be."

183. Olmert, in *Yediot Ahronot*.

184. Danin, interview. For further accounts, see Ethan Bronner, "Olmert Memoir Cites Near Deal for Mideast Peace," *New York Times,* January 27, 2011; also Associated Press, "In Memoirs, Ex-Israeli PM Regrets Failure of Talks," *Washington Post,* January 27, 2011; and, in particular, Bernard Avishai, "A Separate Peace," *New York Times Magazine*, February 13, 2011.

185. Stephen Hadley (former national security advisor), interview with the authors, December 17, 2010, Washington, DC.

186. Walles, interview.

187. Ethan Bronner, "Olmert Says Israel Should Pull Out of West Bank," *New York Times*, September 29, 2008, www.nytimes.com/2008/09/30/world/middleeast/30olmert.html?_r=2&th&emc=th &oref=slogin.

188. Erekat, "The Political Situation in Light of Developments with the US Administration and Israel Government and Hamas' Continued Coup d'etat." Also, emailed answer by American official to author question on May 13, 2012.

189. Abbas put it as follows: "We cannot agree on anything until we have agreed on everything. This is what we have agreed upon with the Israelis." Dealing with issues piecemeal, Abbas added, "would be destroying your cause forever." Abbas, interview with *Al-Sharq al-Awsat*. The mantra has been thoroughly internalized by Americans as well, repeated frequently back to the parties. See Al Jazeera, the Palestine Papers; Ravid and Benn, "Olmert's Negotiator."

190. In retrospect, a senior Israeli negotiator criticized this principle, saying, "In practice, every time someone showed flexibility, the other side tried to pin him down. Therefore, I suggest that the model be changed and that whatever is agreed is implemented." Senior Israeli official, interview with the authors.

191. "Statement by Middle East Quartet," September 26, 2008, United Nations Department of Public Information, News and Media Division, New York, NY, www.un.org/News/Press/docs/2008/ sg2143.doc.htm. According to UNSCR 1850, "irreversibility" refers to the Security Council stressing the necessity of "creating an environment conducive to bilateral negotiations" and that direct talks are vital in order to adhere to the Road Map. Secretary-General Ban Ki-Moon emphasized that all council members must "act today to help set us firmly, finally and irreversibly on the path to peace in the Middle East." See Foundation for Middle East Peace, "Adopting Text on Middle East Conflict, Security Council Reaffirms Support for Annapolis Outcomes, Declares Negotiations 'Irreversible,'" www.fmep .org/resources/reference/united-nations-security-council-resolution-1850.

192. See "Quartet Statement," September 26, 2008, Washington, DC; "UNSCR 1850," December 16, 2008, United Nations, New York, NY.

193. Hadley, interview, December 17, 2010.

194. Although Rice helped draft UN Resolution 1860 calling for a cease-fire in Gaza, the United States later abstained from voting. The resolution passed by a vote of 14–0. Rice was in support of the resolution, but the White House intervened following a call from Ehud Olmert. See Julian Borger, "White House 'behind' US Volte-face on Ceasefire Call," *The Guardian*, January 9, 2009.

195. Mark Landler, "Olmert Says He Made Rice Change Vote," January 12, 2009, *New York Times*, www.nytimes.com/2009/01/13/washington/13olmert.html.

196. See Avishai, "A Plan for Peace That Still Could Be."

197. See Abbas, interview with *Al-Sharq al-Awsat*; Avishai, "A Plan for Peace That Still Could Be."

198. Hadley, interview, December 17, 2010.

199. Emailed answer by American official to author question on May 13, 2012.

200. See Kurtzer and Lasensky, *Negotiating Arab-Israeli Peace*.

201. The terms "nature" and "contours" are borrowed from Condoleezza Rice, "Keynote Address," Saban Forum 2007, www.brookings.edu/events/2007/1103_middle_east.aspx.

202. See Bruce Jentleson, "America's Global Role after Bush," *Survival* 49, no. 3 (2007): 179–200; Jeremy Pressman, "Power without Influence: The Bush Administration's Foreign Policy Failure in the Middle East," *International Security* 33, no. 4 (2009): 149–79.

203. Pressman, "Power without Influence."

204. Bush, *Decision Points*, 410.

Chapter Six

1. Indeed, one former official said he had never seen a president with such massive political capital lose it in the Middle East in as little as nine months. Former U.S. official, interview with the authors.

2. Several of the authors of this volume played roles in the Obama presidential campaign and served in advisory roles during the transition and in the first three years of the administration. This included contributing to the analysis, policies, and speeches of the administration.

3. Barack Obama, "At 60, Israel Has Much to Celebrate," *Yediot Ahronot*, May 11, 2008.

4. Barack Obama, "AIPAC Policy Conference 2008," AIPAC, June 4, 2008, www.aipac.org/~/media/Publications/Policy%20and%20Politics/Speeches%20and%20Interviews/Speeches%20by%20Policymakers/2008/06/PC_08_Obama.pdf.

5. The *Jerusalem Post* reported on this issue as follows: "Barack Obama did not rule out Palestinian sovereignty over parts of Jerusalem when he called for Israel's capital to remain "undivided," his campaign told the Jerusalem Post Thursday. 'Jerusalem will remain the capital of Israel, and it must remain undivided,' Obama declared Wednesday, to rousing applause from the 7,000-plus attendees at the American Israel Public Affairs Committee policy conference. But a campaign adviser clarified Thursday that Obama believes 'Jerusalem is a final status issue, which means it has to be negotiated between the two parties' as part of 'an agreement that they both can live with.' Two principles should apply to any outcome, which the adviser gave as: 'Jerusalem remains Israel's capital and it's not going to be divided by barbed wire and checkpoints as it was in 1948–1967.'" Hilary Leila Krieger, "Obama Backtracks on a United J'lem," *Jerusalem Post*, June 6, 2008.

6. George W. Bush, "President Bush Addresses Members of the Knesset," May 15, 2008, Jerusalem, http://georgewbush-whitehouse.archives.gov/news/releases/2008/05/20080515-1.html.

7. The mention of "appeasement" touched off a controversy in the U.S. presidential election. See Ron Kampeas, "Obama, Democrats Slam Bush on His Speech to the Knesset," *JTA*, May 16, 2008, http://archive.jta.org/article/2008/05/16/2942024/obama-democrats-slam-bush-on-his-speech-to-the-knesset.

8. Former Israeli official, correspondence with the authors.

9. Reuters, "Obama: Gaza War Underscores Need for Immediate Mideast Solution," *Ha'aretz*, January 11, 2009, www.haaretz.com/news/obama-gaza-war-underscores-need-for-immediate-mideast-solution-1.267908.

10. Former American official, interview with the authors.

11. Barack Obama, "Interview with Christiane Amanpour on 'This Week,'" *ABC News*, January 11, 2009, http://abcnews.go.com/ThisWeek/Economy/story?id=6618199&page=1.

12. The so-called Palestine Papers, leaked to Al Jazeera, contain a matrix of Israeli and Palestinian positions, as of January 1, 2009; see www.ajtransparency.com/en/document/4759. This matrix, while unofficial, does indicate a fair amount of congruence in the positions of the parties. It is not known whether this matrix was shared with the Obama team.

13. Condoleezza Rice, *No Higher Honor: A Memoir of My Years in Washington* (NY: Crown, 2011), Kindle ed., 13089.

14. For example, see "Meeting Summary: Dr. Saeb Erekat—Senator George Mitchell," Al Jazeera, the Palestine Papers, October 1, 2009, http://transparency.aljazeera.net/files/4842.pdf; "Meeting Summary: Dr. Saeb Erekat—Senator George Mitchell," Al Jazeera, the Palestine Papers, October 2, 2009, http://transparency.aljazeera.net/files/4844.pdf. These documents report on meetings between Mitchell and the chief Palestinian negotiator, Saeb Erekat, in which there is much discussion of what was and was not agreed in the previous rounds of negotiations.

15. See Bernard Avishai, "A Plan for Peace That Still Could Be," *New York Times Magazine*, February 7, 2011, www.nytimes.com/2011/02/13/magazine/13Israel-t.html?pagewanted=all. Also see Ehud Olmert, "I Told Abu Mazen: It's Hard for Me Too. Take the Pen and Sign It Now," *Yediot Ahronot*, Weekend Supplement, January 28, 2011.

16. Barack Obama, "Remarks at the State Department," January 22, 2010, merln.ndu.edu/archive /NSS/wh/DCPD-200900014.pdf.

17. Former American official, interview with the authors.

18. Ibid.

19. To read a draft of Abbas's letter to Obama, see Al Jazeera, the Palestine Papers, February 2009, www.ajtransparency.com/files/4442.pdf.

20. Former American official, interview with the authors.

21. Netanyahu, in Rory McCarthy, "No Territorial Concessions to Palestinians, Says Netanyahu," *The Guardian*, February 4, 2009, www.guardian.co.uk/world/2009/feb/04/israelandthepalestinians-usa.

22. Hillary Clinton, "Secretary Clinton with Vice President Joe Biden Announce Appointment of Special Envoy for Middle East Peace George Mitchell and Special Representative for Afghanistan and Pakistan Richard Holbrooke," Department of State, January 22, 2009, www.state.gov/secretary/rm /2009a/01/115297.htm.

23. In March, in conjunction with the renewal of American sanctions on Syria, Assistant Secretary Jeffrey Feltman and National Security Council staffer Dan Shapiro visited Syria, but with great symbolism, they entered and exited via Lebanon.

24. Former American official, interview with the authors.

25. "Peace Agreements Digital Collection: Report of the Sharm el-Sheikh Fact-Finding Committee, April 30, 2001," United States Institute of Peace, www.usip.org/files/file/resources/collections/peace_ agreements/sharm_el_sheikh_committee.pdf.

26. Ahmed Aboul Gheit and Hillary Clinton, "Secretary Hillary Clinton, Press Availability with Egyptian Foreign Minister Ahmed Aboul Gheit," Department of State, May 27, 2009, www.state.gov /secretary/rm/2009a/05/124009.htm.

27. Matt Spetalnick, "Obama Meets Abbas, Presses Israel on Settlements," Reuters, May 28, 2009.

28. "Transcript: Obama's Full Interview with NPR," NPR, June 1, 2009, www.npr.org/templates /story/story.php?storyId=104806528.

29. Barack Obama, "Remarks by President Obama at Cairo University, Cairo, Egypt," The White House, June 4, 2009, www.whitehouse.gov/the_press_office/Remarks-by-the-President-at-Cairo -University-6-04-09.

30. The Saudi king reportedly told the president, "Mr. President, whoever advised you to ask me these things, his or her ultimate objective is to destroy the U.S.-Saudi relationship, because my answer to all of this is no." Former American official, interview with the authors.

31. See Al Jazeera, "1967 Border, Land Swaps and Hillary Clinton's Parameters," the Palestine Papers, December 23, 2009, www.ajtransparency.com/files/4950.pdf.

32. Raghida Dergham, "Resolving the Palestinian-Israeli Conflict Would Make the US Troops Less Threatened and Remove the Arguments of Movements: Interview with General David Petraeus by Raghida Dergham," *Dar Al Hayat*, June 1, 2009, www.daralhayat.com/portalarticlendah/22899.

33. Benjamin Netanyahu, "PM's Speech at the Begin-Sadat Center at Bar-Ilan University," Prime Minister's Office, June 14, 2009, www.pmo.gov.il/PMOEng/Archive/Speeches/2009/06/speech barilan140609.htm.

34. For two sides of this debate, see Elliott Abrams, "The Settlement Freeze Fallacy," *Washington Post*, April 8, 2009; Daniel Kurtzer, "The Facts on Israel's Settlements," *Washington Post*, June 21, 2009.

35. James Traub, "The New Israel Lobby," *New York Times,* July 9, 2009.

36. See "Meeting Minutes 9/17/2009: Saeb Erekat and David Hale," Al Jazeera, the Palestine Papers, September 16, 2010, www.ajtransparency.com/files/4827.PDF.

37. The Palestinians maintain that an agreement was reached during a trilateral meeting with Secretary Rice in July 2008 relating to the definition of the territory subject to negotiation: "(A) The basis of negotiations would be the 4 June 1967 Map, including East Jerusalem, the Dead Sea, Jordan Valley, the no-man's land and the Gaza Strip. (b) The principle of land swaps on an agreed basis, including a territorial link between the West Bank and the Gaza Strip. (C) The area of the no-man's land before 4 June 1967, which is 46 km2, would be divided on a 50–50 percent basis between the two States. (D) The goal of the peace process would be to realize the principle of the two-state solution on grounds of this understanding." See "The Political Situation in Light of Developments with the US Administration and Israeli Government and Hamas Coup d'etat," Al Jazeera, the Palestine Papers, December 2009, http://transparency.aljazeera.net/en/document/4928. On the other hand, the Israelis maintain that, during those talks, Rice did not specify the 1967 lines, but rather talked about the gross amount of territory that would add up to the amount of territory Israel had occupied in 1967. The Israelis say they agreed to this number, which then became the baseline for discussion of swaps, but did not agree to use the term "1967 lines." Former Israeli negotiator, interview with the authors.

38. According to a former American official, the Palestinians insisted repeatedly that nothing was agreed until everything was agreed; however, when it came to Secretary Rice's formulation on the extent of territory to be negotiated, the Palestinians wanted to treat this as an agreement, even though the Rice formulation had been put forward as part of discussions that did not result in everything being agreed. Former American official, interview with the authors.

39. "United Nations Fact Finding Mission on the Gaza Conflict," UN Human Rights Council, September 29, 2009, www2.ohchr.org/english/bodies/hrcouncil/specialsession/9/FactFindingMission.htm.

40. "Jones: Middle East Peace 'Epicenter' of Policy," *JTA,* October 28, 2009, www.jta.org/news/article/2009/10/28/1008782/jones-middle-east-peace-epicenter-of-policy.

41. Hillary Clinton and Benjamin Netanyahu, "Remarks with Israeli Prime Minister Binyamin Netanyahu," Department of State, October 31, 2009, www.state.gov/secretary/rm/2009a/10/131145.htm.

42. Hillary Clinton, "Israel's Announcement Regarding Settlements," Department of State, November 25, 2009, www.state.gov/secretary/rm/2009a/11/132434.htm.

43. See "200912 30," Al Jazeera, the Palestine Papers, December 30, 2009, www.ajtransparency.com/files/4990.pdf. This reported U.S. nonpaper specifies draft terms of reference for negotiations, employing Secretary Clinton's formula of reconciling the Palestinian goal of a state based on the 1967 lines with swaps, with the Israeli goal of a Jewish state that meets its security requirements. The nonpaper—whose provenance has not been confirmed by American sources—goes on to list the core issues to be negotiated and lays out some U.S. thinking on the negotiations.

44. Joe Klein, "Q&A: Obama on His First Year in Office," *Time,* January 21, 2010.

45. See Gregg Carlstrom, "Deep Frustrations with Obama," Al Jazeera, the Palestine Papers, January 24, 2011, www.aljazeera.com/palestinepapers/2011/01/2011124113952425385.html.

46. Former American official, interview with the authors.

47. "Palestinian Response to Senator Mitchell's Proposals," Al Jazeera, the Palestine Papers, February 2010, www.ajtransparency.com/files/5043.pdf.

48. Joseph Biden, "Statement by Joseph R. Biden, Jr.," The White House, March 9, 2010, www.whitehouse.gov/the-press-office/statement-vice-president-joseph-r-biden-jr.

49. "Clinton: Israeli Settlement Announcement Insulting," CNN.com, March 12, 2010, http://articles.cnn.com/2010-03-12/world/israel.clinton_1_israeli-president-shimon-peres-prime-minister-benjamin-netanyahu-east-jerusalem?_s=PM:WORLD.

50. "Statement of General David H. Petraeus, U.S. Army Commander, U.S. Central Command, Before the Armed Services Committee on the Posture of U.S. Central Command," Senate Armed Services Committee, March 17, 2010, http://armed-services.senate.gov/e_witnesslist.cfm?id=4425.

51. Benjamin Netanyahu, "Address by PM Benjamin Netanyahu at AIPAC Conference," Israel Ministry of Foreign Affairs, March 22, 2010, www.mfa.gov.il/MFA/Government/Speeches+by+Israeli+leaders/2010/PM_Netanyahu_AIPAC_Conference_22-Mar-2010.htm.

52. See Peter Maer, "Netanyahu to Meet with Obama at White House Next Week," CBSNews.com, May 26, 2010, www.cbsnews.com/8301-503544_162-20006026 503544.html.

53. George Mitchell, Third Annual Dean Acheson Lecture on Foreign Policy, United States Institute of Peace, May 25, 2010, Washington, DC, www.usip.org/acheson.pdf.

54. "Palestinian Authority: U.S. Assistance Is Training and Equipping Security Forces, But the Program Needs to Measure Progress and Faces Logistical Constraints," U.S. Government Accountability Office, May 2010, www.gao.gov/new.items/d10505.pdf.

55. Briefing on Middle East Process, U.S. Department of State, August 20, 2010, www.state.gov/secretary/rm/2010/08/146156.htm.

56. Cabinet Communique, Israel Ministry of Foreign Affairs, August 22, 2010, www.mfa.gov.il/MFA/Government/Communiques/2010/Cabinet_communique_22-Aug-2010.htm.

57. "Remarks by the President in the Rose Garden after Bilaterial Meetings," The White House, September 1, 2010, www.whitehouse.gov/the-press-office/2010/09/01/remarks-president-rose-garden-after-bilateral-meetings.

58. "Briefing by Special Envoy for Middle East Peace George Mitchell on Middle East Peace Talks," U.S. Department of State, September 2, 2010, www.state.gov/p/nea/rls/rm/146750.htm.

59. According to one official at the time, "We went through a variety of ways to persuade the Israelis to extend the moratorium. . . . Is there some way we can offer something of value . . . that would then make it easier to be rationalized or explained why you are extending this." Former American official, interview with the authors.

60. See David Makovsky, "Dear Prime Minister: U.S. Efforts to Keep the Peace Process on Track," Washington Institute for Near East Policy, PolicyWatch No.1707, September 29, 2010; Glenn Kessler, "White House Offers Israel a Carrot for Peace Talk," *Washington Post*, September 30, 2010.

61. Jonathan Broder, "Israel: The Ties That Bind," *Congressional Quarterly Weekly*, October 17, 2011, p. 2159.

62. Itamar Rabinovich, *The Lingering Conflict: Israel, the Arabs, and the Middle East, 1948–2011* (Washington, DC: Brookings Institution Press, 2011), Kindle ed., 2528.

63. See the Palestine Papers, www.ajtransparency.com/en/doc-search-en.

64. Susan E. Rice, "Explanation of Vote by Ambassador Susan E. Rice, U.S. Permanent Representative to the United Nations, on the Resolution on the Situation in the Middle East, including the Question of Palestine, in the Security Council Chamber," U.S. Mission to the United Nations, New York, NY, February 18, 2011, http://usun.state.gov.

65. Susan E. Rice, "Briefing on the United Nations Security Council Vote," U.S. Department of State, February 18, 2011, www.state.gov/p/io/rm/2011/156821.htm.

66. "Palestinian Rivals Hamas and Fatah Sign Reconciliation Deal," *The Guardian*, May 4, 2011, www.guardian.co.uk/world/2011/may/04/palestinian-rivals-hamas-fatah-deal.

67. "Obama, Clinton on Resignation of Middle East Envoy Mitchell," The White House, May 13, 2011, http://translations.state.gov/st/english/texttrans/2011/05/20110513155633su0.6723706.html.

68. Barak Ravid, "Dennis Ross Still Advising Obama on Regular Basis, Despite Stepping Down," Haaretz.com, January 27, 2012, www.haaretz.com/print-edition/news/dennis-ross-still-advising-obama-on-regular-basis-despite-stepping-down-1.409390.

69. "Remarks of President Barack Obama—As Prepared for Delivery—'A Moment of Opportunity,'" The White House, May 19, 2011, www.whitehouse.gov/the-press-office/2011/05/19/remarks-president-barack-obama-prepared-delivery-moment-opportunity.

70. "Statement on US President Obama's Speech," Prime Minister's Office, Jerusalem, May 19, 2011, www.pmo.gov.il/PMOEng/Communication/Spokesman/2011/05/spoketguva190511.htm.

71. The administration apparently considered whether to unveil a more ample set of "parameters" to guide the negotiations, but rejected this approach in favor of one designed to instill confidence

by defining the borders and the security provisions, after which it was thought to be easier to deal with issues such as Jerusalem and refugees. Former American official, interview with the authors.

72. Remarks by the President at the AIPAC Policy Conference, Walter E. Washington Convention Center, Washington, DC, May 22, 2011, www.whitehouse.gov/the-press-office/2011/05/22/remarks -president-aipac-policy-conference-2011. The transcript posted on the White House web page mistakenly has the president nonsensically saying, in the last line quoted in the text, "in joined self-determination", whereas he actually said "enjoying self-determination. . . ."

73. Cf. William B. Quandt, "The Israeli-Palestinian Conflict Now," *Cairo Review*, no.1 (2011): 43–51.

74. This lack of coordination within the administration is disputed by a former official who said that all issues were discussed within the administration before a diplomatic action was undertaken. Former American official, interview with the authors.

Epilogue

1. "Remarks by President Obama in Address to the United Nations General Assembly," United Nations, New York, NY, September 21, 2011, www.whitehouse.gov/the-press-office/2011/09 /21/remarks-president-obama-address-united-nations-general-assembly.

2. Daniel C. Kurtzer and Scott B. Lasensky, *Negotiating Arab-Israeli Peace: American Leadership in the Middle East* (Washington, DC: United States Institute of Peace, 2008).

3. A University of Maryland poll in Egypt in November 2011 indicated that a plurality of Egyptians felt the military was trying to slow or reverse the gains of the revolution (http://newsdesk.umd .edu/bigissues/release.cfm?ArticleID=2561).

4. Arab Public Opinion Surveys, University of Maryland, Anwar Sadat Chair for Peace and Development, November 2011, http://sadat.umd.edu/new%20surveys/surveys.htm.

5. Former American official, interview with the authors.

INDEX